# THE PRICE OF PEACE

Lively political and public debates on war and morality have been a feature of the post-Cold War world. *The Price of Peace* argues that a re-examination of the just war tradition is therefore required. The authors suggest that, despite fluctuations and transformations in international politics, the just war tradition continues to be relevant. However, they argue that it needs to be reworked to respond to the new challenges to international security represented by the end of the Cold War and the impact of terrorism. With an interdisciplinary and transatlantic approach, this volume provides a dialogue between theological, political, military and public actors. By articulating what a reconstituted just war tradition might mean in practice, it also aims to assist policy-makers and citizens in dealing with the ethical dilemmas of war.

CHARLES REED is the International Policy Adviser to the Church of England's Mission and Public Affairs Unit. He is a specialist on the ethics of war and peace and is the author of *Just War?* (2004).

DAVID RYALL is the Assistant General Secretary to the Catholic Bishops' Conference of England and Wales.

# THE PRICE OF PEACE

## Just War in the Twenty-First Century

Edited by

CHARLES REED AND DAVID RYALL

CAMBRIDGE
UNIVERSITY PRESS

CAMBRIDGE UNIVERSITY PRESS
Cambridge, New York, Melbourne, Madrid, Cape Town, Singapore, São Paulo

Cambridge University Press
The Edinburgh Building, Cambridge CB2 2RU, UK

Published in the United States of America by Cambridge University Press, New York

www.cambridge.org
Information on this title: www.cambridge.org/9780521677851

First published 2007

Printed in the United Kingdom at the University Press, Cambridge

*A catalogue record for this book is available from the British Library*

ISBN-13 978-0-521-86051-2 hardback
ISBN-13 978-0-521-67785-1 paperback

# CONTENTS

# CONTRIBUTORS

FRANK BERMAN is a barrister at Essex Court Chambers, international arbitrator and Judge ad hoc of the International Court of Justice. He chairs the Claims Committee of the Austrian General Settlement Fund for Victims of Nazi Persecution. Through the 1990s he was the Legal Adviser to the Foreign and Commonwealth Office and is presently Visiting Professor of International Law at the University of Oxford.

NIGEL BIGGAR is Professor of Theology and Ethics in the School of Religions and Theology at Trinity College, Dublin. He is author of 'On Giving the Devil Benefit of Doubt', in William J. Buckley (ed.), *Kosovo: Contending Voices on Balkan Conflicts* (2000) and editor of *Burying the Past: Making Peace and Doing Justice after Civil Conflict* (2003).

PAUL CORNISH is Carrington Chair in International Security at Chatham House and Head of the International Security Programme.

JEAN BETHKE ELSHTAIN is the Laura Spelman Rockefeller Professor of Social and Political Ethics at the University of Chicago. She has written widely on feminism, women and war. Her books include *Just War against Terror: Ethics and the Burden of American Power in a Violent World* (2003), *Democracy on Trial* (1995) and *Women and War* (1988).

DAVID FISHER was the Deputy Head of the Defence and Overseas Affairs Secretariat in the United Kingdom's Cabinet Office. Prior to that he was the Under-Secretary of State in the Ministry of Defence responsible for defence equipment. He was the Defence Counsellor in the UK Delegation to NATO, where he helped to revise Alliance Defence policies and strategy following the end of the Cold War. He is currently Strategy Director for EDS, the global information technology services company. He regularly contributes to books and journals on defence and ethical issues. He is the author of *Morality and the Bomb* (1985), a study of the ethics of nuclear deterrence written while he was a Research Fellow of Nuffield College, Oxford.

SHANNON E. FRENCH is an Associate Professor of Philosophy in the Department of Leadership, Ethics and Law at the United States Naval Academy. She is the author of *The Code of the Warrior: Exploring Warrior Values, Past and Present* (2003) and numerous articles and book chapters in the field of military ethics.

RICHARD HARRIES is the Bishop of Oxford. He is also President of the Council on Christian Approaches to Defence and Disarmament. He chaired the Church of England's Working Party on *Peacemaking in a Nuclear Age* (1988) and has written a number of books on the ethics of war, most notably *Christianity and War in a Nuclear Age* (1986). He chaired the Church of England's House of Bishops' Working Party on *Countering Terrorism: Power, Violence and Democracy Post 9/11* (2005).

JAMES TURNER JOHNSON is Professor of Religion and a member of the graduate faculty in Political Science at Rutgers University. His books include *Can Modern War Be Just?* (1997) and *Morality and Contemporary Warfare* (2002).

MARY KALDOR is Director of the Centre for the Study of Global Governance at the London School of Economics and author of numerous books on war and democracy. Her recent works include *New and Old Wars: Organised Violence in a Global Era* (2002) and *Global Civil Society: An Answer to War* (2003).

TERRENCE K. KELLY is a Senior Researcher with RAND and a retired army officer. In 2004 he served as the Director for Militia Transition and Reintegration Programs for the Coalition Provisional Authority in Iraq. He is currently serving as the Director for Strategic Planning and Assessment for the US Mission in Iraq.

JOHN LANGAN holds the Cardinal Bernardin Chair of Catholic Social Thought at the Kennedy Institute of Ethics at Georgetown University and is a member of the faculty of the Walsh School of Foreign Service at Georgetown. He edited with William V. O'Brien *The Nuclear Dilemma and the Just War Tradition* (1986) and participated actively in the debate over the US Catholic Bishops' Pastoral Letter *The Challenge of Peace* (1990). He has written extensively on human rights, just war theory and Catholic social teaching.

GWYN PRINS is Alliance Research Professor jointly at the London School of Economics and Political Science and at Columbia University, New York.

He is author of many works on global security, most recently *The Heart of War: On Power, Conflict and Obligation in the Twenty-First Century* (2002).

MICHAEL QUINLAN is a former Permanent Under-Secretary of the United Kingdom Ministry of Defence, and former Director of the Ditchley Foundation. He is currently a visiting professor at the International Policy Institute Centre at King's College, London and a Consulting Senior Fellow for South Asia at the International Institute for Strategic Studies.

CHARLES REED is the International Policy Adviser to the Church of England's Mission and Public Affairs Unit. He is the author of *Just War?* (2004).

DAVID RYALL is Assistant General Secretary to the Catholic Bishops' Conference of England and Wales. He has published articles in journals such as *International Relations, Third World Quarterly* and the *World Today*.

PAUL SCHULTE is a Senior Visiting Fellow at the UK Defence Academy. He was formerly Head of the Post-Conflict Reconstruction Unit in the Department for International Development, Director of Proliferation and Arms Control in the Defence Ministry, and UK Commissioner on UNSCOM (United Nations Special Commission) and UNMOVIC (United Nations Monitoring, Verification and Inspection Commission).

WILLIAM WALLACE is Professor of International Relations at the London School of Economics and a Liberal Democratic peer. He has written widely on European security and the politics of the European Union.

GEORGE WEIGEL is a senior fellow of the Ethics and Public Policy Centre in Washington, where he holds the John M. Olin Chair in Religion and American Democracy and is head of the Catholic Studies project. He is author of *Idealism without Illusions: US Foreign Policy in the 1990s* (1994) and *Moral Clarity in a Time of War* (2003).

MICHAEL O. WHEELER is a consultant and writer on US national security issues and a retired US Air Force officer. He has been the arms control adviser to the Chairman of the Joint Chiefs of Staff and a member of the National Security Council staff, as well as directing the ethics course at the US Air Force Academy in the early 1970s.

# FOREWORD

RICHARD DANNATT

Successive generations in the twentieth century confronted the prospect of war as an ugly but inevitable characteristic of their times. The tone was set by the Boer War, became harsher in the First World War, more universal in the Second World War and took on the potential for total destruction in the Cold War. But then, despite what many saw as the aberration of the first Gulf War in 1990–1, there appeared to be the prospect of an era when swords could indeed be beaten into ploughshares, peace dividends taken and a belief that the likelihood of war – hot or cold, declared or undeclared – had receded. However, 9/11 shattered the last vestiges of that dream. But on reflection, the audit trail to the contemporary security situation had already been marked out.

Although the collapse of the Berlin Wall was the headline event that signalled a switch from the classic focus on Defence to an increasing emphasis on Security, the use of force to achieve political ends did not cease but merely began to change. With certain exceptions in sub-Saharan Africa and in the Middle East, the prospect and incidence of inter-state war sharply declined, while wars amongst the people became a hallmark of the last decade of the twentieth century and on into the first decade of the twenty-first. Moral consciences, pricked by the ubiquity of the international media, have led to a marked increase in military interventions predominantly under the multinational banners of institutions such as the United Nations, the European Union and NATO or within the construct of ad hoc 'coalitions of the willing'. This has certainly been the experience of the British armed forces and also of the armed forces of many Western and former Eastern bloc industrialised nations who have chosen to apply their residual military capabilities not against each other but in support of the less fortunate. The swords have not become ploughshares but in an innovative way more akin to pruning hooks; they are being used to try to contribute to prosperity and stability and not merely to threaten or destroy. If there has been a 'revolution in military affairs' in recent times it is as much about the ways that armed forces are used as about the capabilities available to them.

But an acceptance of the moral responsibility to intervene does not itself provide a solution. Thousands died at Srebrenica and tens, probably hundreds, of thousands died in Rwanda because the military means were not made available in sufficient quantities to support the political intent. 'Never again' was the reaction, and this response has led to a growing acceptance of the responsibility to protect human rights wherever they are threatened. This book is therefore timely as it seeks to re-examine, from first principles, the ethical context of the use of force in the current security climate. Responsible policy-makers and military commanders need the mutual confidence that what they set out to do remains not only legal, but morally and ethically sound.

It is not for me to speak for policy-makers; but from the perspective of the military commander these ethical issues are personal and urgent. Responsibility for a plan or a series of operations can never be delegated. Activity can be delegated to subordinates but never responsibility. Both I and General Sir Rupert Smith, who also addressed the authors' conference at Church House when this book was being shaped, have had first-hand experience of operations in Bosnia, Kosovo and Northern Ireland and know that whereas physical courage is a basic requirement for a soldier – and Private Johnson Beharry VC comes to mind – it is the moral courage to do the right thing that is the harder challenge. A salutary and negative example is that of Major-General Radislav Krstic, the Bosnian Serb Commander of the Drina Corps whose troops carried out the Srebrenica massacres in 1995. I gave evidence at his trial before the International Criminal Tribunal for the former Yugoslavia in The Hague, and by the end of that trial, I believe the prosecution knew, the court knew and even he probably knew that his major failing was not to refuse to carry out the instructions given to him by his superiors which inevitably led to the death of some 8,000 Muslim men and boys. Nuremberg should have taught him that his defence was not a defence. I repeat: responsibility can never be delegated; and seen from where I stand, the moral dimension is highly personal.

If, therefore, the moral dimension to the use of force is of increasing importance in the contemporary security environment then so too is the premium placed on intellectual preparation to take part in modern, post-industrial warfare. A book such as this will contribute significantly to this process, mirroring in part the greater emphasis placed within the British

Army, and the British armed forces generally, on a proper doctrinal understanding of the application of military force.

Until the closing years of the Cold War, the British Army had no formally articulated military doctrine – instead, the basis of belief and conduct was largely rooted in past practice: the army was popularly held to be pretty efficient at preparing for the last war, not too bad at a preparing for the current one but not that good at looking ahead! But in the last fifteen years thought has moved on. Without dwelling unduly on history, in the last decade of the Cold War there was a growing realisation that there had to be an alternative to the cataclysmic nuclear options and more time, thought and resources were put into developing conventional battlefield concepts. Within the British Army, General, then later Field Marshal, Sir Nigel Bagnall led the intellectual charge which culminated in the first comprehensive written doctrine which in turn provided the rationale for an enhanced equipment programme and a new approach to training and war fighting. At the heart of this approach was a deliberate focus on the operational level of war – the level between the strategic and the tactical – the level at which Generalship is exercised and all activity is orchestrated within a single campaign plan.

And this linkage between political intent and the application of force on the ground has served the military well. In each new situation the attempt has been made to plan events beginning with a vision of the end state, identifying the effects that are required to achieve it and working back from there. In parallel to this renewed focus on a doctrinal approach to the application of force has been an intellectual struggle to broaden the debate so as to embrace the challenges of peace-keeping as distinct from war fighting. But heroic attempts during the mid-1990s against the illogical background of the conflicts in the Balkans failed to square the circle and could not provide neat definitions for alternate scenarios. The reality of the early months of the second Gulf War in 2003 showed the unity of all military operations with simultaneous but different activities taking place in adjacent parts of the battlefield, or even city blocks – war fighting, humanitarian relief and peace support operations – the genesis of the so-called 'Three-Block War'.

Such a description of contemporary operations masks the under-lying challenges for the development of the physical means of modern military force. The extent to which any nation can join a 'Revolution in Military Affairs' is ultimately enabled or constrained by the size of the national budget devoted to defence. Successive British governments have set their priorities, challenging defence to be both effective and efficient, and to regard operations with allies and coalition partners as the norm. That said, a small deployment such as that to Sierra Leone in 2000 demonstrated that modest but timely action can bring disproportionate benefit, especially when linked to speedy strategic and operational level decision making. However, the norm will be multinational action often led by the United States, who are forging ahead on all technological fronts. In Britain we accept that we will never fight 'as' the Americans, but we do recognise the requirement to fight 'with' the Americans, and recent experience shows that this is perfectly possible. However, we are all agreed that future warfare will increasingly be intelligence- and information-led, an orchestration of specific effects aligned to specific purposes, and all brought together on a network basis. The day of the 'Big Battalions' is not over, but the synchronisation of the precise use of force is most likely to ensure that our professional skills are turned to our advantage and our conventional mass – still needed in some manpower-intensive circum-stances – does not become our Achilles' heel.

But whatever the means of war, the just war questions remain, promoting a contemporary re-examination of just cause, just conduct and the establish-ment of a just peace – and at the same time there is the realisation that the cast list of key players has also been expanded. The classic understanding of the inter-play between the strategic, operational and tactical levels of war placed greater emphasis and responsibility on those at the upper end of the process. This is not exclusively so today, as the actions of a corporal or a pilot apparently conducting tactical activity can have profound operational and strategic consequences. Thus, the requirement for moral and ethical under-standing becomes more pressing and widespread as the effect of the actions of the 'strategic' corporal or pilot might be as easily visible to the interna-tional media as the actions of the general or the politician. Educating the 'strategic' corporal and pilot to understand his moral responsibilities is now a key challenge for the military leadership.

In past generations it was assumed that young men and women coming into the armed forces would have absorbed an understanding of the values and standards required by the military from their family or from within their wider community. Such a presumption today cannot be made. When a political decision is reached to send a military force on a discretionary intervention there is a conscious or subconscious acceptance that in deploying to a less fortunate part of the world, we do so having publicly adopted a position on the moral high ground. However, when officers or soldiers act in a way contrary to our traditional values and standards and fail to respect the human rights of those they have gone to help, then we risk falling from the high ground to the valley, often in a very public way. The challenge now for the military leadership is to educate and train our young people of today – each one a potential individual decision-maker – so that all concerned understand the rationale behind our core values of selfless commitment, courage, discipline, integrity, loyalty and respect for others, and apply these values to their conduct.

Without an individual moral understanding from all concerned within a military endeavour, from policy-maker to private soldier, then the outcome will be in doubt in both war and peace. But where we get it wrong, when there are lapses in behaviour and conduct, then they must be confronted. Investigation must be thorough. Well-informed decisions must be taken about possible prosecutions and timely disposal through-out the judicial system must follow. Those in the chain of command, from top to bottom, have a duty to support all individuals for whom they are responsible throughout this process; but ultimately individuals must accept responsibility for their own actions. The peculiar conditions and atmosphere of military operations underline why it is imperative that potential offences on operations are tried within a military criminal judicial system according to the burden of civil, military and international law – itself a more rigorous criteria than in civilian life.

But individual moral responsibility and understanding are not suffi-cient of themselves unless the corporate or collective moral understanding is sound too. Napoleon observed in his day that the moral is to the physical as three is to one, and in so doing I believe he was commenting both individually and collectively: the cause must be just, and be under-stood to be just, in order to gain this beneficial multiplier effect that leads to overall success. In the dark days of 1940 the physical odds against Britain were alarmingly high, and in the more sobering moments of the Cold War the military balance was tilted away most unfavourably; but ultimately fascism and communism were defeated. The Second World War and the Cold War were fundamentally moral conflicts – clashes of ideas – 'the difference between truth and lies that makes people commit their best energies and risk their lives and safety in resisting oppression and deceit'. Those were the words of the Archbishop of Canterbury, the

Rt Revd Rowan Williams, in his address at the service in Westminster Abbey on Sunday 10 July 2005 to mark the sixtieth anniversary of the end of the Second World War. It is ironic that the moral challenge to this generation had come to the streets of London only three days before on what we know popularly as 7/7. But Archbishop Rowan Williams also referred to 'the passion that was generated during the darkest days of the War, a passion to see human dignity vindicated after an age of insult and disfigurement. That passion will have been rekindled in recent days.' It is perhaps a sad but inevitable comment on the history of humankind that successive generations must confront the clash 'between truth and lies', but it is most timely that the Church of England Archbishops' Council and the Catholic Bishops' Conference of England and Wales set up their conference and this resultant book entitled *The Price of Peace: Just War in the Twenty-First Century*.[1] I am glad that the contributors have not ducked the difficult issues.

My original invitation to take part in the conference and subsequently the invitation to write this foreword came from the late Major-General the Reverend Ian Durie, tragically killed in a car crash in Romania just a few weeks before the conference. He had commanded the British Artillery in the First Gulf War, subsequently been ordained and at the time of his death was visiting Romania to promote spiritual and moral understanding within their army. Of this conference, to which he had intended to contribute, he expressed his hope to try to 'bring a much better understanding of this critical subject – the theology of just war and its relevance today – to help the Church to speak prophetically into this crucial area'.

Ian Durie felt passionately about the need for a contemporary understanding of what just war permitted and constrained. But at the heart of the matter – the Centre of Gravity, as the military call it – are people. War has traditionally been fought between people, now increasingly it is fought amongst people, but ultimately it is fought by people. The conceptual dimension of war has constantly changed, the physical means of war have become ever-deadlier, but the moral component of war – people – has remained as the central element. What people think they can achieve by war, how people conduct themselves in war and how people set about restoring peace – it is our response to these questions that ultimately defines our humanity.

General Sir Richard Dannatt KCB CBE MC ADC Gen
Chief of The General Staff

[1] Archbishop Rowan Williams, sermon in Westminster Abbey, Sunday, 10 July 2005.

# ACKNOWLEDGEMENTS

Whilst the editors and contributors all write in a personal capacity, this book would not have progressed without the support and encouragement of the Archbishops' Council's Mission and Public Affairs Division and the International Affairs Department of the Catholic Bishops' Conference of England and Wales. Our particular thanks go to Tom Burns, Tom Butler, John Clark, William Fittall, Philip Giddings, Jeremy Harris, Crispian Hollis, Austin Ivereigh, Patrick Kelly, Tim Livesey, Chris Smith, Andrew Summersgill, Frank Turner, Stephen Wall, and especially Ian Linden who moderated the symposium. Thanks are also due to Rupert Smith, Charles Guthrie and Nicolas Maclean. As editors of this collection, and charged with the task of drawing together the contributions, our chief thanks go to all our authors for offering their time so generously to this project. Our task was made immeasurably easier by the goodwill and humour which all contributors displayed throughout the editorial process. This collection was the result of a three-day authors' symposium held in London, in May 2005. This symposium would not have been the success it was without the excellent administrative support provided by Alison Cundiff, Larissa Doherty and Maria Klos. We are also grateful to John Haslam and Kate Brett of Cambridge University Press. Finally, this book would not have been possible without the loving and patient support of our respective friends and family, especially Rebecca and Haleh, Nima and Sophie.

# 1

## Introduction

CHARLES REED AND DAVID RYALL

The genesis of this book lies in a March 2005 symposium on the 'Just War in the Twenty-First Century' and the context for the encounter was the 2003 Iraq War, a conflict that helped to crystallise in the most acute way the recurring moral, political, legal and military tensions that are involved in the recourse to and conduct of war. Historically, the framework used most frequently to explore these issues has been the just war tradition[1] and the symposium aimed to facilitate a transatlantic dialogue involving a diverse range of participants on the ethics of war and peace with a view to investigating and renewing that tradition as part of a broader public conversation.

The starting point of the symposium, as well as of this book, is the premise that the just war tradition remains an indispensable framework for analysing global order, peace and security. In our view, it is critical to see just war thinking as a dynamic tradition for reflecting on the nature of international society rather than as a set of prescriptions to be rigidly applied to crises, a sort of checklist that can be ticked or crossed. Even more fundamental to the volume is the belief that conflict tragically remains an inextricable part of both intra- and inter-state relations. Therefore, trying to understand such a fundamental phenomenon is itself a moral obligation and the just war remains the best way to do so. Allied to this is the sense that moral reflection and action must remain at the heart of politics and that a properly understood just war tradition can play a significant role in shaping public discourse about the values and ends of political communities. Thus, properly understood the tradition becomes,

---

[1] The other element within the Christian tradition is pacifism. Perhaps the foremost British thinker within that strand was the late Sydney D. Bailey. See, for example, *War and Conscience in the Nuclear Age* (Basingstoke: Macmillan, 1987). One of his legacies remains the continuing work of the Council on Christian Approaches to Defence and Disarmament, which he helped to found and to which several of the contributors to this volume belong.

above all, an exercise in practical wisdom about the nature of international society and fundamental questions such as intervention. Yet war remains what it has always been, 'a defeat for humanity' in the words of Pope John Paul II, and just war thinking should never be seen as an attempt to moralise war with the intention of making it easier to fight. Nor can the tradition answer the interlinked security questions that face us about the environmental crisis, disease and poverty and the corresponding moral imperative to realise objectives such as the Millennium Development Goals or more effective conflict prevention. However, focusing on war explicitly allows us to address what remains a fundamental aspect of the human experience and using just war thinking allows, in Bryan Hehir's words, for 'a two–dimensional ethic' that addresses both policy-makers and the conscience of individual citizens.[2]

It is arguable that the just war tradition underwent a narrowing during the Cold War that deformed its utility as a guide to action. The overwhelming shadow of the US–Soviet confrontation understandably shaped the very grammar of our moral language in a way that focused almost exclusively on nuclear weapons. Yet, with the ending of the Cold War and the emergence of radically different threats, the tradition needs to be re-examined. We asked the contributors to this volume to explore whether or not the just war tradition continues to be relevant given the changing nature of international relations. If it is relevant, how can the tradition be reworked in order to provide a framework for practical reflection? The continuing need for dialogue between political and public actors was evident in the fierce debate over the 2003 Iraq War. The symposium sought to encourage such a dialogue by providing a space in which theologians, political and military analysts could consider how a re-energised just war tradition might assist policy-makers and the wider public to grapple better with the moral and political dilemmas of war.

Because that fundamental shift has occurred in the structure of conflicts, away from inter-state 'industrial warfare' to something as yet to be determined, there is an even greater need to explore the relationship between moral theory and practice. In view of this, the book takes an interdisciplinary approach in the belief that the insights from one discipline and culture should usefully contribute to and further the debate in

---

[2] Fr Bryan Hehir, 'The Politics and Ethics of Nonproliferation', *CISAC's Annual Drell Lecture*, Stanford University, 6 December 2005, p. 4.

another. Such an interdisciplinary approach has been central to the long development of the just war tradition as a body of moral reflection, rooted in Christian theology and natural law, that has evolved through a dialogue between secular and religious sources. That conversation between diverse and competing actors, whether theologians, military commanders or politicians, means that the tradition represents more than just a set of moral assumptions or ideals. Participants within this dialogue have always sought to shape and maintain the tradition to give it renewed meaning when faced with new security challenges. This dialogue has shaped methods of statecraft and rules of military engagement while still providing guidance to conscientious individuals grappling with the terrible moral dilemmas posed by war.

In its simplest form, the tradition argues for certain conditions and criteria to be met before any military action occurs. It has two thematic branches, classically denoted by the terms *jus ad bellum* and *jus in bello*. *Jus ad bellum* as generally understood today consists of seven principles, which need to be met to justify the resort to war. They include that war must have a *just cause*, be waged by a *proper authority* and with a *right intention*, be undertaken only if there is *reasonable chance of success* and if the total good outweighs the total evil expected (i.e. overall *proportionality*). It must also be used as a *last resort* and be waged in the *pursuit of peace*. In contrast, *jus in bello* is defined by two concerns: *discrimination*, or avoiding intentional harm to non-combatants, and *proportionality of means*, which implies using such force as is essential to achieve an objective that is itself necessary.

The history of just war thinking suggests that these criteria will atrophy if they are not reworked and then applied afresh in the unprecedented context of the contemporary international environment. One recent example of this reworking is that provided by the philosopher Michael Walzer. *Arguing about War* revisits many of the arguments that Walzer made some thirty years previously in *Just and Unjust Wars*.[3] Faced with the sheer number of recent horrors such as Rwanda, Kosovo and the Sudan, he finds himself defending the right to intervention, a right that he previously opposed. This in turn leads him to sanction long-term

---

[3] Michael Walzer, *Arguing about War* (New Haven: Yale University Press, 2004). Michael Walzer, *Just and Unjust Wars: A Moral Argument with Historical Illustrations* (New York: Basic Books, 1977).

military occupations in the form of protectorates and trusteeships. Taken together, these shifts result in Walzer questioning whether the just war tradition needs to be expanded to include a third branch, namely *jus post bellum*, to help address many of the issues that have arisen in post-conflict situations like East Timor and Iraq.

Walzer's efforts are reflective of a wider uncertainty as to what constitutes a just war in the twenty-first century, as witnessed, for example, by the work of Michael Ignatieff.[4] The traditional image of a country's armed services constituting a war-fighting machine designed and equipped to achieve a decisive military victory on the battlefield in order to 'solve' the original political problem that necessitated the military deployment in the first place sits oddly with post-Cold War reality. It is difficult now to identify not only the battlefield but also who or what is the 'enemy'. Military force is more often than not employed 'in the presence of civilians, against civilians', and most importantly 'in defence of civilians'.[5] Using military force to resolve an international political dispute has increasingly given way to the aim of creating by force the conditions in which peace might be restored and then maintained by non-military means. This is a prolonged and painful process, as, for example, in Bosnia, which takes years, involving political and military skills and equipment quite distinct from those required in the past.

If, as General Sir Rupert Smith argues, the end of the Cold War made obsolete the dominant industrial model of warfare, and with it the industrial army that underpinned it, then it is necessary to rethink what constitutes a justified war, even if war in the conventional sense perhaps no longer exists. The shift from heavy industrial warfare, characteristic of the nineteenth and twentieth centuries, to war amongst the people poses several distinct challenges that need to be resolved as part of a public conversation if military force is to have any moral basis.

Most public and political debate regarding military matters is restricted either to contesting defence budgets or to debating the legality of a particular use of force. These debates are an important part of any

---

[4] Michael Ignatieff, *The Warrior's Honour: Ethnic War and the Modern Consciousness* (London: Vintage, 1999). Michael Ignatieff, *Empire Lite: Nation Building in Bosnia, Kosovo, Afghanistan* (London: Vintage Books, 2003). Michael Ignatieff, *The Lesser Evil: Political Ethics in an Age of Terror* (Edinburgh: Edinburgh University Press, 2005).

[5] General Sir Rupert Smith, *The Utility of Force: The Art of War in the Modern World* (London: Penguin Allen Lane, 2005), p. 5.

functioning democracy. They provide a mechanism for executive accountability and civilian control of the military. However, as in other fields of
public policy, such encounters seem fragmented and episodic and
informed by a cost–benefit culture of positivism that is proving to be
increasingly inadequate. In this context, Christians can play a significant
role in expanding the dimensions of that public conversation so that
fundamental moral questions about ends and means feature more
prominently.

The aim of this volume is to explore the continuing validity of the just
war tradition, and to examine the ways in which it should be updated to
take account of the new security environment. In so doing, the volume
aims to help stimulate a wider and more inclusive debate than has perhaps
existed in this area, without endorsing any one of the diverse and often
provocative opinions expressed. It is concerned rather with the relationship between theory and practice, with the intention of providing a robust
way in which to think and speak about war in the modern world. Running
through this book is the question: 'How can we make the just war
tradition both relevant and accessible to today's moral and political
challenges?'

The book is structured around four themes and concludes with a set of
reflections. In addition to analysing the merits of the just war tradition as a
decision-making model, it examines each of the classical elements of the
just war tradition (*jus ad bellum* and *jus in bello*). Crucially, it also
considers what Walzer calls *jus post bellum*. The intention is to move
beyond recognising that the just war tradition needs rethinking to articulating some of the features of what a reconstituted just war tradition
might mean in practice. This book avoids deliberately the quest for
consensus. Indeed, several of the contributors disagree sharply about
vital contemporary issues, such as the Iraq War. Yet every chapter stands
as a contribution to a wider discussion in which each discipline finds its
own voice in conversation with others.

## A framework for ethical decision making

An important contribution to that debate came on the eve of the 1999
Kosovo War. Tony Blair's speech to the Chicago Economic Club on
22 April 1999 drew heavily on just war criteria to provide a 'Doctrine of
the International Community' that could assist governments in identifying

the circumstances in which they should become involved in other people's conflicts. Similarly, both the *Responsibility to Protect*, a document commissioned by the Canadian Government, following the Kosovo War, and a report by a UN High-Level Panel on Threats, Challenges and Change, following the 2003 Iraq War, affirmed the continuing importance of the just war tradition by using its criteria to frame their deliberations regarding the legitimate use of military force. The concepts of the just war thus form part of our public grammar, but how have governments and international institutions used them? How relevant is a tradition, first developed some twelve hundred years ago, in offering criteria for deciding how new security issues can be appropriately dealt with? Does the use of these criteria suggest that there is a transatlantic consensus as to what the just war tradition means in theory and practice?

In the opening chapter, George Weigel analyses whether a developed just war tradition is evident in the 2002 US National Security Strategy. This is a controversial issue not least because many commentators see this document as providing the ideological framework for the 2003 Iraq War. Weigel acknowledges that the language of the 2002 US National Security Strategy sits uneasily with European sensitivities. However, Weigel argues that when re-read from the perspective of a retrieved and developed just war tradition, a tradition that allows for the morally legitimate first use of armed force, it is an appropriate attempt to respond to the new international reality. Central to Weigel's analysis is the argument that the concept of just cause as defence against aggression already underway, enshrined in the UN Charter's willingness to sanction only the second use of armed force, is inadequate in a world in which rogue regimes or terrorist networks possess or seek to possess weapons of mass destruction (WMD). In certain circumstances, he argues, it might be both necessary and legitimate to use force as a first rather than a last resort, even if the UN does not sanction such action. Weigel admits that while the document addresses the new *ad bellum* issues, it falls short of providing sufficient clarity as to how *post bellum* questions should be resolved.

William Wallace accepts that, unlike their US counterparts, European governments have not yet succeeded in defining the geopolitical context within which they wish to deploy force. As a result, the rules of engagement are more often than not determined at a national rather than a European level. Projecting the argument onto the United States has circumvented to some extent European debates about just war. This has left Europe free to criticise the moral justification for US actions, without necessarily recognising that European governments cannot avoid, at some stage, addressing these issues themselves. Wallace illustrates that events since the end of the Cold War, most notably in the Balkans and more recently in Afghanistan and Iraq, have forced European governments along a painful learning process in containing conflict and in post-conflict reconstruction. All major European states have contributed troops to the Balkans, Afghanistan or Iraq, but the majority have contributed to post-conflict operations rather than to the initial stages of military intervention. According to Wallace, Europe must develop the skills and capabilities to move beyond civilian nation-building exercises to active military enforcement operations. He recognises, however, that such a move remains difficult given the absence of any Europe-wide public and political debate about strategic priorities and geopolitical interests.

The contributors in chapters 4 and 5 examine the impact of just war thinking upon the churches' understanding of the use of military force as a tool of statecraft. How have British and American churches used or rejected the just war tradition at times of international crisis? Why are some within the churches increasingly disenchanted with this tradition? What factors have contributed to this situation and how should Christians respond? How can the churches revitalise what has been their dominant way of understanding, judging and limiting violence? Are there alternative ways of analysing conflict that would supplant the just war framework?

Nigel Biggar's controversial analysis of the various statements and reports issued by churches following the end of the Cold War argues that whilst the language of just war features prominently, the moral reasoning that binds the tradition together is noticeably absent. Many within the churches do not deny that a justified war is possible, but they do often raise the bar so high that no conflict could ever qualify. Biggar attributes this to broader cultural influences: the suspicion of 'power', post-imperial Western self-loathing and a belief that something as terrible as war must be avoided at all costs. In Biggar's analysis, the repudiation of the just war corpus takes one of several forms of 'anti-Americanism'. Biggar argues that the just war tradition is capable of further development to respond to international public life, but he mourns the fact that many within the churches, like most of civil society, seem reluctant to participate in such an agenda-setting exercise.

Much of Biggar's analysis mirrors James Turner Johnson's consideration of American churches. Johnson shows that, with the exception of the evangelical Protestant churches, American churches have for the most part interpreted just war thinking as assuming a presumption against using military force rather than seeing it as a legitimate tool of statecraft that has utility in maintaining and restoring peace and order. Johnson suggests that this reflects the emergence of a form of functional pacifism within the churches that owes its origins to the nuclear debates of the 1970s and the Civil Rights movement of the 1960s. Catholic and mainstream Protestant churches began identifying themselves less and less as an integral part of the existing social and political order and more and more in opposition to the state and to society. The public moral leadership role that these churches had traditionally played in such policy debates has increasingly been assumed by evangelical Protestant churches.

## Responding justly to new threats

International security has fundamentally changed since the end of the Cold War. New security threats have emerged (such as mass-terrorism, 'rogue regimes' and proliferation of weapons of mass destruction) that affect the way states view the use of force as an instrument of foreign policy. Ideas about preventative war and regime change have added another layer of complexity to the conduct of international relations. The use of force by some Western governments resembles a form of police action more than a traditional model of warfare. International law has been slow to adjust to this new security environment with the result that state practice can appear at odds with the UN Charter. This discrepancy is deeply problematic because it has eroded the international consensus as to when it is right and proper to use force. If the old rules governing state behaviour no longer seem particularly relevant, it is far from clear what the new rules are, or even who should draft or enforce them.

From a *jus ad bellum* perspective, the emergence of new security threats challenges the 1945 consensus, as enshrined in the UN Charter, that military force should only be used in self-defence. This consensus was a reaction to the horrors of the First and Second World Wars and reflected a significant narrowing in the just war understanding of what constituted just cause. Prior to the political transformations in Europe following the treaties of Westphalia just war jurists, such as Hugo Grotius, recognised the state's right to use force to inflict punishment on those that transgressed universal values. In the absence of clearly defined rules, and in a global environment that is now distinctively post-Westphalian, how helpful is it to revisit pre-Westphalian understandings of the just war tradition?

Redefining what just cause means has implications for the other *jus ad bellum* criteria, most notably last resort and competent authority. If classical just war thinking has at times sanctioned anticipatory self-defence and humanitarian intervention, it has been more reticent about the benefits of preventive and pre-emptive military action. If it is accepted that the nature of the contemporary threats requires early intervention, can the just war tradition provide insights into when such action is both necessary and legitimate? Alternatively, will such action always constitute a breach of the peace and therefore be open to abuse? Finally, if, under certain circumstances, it might be legitimate to resort to unilateral action, what are the boundaries of such action?

In chapter 6, David Fisher examines the moral and political dilemmas that arise when contemplating using military force for humanitarian purposes. Fisher argues that while the classical notion of just war always recognised that there existed a legitimate right to intervene in the internal affairs of another nation-state, this right was overtaken by developments in international law following Westphalia and the creation of the states' system. He argues, however, that international law needs amendment to reflect the growing international moral consensus in favour of intervention where human rights are seriously under threat. He suggests that the just war tradition provides a robust framework to help determine when such an intervention is necessary, whilst also ensuring that this new-found right of intervention is not open to abuse. He concludes by underlining the urgent moral necessity for action to prevent tragedies such as the Rwandan genocide and the horrors now unfolding in Darfur.

Jean Bethke Elshtain's analysis of the historical and ethical roots of the just war tradition leads her to reject vigorously the claim that just war thinking is applicable only to conflicts between states. She argues that while a just response to terrorism will not be narrowly and exclusively military, military means might be necessary where a legal–criminal paradigm is found wanting, such as when a terrorist organisation works from a failed or failing state. Controversially, she argues that the modern-day complexity of terrorism requires a flexible nuanced response that may at times skirt the edges of law and restraint, but that just war thinking remains crucial if politics and ethics are not to diverge.

In the subsequent chapter, Paul Schulte argues that the presumption against the first use of force is no longer sustainable when a nexus of threats such as terrorism, 'rogue regimes' and weapons of mass destruction threaten world order. Schulte lists a number of defining characteristics of what constitutes a rogue regime that helps to ward against cultural demonisation, although he recognises that the term remains problematic. Despite the threat posed by rogue regimes, only a handful of states can undertake regime change. Such states, he believes, will make a decision on a case-by-case basis and the overriding ethics in such decisions will invariably be prudential, requiring a significant dosage of moral luck. Using a utilitarian analysis, Schulte provides a provisional schema that might help to ensure that those states that do respond with military action without international authorisation can ensure that their actions more closely approximate 'wars of enforcement', that is, military interventions intended to reinforce world-ordering principles.

The brief overview of the above chapters points to a willingness amongst many of the contributors to assume that moral outrage can and should act as driver for the formation of new laws by either treaty or custom. Taken to the extreme this can lead to the conclusion that in the absence of clearly defined legal rules it is legitimate, even necessary, to fall back on natural law. In chapter 9, Franklin Berman examines in closer detail the correlation between compliance and enforcement, which is fundamental to the functioning of any legal system. Berman argues that the question 'Is there a right of intervention?' is misleading because it confuses the 'right holder' and the 'obligee'. If the question is reframed as 'Who is entitled to intervene?' a more fruitful discussion can be had as to the question of values (justice, welfare and peace) and agency in the international law context. This discussion leads him to the formidable combination of obstacles that confront the construction of a viable legal regime of ethical intervention.

## Fighting wars justly

Changes in international security have accompanied a revolution in military affairs. The emergence of network centric warfare and effects-based warfare has given rise to such language as the 'intelligent battlefield'

and even 'humane warfare'. Historically, developments in military technology have been followed by a revision of the international laws of war. It
is therefore important to ask how the language of law and morality is
responding to the challenges of new military technology. Allied to
this inquiry is the question of whether the increasing technological
superiority of Western countries creates its own military and moral
dilemmas through the development of asymmetrical warfare and even
'asymmetrical morality', in which a combatant eschews the traditional
battlefield in favour of low-intensity conflicts which pay scant regard to
the laws of war.

The following questions are of particular relevance. How does the
revolution in military affairs impact upon just war understandings of
proportionality and discrimination? In what ways will these developments
shape our political, if not our moral, understanding as to when it is
legitimate to resort to military force? Is it possible to imagine an 'intelligent' or even 'humane battlefield'? If so, what are the ethical and political
challenges of such a development? Is the emergence of asymmetrical
warfare and asymmetrical morality a side effect or an intended consequence of this military revolution? If so, is it reasonable to expect combatants fighting in low-intensity conflicts to abide by the humanitarian rules
of law? If humanitarian laws remain relevant, how should they be
strengthened?

Effects-based warfare represents a transformation from the largely
static armed forces that characterised the Cold War to a lighter and
more responsive military as deployed in Afghanistan and Iraq. Paul
Cornish examines the impact of this transformation on the *jus in bello*
criteria of proportionality and discrimination. He argues that there is a
danger that the long-distance micro-management of military operations
leads to a compression of ends and means that reduces the role of the
solider as a moral agent at the tactical level. Cornish questions whether the
just war tradition can survive the homogenisation he perceives of *jus ad*
and *jus in bello* considerations. He argues that either greater effort is
needed in maintaining the boundaries between the two branches or it is
necessary to devise a new unicameral model of just war in which authority
and responsibility are more clearly defined.

In chapter 11, Terrence Kelly examines the moral and political challenges that arise when military force is used in civilian areas, such as
Baghdad. He recognises that emergency ethics is sometimes claimed to

override considerations of proportionality and discrimination, but that such a strategy could prove counterproductive in the battle to win hearts and minds. This poses a significant challenge for US military doctrine and culture, which he argues is still geared to fighting conventional industrial wars rather than wars amongst civilians. Without a radical reappraisal of US military thinking, which reconnects *ad bellum* and *in bello* considerations, US counter-insurgency strategy in Iraq and elsewhere is doomed to failure. It follows morally that if the United States cannot be reasonably assured of success then there is an absolute moral obligation to refrain from fighting the war in the first place.

## Securing peace justly

From a just war perspective the type of community for which war is being fought is all-important. In this sense, the *jus ad bellum* and *jus in bello* can be considered subordinate to a wider *jus post bellum*. An imperial order where one state seeks to dominate another is not a just and well-ordered community because it requires the absolute supremacy of one community over another. The peace that must be the goal of a justified war is neither a purely military victory nor the absence of violence, but the restoration of community. Yet the harsh and intensely difficult reality of creating viable political communities in Kosovo, Afghanistan and Iraq appears to generate, or even legitimate, a form of imperial oversight. Attempting to reconcile the tension between theory and practice helps to articulate what constitutes *jus post bellum* and how it might relate to *jus ad bellum* and *jus in bello*.

Central to this debate is the problem of how, or if, military power can secure a just peace. Are there natural limits and constraints to the way in which states exercise in peace that power accrued through military conflict? How do those states that are victorious on the battlefield avoid promoting their own particularistic agenda over and above a peace that furthers the global common good? Are there recognisable steps that states can take to transform their post-war position in a way that commands not only the allegiance of other states but also the population of the weaker and defeated state?

In chapter 12, John Langan examines the altered network of relationships between combatants and among nations that arises at the end of hostilities. He is less concerned with how wars end but rather with the different ways of conceiving this new network of relationships. Langan examines the various conceptions of international order that could be actualised at the end of a conflict. This leads him to question how these conditions relate to the traditionally recognised norms of just war. In so doing Langan shows that different understandings of what constitutes a just peace radically affect the way that *ad bellum* and *in bello* considerations are assessed and addressed.

Langan's philosophical treatise on *jus post bellum* contrasts with Gwyn Prins's robust exploration of the relationship between the conditions in general and the applied moral considerations in particular for the legitimation of imperial rule following a just war, fought justly. Prins argues that judgements regarding the character of a regime must be subordinate to the capacity of that regime to deliver and uphold the social contract in a way seen as legitimate by its subjects. Using a performance-based criterion, Prins argues that the predicament in post-war Afghanistan and the tragedy of Iraq, unlike the situation in the Balkans, is due to poor planning and management. This has undermined the legitimacy of the 'imperial' project, with the result that the United States and its allies are dependent upon hard rather than soft power to maintain effective control. For Prins, the problem is less that America is an imperial power, but that it refuses to accept the responsibilities that such power entails.

When viewed from the perspective of the on-going insurgency in Iraq, the need for all governments to develop an adequate peacemaking capability becomes a political as well as a military imperative. Mary Kaldor argues that neither the US model of war fighting nor the European model of peace-keeping is relevant to today's interconnected world where the traditional friend–enemy distinction no longer holds. Indeed, Kaldor poses a fundamental challenge in that her approach, which draws on the just war but attempts to transcend it, offers a radically different analysis about the morality of force. Rather than favouring the language of just war, she argues for the concept of 'human security'. Using Britain's experience of counter-terrorism in Northern Ireland as a case example, she suggests that while some just war principles are relevant to an understanding of human security, its language impedes the development of new ethical approaches which centre on and protect the rights of the individual rather than the rights of states. Developing such a human-security strategy would help to avoid, as in Iraq and Afghanistan, a friend–enemy distinction that attracts disaffected people to extremist causes.

## Reflecting on just war

Rather than attempting a definitive conclusion as to what the just war means today, this book concludes with five reflective chapters that mirror the different voices captured by the preceding conversation. Michael Wheeler takes up the argument made by George Weigel and James Turner Johnson, that to reflect on the just war tradition is to reflect on the use of power in the world. He poses the question, 'What does that tradition suggest for the twenty-first century?' Wheeler argues that while the *ad bellum* and *in bello* branches of the laws of war were developed in response to the experiences of war in the nineteenth and twentieth centuries, it is likely that the twenty-first century will see significant transformation in the tradition's understanding of *jus in pace*. Wheeler suggests that the nature and shape of this peace will depend not only on how America exercises power but also on how others react to the exercise of this power.

To Michael Quinlan the just war tradition represents the most thoroughly developed account of moral discipline governing the use of armed force. Though its origins reside in Christian reflection, it can command widespread acceptance as a way of thinking about war. Echoing Wheeler, Quinlan argues that the tradition's development cannot be the result of the preferences of the powerful. Quinlan explores three areas where he believes there exists a transatlantic divergence in the understanding and application of just war thinking: proportionality, right authority and right intent. Without further bridge building in these areas, transatlantic differences will continue to impede any international consensus as to when it is acceptable to deploy and employ military force.

Shannon E. French reminds us that debates regarding just war are not of mere academic interest but are of vital importance to those men and women who do the actual war fighting. Equipping members of the armed services with the necessary ethical tools with which to make a just decision on the battlefield is sometimes as important as, if not more important than, equipping them with the necessary armaments with which to achieve their mission. Without such ethical training, the boundary between warriors and murderers or between *bellum* and *duellum* is all too easily eroded. French argues that while governments have a responsibility not to commit troops to an unnecessary and immoral war, they also have a responsibility to ensure that a permissive environment does not emerge which legitimates acts, such as torture, that are inconsistent with a 'warrior's' code of conduct.

Richard Harries concludes by subjecting his own theological and political understanding of what constitutes the just war criteria to a re-examination in light of the analysis provided by preceding chapters. He rejects the claim that the just war tradition is outmoded and no longer applicable to the conditions of modern warfare by arguing that anyone who makes a judgement about the rightness or wrongness of a particular military conflict will, whether they are aware of it or not, be using principles and criteria which are basic to the just war tradition. While he takes issue with some of the arguments made by American contributors, he accepts that the criteria of the just war tradition have to be applied afresh in the face of very different contemporary challenges, whether of humanitarian crises, proliferation or terrorism. However, he maintains that, properly thought through, those criteria remain indispensable.

The contributors, of course, do not manage to settle the complex problems involved in attempting to think afresh what constitutes the legitimate or illegitimate use of force in the twenty-first century. However, they do demonstrate the enduring relevance and value of the just war tradition in helping us address those challenges. Our hope as editors is that in setting out and discussing some of the complex and controversial theoretical and practical problems that arise in relation to conflict, using what remains a vital conceptual framework, this volume will contribute to a wider public conversation about the nature of moral responsibility in this critical area.

# PART I

A framework for ethical decision making: state and civil society-based approaches

# 2

# The development of just war thinking in the post-Cold War world: an American perspective

GEORGE WEIGEL

The just war tradition has been the normative Christian method of moral reasoning about the responsible use of armed force in world politics by legitimate public authorities for some fifteen hundred years. Over a millennium and a half, and even as its central ideas have endured, the tradition has developed in response to political and technological innovation. In times like our own, which feature rapid political and technological change, the development of the just war way of thinking must, of necessity, accelerate. The purpose of this essay is to identify the changes in world politics and in weapons technology that require a development of the tradition in the early twenty-first century; to note the obstacles to that development posed by certain defective understandings of the just war tradition; to suggest several areas in which the tradition needs development, while proposing lines along which that development might take place; and to ask whether one might see such a developed tradition shaping and indeed being unfolded in US national security policy.

While the roots of the just war tradition reach back to Greek and Roman political theory, a specifically Christian idea of the just war was first enunciated by Augustine in *The City of God*, and was only later systematised: canonically by Gratian and his successors, the Decretists and the Decretalists; theologically, by Thomas Aquinas. Refined in subsequent centuries through reflection on the experience of statecraft, the code of chivalry and the evolving norms of Christian society, the just war way of thinking was, in James Turner Johnson's terms, 'the collected consensus of the Christian culture of the west on the justified use of force, set squarely within a normative consensus on the purpose of political order' – a consensus shared by Vitoria, Suarez and Molina, by Martin Luther and Hugo Grotius.[1]

---

[1] James Turner Johnson, 'Just War, as It Was and Is', *First Things* 149 (2005): 14.

It is crucial to a proper understanding of the tradition to recognise that, along this line of development from Augustine to the early moderns, this way of thinking was understood as one component of a more comprehensive theory of politics and statecraft. Peace, on this understanding, was *tranquillitas ordinis* (the 'tranquillity of order'), the 'order' in question being composed of justice and security (to which contemporary theorists would add freedom).[2] The proportionate and discriminate use of armed force to defend or promote *tranquillitas ordinis* gave war its particular moral texture; indeed, within the classic just war tradition *bellum* (war) is to be rigorously distinguished from *duellum*, the private use of armed force for private ends. According to the just war tradition, *bellum* can be good or bad, just or unjust, depending on other considerations; *duellum* could only be unjust. The just war way of thinking, in other words, is a method of moral reasoning within a broader conception of morally grounded and responsible statecraft. It is a way of thinking politically about the possible use of armed force in the pursuit or defence of *tranquillitas ordinis*, while taking full account of the moral imperatives involved in any just politics and in any justified use of armed force.

The just war tradition underwent little development in the first centuries of what we call 'modernity', thanks to the fissure of Christendom in the Reformation and the rise of secular philosophy. Following the Second World War, however, it was revived in the United States by a diverse group of thinkers including the Protestants Paul Ramsey, James Turner Johnson, James Childress and David Yeago; the secular Jewish political theorist Michael Walzer; and Catholics John C. Ford, John Courtney Murray, William V. O'Brien and J. Bryan Hehir. Their various contributions to the discussion underscore the fact that the just war way of thinking remains a developing tradition, a method of moral reasoning that has evolved, amidst considerable debate, to meet the political, technological and military challenges placed before it by history.

### The new world disorder

Development of the tradition is also imperative today, as new circumstances demand an evolution of the just war way of thinking for scholars

---

[2] See George Weigel, *Tranquillitas Ordinis: The Present Failure and Future Promise of American Catholic Thought on War and Peace* (New York: Oxford University Press, 1987), pp. 25–32.

and statesmen alike. What are the 'new things' in the post-Cold War world that require a development of moral reasoning within the just war tradition today? The first of these 'new things' is the fact that non-state entities are now crucial actors in world politics. The emergence of international and regional legal and political institutions and transnational economic and financial entities has compelled fresh thinking among international relations theorists on the actors and their interaction within the international system. For just war theorists and responsible public officials, though, the most drastic change involves the rise of non-state actors capable of politically consequential force-projection over long distances. The nation-state remains a crucial actor, and often the most important global actor, but it is no longer the only consequential actor capable of shaping the course of history.

The second 'new thing' involves the question of the location of international public authority. Following the Second World War some just war theorists and many churchmen imagined that national sovereignty in its post-Westphalian form would gradually wither away as decision making about global politics increasingly took place through the UN system (and through regional transnational organisations). Pope John XXIII, for example, seemed to envision a transfer of sovereign authority on at least some questions of international public life to what he called a 'universal public authority'.[3] The new openness of world politics after the bipolarity of the Cold War, coupled with the depoliticisation of European consciousness, seems to have revived this vision in the post-Cold War world, especially in Western Europe. That vision has, however, been challenged empirically by some of the hard facts of post-Cold War international public life.

To take the obvious examples: the manifest incapacities of international and regional institutions in preventing genocide (the UN in Rwanda and Sudan) and/or brokering non-violent political change (the EU in post-Yugoslavia), and the relationship between the internal corruptions of the UN system and the UN's incapacities in monitoring weapons non-proliferation (as in the oil-for-food scandal in pre-2003 Iraq), raise important new questions about the locus of war-decision authority. Can the claim of some theologians and political commentators

---

[3]  *Pacem in Terris: Encylcical of Pope John XXIII on Establishing Universal Peace in Truth, Justice, Charity and Liberty*, 11 April 1963.

that the UN Security Council alone possesses the moral authority to legitimate the use of armed force be sustained? If not, what other focal points for war-decision authority might be envisioned?

The third 'new thing' involves technology, at both the high and low ends of the spectrum. Advances in weapons technology, real-time intelligence capabilities, and global satellite-guidance systems have created a battlefield environment in which the most developed states can observe the just war *in bello* principles of proportion and discrimination far more scrupulously. At the same time, the use of low-technology weaponry for purposes of murder and/or political intimidation has become a virtually daily occurrence in many parts of the world. The new phenomenon of the suicide bomber, who marries distorted religious conviction to nihilism and low-technology weaponry to produce lethal personal effects and critical political effects is the obvious example. What developments in the classic *in bello* principles, and in responsible governments' use of those principles to guide decision making, might be required by these new realities which, considered together, produce the phenomenon sometimes called 'asymmetrical warfare'?

The fourth 'new thing' involves the character of certain contemporary political regimes. Just war thinking in the post-Westphalian period virtually ignored the character of regimes in thinking through the *ad bellum* questions of just cause and last resort. In addressing the question of whether a morally legitimate *casus belli* existed and whether all non-military options for resolving the conflict had been exhausted, all regimes were assumed to be equal for purposes of moral analysis. In a world in which rogue states seek or possess weapons of mass destruction (WMD) and ballistic missile capability and have close links to international terrorism, are there circumstances in which regime character and technological capability combine in a clear and present danger, such that last resort might mean the morally legitimate first use of armed force? Can the post-1945 identification of just cause with the second (and only the second) use of military force be sustained? How, in other words, is the regime factor to be weighed in the moral calculus of just war reasoning and governmental decision making?

## Defective ideas have consequences

These, then, are the 'new things' that compel a development of just war thinking. A proper development is unlikely, however, unless three defects in the recent just war debate are confronted. The first defective notion regularly encountered in the contemporary debate is a misunderstanding of the nature of just war thinking itself as essentially a matter of casuistry. Here, the tradition is (mis)conceived as a set of hurdles set before statesmen by just war analysts. If the statesman in question successfully leaps the hurdles, the analysts are obliged to concede the justice of a particular use of armed force. Prior to the recent wars in Afghanistan and Iraq, this defective understanding of the just war way of thinking was ubiquitous, not least in the commentary of those who seemed more worried about restraining the allied use of armed force than about the terrible damage done to world order by al-Qaeda and by a rogue regime like Saddam Hussein's Iraq.

As a tradition of statecraft and as an expression of Augustinian moral realism, the just war tradition recognises that there are circumstances in which the responsible statesman's first and most urgent obligation in the face of evil is to stop it. There are times when waging war is not only morally permissible, but also morally imperative to defend the innocent and to promote the minimum conditions of international order. This does not require us to be 'pagans', as political commentator Robert Kaplan suggests.[4] It only requires us to be morally serious and politically responsible. It requires us to make the effort to connect the dots between ends and means, between the political good of peace and the means necessary to achieve that good.

In developing further the just war way of thinking, the tradition is best understood as its classic formulators understood it – as an attempt to relate the morally legitimate use of proportionate and discriminate military force to morally worthy political ends. In this sense, the just war tradition shares Clausewitz's view of the relationship between war and politics: unless war is an extension of politics, it is simply wickedness. Some may consider Clausewitz the archetypal pagan. But on this crucial point, at least, Clausewitz was articulating a thoroughly classic just war view of the matter. Good ends do not justify any means. But as Father John Courtney Murray liked to say, in his gently provocative way, 'If the end doesn't justify the means, what does?' From a just war perspective, what justifies the resort to proportionate and discriminate armed force – what

---

[4]  Robert Kaplan, *Warrior Politics: Why Leadership Demands a Pagan Ethos* (New York: Random House, 2002).

makes war make moral sense – is precisely a question of the morally worthy political ends being defended and/or advanced. That is why the just war tradition is a theory of statecraft, not simply a method of casuistry. It is a method of moral reasoning about politics, not a matter of theologians and political commentators setting hurdles for statesmen.

The second difficulty frequently encountered in the contemporary just war debate has to do with the just war tradition's starting point. The distinction between *bellum* and *duellum* is critically important in the classic just war way of thinking. *Bellum*, rightly conceived, is the use of armed force for public ends by legitimate public authorities who have an obligation to defend the security of those for whom they have assumed responsibility. *Duellum*, on the other hand, is the use of armed force for private ends by private individuals. To grasp this essential distinction is to understand that, in the just war tradition, war *is* a moral category. It is not inherently suspect morally. Rather, armed force is something that can be used for good or evil, depending on who is using it, why, to what ends and how.

Those who claim that the just war tradition begins with a presumption against war are mistaken. It does not begin there, and it never did. To suggest that the just war tradition begins with a 'presumption against war' – in anything other than the limited sense that all morally serious people prefer that there not be wars rather than that there be wars – is not merely a matter of misreading intellectual history; it also inverts the structure of moral analysis in ways that lead to dubious moral judgements and distorted perceptions of political reality. Classic just war thinking begins with the moral judgement that rightly constituted public authority is morally obliged to defend the security of those for whom it has assumed responsibility. This explains why Paul Ramsey described the just war tradition as an explication of the public implications of the Great Commandment of love of neighbour (even as he argued that the commandment sets limits to the use of armed force).

If the just war tradition is a theory of statecraft, to imagine that its method of moral reasoning begins with a presumption against war is to begin at the wrong place. The just war tradition begins somewhere else. It begins by defining the moral responsibilities of governments, continues with the definition of morally appropriate political ends and then takes up the question of means. By reversing the analysis of means and ends, the presumption against war starting point collapses *bellum* into *duellum* and ends up conflating the ideas of violence and war. This strips warfare of its distinctive moral texture. Indeed, the very notion of warfare as having a moral texture seems to have been forgotten in some quarters today.

The presumption against war starting point is also theologically dubious. In several instances, its effect in moral analysis has been to turn the tradition inside out, such that *in bello* questions of proportionality and discrimination take theological precedence over what were traditionally assumed to be prior *ad bellum* questions. This helps to explain why, after the terrorist attacks of 9/11, considerable attention was paid by many ecclesiastical and political commentators to the necessity of avoiding indiscriminate non-combatant casualties in the war against terrorism, while little attention was paid to the prior question of the moral obligation of government to pursue national security and world order, both of which were directly threatened by the terrorist networks. This inversion is theologically problematic because it places the heaviest burden of moral analysis on what are inevitably contingent judgements. There is nothing wrong, per se, with contingent judgements; but they are contingent. In the nature of the case, we can have less surety about *in bello* considerations than we can about certain *ad bellum* questions. The just war way of thinking logically starts with *ad bellum* questions because, as indicated previously, it is a tradition of statecraft: a tradition that attempts to advance morally worthy political ends. But there is also a theo-logic – a theological logic – that gives priority to the *ad bellum* questions, for these are the questions on which we can have some measure of moral clarity.

The claim that a presumption against war is at the root of the just war tradition cannot be sustained historically, methodologically or theologically; moreover, the presumption tends to distort the political analysis of those who adopt it. To begin here is to begin at the wrong place. And beginning at the wrong place almost always means arriving at the wrong destination. Thus the development of just war thinking in the post-Cold War world must include a recovery of the classic structure of just war analysis, which begins with the question of the moral obligations of legitimate public authority.

A third impediment is the functional pacifism displayed by Church leadership in both North America and Europe. By functional pacifism, I mean an approach to just war in which it is assumed that the hurdles to be overcome by statesmen are so high that the morally appropriate use of armed force is virtually inconceivable. Functional pacifism distorts reality to the point where moral vision becomes blurred. This blurring has been amply displayed since 11 September 2001. It was evident when commentators used words like 'tragedy' or 'crime' to describe what moral realism would have instinctively understood to be acts of war. It was evident when the overwhelming majority of American religious leaders and intellectuals prioritised the imperative of avoiding non-combatant casualties in the national response to terrorism. It was evident when American and European politicians and commentators alike deplored the 'root causes' of terrorism – an analysis that seemed unacquainted with the history of modern terrorist politics, that ignored the empirical facts of 9/11 (when the perpetrators were well-educated, amply funded middle-class people), and that implied a demeaning and deterministic reading of others' moral capabilities (as if the perpetrators of 9/11 were people who just did not know any better). It was also evident in the warnings heard from European and American religious leaders and intellectuals about 'violence begetting violence' – as if a proportionate and discriminate use of military force in a just cause were the moral equivalent of turning a 767 into a weapon of mass destruction. Finally, a blurring of moral vision has been evident at the local congregation level: how many prayers for the vindication of justice, much less for victory in the war against terrorism, have been heard since 9/11? Some perhaps, but not many. Somehow, to 'pray for peace' has come unglued from 'praying for justice'. This functional pacifism, which has been discernible in American ecclesiastical life as well as some quarters of American political life for more than thirty years, is one reason why the just war way of thinking is taken far more seriously in America's service academies and armed forces' graduate schools than it is in America's seminaries. The interest in classic just war thinking in the officer corps and throughout the armed forces is surely to be welcomed; its diminishment in graduate schools of theology is not.

## The issues revisited

Developing the just war way of thinking today requires both retrieval and development. Just war thinkers must retrieve the idea of the just war tradition as a tradition of statecraft, the classic structure of just war analysis and the concept of peace as *tranquillitas ordinis*. They must also develop and extend the tradition to meet the political exigencies of a new century and to address the international security issues posed by new weapons technologies. There are three areas in which the *ad bellum* criteria of the just war tradition require development in response to the four 'new things' in the post-Cold War international environment noted above.

### Just cause

In the classic just war tradition, just cause was understood as defence against aggression, the recovery of something wrongfully taken, or the punishment of evil. As the tradition has developed since the Second World War, the last two notions have been largely displaced, and defence against aggression has become the primary, even sole, meaning of just cause. This theological evolution has parallels in international law: the defence-against-aggression concept of just cause shapes Articles 2 and 51 of the United Nations Charter. New weapons capabilities and rogue states require a development of the concept of defence against aggression. In light of contemporary security realities, it is imperative to reopen this discussion and to develop the concept of just cause. Can it be said that, in the hands of certain kinds of states, the possession of WMD constitutes an aggression – or, at the very least, an aggression waiting to happen?

WMD are clearly not aggressions-waiting-to-happen when they are possessed by stable, law-abiding states. No Frenchman goes to bed nervous about the UK's nuclear weapons, and no sane Mexican or Canadian worries about a pre-emptive nuclear attack from the United States. Every sane Israeli, Turk or Bahraini, on the other hand, was deeply concerned about the possibility of an Iraq with nuclear weapons and medium-range ballistic missiles. If this regime factor is crucial in the moral analysis, then the first use of armed force to deny the rogue state that kind of destructive capacity does not contravene the defence-against-aggression aspect of just cause. Indeed, it would do precisely the opposite, by giving the concept of defence against-aggression real traction in the world we must live in, and transform.

Does a development of just cause along these lines violate the principle of sovereignty and risk a global descent into chaos? A developed just war tradition would recognise that the post-Westphalian notions of state equality and sovereign immunity assume at least a minimum of acquiescence to minimal international norms of order, an assumption that it would be imprudent to grant to states seeking to break out of international nuclear non-proliferation regimes. To deny rogue states the capacity to create lethal dis-order, precisely because their possession of weapons of mass destruction would threaten the minimum conditions of order in international public life, strengthens the cause of world order; it does not undermine it. The lessons of the 1930s are pertinent here.

A developed just war tradition would also take up the question of the relevant actors in world politics. Since 9/11, some analysts have objected to describing the Western response to the international terrorist networks as war because, they argue, al-Qaeda and similar networks are not states, and only states can, or should, wage war, properly understood. There is an important point at stake here, but the critics misapply it. By limiting the legitimate use of armed force to those international actors who are recognised in international law and custom as exercising sovereignty, the just war tradition has had an important influence on world political culture and law. Over a period of centuries, the classic distinction between *bellum* and *duellum* has been concretised in international law. Yet it does not fudge this distinction to recognise that al-Qaeda and similar networks function like states, even if they lack certain attributes and trappings of sovereignty. Indeed, terrorist organisations provide a less ambiguous example of a legitimate military target, because unlike conventional states the parasite states that are international terrorist organisations are unmitigated evils whose only purpose is wickedness – the slaughter of innocents for ignoble political ends. These new realities require us to recognise that a state properly described from a moral point of view as *bellum* can exist between states and non-state actors – a recognition that strengthens the distinction between *bellum* and *duellum*.

## Competent authority

That the *ad bellum* criterion of competent authority needs development is obvious from the debate throughout the entire post-Cold War period, and most especially in the debate prior to the 2003 Iraq War. From the point of view of moral reason, must any legitimate military action be sanctioned by the UN Security Council? Or, if not that, then are those states that bear a large responsibility for world order obliged, not simply as a matter of political prudence but as a matter of moral principle, to gain the agreement of allies (or, more broadly, coalition partners) to any use of armed force in response to terrorism, or any military action against aggressive regimes possessing or actively seeking WMD? That the UN Charter itself recognises an inalienable national right to self-defence suggests that the Charter does not claim for the Security Council sole authority to legitimate the use of armed force. According to the UN Charter, one does not have to wait for the permission of the veto-wielding powers on the Security Council to defend oneself. The manifest inability of the UN to handle large-scale international security questions suggests that assigning a moral veto over any possible military action to the Security Council would be a mistake. Furthermore, what kind of moral logic is it to claim that the US Government must assuage the interests (including financial interests) of the French Foreign Ministry and the strategic aims of the repressive Chinese Government – both of which are in full play in the Security Council – in order to gain international *moral* authority for the war against terrorism and the defence of world order against rogue states possessing or seeking WMD?

Building coalitions of support is politically desirable (and in some instances militarily essential). But it is not morally imperative from a classic just war point of view – and a developed just war tradition would recognise that. It is not an exercise in 'American exceptionalism' but a matter of empirical fact to recognise that the United States has a responsibility for leadership in the war against terrorism and the struggle for world order. That responsibility may have to be exercised unilaterally, or in concert with allies but without UN approbation, on occasion. Defining the boundaries of such action while defending its legitimacy under certain circumstances is one crucial task for a developing just war tradition.

### Last resort

The classic *ad bellum* criterion of last resort is defined by functional pacifists in virtually mathematical terms: the use of proportionate and discriminate armed force is the last point in a series of options, and prior, non-military options (legal, diplomatic, economic, etc.) must be serially exhausted before the criterion of last resort is satisfied. This is an excessively mechanistic understanding of last resort and a prescription for danger. The case of international terrorism again compels a development of this *ad bellum* criterion. For what does it mean to say that all non-military options have been found wanting when we are confronted with a type of international actor that recognises no other form of power except the use of violence and that is largely immune (unlike a conventional state) to international legal, diplomatic and/or economic pressures? The charge that American-led military action in Afghanistan and Iraq was morally dubious because all other possible means of redress had not been tried misreads the nature of terrorist organisations and the nature of rogue regimes. The 'last' in last resort can mean 'only', in circumstances where there is plausible reason to believe that non-military actions are unavailable or unavailing. As for rogue states developing WMD, an updated just war tradition would recognise that here, too, last resort cannot be understood mathematically, as the terminal point of a lengthy series of non-military alternatives. Can we not say that the criterion of last resort has been satisfied in those cases when a rogue state has made plain, by its conduct, that it holds international law in contempt and that no diplomatic solution to the threat it poses is likely, and when it can be demonstrated that the threat the rogue state poses is intensifying? How, in other words, might we begin to refine the just cause and last resort criteria, such that the first use of armed force could be deemed morally justifiable because of a responsible judgement that aggression was indeed underway?

In early 2003, Anne-Marie Slaughter, the president of the American Society of International Law (who is comfortably situated on the port side of the American political spectrum) suggested that aggression could reasonably be said to be underway when three conditions had been met. First, when a state possessed WMD or exhibited clear and convincing evidence of intent to acquire them. Second, when grave and systematic human rights abuses in the state in question demonstrate the absence of internal constraints on that state's behaviour internationally. Third, when the state in question had demonstrated aggressive intent against others in the past. These three criteria set a high threshold for the first use of armed force in the face of aggression, while recognising that there are risks too great to be countenanced by responsible statesmen.[5] The future development of the just war tradition requires engaging with this proposal and refining it further. Some states, because of their manifest aggressive intent and the lack of effective internal political constraints on giving lethal effect to that intent, cannot be permitted to acquire WMD. Denying them those weapons through proportionate and discriminate armed force – even displacing those regimes – can be an exercise in the defence of the peace

---

[5]  See Anne-Marie Slaughter, 'A Chance to Reshape the UN', *Washington Post*, 13 April 2003, p. 7.

of order, within the boundaries of a developed just war tradition. Until such point as the international political community has evolved to the degree that international organisations can effectively disarm such regimes, the responsibility for the defence of order in these extreme circumstances will lie elsewhere.

## The 'new things' and the United States government

American governmental wrestling with the 'new things' shaping international public life did not begin with the administration of President George W. Bush. Regime change had been the declared policy of the United States toward Iraq in the Clinton administration.[6] President Clinton has also stated that his first thought, on hearing of the 9/11 attacks, was Osama bin Laden. That there were new threats to national and international security in the post-Cold War world, including terrorists capable of unleashing vast damage and rogue regimes like Iraq, was certainly one aspect of Clinton's foreign policy analysis that the new Bush administration shared on coming to office in 2001. Yet the Clinton administration, while recognising these 'new things', was not prepared to think beyond the conventions of post-1945 international public life. Neither was the Bush administration, in its first eight months in office. The 9/11 attacks convinced the Bush administration, beginning with the President himself, that the national security strategy of the United States needed comprehensive re-examination. The result of that re-examination was a much-debated document, *The National Security Strategy of the United States of America* (*NSS-2002*), issued in September 2002.[7] Read carefully (rather than through the prism of cartoons about American cowboys, influenced by apocalyptic evangelical theology, running riot in the world), *NSS-2002* emerges as a serious, although imperfect, attempt to think through the four 'new things' of international public life in a way that meets the tests of moral reasoning that a developed just war tradition would pose to responsible governments.

---

[6] Kenneth Pollack, *The Threatening Storm: The Case for Invading Iraq* (New York: Random House, 2002), pp. 94–5, 97, 99, 101–2, 188.

[7] *The National Security Strategy of the United States of America*, President George W. Bush, The White House, 17 September 2002 at www.whitehouse.gov/nsc/nss.pdf (hereinafter, *NSS-2002*).

The tone of *NSS-2002*, with its blunt affirmation of 'unprecedented' and 'unequalled' American strength and influence in the world, is undoubtedly grating at points, even (perhaps especially) on allies. The document's determination to advance a 'distinctly American internationalism that reflects the union of our values and our national interests' raises immediate cautions in the mind of anyone schooled by Augustinian realism to recognise that politics often involves hard choices among lesser evils, and that even the best of intentions will come into conflict with unavoidably imperfect policy options from time to time.[8] Read as a whole, however, *NSS-2002* is emphatically not a sermon, nor is it an exercise in triumphalism; but rather, it is a sober-minded attempt to define a morally sound security strategy by which the United States and its allies can advance the cause of the peace of order in the twenty-first century.

*NSS-2002* underscores an empirical point that any analysis of world politics shaped by moral realism must recognise. The axis of conflict in the world has shifted; the twentieth-century confrontation between various totalitarianisms and the democracies has been replaced by a new confrontation between Western democracies, on the one hand, and terrorist networks often supported by rogue states, on the other. In the new international environment, failed states are as much a present danger as states bent on conquest were in the past.[9] Experience has taught the hard lesson that the status quo is unacceptably volatile in certain parts of the world, including the Middle East. Prudent efforts to change this status quo by advancing the development of civil society and responsible self-government in that region are essential. In expanding the zone of political freedom in the world, the United States is acting, not according to 'exceptional' American insights, but according to principles of 'liberty and justice ... [that] are right and true for all people everywhere'.[10]

According to *NSS-2002*, the strategy of deterrence that saw the free world through to safety in the Cold War is unavailing against terrorist organisations and networks and against the most extreme rogue states. To rely solely on a reactive posture is too dangerous. Thus the first use of military force must therefore be considered an available option under the doctrine of imminent danger that international law has recognised for centuries. While the United States 'will not use force in all cases to pre-empt emerging threats', the United States 'will, if necessary, act

---

[8] *NSS-2002*, p. 1.    [9] *Ibid.*    [10] *Ibid.*, p. 3.

pre-emptively'.[11] Such first use of military force will be one of the means by which the United States seeks to defend the order that exists in international public life and to expand the zone of freedom (and hence of order) in the world. Other available means include public diplomacy, foreign aid and coalitional activity with allies whose purposes in the world are the same.[12]

Criticism of NSS-2002 has focused primarily on its call for pre-emptive military action. NSS-2002 spends far more time discussing co-operative international diplomatic, economic and political activity in support of the peace of order than it does discussing pre-emptive military action. Pre-emption was, however, the strategic 'new thing' proposed by the US Government in response to the four 'new things' of international public life. That, plus the fact that the word pre-emption seemed to imply a settled contempt for the role of international legal and political institutions in managing conflict, made it likely that pre-emption would be perceived as the centrepiece of NSS-2002. Suppose, however, that NSS-2002 had adopted language derived more explicitly from the just war tradition – which can indeed imagine the morally legitimate first use of armed force – rather than the language of pre-emption? Substituting this just war-derived language for the words 'pre-emption' and 'pre-emptively' (and their synonyms) in the relevant passages of NSS-2002 yields the following interesting results:

> While the United States will constantly strive to enlist the support of the international community, we will not hesitate to act alone, if necessary, to exercise our right of self-defence by *the first use of armed force* against such terrorists, to prevent them from doing harm against our people and our country.[13]

> For centuries, international law recognized that nations need not suffer an attack before they can lawfully take action to defend themselves against forces that present an imminent danger of attack. Legal scholars and international jurists often condition the legitimacy of *the first use of armed force* on the existence of an imminent threat.[14]

> The United States has long maintained the option of *the first use of armed force* to counter a sufficient threat to our national security. The greater the threat, the greater is the risk of inaction – and the more

---

[11] *Ibid.*, p. 15.    [12] *Ibid.*, pp. 4, 6, 25–8.    [13] *Ibid.*, p. 6.    [14] *Ibid.*, p. 15.

compelling the case for *the first use of armed force*, even if uncertainty remains as to the time and place of the enemy's attack. To forestall or prevent such hostile acts by our adversaries, the United States will, if necessary, *engage in the first use of armed force*. The United States will not use force in all cases to *forestall* emerging threats, nor should nations use *[our] first use of armed force* as a pretext for aggression.[15]

We will always proceed deliberately, weighing the consequences of our actions. To support options *involving the first use of armed force*, we will ... build better, more integrated intelligence capabilities ... coordinate closely with allies ... [and] continue to transform our military forces. The purpose of our *first use of armed force will* always be to eliminate a specific threat to the United States or our allies and friends. The reasons for our actions will be clear, the force measured, and the cause just.[16]

If this more traditional just war language is substituted for the language of 'pre-emption' in the relevant sections of the document, *NSS-2002* emerges more clearly as what its authors intended it to be: an effort to describe a morally serious and politically feasible national security strategy in which the use of armed force, as one necessary instrument of statecraft, is understood according to the canons of a developed just war tradition. Given the political and media contexts into which *NSS-2002* was launched, however, the sound-bite language of pre-emption readily fed the perception that *NSS-2002* marked a breach with the just war tradition and with the tenets of international law. Using the classic language of the morally responsible first use of armed force would have been truer to the logic of *NSS-2002*, and might have accelerated fresh thinking among just war analysts and European political commentators.

*NSS-2002* would have been further strengthened had it addressed more thoroughly another of the classic *ad bellum* criteria, namely, the criterion of right intention. Right intention is where the political goal of peace intersects with the means of proportionate and discriminate armed force in the just war way of thinking. A rightly intended use of armed force is not only one in which an immediate or on-going threat is addressed; a rightly intended use of armed force must be completed by efforts to secure the peace of order in the affected country. Thus war planning congruent with the just war way of thinking would take post-war planning for

---

[15] *Ibid.*    [16] *Ibid.*, p. 16.

economic and political reconstruction seriously – as seriously as military planners take their planning for actual war fighting. There will, of course, always be an element of the unexpected in post-war situations. But effective post-war planning would attempt to anticipate contingencies, and match capabilities and resources to those contingencies. Had moral theologians, churchmen and other analysts pressed this question of building the post-war peace into the debate more vigorously in the years after 9/11, *NSS-2002* might have included a more developed statement on these urgent *post-bellum* questions, even as it thoughtfully addressed the new *ad bellum* issues raised by the transformed international environment of the twenty-first century. If this had occurred then the results in Iraq might have reflected that more careful anticipation of the demands of securing the peace after an overwhelming victory in war.

Its not altogether satisfactory suggestion of a rather simple congruence between 'values' and 'interests' notwithstanding, *NSS-2002* also advanced the just war way of thinking by reminding its readers that questions of national interest can never be abstracted from moral scrutiny. Foreign policy realists seem to assume that the determination of the national interest is an exercise in casuistry, in which policy-makers determine the best way to achieve something already well known and perfectly understood. As *NSS-2002* illustrates, however, the determination of the national interest is a calculus of political judgement and moral judgement in which resources and capabilities, imperatives and commitments, aspirations and traditions are all in play. Or, to put it another way, the determination of the national interest and the best means to achieve it is an exercise in prudence, one of the four cardinal virtues and the first of political virtues.

## Concluding thoughts

It is, of course, far too early to tell whether the approach to the 'new things' of international public life outlined in *NSS-2002* will be successful in securing 'a balance of power that favours freedom' in championing 'the cause of human dignity', and in opposing 'those who resist it'.[17] Developments in Afghanistan, Iraq, Lebanon and the Holy Land, the transformation of Pakistani foreign policy and Libya's agreement to abandon its nuclear weapons programmes are one side of the coin. The

[17] *Ibid.*, pp. 1–3.

carnage caused in Iraq by Islamist terrorists and their Baathist allies is the other. Yet a careful reading of *NSS-2002* suggests that the US Government, unlike some others in the West, has been prepared to take the 'new things' of international public life with the seriousness they deserve. It has framed its response in ways that reflect a serious reception of the just war way of thinking in American public life, despite the difficulties noted earlier in this essay. *NSS-2002* thus challenges just war thinkers in the Church and in the academy to develop their own discipline to meet the demands of this new and dangerous period in world history – a period, however, in which new dangers could be the impetus to making real strides in the building of *tranquillitas ordinis*.

# 3

# Is there a European approach to war?

WILLIAM WALLACE

The just war tradition is concerned with defining the justification for resort to force, with limitations on the use of force, and with the obligation to use force in certain circumstances. Institutionalised Europe, which was successfully constructed on the basis of excluding force as an element in inter-state relations in the wake of two destructive continental wars, has found it easier to focus on the limitations than on the moral obligation. The enlarged European Union has become a 'zone of peace', freed since the demolition of the Berlin Wall and the retreat of the Red Army from any direct threat. The concept of 'just peace', propounded by the German Bishops' Conference in September 2000, seems much more appropriate to this ordered region, with its references to 'non-violence as a liberating concept' and 'conflict consultations ... aimed at preventing the use of force'. European governments and political leaders in the post-Cold War world have struggled to justify to their publics expenditure on military forces and equipment, and the deployment of those forces in response to indirect threats outside the European region: the duty to intervene, the responsibility to protect, the obligation to contain internal conflicts, and to remain committed after immediate conflicts subside to rebuilding states, societies and economies.

During the Cold War, most European governments and publics did not have to confront issues of projecting power beyond their boundaries. NATO managed security, while the EU was a 'civilian power'. Military forces were focused on the defence of Western Europe against Soviet attack: conventional forces played their part in the 'spectrum of deterrence' that stretched from local resistance to massive nuclear retaliation. Issues of justification for war scarcely arose when the expectation was that forces would be defending national territory, or the territory of allies, against attack. Questions of 'proportionality', of the appropriate application of force, focused on whether nuclear weapons were a legitimate element in the spectrum of deterrence. Britain and France, exceptionally, maintained limited capabilities for intervention outside Europe – the shrunken legacies of imperial power, now justified in terms of their status as permanent members of the United Nations Security Council (UNSC), and as the contribution of 'responsible' powers to the maintenance of Western-led international order. Some other West European governments developed extensive experience and skills in peace-keeping, through participation in UN missions. There were Swedish troops in the Congo in 1960, as well as in 2004; Danish, Norwegian, Finnish and Irish soldiers served in Lebanon, in Cyprus, in Sinai and in smaller numbers in observer missions across the globe. The rules of engagement for such missions, however, were very restrictive, and the legitimacy of their presence established under UN mandate. Use of weapons was relatively rare, and weaponry was almost entirely light.

Once the initial post-1945 idealism about European federation had subsided, European integration was led by elites and sustained through institutions. Underlying objectives were left unspoken; the European Community was declared to be a 'project', a 'journey to an unknown destination', a process of co-operation through which common interests might be discovered. National publics were largely uninvolved in these processes of elite negotiation; their 'passive consent' was assumed so long as the system delivered prosperity. Indirection, absence of public debate about political dilemmas and long-term objectives, was thus a structural characteristic of European policy-making. Common policies emerged out of complex negotiations within institutional frameworks, as elaborate compromises among divergent governments: manageable when negotiating economic regulations or trade packages, but a flimsy basis for common foreign or defence policies. Thankfully NATO, under US leadership, provided for the common defence.

The concept of 'civilian power Europe', which had developed in the 1970s, carried comfortable connotations of moral superiority: America focused on force, while Europe spread prosperity and democracy. It was, from the outset, an illusion; the security of Western Europe rested on the projection of American power. The European Union's self-image, however, was constructed around this separation of 'soft' civilian power – the power of attraction, reinforced by trade incentives and financial assistance – from hard military power. Sanctions – as on apartheid South Africa, or on Greece and Turkey when under military rule – were depicted as the withdrawal of Europe's usual generosity, with rewards (including even the promise of EU membership) to follow a change of regime.

## Rethinking Europe's international responsibilities?

The end of the Cold War thus raised difficult questions both about the international responsibilities of West European states, and about the future rationale for their military forces. As the direct perceived threat shrank, defence establishments in Germany and Belgium, for example, faced the almost existential question of how to justify their continued existence when their national territories were no longer threatened. The Belgian Government's enthusiasm for joining *both* the Eurocorps *and* the (British-led) NATO Rapid Reaction Force was driven by the sense that multilateral engagement was the only way to provide a new role for their national military. General Naumann, the Inspector-General of the Bundeswehr, played a leading role in the domestic debate within Germany in 1991–2 on the admissibility of deploying German forces beyond national territory, for the same reason. Military officers turned their attention to the contribution their forces might make to the management of distant conflicts; but few outside the defence community wished to follow their logic.

West European governments were preoccupied in the years after the Berlin Wall came down with the reunification of Germany, with carrying through the commitment to a single currency in conditions of slow economic growth and with meeting the demands from ex-socialist governments to move towards joining the EU. There was little inclination to address broader issues of security and strategy within the European region itself, even the awkward issues arising out of the disintegration of Yugoslavia – let alone wider questions about collective responsibilities for promoting global order or containing disorder.[1] NATO and the EU were both based in Brussels, with substantially overlapping membership; but there was almost no communication between the two, even between the separate missions of the same member governments. Institutionalised Europe, its proponents came to claim, was (and is) a force for good, for spreading civilised values across the globe, promoting human rights and

---

[1] Robin Niblett and William Wallace (eds.), *Rethinking European Order: West European Responses, 1989–1997* (Basingstoke: Macmillan, 2001).

opposing the death penalty.[2] It was relatively easy for Robert Kagan to portray this comfortably self-regarding Europe as believing in a Kantian world, while America coped with a Hobbesian one.[3]

Fifteen years after the end of the Cold War, European governments *have* partly adjusted to the challenges of projecting force beyond their national territories – though without explicitly defining the conditions under which they should be deployed. In 2003–4, 60,000 to 70,000 European troops were deployed outside the boundaries of the EU and NATO.[4] The largest and most long-standing commitments were in south eastern Europe – in Bosnia, Macedonia and Kosovo, where the EU was progressively taking over civilian and military responsibilities from NATO, and where European police and gendarmerie were slowly displacing heavier military forces. But contingents from a wide range of European states were also serving in Afghanistan, both in the International Stabilisation Force in Kabul and in Provincial Reconstruction Teams and other operations elsewhere. British, Spanish, Italian, Polish, Dutch and other contingents were stationed in post-conflict Iraq; though only the British had taken part in the invasion, and in the course of 2004 first the Spanish and then other contingents began to be withdrawn. Operation Artemis, the EU's first rapid-response deployment, had deployed 1,200 troops to the eastern Congo: French-led, with significant British, Swedish and German contributions, its deployment under way within seven days of the request for assistance from the UN Secretary-General. British and French troops were also deployed in west Africa, on a formally national basis (but with discreet co-ordination, in facing untidily trans-border conflicts); Nordic troops were deployed in Liberia, under a UN mandate, though linked to the same set of overlapping conflicts.

From 1998–9, furthermore, West European governments had explicitly addressed the issue of shared security and defence policy within a European – as opposed to US-led, Atlantic – framework, with the development of a European Security and Defence Policy (ESDP). The British and French governments were clearly the leaders in this process, with the

---

[2] Thomas Diez, 'Constructing the Self and Changing Others: Reconsidering "Normative Power Europe"', *Millennium* 33/3 (2004): 22–33.

[3] Robert Kagan, *Of Paradise and Power: America and Europe in the New World Order* (New York: Knopf, 2003).

[4] Bastian Giegerich and William Wallace, 'Not Such a Soft Power? The Deployment of European Troops outside Europe', *Survival* 46/2 (2004): 163–82.

German Government (or, at least, the German defence and foreign ministries) a willing follower. The thrust of the 1998 St Malo Initiative was to promote the reshaping of European armed forces around the British model, which the French had already adopted: smaller, professional forces instead of large, conscripted armies, with the equipment, transport and logistical support to operate at a distance from their home base. The fifteen governments of the EU committed themselves under the 1999 'Helsinki Target Goals' to provide collectively a force of 60,000 troops, deployable outside their combined territories within sixty days and sustainable as deployed for up to twelve months – which implied reserves for rotation and replacement, and a high-quality logistical chain. The target was not reached by its declared deadline, of the end of 2003, though (as has been noted) a comparable number of European forces were by then deployed on active missions. It has since been supplemented by a further British–French initiative, in February 2004, to organise for rapid deployment a series of European 'battle groups' (on the Operation Artemis model), some 1,200–1,500 troops including support for sustained deployment, challenging other European governments to demonstrate their ability to provide troops and equipment to the required standard. By December 2004 some thirteen battle groups had been pledged (some on a combined basis, as between the Swedes and Finns – with Norwegian participation under negotiation), to be ready for deployment by 2007.

European governments, through the EU, are thus becoming a collective military actor, alongside NATO and to a limited degree autonomously from NATO. There is, of course, no prospect that the EU will develop into a military power comparable to the United States, let alone competitive with the United States. Dependence on the United States for external security, and for the maintenance of global order, remains a deeply ingrained assumption. The pacifistic publics of democratic Europe resist increases in defence spending, in the absence of any clear and present danger; the combined defence spending of EU member states is now barely half that of the USA. European governments, furthermore, lack a coherent approach to the use of force, to support the role that they are gradually assuming. It has been characteristic of the indirection with which EU member states approach difficult issues of integration that ESDP was launched without an agreed strategic concept, without any open discussion on the threats to be faced or the appropriate actions to be taken in responding to them. The European Security Strategy (ESS),

*A Secure Europe in a Better World*, was drafted nearly four years after ESDP was launched. It was adopted by EU heads of government in December 2003, after months of discreet discussion among officials, with no encouragement of public debate in national capitals.[5] It remains a largely unnoticed document outside the small community of strategic experts in foreign and defence ministries and associated think-tanks and university departments.

No European approach to war has yet been agreed among national governments, nor accepted by national publics. Yet European governments have gone a long way towards addressing the obligation to use force and to intervene in external conflicts in particular situations, without spelling out the full extent of their commitments or the implications for future policy. The EU now exercises trusteeship powers over Bosnia, and (much less clearly or successfully) over Kosovo. Rules of engagement, however, differ among national contingents, and readiness to commit or to maintain forces (and to procure the equipment needed to commit forces more effectively in the future) varies considerably. Questions such as these are, after all, deeply embedded within national 'strategic cultures': understandings of national roles, responsibilities and identities, and of the place of military force within them.[6] Governments can only change national strategic cultures over time, through active and sustained political leadership, unless the perception of acute crisis alters the framework for national debate. As Nigel Biggar notes in his contribution to this volume, political elites do not find it easy to focus public attention on moral obligations in international relations, except on a case-by-case basis.

There is a very large question about whether or not it is possible for a non-state entity like the EU to develop a shared sense of international interests and responsibilities, or a shared sense of direct and indirect threats. The EU lacks a 'Demos', a political community with a common set of myths and symbols and a shared public debate (what the Germans call a *Schicksalgemeinschaft*). Some optimists have nevertheless argued that the EU is developing a European strategic culture, seeing the process

---

[5] Alyson Bailes, *The European Security Strategy: An Evolutionary History* (Stockholm: SIPRI, 2005).
[6] Peter Katzenstein (ed.), *The Culture of National Security: Norms and Identity in World Politics* (New York: Columbia University Press, 1996).

of European integration in this field (as in others) as 'a joint exercise in norm-setting and institution-building', in which the evolution of ESDP since 1998 is creating an underlying consensus on means and ends.[7] This may at best, however, represent 'the beginnings of a European strategic culture', among the small group of professionals and specialists engaged in the construction of the limited agreements and institutions so far established.[8] Most members of national parliaments, let alone mass publics, remain, however, largely unaware of what has been agreed or jointly ventured. The prevailing mood amongst most European publics is to celebrate peace, and to resist addressing the moral dilemmas of their shared responsibilities for ordering a disordered world. The rainbow-coloured flags emblazoned with 'Peace' in different languages that were carried in demonstrations and flew from houses and churches across Europe, in the wake of the invasion of Afghanistan and the highly controversial intervention in Iraq, symbolised this deep and widespread commitment to the avoidance of force.

## The painful evolution of a European approach

During the Cold War, the undertones of moral superiority among progressive West European elites paralleled substantially lower levels of defence spending than the alliance's dominant power, on which the West European allies depended for their security. France's ambivalent relationship with NATO's integrated military structures allowed some enthusiasts for European integration to envisage an integrated Western Europe disengaged from its encompassing alliance, disregarding the heavy dependence of Germany on US forces, and the dominant role that American ships and aircraft played in policing the Mediterranean (with implications for American influence over Italian, Spanish, Greek and Turkish domestic politics). There were internal contradictions in the stance that Belgian, Luxembourg, German, Italian and French political leaders adopted on the EU's developing international role. These states, to one degree or another, supported the extension of co-operation in foreign policy to defence, and negotiated into the Maastricht Treaty of European

---

[7] Gilles Andreani, 'Why Institutions Matter', *Survival* 42/2 (2000): 83.
[8] Paul Cornish and Geoffrey Edwards, 'Beyond the EU/NATO Dichotomy? The Beginnings of a European Strategic Culture', *International Affairs* 77/3 (2001): 587–603.

Union (1992) a clause that committed the EU to a 'common foreign and security policy [which] shall include all questions related to the security of the Union, including the eventual framing of a common defence policy, which might in time lead to a common defence' (Article J.4).

This clause had been carefully negotiated between the French and the Americans, with other European governments in between, in the course of redefining a new NATO 'Strategic Concept', in parallel to the Inter-Governmental Conference that led to the Maastricht Treaty. And the US Government then in effect challenged its European partners to demonstrate their capability. In the course of 1990–2, the number of US forces stationed in Europe halved, from over 300,000 to around 150,000. American policy-makers made it clear that the disintegration of Yugoslavia was a regional matter for which European states themselves should take responsibility; indeed, the Luxembourg foreign minister, then acting as president of the EU Council of Ministers, rashly declared, on a visit to Sarajevo, that 'now is the hour of Europe, not of the United States'. There followed a classic illustration of the consequences of willing the ends without the means. At one Council of Ministers meeting in September 1991, the German foreign minister is said to have insisted that 'we must send troops' to protect Bosnian Muslims from Serb attack. 'You mean, *you* want to send *British* troops', the British Foreign Secretary replied.

The bitter experience of Bosnia, between 1991 and 1996, provided the painful learning experience that forced European governments and elites to confront the hard choices of deploying military power. The French, with fewest inhibitions about the projection of military force, would have sent in troops at an early stage in the conflict, which in retrospect might well have contained the conflict at a far lower level of casualties. But there was no consensus on the purposes or limits of intervention, or willingness from other governments to contribute to a joint force with robust rules of engagement. The British hesitated to intervene, partly because their experience in Northern Ireland had taught them that intervention in civil conflict risked stretching into long-term engagement in containing violence, in reconciliation and reconstruction. The United Nations Protection Force (UNPROFOR) was sent in with very limited rules of engagement, and with relatively light weapons – though within two years not only the British and French, but also the Danes, were following a more robust rulebook in containing Serb forces, with artillery and armoured vehicles. The Dutch company in Srebrenica, with only light weapons and without air support or reinforcement, discovered the limits of peace-keeping operations when faced with well-equipped hostile forces, and stood by as the population it was tasked to protect were taken away to be shot. German politicians, meanwhile, were anxiously debating whether it was compatible with Germany's limited military responsibilities for air force personnel to serve on NATO's multinational AWACs (airborne early warning) aircraft over Bosnian territory.

While different dilemmas were being debated within different domestic political systems, officials of Europe's weak security institutions attempted to provide some focus for inter-governmental debate. National defence ministers within the (then) ten-member Western European Union (WEU), in June 1992, agreed the Petersberg Declaration, which spelled out what became known as 'the Petersberg tasks'. Apart from contributing to the common defence in accordance with Article 5 of the Washington Treaty and Article V of the modified Brussels Treaty respectively, military units of WEU member states, acting under the authority of WEU, could be employed for: humanitarian and rescue tasks; peace-keeping tasks; tasks of combat forces in crisis management, including peacemaking. These rapidly passed into the jargon of European policy-making, with references to 'top-end Petersberg tasks' acting as code for preparedness to use military force in an active as well as passive way, to 'make' peace as well as to 'keep' it. The 1997 amendment to the Treaty of Maastricht (the Amsterdam Treaty, new Article 17.2) incorporated these tasks into formal treaty language.[9]

Operations in Bosnia were a painful learning experience also for the USA, and for the United Nations as a multilateral organisation. In Bosnia (and later in Kosovo) US forces had in some ways much more constricting rules of engagement than their European counterparts; force protection (the avoidance of American casualties) was ranked far more highly in their criteria than in instructions to British, French or Danish troops. The USA

---

[9] The text of the Constitutional Treaty, however, waters down these references to the 'tasks of combat forces', replacing them (Article I-41.1) with less explicit phrasing: 'The common security and defence policy shall be an integral part of the common foreign and security policy. It shall provide the Union with an operational capacity drawing on civil and military assets. The Union may use them on missions outside the Union for peace-keeping, conflict prevention and strengthening international security in accordance with the principles of the United Nations Charter. The performance of these tasks shall be undertaken using capabilities provided by the Member States.'

demonstrated a strong preference for the use of air power, to intimidate hostile forces into withdrawal or surrender, supplemented by training and arming local forces – an approach which it followed later in Kosovo and then in Afghanistan, as the approach was consolidated into the 'Revolution in Military Affairs' and the concept of 'Shock and Awe'. Committed European forces – the British and French, most significantly, but also some other contingents in Bosnia – placed much more emphasis on occupying the ground, and on establishing contact with the local population.

This preference for peacemaking and nation building has emerged as a distinction between the American and the European approach to war – reinforced by American preoccupation with exit strategies and dismissal of post-conflict nation building. There are, however, two limitations to this European approach. First, it is open to the American charge that the European allies are capable only of managing the more limited tasks of policing and nation building, after hard power has achieved its initial impact. The air war over Bosnia and Kosovo was overwhelmingly American, given the limited abilities of European air forces to identify targets or direct bombs accurately at them; the projection of force much above the 'top-end Petersberg tasks' was beyond the capacity of most European states. Second, few European states were able to mobilise and move ground forces in sufficient numbers to occupy even the limited territory of Kosovo (the same size and shape as Northern Ireland) effectively, in spite of its geographical closeness to Western Europe. Only the United Kingdom's promise to commit 50,000 of its own ground forces – nearly half the British Army – to a ground invasion, as the core of a joint US–European force, persuaded Washington that a ground invasion was a viable option.[10]

The experience of Kosovo, confirming the immobility and inappropriate 'legacy' equipment of most European armed forces, set the context for the British–French initiative on ESDP. Their aim was to push their partners towards reorientation of armed forces towards the more likely threats that they would face, outside their shared borders and, with increasing likelihood, outside the European region itself. It is important to emphasise how reluctant European governments and foreign policy

[10] Lawrence Freedman, 'Can the EU Develop an Effective Military Doctrine?', in Charles Grant (ed.), *A European Way of War* (London: Centre for Reform, 2004), p. 19.

elites have been to accept that distant conflicts may represent indirect threats, even when the spillover of refugees and transnational crime reaches their domestic territory. The UK, as well as most other West European governments, refused to recognise that the collapse of domestic order in Albania in 1996–7 represented a common threat, in spite of the spread of Albanian refugees across Europe. It was left to the Italian Government to lead a limited coalition of the willing in a successful intervention, with other European governments joining in to contribute to post-conflict reconstruction. The St Malo Initiative was accepted by other governments in its initial stages on condition that its proposers did not spell out specifically where beyond Europe's immediate borders common forces might be deployed; leaving discussions to focus on force structures and institutions, without scenarios for deployment. German officials, in particular, resisted the idea that common European forces should be deployed to sub-Saharan Africa, where British and French policy-makers were still struggling to reconcile their different national priorities.

The intervention in Kosovo, it should be noted, was made without UN authorisation. The Russian veto in the Security Council was accepted as blocking a near-consensus from the rest of the 'international community', with NATO authorisation as the relevant regional security organisation serving as a substitute. This was, however, a reluctant concession for some national parliaments; Joschka Fischer, as German foreign minister, elo-quently swung initially sceptical German political opinion behind the case for intervention. It is, however, not at all evident that European govern-ments or parliaments would accept future projections of force without specific authorisation from the UNSC. Inclusion in the Constitutional Treaty of additional references to the use of force 'in accordance with the principles of the UN Charter' represents continuing reluctance to con-template any pre-emptive actions, or the projection of force in circum-stances where major states are divided about its use.

Without an open debate about strategic priorities and geopolitical interests, the restructuring of European armed forces was a procedural exercise, driven by formal commitments negotiated within multilateral institutions, rather than by recognition of need. Hardly surprisingly, such restructuring moved slowly between 1999 and 2003. Defence budgets stopped falling, but there was no accepted rationale for any increase. The German Government repeatedly delayed committing itself to procure the transport aircraft, which were key to the despatch and support of forces outside Europe, as it struggled with other demands on its budget; the Berlusconi administration in Italy cancelled its order when it came into office, without proposing any alternative arrangements. Peace-keeping contingents from European states were accustomed to travelling to their missions by chartered civilian aircraft, either without heavy weaponry or with armoured vehicles transported by sea or in US or Ukrainian heavy air transport. They operated within a UN timescale which allowed at least thirty days for a force to be assembled, usually more. In practice, few defence establishments were planning to send substantial contingents much further than south-eastern Europe. National governments resisted the EC Commission's efforts to include the southern Caucasus within the remit of Europe's 'Neighbourhood Policy' in 2002–3, for example, leaving support for the weak states of Georgia, Armenia and Azerbaijan to the USA. They were more open to contingency plans for peace-keeping forces to be sent to Moldova, discussed within the NATO framework in 2003, because it was possible to reach Moldova by land. When German troops were despatched to Afghanistan in 2002, a significant number were temporarily stranded in Turkey, because of the non-availability of the Ukrainian transport aircraft on which they depended.

Until the attacks of 9/11, therefore, European approaches to war were evolving through the accumulation of experience in south-east Europe, without agreement to apply that experience at greater distance from their borders. Within the western Balkans, it is striking how far European governments were willing to accept the responsibilities of occupation and directed state reconstruction. In different ways in Bosnia and Kosovo, representatives of the EU assumed directing authority over domestic populations – collective trusteeship, or collective empire, depending on one's perspective. In accordance with EU ambitions and US exit strategies, troop numbers and responsibilities have progressively been transferred from the United States (within NATO) to its European partners (within the institutional EU): a process that has culminated in the transfer of responsibility for Bosnia from NATO to the EU at the end of 2004, while military and civilian missions in Macedonia and Kosovo are now also EU-led. Alongside this long-term commitment to reconstruction, EU governments had in effect accepted that the western Balkans, like their eastern counterparts, were part of the wider European community;

the South-East Europe Stability Pact offered all these weak states the prospect of eventual membership of the EU. This, in effect, implied also that military and police contingents within these states were no longer operating outside Europe's borders; they represented no longer the projection of power, but rather support to neighbours who would in due time become partners.

Robert Kagan's characterisation of European attitudes to hard power as that of Venus compared to an American Mars caused outrage among European elites. It was, however, largely accurate. The evidence of European military structures and capabilities, levels of spending and of declared strategic planning, as of the summer of 2001 – with the exception of Britain and France – indicates a group of governments deeply reluctant to address potential threats or to prepare to meet them. It is, for example, striking that there was so little linkage in national or EU-level policy between the development of intensive co-operation on internal security, including the management of immigration and asylum flows, and the development of external security policy. The Tampere European Council in 1999, which launched a five-year programme for the development of common policies for internal security (or 'Freedom, Security and Justice', as the EU labelled it), received a series of papers on the situation within states from which the greatest numbers of asylum-seekers came. Interior ministers agreed on the need to tackle the causes of forced migration 'at the root'; but foreign and defence ministers appear not to have received the unwelcome message that engagement with weak and failed states outside Europe was now a necessary response to the indirect threat to Europe's domestic order that continued flows of desperate migrants posed.

Nor was there a consensus on the relationship between political and economic development and the provision of military support and training. Within Britain, certainly, there has since 1997 been much reorientation of policy towards the security foundations for nation building, led as much by the Department for International Development as the Ministry of Defence. There was a singular precedent for such a linkage in the early stage of the Somalia crisis, when the Belgian Government successfully negotiated reimbursement from the European Development Fund for the deployment of a battalion there, on the grounds that aid could not be distributed without military protection. But that lesson has had to be relearned in Darfur, where small contingents of European troops have attempted to support an African Union peace-keeping force, in protecting the provision and distribution of aid.

Until 11 September 2001 there was no substantial debate among European governments about the international implications of transnational terrorism, nor about the problem of weapons of mass destruction. Both of these were dossiers on which the Americans led, with limited consultations through NATO. National capabilities for intelligence collection and analysis were limited in most European states; Britain and France, the best supplied in this respect, hesitated to share information with partners less careful to maintain secrecy. The attacks of 9/11 were thus a shock to European foreign and defence ministries, as well as to wider publics. European responses since then have indicated the potential, and the limits, of the slowly developing European approach to post-Cold War disorder. There has been a remarkable transformation in attitudes to the deployment of troops beyond Europe. The German–Dutch corps has commanded ISAF (International Security Assistance Force); there are Danish troops in Iraq, Icelanders manning air traffic control at Kabul airport. Thirteen of the fifteen pre-2004 EU member states have sent forces to Afghanistan, nine to post-conflict Iraq. A great deal of this, however, has been in response to American pressure, rather than the outcome of shared European analysis and agreement. The intervention in Iraq and its aftermath has been a source of sharp disagreement among EU governments. NATO, it seems, under dominant American leadership, still defines Europe's security agenda, at least as far as Asia (west and central) is concerned. The African continent is the region in which the USA is content for European states to operate autonomously; but many European states are themselves unsure how far they wish to shoulder security responsibilities in Africa south of the Sahara.

## Is there yet a European approach?

The development since 1999 of security and military staffs in Brussels (now including a European Defence Agency, to promote shared procurement and capabilities) has been remarkable: institutions and procedures at least, though not necessarily leading to policies and outputs. The deployment of forces outside Europe has also risen, to a level unthinkable five years before. But only in south-eastern Europe, and in the brief and modest deployment to the eastern Congo, has this been within an agreed

European framework. Forces in Afghanistan have operated partly under bilateral arrangements and partly under NATO, while in Iraq disagreement among European governments has unavoidably made for ad hoc agreements within a US framework. A cumulative learning process has, however, been under way, for all contributing governments. What have they learned, and what issues remain unresolved?

The European Security Strategy represents both a declaration about what foreign and defence policy-makers would like European governments to accept, and a statement of the limited consensus so far achieved. Whereas the American National Security Strategy of 2002 spelt out the power priorities of an established power, the ESS set out to justify why collective Europe needed more effective military capabilities, and when it should be willing to use them. Its introduction declares that 'Europe still faces security threats and challenges', and that 'the European Union is inevitably a global player ... Europe should be ready to share in the responsibility for global security and in building a better world.' It identifies terrorism, the proliferation of weapons of mass destruction, regional conflicts among and within states, 'state failure ... the collapse of state institutions' and organised crime as the key threats, while noting the frequent overlap between these different categories. It stresses the importance of strengthening the multilateral institutions of international order, both global and regional. It argues that it is a European interest to promote good governance and political and social reform. 'The best protection for our security is a world of well-governed democratic states.' This short and outline document leaves a great deal to be inferred from the evolution of practice on the ground, and from the response of EU member governments to parallel discussions in other multilateral contexts: the 2004 report of the UN High-Level Panel, with its similar emphasis on security challenges, and the March 2005 report of the Commission for Africa, *Our Common Interest*, which contains a substantial chapter (not much reported in media coverage on publication) on 'The Need for Peace and Security'. A number of Europeans served on the UN High-Level Panel, while the British Prime Minister chaired the Africa Commission; domestic sensitivities over the future development of European integration, and over its extension into defence, mean that it has been easier in some countries and political circles to promote open discussion around these other reports. The Common Foreign and Security Policy (CFSP) Secretariat has continued to press the expert debate forward. The EU Institute of Security Studies, in Paris, has published a series of reports and papers, while the Centre for Global Governance at the London School of Economics published *A Human Security Doctrine for Europe* (in September 2004) with the CFSP Secretariat's support.

There is, as yet, no coherent or explicit European approach to the new security challenges or to the role of military force in countering them. Some indications of an emerging consensus are, however, emerging. There are, for example, significant differences in European employment of force from the American, in terms of proportionality, and relations with civilian populations: evident in Iraq and Afghanistan as in south-eastern Europe. European rules of engagement assign a lower priority to force protection, and a higher priority to protecting, and gaining the confidence of, civilian populations. These rules, it is true, have not yet been tested in such difficult conditions as counter-insurgency; the reaction of French troops in Kosovo to aggressively hostile (but largely unarmed) crowds in the summer of 2004 suggests that most are unprepared for containing resistance that threatens to slip beyond control. There are also specific and delicate issues about European special forces – which include German, Swedish and Danish special forces, as well as French and British – and the compatibility of special force rules of engagement with European assumptions about minimum use of force. Divergences between national rules remain significant and represent an important obstacle to joint operation.

European governments find it easiest to operate at the lower end of the Petersberg tasks. They are most comfortable with peace-keeping and nation building, even though they have not yet agreed an approach to the deployment of forces to failed states to provide basic security while political and economic structures are rebuilt. In this respect, European approaches fit American assumptions: that hard power and heavy conflict is beyond their capabilities or intentions, while post-conflict reconstruction and stabilisation are European skills. Few Europeans are prepared to admit explicitly that they continue to depend on the USA to counter direct threats from aggressive states (as in the expulsion of Iraq from Kuwait in the First Gulf War of 1991), but this is implicit in the scale of European military expenditure and procurement. The majority of EU member governments are evidently more comfortable with civilian nation building than military peace-enforcement. The final version of the ESS, in

December 2003, laid greater emphasis on peace building, and weakened the earlier draft reference to 'preventive' action.

European governments have not yet succeeded in defining the geopolitical context within which they wish to deploy force. Following the publication of the draft European Security Strategy, the Council Secretariat also produced a draft paper on WMD and European responses, which met a similarly limited response from member governments. European policies towards Russia and the Middle East – the two most threatening neighbouring regions – remain hesitant, even incoherent. National interests and ambitions pull different governments in different directions; the European Council was unable even to present a united welcome to the newly elected President of Ukraine in December 2004, and the French and German governments continued in 2004–5 to pursue much friendlier relations with Moscow than their Polish or British partners. Linkage between the external and internal security agendas remains weak and is also driven by divergent domestic circumstances and perceptions. Migration and asylum policies have become matters of intense domestic sensitivity, but not of combined external action. Rising opium production in Afghanistan, with a consequent increase in heroin supplies to Europe, had not led to a significant increase in the scale of European commitment to security and reconstruction across that country.

Attitudes to the necessary authorisation of force still differ. Britain and France are willing to deploy forces, if necessary, without UN (or EU) authorisation, if faced with a perceived crisis in which their interests are at stake; most other governments expect and assume UN authorisation. The sense of obligation to contribute forces remains contested. Nordic states, alongside France and Britain, share a sense of international responsibility for the maintenance of international order which inclines them to respond to UN requests; some other states have a notably lower sense of obligation. The most distinctive European approach, evident within the western Balkans, is the commitment to nation building and reconstruction over the long term. But there is not yet enough evidence from other deployments to support any generalisation from this experience. It has proved difficult to persuade European governments to sustain a commitment to Afghanistan anywhere close to the level asked for by the UN Secretary-General. Deployment to central Africa, into which it would be possible to deploy very large numbers of troops without succeeding in establishing and maintaining civil order, has been carefully limited both in numbers and in time span. The integration of military forces with civilian police and reconstruction teams has moved ahead in south eastern Europe, and in plans for the future development of ESDP, but has not yet been tested in failed states further south.

There is, therefore, only a muffled debate so far on the use of force across Europe, conducted largely through the communiqués and negotiated compromises of European institutions. Tentative steps to promote a more open European debate have so far failed to arouse a response. Even within the Roman Catholic Church, one of the strongest transnational organisations within Europe, different national bishops' conferences have addressed distinctive national concerns. Shared experience has, however, promoted convergence of national assumptions, and a more limited convergence of national capabilities. A European approach to war is slowly emerging out of the separate strategic cultures of different European states. So far, however, the outlines of a common approach must be traced through the accumulation of responses to crises, of reactions to American demands and the gradual accretion of shared declarations and institutions.

# 4

# Between development and doubt: the recent career of just war doctrine in British churches

NIGEL BIGGAR

The career of the doctrine of just war in British churches since the Second World War has been mixed. In some quarters it has enjoyed revival and development, but in others it has suffered doubt and suspicion. The task of this chapter, then, is to demonstrate past and present growth, to track the roots of current scepticism and to comment on what these imply for the future role of the churches in public debate about peace and war.

## The development of the doctrine since the Second World War

During the Second World War just war doctrine was alive in the minds of some prominent members of British churches: for example, the Roman Catholic philosopher Elisabeth Anscombe explicitly employed its criteria in her 1939 essay, 'The Justice of the Present War Examined'.[1] In the Church of England of this period, however, acknowledgement of the doctrine is harder to find. Traces do appear in the writings of William Temple, Archbishop of Canterbury, when he stipulates that Christians should enter upon war, not out of hatred for the enemy, but only with the intention of restoring a just peace; and when he makes use of the principle of double effect to argue that airmen who aim their bombs at factories and harbours cannot be blamed for any civilian deaths that might result, since these were not directly intended. On the other hand, Temple can also be found to brush aside any principle of discrimination, arguing that all citizens are implicated in the actions of the modern state, and that civilians may therefore be directly attacked if strategic considerations

---

[1] G. E. M. Anscombe, 'The Justice of the Present War Examined', in Richard B. Miller (ed.), *War in the Twentieth Century: Sources in Theological Ethics* (Louisville, KY: Westminster/John Knox Press, 1992), pp. 125–37.

require it.[2] Indeed, in respect of the conduct of war he displays symptoms of the very consequentialist tendency in Protestant ethics that would later provoke Paul Ramsey into helping to revive just war thinking in the USA in the 1960s.[3]

During that same period, British churches were beginning to wrestle with the morality of the uses of nuclear weapons and of guerrilla insurgency. One sign of this growing engagement was the founding in 1963 of the Council on Christian Approaches to Defence and Disarmament by the Anglican military historian, Michael Howard, and the Quaker expert on the United Nations, Sydney Bailey. Two years later Joan D. Tooke was moved to plumb the historical depths of the just war tradition in her study, *The Just War in Aquinas and Grotius*.[4] In the 1970s Oliver O'Donovan put the case for just war thinking to evangelical Anglicans in his booklet, *In Pursuit of a Christian View of War*.[5] Five years later appeared one of the most substantial Anglican treatments of war and peace ever written, *The Church and the Bomb*.[6] This applies and interprets just war criteria – in particular, the *jus in bello* ones of proportionality and discrimination – with some care, developing them especially in relation to a policy of deterrence by bluff. In the same year Richard Harries published *Should a Christian Support Guerrillas?*,[7] following it four years later with *Christianity and War in a Nuclear Age*.[8] In both of these Harries draws directly upon the just war tradition, as well as upon its American interpreters.

In the mid- to late 1980s there appeared several other volumes on the ethics of nuclear deterrence, all of them operating within just war terms. David Fisher, civil servant in the Ministry of Defence and member of the Church of England, put the case for a policy of deterrence in *Morality and*

---

[2] Here I rely on Stephen Lammers's study of the debate within the Church of England about the bombing of German cities during the Second World War. Stephen Lammers, 'William Temple and the Bombing of Germany: An Exploration in the Just War Tradition', *Journal of Religious Ethics*, 19/1 (Spring 1991): 72–82.

[3] Paul Ramsey, *War and the Christian Conscience* (Durham, NC: Duke University Press, 1961).

[4] Joan D. Tooke, *The Just War in Aquinas and Grotius* (London: SPCK, 1965).

[5] Oliver O'Donovan, *In Pursuit of a Christian View of War* (Bramcote, Nottingham: Grove Books, 1977).

[6] *The Church and the Bomb: Nuclear Weapons and Christian Conscience*, report of a working party of the Board for Social Responsibility of the General Synod of the Church of England (London: Hodder and Stoughton, 1982).

[7] Richard Harries, *Should a Christian Support Guerrillas?* (Guildford: Lutterworth, 1982).

[8] Richard Harries, *Christianity and War in a Nuclear Age* (London and Oxford: Mowbray, 1986).

*the Bomb,*[9] while the Oxford philosopher and one-time Roman Catholic Anthony Kenny put the contrary case in *The Logic of Deterrence.*[10] Shortly afterwards, Kenny's jurisprudent colleague John Finnis added his voice to the anti-deterrence chorus in *Nuclear Deterrence, Morality and Realism.*[11] And in 1989 Oliver O'Donovan published on the matter in *Peace and Certainty: A Theological Essay on Deterrence.*[12]

Since the end of the Cold War, Anglicans have continued to contribute to the doctrine's development. O'Donovan has emphasised its retributive dimension and re-examined such topics as counter-insurgency and economic sanctions in *The Just War Revisited;*[13] Nigel Biggar has written articles on morality and the authority of international law in the case of Kosovo, on what just war doctrine says about weapons of mass destruction, and on the application and development of the doctrine in the Church of England;[14] General Sir Hugh Beach has applied just war criteria systematically to Kosovo;[15] and Charles Reed has tracked the treatment of just war thinking by British churches with regard to the Gulf War of 1990–1 and the Iraq War of 2003 in *Just War?*[16]

However, notwithstanding the appropriation and elaboration of just war doctrine in Britain by some churchmen – as well as by some philosophers and public intellectuals – regard for it in British churches remains, at best, equivocal. The reasons for this are several. One of them can be found in a cluster of critical attitudes that, for want of a more nuanced collective title, may be called 'anti-Americanism'.

---

[9] David Fisher, *Morality and the Bomb: An Ethical Assessment of Nuclear Deterrence* (London: Croom Helm, 1985).

[10] Anthony Kenny, *The Logic of Deterrence* (London: Firethorn, 1985).

[11] John Finnis, Joseph M. Boyle and Germain Grisez (eds.), *Nuclear Deterrence, Morality and Realism* (Oxford: Clarendon Press, 1987).

[12] Oliver O'Donovan, *Peace and Certainty: A Theological Essay on Deterrence* (Oxford: Clarendon Press, 1989).

[13] Oliver O'Donovan, *The Just War Revisited* (Cambridge: Cambridge University Press, 2003).

[14] Nigel Biggar, 'On Giving the Devil Benefit of Law in Kosovo', in William Joseph Buckley (ed.), *Kosovo: Contending Voices on Balkan Interventions* (Grand Rapids, MI: Eerdmans, 2000), pp. 409–18. Nigel Biggar, 'Christianity and Weapons of Mass Destruction', in Sohail Hashmi and Steven Lee (eds.), *Ethics and Weapons of Mass Destruction* (Cambridge: Cambridge University Press, 2004), pp. 168–99.

[15] Hugh Beach, 'Interventions and Just Wars: The Case of Kosovo', *Studies in Christian Ethics* 13/2 (2000): 15–31.

[16] Charles Reed, *Just War?* (London: SPCK, 2004).

## 'Anti-Americanism'

Because most of the wars in which Britain has been involved since 1989 have been led by the USA, the attitudes of contemporary Britons towards war are bound up with their views of America. These are ambivalent, as any American who lives in England quickly learns. On the one hand, the British share with Americans a view of the Second World War as a just war, and therefore also the assumption that sometimes the use of military force is necessary to fend off great injustice. In addition, Britain's not so distant imperial experience, now enjoying a more positive press than at any time since the 1960s, inclines some British commentators to appreciate the need for a global policeman; and, given the evident impotence of the United Nations, to urge America to take up today's imperial task with both hands.[17]

On the other hand, there remains in Britain a widespread, if not overt, resentment at being deliberately supplanted on the world stage by a former colony and at having its own historic role as a matrix and beacon of political liberty written out of the script by an American popular rhetoric in which 'freedom' is the invention and monopoly of the United States. In some quarters this is intensified by a left-wing hatred of American capitalism, often combined with a moral-aesthetic loathing of American consumerism. In John Le Carré's novel, *Tinker, Tailor, Soldier, Spy*, we are told that after he had been exposed as a Soviet spy in the British intelligence service, Bill Haydon 'spoke not of the decline of the west, but of its death by greed and constipation. He hated America very deeply.'[18] Similar sentiment is evident in the statement by the playwright Harold Pinter, who explained NATO's intervention in Kosovo as follows: 'The truth is that neither Clinton nor Blair gives a damn about the Kosovar Albanians. This action has been yet another blatant and brutal assertion of US power using NATO as its missile. It sets out to consolidate one thing – American domination of Europe.'[19]

In addition to resentment at American power and pretensions and (in some cases) ideological hatred, British attitudes towards America are sometimes further coloured by a more virtuous 'Burkean' suspicion of

---

[17] E.g. Robert Cooper, 'The Next Empire', *Prospect* (October 2001): 22–6.
[18] John Le Carré, *Tinker, Tailor, Soldier, Spy* (New York: Alfred A. Knopf, 1974), p. 342.
[19] As reported in the *Guardian*, 7 June 1999, p. 2.

grandiose revolutionary ambitions, and by a post-imperial awareness both of the moral ambiguities of *missions civilitrices* and of the limited capacity of even predominant imperial power to achieve them. As a consequence, many contemporary Britons find suspect and alienating the tendency of much American public rhetoric to represent the United States as the Chosen People born in original righteousness and manifestly destined to mediate the Kingdom of God to the rest of the globe.[20] Recently, this distaste has found expression in a minor spate of British deconstructions, both televisual and literary, of the American Foundation Myth[21] and of the messianic dimension of popular American self-understanding.[22]

These various strains of 'anti-Americanism' help to explain some of the reluctance of many British church people to identify as 'just' any of the recent wars in which the United Kingdom has been involved. Another, probably more important cause, however, is the high incidence of 'virtual' or 'practical' pacifism.

## 'Practical pacifism'

All British churches include members who are pacifists in principle, supposing war to be morally wrong as such; but these would be few in number. Far more numerous are the 'virtual' or 'practical' pacifists, who do not deny that a just war is possible in theory but raise the bar so high that no actual war could ever qualify. They assume that war is so evil that there *must always* be a better alternative. Such an attitude is more common

---

[20] Late-Victorian and Edwardian Britons would have found such absolutely self-confident rhetoric far less alien – except, of course, that they would have used it of Britain. What changed British sensibilities? The obvious candidate is the slaughter of the First World War, whose sobering impact may be measured by the different manner in which Britons went to war in 1939 as compared to 1914. Writing of the letters of a friend killed in the Battle of Britain in 1941, Kenneth Pinnock observes that 'they seem to me to encapsulate the spirit in which so many of my contemporaries went to war – with not a hint of the patriotic fervour which inspired their fathers in 1914, but instead a grim determination to shoulder the unwelcome task that history had thrust upon them' ('November Thoughts', *Oriel Record 2002* (Oxford: Oriel College, 2002): 38).

[21] For example, the BBC TV series 'Rebels and Redcoats' (2003), and its accompanying book by Hugh Bicheno (*Rebels and Redcoats: The American Revolutionary War* (London: HarperCollins, 2003)).

[22] For example, Clifford Longley, *Chosen People: The Big Idea that Shaped England and America* (London: Hodder and Stoughton, 2002).

in continental Europe than in Britain. Take for example the permanent exhibition at the German military cemetery at Maleme in Crete, which ascribes the poignant deaths of the many young Germans buried there to 'War'. War was responsible. War is the enemy. War is the great evil that we can and must forever forswear. The exhibition does not trouble itself to ask what young beweaponed Germans were doing parachuting onto western Crete in 1941. Nor does it enquire what would have become of the world had others not taken up arms against them and their like. What is true of the *Soldatenfriedhof* at Maleme is equally true of the Imperial War Museum's northern outpost near Manchester: the moral of its story is the terrible, futile evil of all war, simply. Pacifist conclusions are not explicitly drawn, but no moral ambiguities are let speak that might hinder the drawing of them.

If practical pacifism flourishes in at least one major British cultural institution whose subject is war, it is also alive and well in some British churches. Judging by the reports of its Committee on Church and Nation, the Church of Scotland is inclined to believe that war can only ever be a simple evil. Thus on the war in Afghanistan the Committee wrote:

> Answering violence with more violence rarely overcomes the complex international problems which blight humanity. We recall again that the General Assembly of the Church of Scotland has consistently opposed the solving of international disputes by resort to violence. The killing of thousands is not to be answered by killing thousands more.[23]

> We would strongly question whether such a policy [of military intervention] offers a lasting solution.[24]

Lest it be thought that practical pacifism is the peculiar property of Protestant churches, we should note that while the leadership of the Catholic Church in England and Wales has consistently affirmed 'the tragic necessity' of just war, Pope John Paul II himself did not.[25] In relation to the Gulf War of 1991 he declared that 'a peace obtained by

---

[23] Committee on Church and Nation, 'Statement on the Military Campaign in Afghanistan', 1 November 2001, p. 3.

[24] Committee on Church and Nation, 'The Terrorist Attacks on the United States of America and the War in Afghanistan', Supplementary Report to the General Assembly (2002), 6.5.1.

[25] Thus Cardinal Basil Hume in his homily at Westminster Cathedral on 20 January 1991 (*Briefing* (London: Catholic Media Trust), 21/3 (31 January 1991): 17).

arms could only prepare new acts of violence'; that '[t]he "needs of mankind" today require that we proceed resolutely towards outlawing war completely';[26] and that '[w]ar cannot be an adequate means for completely solving the problems that exist among nations. It never has been and it never will be.'[27] And on the war in the former Yugoslavia, the Pontifical Council for Justice and Peace asserted that peace 'is always possible, if truly desired, and if peace is possible, it becomes an imperious duty'.[28]

Proponents of just war thinking do not disagree with practical pacifists that war causes terrible evils. Nor do they disagree that war by itself is no foundation for a lasting peace. Where they do disagree is with the claim that, because war cannot provide a lasting solution to civil or international conflicts, therefore it cannot provide a provisional one. And they also quarrel with the assertion that peace is always possible if truly desired, in so far as it implies that conflict should always be avoided. Of course every party to a conflict wants 'peace', but each party means something different by it – otherwise there would be no conflict. And sometimes the 'peace' that one side wants spells 'injustice' for the other side; and sometimes that injustice is not only perceived, but real; and sometimes it is not only real, but so grave and persistent as to warrant armed resistance. To claim that peace is always possible if truly desired obscures the fact that some kinds of 'peace' we should not desire at all. It is hard to avoid the conclusion that the practical pacifism expressed in the statements of the Church of Scotland and the Vatican reaches its anti-war judgements by way of non-sequiturs and equivocation, and propelled by a strong gust of unrealism.

## Consequentialism

A third cause of scepticism about the possibility of just war is evident in the character of the moral reasoning conducted by practical pacifism: its almost exclusive focus on consequences and its pretension to be able to

---

[26] Pope John Paul II, 'Address to the Diplomatic Corps', 12 January 1991, in *ibid.*, 21/1 (14 February 1991): 3–4.

[27] Pope John Paul II, 'Address to the Vicariate of Rome', 16 January 1991, in *ibid.*, 21/3 (31 January 1991): 15.

[28] Pontifical Council for Justice and Peace, 'Peace is Possible in the Balkans', in *ibid.*, 24/2 (27 January 1994): 14.

predict and evaluate what these might be. Now, the consideration of consequences has its place in just war thinking: when embarking upon a war one must consider whether there is some kind of 'proportion' between the evils incurred and the good pursued; and in the midst of conducting a war there must be 'proportion' between military objectives and means. To what extent this moment in just war thinking involves the comparative 'weighing' of consequent goods and evils, and with what rationality, we will consider later. Suffice it to say at this point that the consideration of consequences here is but a *moment* in a larger process of reasoning, and only if certain non-prudential criteria – just cause, right intention, legitimate authority, last resort – have already been met does this moment arise at all.

In contrast, the moral reasoning employed by the Committee on Church and Nation has its centre of gravity in the consideration of consequences and reaches its judgements on the back of a doubtful 'calculation' of costs and benefits. That is to say, its reasoning is 'consequentialist'. So in the committee's report, 'The Legacy of the Kosovo War', for example, the *only* moral (as distinct from legal) criterion that is invoked is that 'any recourse to warfare should have as its ultimate goal the greater promotion of peace and justice in the region of conflict'.[29] The report then proceeds to ask 'whether the Balkans is a more secure, more peaceful and more just area than it was before the conflict started'. The answer that it gives to this question is a litany of the war's evil consequences – physical, environmental, political. The facts that a state-sanctioned policy of murderous 'ethnic cleansing' had been stopped, that an oppressive Serbian army had been made to withdraw and that the political stability of Macedonia had been maintained found no place in the equation – illustrating one of the weaknesses in consequentialist moral reasoning, namely, the inevitable selection of consequences to be considered. What is mentioned is that, six months after the end of the war, Slobodan Milosevic was still in power, and this is used to throw doubt on 'the effectiveness of a military approach to removing dictators'.[30] The fact that Milosevic was subsequently overthrown and delivered to the International Criminal Court in The Hague illustrates a further weakness

---

[29] Committee on Church and Nation, 'The Legacy of the Kosovo War', Supplementary Report to the General Assembly (1999), s. 3.
[30] *Ibid.*, ss. 6.1, 8.1.

in consequentialism, namely, the inevitability of considering only those consequences that are visible.

Such consequentialism is more than a passing phase in the Church of Scotland's thinking. It appears again in the Committee on Church and Nation's 'Statement on the Military Campaign in Afghanistan', which tells us in the opening paragraphs that 'we believe that it [the campaign] is doing more harm than good'.[31] In support of this the committee invokes civilian casualties, the exacerbation of the refugee crisis and the stimulus given to Muslim anti-Westernism. All of these are undoubted evils, but nowhere is it made clear quite how the committee 'calculated' that these 'outweighed' the realisation of the possible goods of the dislodgement of a ruthless terrorist group from one national haven, the discouragement of other states from offering it a fresh one, and the overthrow of an extremely oppressive regime in Afghanistan. It is true, as the committee points out, that '[t]here is no absolute guarantee that a new regime will not eventually degenerate into the same level of brutality as the Taliban'. But since when did absolute guarantees ever deign to dwell in the world of human affairs?

Judging by these instances of the Church of Scotland's moral reasoning, it seems that 'the problem of Protestant ethics' – as Paul Ramsey saw it in 1961 – is still with us.

## Misunderstandings

In addition to 'anti-Americanism', practical pacifism and a consequen-tialist tendency, a number of misunderstandings of the criteria of just war doctrine have also jaundiced its reception in British churches.

### Just cause

One of the most important developments of just war doctrine in the 1990s is the extension of the concept of a just cause for war to encompass the atrocious oppression of a people by its own government. The proposal is that military intervention in the affairs of a 'sovereign' state for human-itarian reasons should be regarded as just – under certain conditions. This is now widely, but not universally, accepted, and the attending

[31] Committee on Church and Nation, 'Statement on the Military Campaign in Afghanistan', p. 1.

conditions are the subject of debate. A common criticism of invocations of this humanitarian cause argues that they must be insincere, since a genuine concern to end the atrocious violation of human rights would manifest itself in a commitment to intervene wherever such violation is current. 'If Kosovo and Iraq', so the rhetorical question goes, 'then why not Rwanda and Chechnya?' And the implicit answer is: because vengeance or oil or geopolitical strategy, not the maintenance of human rights, is the real concern. Thus on the 2003 Iraq War, the Church of Scotland's Committee on Church and Nation:

> The reasons for attacking Iraq changed from the need to 'remove weapons of mass destruction' (still not located at the time of writing) to 'regime change' and then to the moralistic argument of 'liberating the Iraqi people'. On this basis, the US and the UK should now engage in military conflict with many other regimes in the world which lack democracy and do not respect human rights. These could include Saudi Arabia, Burma, Zimbabwe, North Korea and even China.[32]

The first response to this argument is that the gravity of human rights violation is not the only determinant of the morality of intervention. There are also prudential considerations. Not all interventions have equally good prospects of success and some incur greater risks of escalation – and so of disproportionate evil – than others. There were therefore good reasons why NATO did not intervene in Hungary in 1956 and in Czechoslovakia in 1968. And there are good reasons why the USA does not intervene in Chechnya. Second, the presence of other motives – for example 'national interests' – does not in itself render fraudulent a vaunted concern for human rights. Most human action, whether individual or collective, is subject to multiple motivation. And third, even if intervention in one case cannot be squared ethically with inaction elsewhere, surely it is better to be inconsistently responsible than consistently irresponsible.

## Legitimate authority

Many of those who have opposed recent wars have done so on the ground that these have lacked authorisation by the United Nations, and that the

---

[32] Committee on Church and Nation, 'The War in Iraq', Supplementary Report to the General Assembly (2003), 3.4.4.

UN is the only body fit – legally and morally – to give such authorisation. On the eve of the 2003 Iraq War the Archbishop of Canterbury, Rowan Williams, and the Cardinal Archbishop of Westminster, Cormac Murphy-O'Connor, pressed that '[i]t is vital . . . that all sides in this crisis engage through the United Nations – fully and urgently – in a process . . . that could and should render the trauma and tragedy of war unnecessary'.[33] The Church of Scotland's Committee on Church and Nation followed suit: 'War must have the backing of the international community through the United Nations and only be undertaken when there is a direct threat to a member state or in self-defence. The war was not undertaken through a specific mandate of the United Nations Security Council.'[34]

This identification of the just war criterion of legitimate authority with international law and the UN in its current form is problematic. Statutory international law reserves to the UN the sole power to authorise war, except in cases of self-defence. If we could be sure that this power would be exercised when warranted, then legal authority would amount to moral authority. As it is, however, the UN's capacity to uphold the law is severely compromised by the politics of the Security Council, where a single veto cast to protect the dubious interests of a member state can paralyse the UN as an effective global policeman. This is what happened in 1999 over Kosovo. NATO did not obtain Security Council authorisation for military intervention to stop Milosevic's 'ethnic cleansing' and prevent civil war in Macedonia and further Balkan meltdown, because it did not seek it. And it did not seek it, since it was clear that Russia would have vetoed it. Why? Because Moscow did not want to set any legal precedent that might tie its hands in Chechnya. How, then, should the Security Council react the next time a Hitler constitutes a threat to regional stability when rather than invading a neighbour he decides upon a Final Solution for a minority group within the borders of his own state and is not dissuaded from this policy by diplomatic or economic pressure? If the politics of the Security Council preclude sufficient unanimity to authorise armed intervention, should the *letter* of *statutory* international law require us to stand by and watch?

This is not to deny that serious efforts should be made to abide by the letter of international law: any deliberate breach of positive law, even if

---

[33] Catholic and Anglican Archbishops' Joint Statement on Iraq, 20 February 2003.
[34] Committee on Church and Nation, 'The War in Iraq', 3.2.3.

morally justified, weakens its authority and therefore its power to constrain those who deserve to be constrained. Nevertheless, while it is true
that transgression of the law weakens its authority, it is no less true that
this authority is also weakened by a chronic failure to enforce the law.
Think Rwanda. Think Srebrenica. Nor do we mean to deny that UN
authorisation should be sought, where the law requires it. The concern
that lies behind the criterion of legitimate authority is that any military
action be undertaken for the common good, and not for the sake of some
selfish, private national interest; and the approval of the UN amounts to
weighty evidence that this is the case. Nevertheless, given the political
limitation of its power to enforce international law, the absence of UN
approval is not by itself enough to decide the morality of the use of armed
force.

### Last resort

Sometimes it is supposed that just war doctrine requires every possible
non-military solution to have been pursued before going to war is justified. Thus Cardinal Basil Hume in regard of the 1991 Gulf War: the
criterion of last resort requires, he wrote, 'a determination to pursue
every opportunity for a diplomatic solution'.[35] The Committee on
Church and Nation took a similar view: 'The dominant criterion of last
resort requires that all efforts to reach a peaceful settlement must be
exhausted with no alternative left.'[36] And then again on the 2003 Iraq
War: 'War should be undertaken as a last resort. It is clear that this was not
the case in regard to Iraq, since the weapons inspectors had not yet
completed their work and the United Nations had not exhausted
diplomacy.'[37]

Common sense knows, however, that diplomacy is futile if one party is
negotiating in bad faith, using what appears to be an attempt to reach a
settlement as a means of gaining political or military advantage. It also
knows that it is foolish to extend benefit of doubt to a negotiating party
who carries a record of manipulation. Moreover, if just war doctrine

---

[35] 'Points made by Cardinal Hume in a Letter to Mr Patten', *Briefing* 21/3 (31 January
1991), p. 12.
[36] General Assembly of the Church of Scotland, *Report of the Proceedings* (1991), Committee on
Church and Nation, 'The Gulf Crisis', 2.79.
[37] Committee on Church and Nation, 'The War in Iraq', 3.2.1.

warns against embarking upon the hazardous venture of war too soon, then common sense – educated by the 1990s, if not by the 1930s – also warns against embarking upon it too late. The point is made by Richard Harries, speaking on Kosovo to the Church of England's General Synod: 'Terrible things happened earlier, especially in Bosnia. Should we have intervened earlier, at that point? If we did not intervene at that point and we should have done, how much responsibility do the churches bear for failing to face up to evil and support the necessary stern measures?'[38] Just war doctrine should not be read as enjoining the defiance of common sense. Its criterion of last resort requires only the pursuit in good faith of every *realistic* possibility of a genuine, non-military solution.

## Discrimination

One of the most common misunderstandings of just war doctrine attends the criterion of discrimination. Sometimes this is thought to imply 'a fundamental injunction on any military operation that it should avoid civilian casualties'.[39] At other times it is taken to mean, more strongly, 'non-combatant immunity'[40] – such that '[t]here is no moral distinction between the death of a civilian in Afghanistan and that of the innocent who died on September 11th [2001]'.[41] Both views, however, render just war virtually impossible, since one cannot expect to wage war successfully without incurring civilian casualties, and one cannot wage war justly when one has no hope of succeeding. This may be an implica-tion that practical pacifists want, but it is presumably not what the doctrine intends. As Robert Runcie, Archbishop of Canterbury during the 1991 Gulf War, commented:

> The doctrine of just war has been much invoked and variously interpreted. Sometimes the distortion of the doctrine has gone to extraordinary lengths. For example, some have argued that an essen-tial part of the doctrine is the rule that in a 'just war' non-combatants must not be hurt. That quite frankly is an absurdity, it is a doctrine

---

[38] General Synod of the Church of England, *Report of the Proceedings* (London: Church House, 1999), 12 July 1999, p. 313.
[39] Committee on Church and Nation, 'Kosovo Press Release', 2000.
[40] General Assembly of the Church of Scotland, 'The Gulf Crisis', 2.79.
[41] Committee on Church and Nation, 'Statement on the Military Campaign in Afghanistan', p. 2.

of near perfection that has been unattainable save in the most exceptional circumstances.[42]

Actually, the criterion of discrimination needs to be interpreted in terms
of the theory of double effect. According to this, it is morally permissible
to decide upon a course of action that one foresees will possibly, probably,
or certainly produce evil consequences (effects), provided that by means
of the act one intends to realise good effects; that any evil effects it also
realises are not 'disproportionate' to the good ones; that one does not
want the evil effects, and only accepts them with due reluctance; and that
this reluctance manifests itself in earnest attempts to avoid or minimise
them. In the light of this theory, the criterion of discrimination only
requires military operations not to intend civilian deaths and to seek
earnestly to avoid or minimise them as far as possible.

The misreading of the criterion of discrimination reflects a measure of
ambivalence over the theory of double effect. This finds expression in the
Committee on Church and Nation's report on the war in Afghanistan:

> [T]he US government argues that unlike those who carried out the
> September 11 atrocity, it did not target civilians, and their deaths and
> injuries were unintended. We would point out that the terror expe-
> rienced by Afghan civilians was not somehow lessened because their
> village happened to be an unintended target of a bomb, but we fully
> accept the argument that the motivation behind inflicting such terror
> was fundamentally different in nature from those who undertook the
> attacks of September 11 ... While it may be the case that the US did
> not deliberately target civilians, its policy was such that it chose to risk
> the lives of many innocent people by bombing targets where they were
> liable to be.[43]

If this last point is intended as a criticism, then it falls short of its target.
Any choice of an act that one foresees might or will result in evil effects
(e.g. the deaths of the innocent) as well as good ones involves a *choice* of
the former as well as the latter – a choice for which one is responsible and
for which one must give an account. According to the doctrine of double
effect, however, it is possible to give a morally justifying account that

---

[42] General Synod of the Church of England, *Report of Proceedings* 21/3 (1990), p. 927; quoted by
Reed in *Just War?*, p. 74.
[43] Committee on Church and Nation, 'The Terrorist Attacks on the United States of America',
6.1.3, 6.2.5.

shows that responsibility here does not amount to culpability – provided that one's 'choice' of the evil effects was a reluctant acceptance rather than a positive desiring, and provided that this reluctance was demonstrated in reasonable steps taken to try to avoid or minimise the evil. Since the committee does not make the case that US policy failed to demonstrate an appropriate degree of reluctance in its choice to accept the risk of civilian deaths, its critical remark lacks force.

## Outstanding questions

Some of the ambivalence with which just war doctrine has been received in British churches may be attributed to the misunderstandings that we have just discussed. In fairness, however, some of it must also be laid at the feet of three outstanding questions that arise within the doctrine itself, and to which entirely satisfactory answers have yet to be found.

### Just cause

One of the controversial questions that the 2003 Iraq War has raised is whether, and to what extent, one may go to war to fend off a *threat*. This is the question of the justice of war that intends to 'pre-empt' or 'prevent' an attack. In some moments of the Anglican discussion, no clear distinction has been drawn between (moral) pre-emption and (immoral) prevention. Thus Peter Price, Bishop of Bath and Wells: 'There is a deep sense that unilateral pre-emptive action would lower the threshold of war below acceptable levels.'[44] In other moments, however, a distinction has been drawn. For example, in its 2002 report on Iraq the Board for Social Responsibility distinguished between just war to fend off an imminent attack ('anticipatory self-defence' or pre-emptive war) and unjust war to prevent a threat that was merely growing or an attack that had yet to materialise ('preventative war').[45] Seven months later the Board for Social Responsibility (now renamed the 'Public Affairs Unit') developed its thought further: '[T]he justice of a pre-emptive attack requires

[44] General Synod of the Church of England, *Report of Proceedings*, 11 November 2002, p. 20.
[45] Board for Social Responsibility of the General Synod of the Church of England, *Iraq: Would Military Action Be Justified? The Church's Contribution to the Debate*, GS Report 1475 (London: Church House, 2002), ss. 54, 46.

demonstrable and compelling evidence of the hostile intent and capability of a perceived aggressor ... [I]t is crucial that states considering pre-emptive action have more than probable cause to believe they must attack. Otherwise, questions will always be asked as to whether a pre-emptive attack was itself nothing more than an act of aggression.'[46]

This thinking is helpful as far as it goes, but it leaves hanging the crucial questions of what differentiates a 'more than probable' cause from a 'probable' one, and why a merely 'probable' threat is not a sufficient justification. Surely the very probability (as opposed to the mere possibility) of the materialisation of a threat could be sufficient to warrant pre-emptive action, if its gravity were very high. Would it not also be sufficient if the threat were simply grave (as distinct from very grave), but the window of opportunity for fending it off were very narrow (perhaps because effective military action would be rendered impossible by a change in climate, whether atmospheric or political)? And in estimating whether a threat is probable rather than just possible, and whether the evidence for it is 'demonstrable and compelling', would it not be perfectly reasonable to withhold any benefit of doubt from a threatening source that carries a public record of aggressive intent and of serial bad faith?

We need to refine further our distinction between morally legitimate and illegitimate anticipatory action. We could start by ceasing to speak of a distinction between (moral) 'pre-emption' and (immoral) 'prevention'. The distinction is not immediately obvious because the word 'prevention' carries no naturally pejorative connotation. A more obvious verbal contrast is provided by a distinction between 'pre-emptive' and 'premature' action. Having settled on these terms, we need next to articulate what distinguishes their moral content. It seems reasonable that a threat that is 'immediate' and 'serious' should be met with 'pre-emptive' action. What would constitute 'premature' action? Most certainly, action against a threat that is non-existent. When is a threat 'non-existent'? Most certainly, when no one is posing it or intending to pose it, and when the aggressor invents it as a pretext – for example, the 'threat' that Poland posed to the border of Nazi Germany in 1939. Certainly enough, when a threat has been verbally posed but is not being realised. Equally, when

---

[46] Public Affairs Unit of the General Synod of the Church of England, 'A Submission to the House of Commons' Foreign Affairs Select Committee's Inquiry into the Decision to Go to War in Iraq', 9 June 2003.

a threat has not merely been stated (it could be a bluff) but is also clearly intended, and yet is not being realised.

But what about a threat that is clearly intended and is in the early stages of preparation? Would it be premature to act against that? Not obviously, if the threat is serious enough to warrant the hazards of military action. If that is so, then we should note that such a threat is not 'immediate'. 'Pre-emptive' action would then be permissible against threats that are 'clearly of sufficient seriousness and in the process of being realised'. The issue is not really the immediacy of the threat. It only seems that way because an immediate threat is most visible – most 'clear'. The issue is whether there is sufficient reason to believe that a serious threat is real: is it '*clearly* ... being realised'? Now, there could be a clearly serious and emergent threat, and yet it would be premature to meet it with military force – because effective alternatives are available. So we need to add that 'premature' military action is also that which is directed against a serious and emergent threat before all other effective alternatives have been tried.

In the end, then, we arrive at the following definitions: morally permissible 'pre-emptive' military action is that which is directed against a threat whose seriousness and emergence is sufficiently clear, and where no effective non-military alternatives are available; morally impermissible 'premature' military action is that which is directed against a threat whose seriousness and emergence are not sufficiently clear, or where effective non-military alternatives are available. This, of course, raises the question of what degree of clarity is 'sufficient'. Here as elsewhere satisfying answers must wait upon the casuistical analysis and comparison of concrete cases, identifying those threats whose clarity we deem 'sufficient', comparing them with those that we deem 'insufficient', and explicating the implicit grounds for our differing judgements.

## Right intention

I asserted above that in addition to a genuine concern to maintain human rights, a government's decision to go to war might well be shaped by what are perceived to be national interests; and that this need not invalidate the moral justification of its decision. What I did not explain was that this could be so for two different reasons. One is that the 'altruistic' humanitarian concern with human rights is in some sense primary, while the 'selfish' national interests are secondary. The other reason is that national interests need not be selfish at all. It is this second reason that needs development in the field of thought about international justice generally and about just war specifically. It is commonly assumed in discussions of international relations that in order to be moral, conduct must be altruistic. Those who believe this to be possible regard all self-interested policies as immoral; whereas those who consider altruistic conduct in international relations to be hopelessly unlikely regard base self-interest as the only realistic determinant of international behaviour. The choice presented, then, is between an impractical Kantian idealism and an amoral Hobbesian realism. However, the tradition of ethics stemming from Aristotle via Thomas Aquinas suggests a third option: the possibility of appropriate, indeed obligatory, self-interest. As individuals have a moral duty to take proper care of themselves, so governments have a moral duty to serve the well-being of the people they govern. They have a duty to serve the well-being in which their people have a morally legitimate *interest*.

Lest this still sound too base and ignoble, let us make clear that to serve a people's well-being involves more, *pace* Hobbes, than keeping them secure and fat. For example, human individuals and peoples also care about being just. They are moved by appeals to 'justice'. They have an interest in maintaining their moral self-respect. And sometimes for the sake of that self-respect – among other things, no doubt – they will sacrifice their security. A government that aspires to be genuinely realistic, and not merely reductionistic, will bear this in mind.

If we grant the possibility of a morally legitimate national interest, then it is no longer enough to be told, for example, that military action against Iraq to secure oil supplies vital to the West's economy is self-interested (and by implication wrong). We also need an explanation of what is supposed to make this self-interest immoral. One explanation could be that Iraq has a legal right to the oil that the West wants for itself. Another explanation could be that while the West has legal entitlement, that entitlement is undermined morally by the gross unfairness of the terms that it has forced upon the producers. A third explanation could be that while the West has legal entitlement through a contract that was not merely 'free' but fair, other nations have far greater need of the oil and could put it to far better use. The point here is that, while a government has a duty to preserve and promote the well-being of its people, it may not do so *at all costs*. Its pursuit of legitimate national self-interest should be constrained by the rights of others and by considerations of fairness – and even charity – towards them. Still, in the absence of any infringement of rights or of the claims of fairness or charity, a government's pursuit of the genuine interests of its people is not only not immoral, but morally obligatory.

## Proportionality

Perhaps that aspect of just war doctrine that needs most urgent attention is the criterion of proportionality. This requires that there be no 'dispro-portion' between evils of the war one is about to embark upon and the goods one hopes to secure by it, or between the destruction a particular military operation will wreak (e.g., civilian deaths) and the military advantage it intends to gain. There are two interpretations of this criterion that enable it to be sensibly applied. First, an evil may be said to be disproportionate if it is such as to destroy the very good that one hopes to gain by it. One example of this would be a case where a nation's use of nuclear weapons in self-defence might provoke a counter-strike that would not only devastate its own territory but render it uninhabitable for gener-ations. Second, an evil may be said to be disproportionate where it is avoidable. An example of this would be a case where a field commander takes risks with civilian lives that his military purposes don't require.

However, beyond these limited kinds of case the application of the criterion of proportionality is problematic. How are we to gauge with any rigour at all whether or not the risks of inciting Muslim terrorism and kindling civil war were worth the possibility of establishing some kind of responsible government in a stable, pluralist Iraq? Or to move onto the battlefield, granted that a military objective cannot be achieved without civilian deaths, how can we use the relative importance of the objective to set a limit to the number of deaths? Certainly, we can say that the criterion of proportion is well known to moral common sense, and that it can be effective in ruling out certain belligerent actions as clearly *dis*proportionate. The question remains, however, as to whether it has any useful, rational application beyond that. Too often, arguments over the proportionality of military action appear to involve little more than subjective construals, some pessimistic, some optimistic, all equally – and unavoidably – speculative, and usually claiming a greater measure of rationality than they have a right to.

## Conclusion

The fact that just war doctrine stands in need of further elaboration does not suffice to explain its doubtful reception in certain reaches of British churches. No body of human thought is complete; and any body of moral concepts designed to help us tell right from wrong conduct will need periodic refinement and extension in the face of novel phenomena or of old questions that have taken on new life. But when to the inevitable loose ends of just war doctrine are added a series of misunderstandings, then it begins to appear not merely imperfect but unworkable.

So why has the doctrine been misunderstood? The reason lies in two sets of cultural assumptions and prejudices: 'anti-Americanism' and, more important, practical pacifism. Together these incline many Britons – both within and without the churches – to be acutely alert to the temptation that faces those (like Americans) who possess military hammers: namely, to perceive every problem as a nail. But they also incline the same people to be stubbornly oblivious to the temptation that faces those (like Europeans) who lack military hammers: namely, to pretend that nails do not exist. The truth is that temptation lies on both sides, and wilful arrogance is not the only form that vice in international politics can take. Wilful blindness is another.

What this implies for the future conduct of British churches in debates about war and peace is the need to be careful not to assume that prophecy always comes from the Left, and that the exercise of military power by America or Britain always deserves to be one of its targets. Karl Barth was absolutely correct: the prophecy that really speaks the Word of God is the poodle of no ideology, whether of the Left or of the Right.[47] Of course it is true that American and British governments can abuse the military power of the state for ignoble ends, or use it imprudently for noble ones. But it is equally true that the British public can be spellbound by the power of comfortable and irresponsible illusions. Among these is the belief that tyrants, terrorists or insurgents threaten violence only because of justified grievances, and that a just peace can always be negotiated without recourse to armed force.

---

[47] Karl Barth, 'The Christian Community in the Midst of Political Change', in *Against the Stream: Shorter Post-War Writings, 1946–52* (New York: Philosophical Library, 1954), pp. 77–93.

In contrast to some members of British churches who confuse Christian witness with anti-establishment politics, just war doctrine embodies a supple and discerning prophecy. On the one hand, it demands of those who would use lethal violence that they have the patience to meet the demands of a system of elaborate moral criteria. But on the other hand, it requires of those who rightly fear the awful horrors of war, the courage to admit that sometimes, tragically, just peace can be bought at no lesser price.

# 5

# Just war thinking in recent American religious debate over military force

JAMES TURNER JOHNSON

During the two decades beginning with Paul Ramsey's *War and the Christian Conscience* and *The Just War*, including Michael Walzer's *Just and Unjust Wars*, and concluding with the United States Catholic bishops' *The Challenge of Peace*, the just war idea underwent a remarkable recovery and entry into American public debate over the uses of military force.[1] As the cases of Ramsey and the US Catholic bishops testify, much of the effort to recover and apply just war thinking to contemporary issues was Christian in motivation, and though both Ramsey and the Catholic bishops also addressed the secular policy community and engaged people within that community, much of the debate took place within the spheres of Christian ethics and Church reflection on social justice.

In recent debates the picture in religious circles regarding the use of just war reasoning is more mixed. The US Catholic bishops have reiterated their understanding of the tradition and they have entered into the policy forum using this as their basis in statements on recent uses of US military force. At the same time, the just war idea has been taken up in evangelical Christian circles in the USA and applied in policy debates. But the 'mainline' Protestant churches have responded variously. Some have not accepted it at all, others have accepted it only in part, others have sought to 'go beyond' it, or have taken up the call for 'positive peace-making', defined in opposition to the idea of just war. Pacifism, as the only truly Christian position, is strong in certain sectors of American

---

[1] Paul Ramsey, *War and the Christian Conscience: How Shall Modern War Be Conducted Justly?* (Durham, NC: Duke University Press, 1961). Paul Ramsey, *The Just War: Force and Political Responsibility* (New York: Charles Scribner's Sons, 1968). Michael Walzer, *Just and Unjust Wars* (New York: Basic Books, 1977). National Conference of Catholic Bishops (NCCB below), *The Challenge of Peace: God's Promise and Our Response* (Washington, DC: United States Catholic Conference, 1983).

Protestantism and Catholicism. Meanwhile attention to just war thought has grown in secular circles: think-tanks, the academic world and the US military. The purpose of this paper is to examine the specifically Christian use, abuse and outright rejection of just war thinking in recent policy debates: to outline the dimensions of this, to show what may explain it, to chart some of the controverted points in recent Christian just war usage, and to suggest what all this implies for Christian entry into public debate over the use of military force in the United States.

## Background and context

During the 1960s and 1970s the just war idea underwent a remarkable rediscovery and entry into American public debate over the uses of military force. It was necessary that there be such a rediscovery, as the just war idea had disappeared in religious moral discourse for some time. While this idea remained in the official teachings of Protestant and Catholic churches alike, much Christian energy, especially from the nine-teenth century forward, had shifted towards pacifism. When Christian thinkers, leaders and laity accepted war, they did so not on just war terms but in the terms of a crusade, as in the case of the Civil War and both world wars. Beginning in the 1930s, Reinhold Niebuhr added Christian realism to the mix, but though this position accepted uses of armed force in the service of statecraft, it regarded this as reflecting the sinfulness endemic to human life and institutions, and it did not in any way seek to engage the Christian tradition of just war.

When Ramsey started to recover just war thinking for Christian ethical discourse in the 1960s, he did so in a context in which opposition to all war was strong. This resistance was fuelled by opposition to nuclear weapons and by optimism about the possibilities of a world without war under the aegis of the United Nations. Within this environment Ramsey drew a version of just war out of the concept of Christian love of neigh-bour. This placed him in the conversation between a love-based Christian pacifism and the emphasis on love as the premier Christian ethical ideal, as defined and used by Niebuhr and those influenced by him. Ramsey's use of an important historical just war thinker like Augustine, as a result, was very much of a piece with contemporaneous Protestant (and some Catholic) theological understandings of Augustine which emphasised his conception of the primacy of charity as the central normative base of

Christian ethics. The downside of this approach was that Ramsey's conception of just war did not connect with the historical just war tradition.

Ramsey answered his own question, 'How shall modern war be conducted justly?' by introducing two moral principles. First, discrimination, which he held to follow directly from the obligation of love of neighbour and understood to define an obligation without exceptions. Second, proportionality, a prudential calculation of the moral gains and losses to be expected from a particular course of action in combat. This way of defining the *jus in bello* – by means of the moral principles of discrimination and proportionality – has since come to dominate moral discourse on just war. Ramsey's emphasis on the principles of discrimination and proportionality and his lack of attention to the question of a *jus ad bellum* was almost immediately turned against him by contemporary pacifists, who held that modern war is inherently indiscriminate and disproportionate. Although Ramsey rejected this judgement about the use of armed force in the contemporary world, this line of argument has persisted.

A new plateau of engagement was reached, however, when the American Catholic bishops began their work towards a pastoral letter on the subject. Front-page treatment by the *New York Times* and the *Washington Post* of the second draft of the document opened the bishops' thinking to a broad readership. Responding to the Catholic bishops' efforts, considerable public attention was given to examining the concept of just war and how it should be understood as applying to contemporary warfare. Numerous conferences were held on the subject in college and university campuses, policy and military study groups, and a major session of the US Army's annual Major Command Chaplains' Conference was devoted to this subject in 1982. Spurred on by the Catholic example, major Protestant bodies followed suit. The interest continued after *The Challenge of Peace* was issued in 1983, with conferences organised at a variety of institutions including the United States Military Academy and Princeton University. Various articles and books have subsequently emerged that either build on what the pastoral letter said or critique it in some way.

Attention to the just war idea has continued to grow in secular circles, including think-tanks, the academic fields of political science and philosophy, and far from least in the US military, where just war is now part of the curriculum at all the service academies and the war colleges.

The picture is more mixed among the churches. The American Catholic bishops have continued to employ the concept of just war they laid out in *The Challenge of Peace*. At the same time, just war thinking has been taken up and used in some Protestant evangelical circles. But among the more theologically and socially liberal Protestant denominations, even when statements of doctrine or discipline refer to the idea of just war, denominational leaders have avoided this concept.

## From *The Challenge of Peace* to the war against Saddam Hussein

*The Challenge of Peace* undertook to provide its own conception of just war. While it noted the presence of this idea in historical Catholic thought, it dismissed the thought that this was a settled doctrine with the assertion that '[t]he just-war argument has taken several forms in the history of Catholic theology'.[2] Yet there was in fact a settled doctrine which had been recognised and used by early modern theorists, Catholic and Protestant alike. This is what one found in Catholic canon law, the Catechism, or *The Catholic Encyclopaedia* right down to the time *The Challenge of Peace* was written. Striking out on its own route, though, *The Challenge of Peace* created a version of just war with its own particular characteristics.

*The Challenge of Peace* was written and adopted in a context in which many people were concerned with preventing nuclear war and feared that any war involving the superpower blocs would escalate to a nuclear exchange. Its version of just war represented a compromise between nuclear and other pacifists, and proponents of traditional just war thinking on the drafting committee and among the bishops as a whole. It closely followed, not the settled traditional concept of just war, but a theory of just war based on the idea of the prima facie duty of non-maleficence defined by James F. Childress, an academic ethicist of Quaker background, in an article published a few years earlier in *Theological Studies*.[3] Though representing itself as faithful to Catholic teaching on war, it was at odds with the historical just war tradition. It represented Childress's principle of non-maleficence as the content of love of

---

[2] *Challenge of Peace*, par. 82.
[3] James F. Childress, 'Just War Criteria', *Theological Studies* 39 (1978): 427–45.

neighbour as found in Augustine.[4] It advanced the claim that '[j]ust-war teaching has evolved as an effort to prevent war', though the traditional teaching had clearly envisioned the possibility of just resort to armed force as positively serving justice, order and peace.[5] It set this interpretation within the frame of an assertion that Catholic teaching 'establishes a strong presumption against war' and it provided a list of just war criteria in which the function of the *jus ad bellum* was described as to determine when this presumption could be overridden.[6] Ironically, the listing of just war criteria in *The Challenge of Peace* did not include the classic requirement of the end of peace, which was central to the traditional conception of just war. The US Conference of Catholic Bishops have repeatedly utilised this conception of just war to seek to influence opinion and policy on the use of armed force in such contexts as the debates over Iraq in 1990–1 and in 2002–3 and those over economic sanctions and humanitarian intervention in the early 1990s.

### The 1990–1991 Gulf War

Late in 1990 representatives of the United States Catholic Conference used *The Challenge of Peace* to argue against the use of military force to remove occupying Iraqi troops from Kuwait. The fullest statement was that of Archbishop John R. Roach, chairman of the Conference's International Policy Committee, in testimony to the Senate Armed Services Committee in December 1990.[7] 'In our tradition,' he wrote, 'moral reasoning about the relationship of politics and war begins with a presumption against the use of force.' Though this ethic 'has been called the just war tradition,' he continued, 'its purpose is not to facilitate the choice for war, but to make that choice both difficult and rarely used'. As Roach continued, it was clear that in his conception the moral problem was the possible use of force, not the Iraqi aggression. Any sense that the use of force might be a moral tool to right a wrong done, to punish evil-doing and to establish a more just and peaceful order – all parts of the traditional concept of just war – was absent in his testimony.

---

[4] *Challenge of Peace*, pars. 80–1.   [5] *Ibid.*, par. 83.   [6] *Ibid.*, par. 70.
[7] Testimony of Archbishop Roach before the Senate Armed Services Committee, in James Turner Johnson and George Weigel (eds.), *Just War and the Gulf War* (Washington, DC: Ethics and Public Policy Centre, 1991), pp. 117–29.

Though Roach referred to 'Iraq's aggression' and 'Iraq's flagrant violation of international law', he overlooked the fact that positive and customary international law allow both individual and collective use of force in self-defence to respond to such aggression. Indeed, collective self-defence against a continuing 'armed attack' by Iraq was the fundamental international law justification for military action to eject the Iraqi forces and to restore Kuwait. Roach's argument, though, dwelt on certain US policy objectives that, he believed, did not provide just cause for use of force. The policy option he offered, connecting it to *The Challenge of Peace*'s requirement of last resort, was to give the economic embargo on Iraq more time to work. Apart from the fact that he, as a Catholic bishop, had no special expertise in making the judgement that, given time, the embargo might lead to an Iraqi withdrawal and restoration of Kuwaiti sovereignty, embargoes are themselves morally problematic because they are inherently indiscriminate. Why they should be preferred to a discriminate and proportionate use of armed force is not apparent – unless, as implied by the 'presumption against force', force is always to be avoided if at all possible. Finally, under the rubric of the criterion of proportionality, Roach did not in fact weigh the opposing goods and evils of the use of force and not using force in this case; instead, he dwelt on the possible evils the use of force might cause. In so doing he painted a worst-case scenario of what might happen if military action were used. He suggested that the war would not be 'swift, neat, and clear-cut'. He forecast that the war could not be confined to Kuwait and Iraq but that it might inflame the 'region laced with interlocking conflicts'. And he questioned whether the end of the war would 'leave the people of Kuwait, the Middle East and the world, better or worse off'. If the criterion of proportionality is to be understood only in terms of worst-case projections, one may wonder whether any case could ever exist in which the 'presumption against war' could be overturned.

### Economic sanctions and humanitarian intervention

Three years later the Catholic bishops issued a new collective statement, *The Harvest of Justice Is Sown in Peace*, to mark the tenth anniversary of *The Challenge of Peace*.[8] This document affirmed the 1983 conception

---

[8] NCCB, *The Harvest of Justice is Sown in Peace* (Washington, DC: United States Catholic Conference, 1993).

of just war though it made certain changes. It recast the 'presumption against war' as a more restrictive 'strong presumption against the use of force'. It lowered what it now called 'legitimate authority' from second to third place in the *jus ad bellum* listing, placing it behind both just cause and comparative justice. Though it added the requirement of the aim of peace, it made this part of the *jus in bello*, rather than the *jus ad bellum* requirement of right intention as in the traditional just war concept. The context of the 1993 statement was different from that of the 1983 pastoral. The Berlin Wall was down, and the threat of superpower nuclear war had receded. While *The Harvest of Justice* addressed the issue of nuclear weapons this was no longer the primary focus of the statement. Rather discussion of nuclear weapons appeared as one of several 'special problems' identified in a section titled 'Building Co-operative Security'. Among the other 'special problems' treated was the question of economic sanctions. Here the bishops noted that they had supported such sanctions in three cases (including the sanctions against Iraq in 1990) despite the 'inherent dilemma' in them, observing that they took 'very seriously the charge that sanctions can be counterproductive and sometimes unjustifiably harm the innocent'. Yet they posited no 'presumption against sanctions', continuing to uphold sanctions as morally preferable to war.

Those who understand the just war tradition as not simply having to do with how to prevent the resort to force, but as expressing a broader theory of statecraft – an idea championed by Ramsey – would insist that the various moral criteria defined there apply to other forms of statecraft as well, including sanctions. By this test the usual impact of sanctions – lack of discrimination and disproportionate harm to the civilian population of the targeted country – makes them morally problematic. The bishops addressed these problems under the rubric of proportionality, though their solution – targeted sanctions – was that they should be more discriminate. They did not consider the possibility that there may be instances in which military force might be more discriminate and proportionate than sanctions, and thus morally preferable. There is thus a tension in their moral reasoning on sanctions: despite the moral problems with sanctions, the 'strong presumption against the use of force' effectively takes this tool of statecraft off the table in favour of any other options, including economic sanctions.

The tension is sharpened in the bishops' discussion of another of the 'special problems' in *The Harvest of Justice*, humanitarian intervention.

The document starts by citing the words of Pope John Paul II that 'humanitarian intervention be obligatory where the survival of populations and entire ethnic groups is seriously compromised'. Later, albeit after numerous qualifications, they stated as their own position that 'military intervention may be justified to ensure that starving children can be fed or that whole populations will not be slaughtered'. In so doing they set a much higher hurdle for justification than the Pope, and indeed a much higher hurdle than that set in the Genocide Convention. Yet even so, the bishops further qualified the right they had just admitted: 'We must be wary that the outstretched hand of peace is not turned into an iron fist of war.' While the bishops affirmed in this document that they had supported economic sanctions in three cases, they have never supported the use of force even to respond to the most serious humanitarian need. Indeed, the only times they have addressed the use of military force in public debate they have done so to oppose it. Their 'presumption against war' version of just war theory has proven to translate into a functional pacifism, in which resort to military force is always wrong and cannot be considered objectively alongside other options, using the same moral criteria.

## 2003 Iraq War

Finally, I turn to the bishops' position in the debate of 2002–3 on the use of military force to oust Saddam Hussein and his regime. There are two particular documents to consider: a letter written in mid-September 2002, by Bishop Wilton C. Gregory, President of the Conference of Catholic Bishops, to US President George W. Bush, and the 'Statement on Iraq' from the Conference as a whole, issued in mid-November.[9] Bishop Gregory opened his September letter by invoking the Catholic bishops' trademark conception that there is always a moral 'presumption against war' and that just war theory functions to determine when overriding that presumption is justified. He followed by listing six just war criteria – just cause, right authority, right intention, reasonable hope of success, proportionality and non-combatant immunity. This listing did not include

---

[9] Bishop Wilton C. Gregory, 'Letter to President Bush, September 13, 2002', at http://www. usccb.org/sdwo/international/bush902.htm. United States Conference of Catholic Bishops, 'Statement on Iraq', http://www.usccb.org/bishops/iraq/shtml.

all the criteria laid out in *The Challenge of Peace* and *The Harvest of Justice*. It also used the *jus in bello* criterion of non-combatant immunity (discrimination) as if it belonged to the *jus ad bellum*. Bishop Gregory interpreted all these criteria to argue against resort to force against Iraq.

A few days before this letter was sent, President Bush, in his speech to the United Nations, 12 September 2002, outlined three justifications for using force against Iraq: to pre-empt possible use of weapons of mass destruction; the frequent, flagrant and continuing violation of international law, and the on-going violation of fundamental human rights. Bishop Gregory did not mention either of the last two of these justifications, arguing only that pre-emption did not satisfy the just war requirement of just cause. It would have been interesting to see what he might have said about the case for armed intervention to respond to the Saddam Hussein regime's egregious violations of basic human rights, given the discussion of humanitarian intervention in *The Harvest of Justice*.

As in 1990, the international law case for armed action against Iraq was entirely ignored. In the US Catholic bishops' usage, international law regarding the use of force has been cited only when it serves the purpose of denying the right to use force, as when the requirement of 'legitimate authority' is interpreted to require a specific UN resolution that has not been given. Otherwise it simply does not appear in the reasoning offered. In discussing the other just war criteria treated in this letter, Bishop Gregory included the same sort of worst-case prognosis of the evils the use of force could be expected to cause, with no mention of the evils the use of force might remedy. The aim here was not to consider even-handedly whether in this case the various just war criteria could be satisfied, so that they would override the 'presumption against war', but to argue that the criteria could not be satisfied. As in 1990, this letter used the conception of just war to foreclose the possibility of overriding the 'presumption against war'.

The November 'Statement on Iraq' from the Conference of Catholic Bishops mirrored the Gregory letter, though it listed the just war criteria in still another way: just cause, legitimate authority, possibility of success and the need for proportionality (named together), and 'norms governing the conduct of the war', identified as 'civilian immunity and proportionality'. Again, the discussion of just cause focused on the morality of pre-emptive use of military force, making no mention of the other two justifications President Bush had put forward. The discussion of legitimate authority identified this as requiring further Security Council action and that the use of force only take place 'within the framework of the United Nations'. The commentary on both the remaining named criteria spoke of 'unpredictable consequences' expected to be bad, from the use of force against the Saddam Hussein regime, while not mentioning any evils the use of force might remedy.

Missing in both these statements was any consideration of the traditional just war requirement that justified use of force must aim at a just and orderly peace. The heavy emphasis on the 'presumption against war' means that it is difficult to grant that resort to war might justly aim at restoring peace. In a statement issued in February 2003, Bishop Gregory took up the theme of the end of peace. The statement called for 'a long-term commitment to reconstruction, humanitarian and refugee assistance, and establishment of a stable, democratic government'.[10] But he did not connect this to the idea of just war. Even this reference to the moral aim of establishing peace, then, reinforces the central theme of the US Catholic bishops' conception of just war: that the use of armed force itself is the evil to be avoided, and establishing peace is a separate issue, to be considered only in the absence of war.

### Just war thinking and American Protestantism: two contrary examples

While American Protestantism is diverse almost beyond cataloguing, a frequent and fairly useful division is between those denominations that are theologically and politically liberal and those generally called 'evangelical', which are theologically and politically conservative. The denominations belonging to the former group represent the Protestant 'establishment' that, until recent decades, dominated American religious life and provided social and political leadership from the local to the national level. The influence of these denominations has waned significantly since the 1950s, with social and political leadership today more frequently coming from the Catholic and evangelical churches. As to the latter, 'evangelical' refers to a mixed grouping of large denominations of various backgrounds, looser confederations of congregations, individual

---

[10] Bishop Wilton W. Gregory, 'Statement on Iraq', at http://www.usccb.org/sdwp/international/itaqstatement0203.htm.

churches including independent 'mega-churches' and various organisations defined around a special purpose, such as Focus on the Family and Prison Fellowship Ministries. The following discussion examines the United Methodist Church for the former and the Southern Baptist Convention for the latter.

## The United Methodist Church

The United Methodist Church's relation to just war thinking is mixed at best. Like other Protestant denominations it employs just war language in its official teachings, as exemplified in this resolution from the denomination's 1992 General Assembly:

> The United Methodist Church calls upon all who choose to take up arms or counsel others to do so to evaluate their actions in accord with historic church teachings relating to war, including questions of proportionality, legal authority, discrimination between combatants and non-combatants, just cause, and probability of success.[11]

These 'historic church teachings' are in fact criteria frequently used in recent versions of just war thought, though the term 'just war' is not employed, and the criteria are listed in an unusual order and without any distinction between those having to do with the decision to resort to war and those having to do with war-conduct. Adopted during the period when American churches were leaning towards an acceptance of the idea of armed humanitarian intervention, this statement opens the door to this possibility, while using these criteria to caution those inclining in this direction to weigh their position against 'historic church teachings'. The resolution does not caution those against the use of force to weigh their position similarly, which suggests that the aim is to oppose use of force, not to present it as a moral alternative.

However the use of just war criteria here was intended, there is a strong current in United Methodist teaching that amounts to a functional pacifism. This is exemplified in the following statement from the denomination's Social Principles adopted by the 1972 General Assembly:

---

[11] From a Resolution entitled 'Consequences of Conflict' adopted in 1992, found at http://www.umc.org/interior.asp?ptid=1&mid=1036.

We believe war is incompatible with the teachings and example of
Christ. We therefore reject war as a usual instrument of national
foreign policy and insist that the first moral duty of all nations is to
resolve by peaceful means every dispute that arises between or among
them; that human values must outweigh military claims as governments determine their priorities; militarisation of society must be
challenged and stopped; that the manufacture, sale, and deployment
of armaments must be reduced and controlled, and that the production, possession, or use of nuclear weapons be condemned.[12]

Opposition to war as such and uneasiness with the idea of just war were
also the thrust of a collective statement made by the bishops of the United
Methodist Church in 1986 under the title *In Defense of Creation*.[13] While
the polity of the United Methodist Church provides that only the General
Assembly, not the bishops, can take positions on behalf of the denomination, this 1986 statement was clearly intended to parallel *The Challenge
of Peace*. The 1986 statement effectively dismissed the just war tradition as
a guide for Christians, calling for Christians to 'move beyond' it and
instead to work for peace. Peace is defined in terms of the ideal *shalom*
of the Old Testament prophetic tradition. As in the Catholic position, this
document rejected any connection between the just war idea and the end
of peace. It quoted with approval the passage given above from the Social
Principles adopted in 1972, making the bishops' own the assumptions
about the incompatibility between 'human values' and 'military claims',
their fears about 'the militarisation of society', and the rejection of war 'as
a usual instrument of foreign policy'. Paul Ramsey (a United Methodist),
commenting on this last point, countered that 'the war we should really
worry about is a war that is not and cannot be an instrument of national
policy'.[14] This observation fits well with the just war idea of justified use of
force: to protect and defend the political community from aggression and
other injustice. But the United Methodist position is that national interest
is suspect, and 'military claims' even when attached to the preservation of

[12] From *The Book of Discipline of the United Methodist Church, 2000*, cited at http://www.
gbgm-umc.org/umw.statement_iraq.html.
[13] United Methodist Bishops, *In Defense of Creation: The Nuclear Crisis and a Just Peace*
(Nashville, TN: Graded Press, 1986).
[14] Paul Ramsey, *Speak Up for Just War or Pacifism: A Critique of the United Methodist Bishops'
Pastoral Letter 'In Defense of Creation'* (University Park, PA, and London: Pennsylvania State
University Press, 1988), p. 9. From a Resolution entitled 'Consequences of Conflict', adopted
in 1992, found at http://www.umc.org/interior.asp?ptid=1&mid=1036.

national interests are at odds with 'human values'. The upshot is a denominational position that leaves no room for an idea of just war, unless it serves to provide reasons to oppose the use of armed force.

## Evangelical Protestantism

On 3 October 2002, on the letterhead of The Ethics and Religious Liberty Commission of the Southern Baptist Convention (the largest Protestant body in the United States), a letter was sent to President Bush affirming his stated policy regarding use of force against Saddam Hussein, using just war principles to do so.[15] The letter was signed by five prominent evangelicals, all of whom have had leadership roles in recent political and social debates. The lead signatory was Richard D. Land, President of The Ethics and Religious Liberty Commission. He was joined by: Chuck Colson, Chairman of Prison Fellowship Ministries; Bill Bright, founder and Chairman of Campus Crusade for Christ; D. James Kennedy, President of Coral Ridge Ministries Media, and Carl D. Herbster, President of the American Association of Christian Schools. This list reflects how the evangelical movement is defined not just by denominations but by a variety of special-purpose organisations that cut across denominational lines and may explicitly describe themselves as non-denominational Christian.

The letter affirmed the idea of just war as Christian teaching and worked systematically through the just war criteria. On every point this letter reached a position opposite to that of the US Catholic bishops. More significant, I think, especially since the Southern Baptist Convention is not historically a 'just war church', is that the just war criteria cited were used with respect for their traditional meaning. Further, this letter is the only denominational entry into the debate of 2002–3 to take account of all three of the reasons for using force put forward by President Bush in his 12 September UN speech. It adhered to the traditional conception of the authority to use force as 'the authority of the sovereign', that is, in this case, the authority of the US Government, not the UN. On proportionality the language of the letter was that of balancing alternatives – 'We believe that the cost of not dealing with this threat now will only

---

[15] Richard D. Land *et al.*, 'Letter to President Bush on "Just War" ': http://www.christianity.com/partner/Article_Display_page/0,,PTID314166.

succeed in greatly increasing the cost in human lives and suffering . . . in the not too distant future' – and not that of imagined worst-case or even best-case scenarios. War here is not the moral problem to be avoided; Saddam Hussein's past evil actions and his present threat are identified as the moral problem. The letter concludes that the use of force is the proper moral response.

This letter, like the other examples treated above, does not distinguish between the requirements for deciding to use armed force and those for conduct in using the force that has been determined to be justified. Nor does it refer to the historical just war tradition, and its list of just war criteria is substantially similar to those employed by the Catholic and liberal Protestant churches. But there is no 'presumption against war' here; the argument of the letter assumes, in accord with the broader historical just war tradition, that resort to force may be an instrument of positive good. Nor is there any visible fear of the state or imputation of evil motives to it: the American Government is treated as able to act responsibly and for good. Rather than laying out a worst-case scenario expected from resorting to force, the letter highlights Saddam Hussein's record of evil-doing as needing to be dealt with and anticipates that the US use of force will meet the criteria of non-combatant immunity and proportionality. In short, though this letter uses essentially the same list of just war criteria as used by the other churches treated above, it employs them without imposing a 'presumption against war', without referring to 'peacemaking' as something inherently at odds with use of military force and overall in a way that represents the justified use of force as a responsible tool of statecraft when dealing with evil-doing that has resisted other approaches. As a policy statement this letter more closely reflects the normative assumptions, content, form and intent of historical Christian just war tradition than those of the other American Christian bodies treated.

### Factors influencing the churches' positions on war

Why have these churches taken the positions they have taken? What factors have influenced them, and what have they understood to be their role in entering the public debate over the use of armed force? The answers to these questions are as different as the churches themselves; yet there are also important common themes.

## The influence of pacifism

At the beginning of *War and the Christian Conscience*, Paul Ramsey refers to 'the pacifism which between the world wars spread widely in the non-peace churches', though he thought then that this influence had waned.[16] He later realised that it had returned, if it had ever left. When giving the title *Speak Up for Just War or Pacifism* to his book-length critical analysis of the United Methodist bishops' *In Defence of Creation* and the Catholic bishops' *The Challenge of Peace*, he intentionally drew attention to the presence of pacifist thought in these statements alongside just war thinking and in tension with it.

In similar vein, I have several times in this chapter called attention to how just war language has been used in recent American churches' statements on war to reach what I have called 'functionally pacifist' conclusions. I have observed how the 'presumption against war' imposes a kind of pacifist premise on just war theory, so that the debate over the use of force is turned into one of whether to use evil to oppose evil. Pacifism in various forms has been one of the most important influences in recent American churches' public positions on the use of armed force, and this has distorted conceptions and uses of just war language in these public positions.

Four distinguishable forms of pacifist attitudes towards military force can be recognised in recent American Christian thinking on war: rejection of violence as evil in itself, rejection of war and military force as morally tainted by the evil of the state, rejection of modern forms of war as inherently so indiscriminate and destructive that the use of military force can never be moral, and rejection of war and military force as an element of commitment to international order. These can be discerned in the official Catholic and United Methodist positions discussed above. All of them are inimical to the kind of thinking about the possible use of force found in just war tradition, where force itself is not evil, and the good of the political community is understood as a value needing to be protected. No behind-the-scenes pacifism is visible through the evangelical statement treated above, and this is one of the reasons I have concluded it is the only one of the positions

---

[16] Ramsey, *War and the Christian Conscience*, p. 3.

examined to treat the just war idea in a way consistent with historical meaning.

## The Civil Rights movement

For many socially and theologically liberal American Christians, Protestants and Catholics alike, the Civil Rights movement of the 1950s and 1960s stands as an iconic example of how organised non-violence may be used effectively against social injustice and may bring about lasting social change. The theory of non-violent resistance put forward by Martin Luther King, Jr was explicitly Christian in character, tied to Jesus' command to his followers to love their enemies. That the racist structures the Civil Rights movement sought to change were often symbolised by brutal policemen and by killings and other violence perpetrated by members of the Ku Klux Klan reinforced the sense of moral superiority that acting non-violently gave.

But given this, why still accept the use of force at all, even if only as a very last resort? One answer is that some Christians did not do so; they became pacifists. This was the route taken by proponents of the 'Catholic peace tradition' as applying in principle to all Catholics and not just to those in religious life.[17] For these the compromise represented by *The Challenge of Peace* theoretically gave them a common ground with just war Catholics: they could unite under the banner of a common 'presumption against war'. But while the just war Catholics could admit in theory that this 'presumption' might be overturned, the genuine pacifists committed to non-violence could not; they remained (and remain) a powerful internal force within American Catholicism opposed to the idea that the 'presumption against war' can ever be overruled. For Protestants the answer is more elusive. Clearly vocational pacifism is no longer the province of the 'peace churches' alone. United Methodist theologian Stanley Hauerwas is a prominent example of a pacifist within the frame of mainline Protestantism, and he is hardly alone, particularly among those who remain committed to the cause of non-violence as developed and experienced in the Civil Rights movement.

---

[17] On this position see further Ronald G. Musto, *The Catholic Peace Tradition* (Maryknoll, NY: Orbis Books, 1986).

## The nuclear debate

The debate over nuclear weapons has coloured much American religious thinking on war. *The Challenge of Peace* and *In Defense of Creation* both reflect a reaction to the Reagan administration's build-up of American strategic nuclear capacity and various forms of new weapons development. The 1983 pastoral letter explicitly rejected such new technologies and repudiated the entire idea that nuclear weapons might be part of a 'war-fighting' concept. Indeed, they came close to denying that nuclear weapons had any moral use at all, taking the position that such weapons might be stockpiled for deterrence purposes but could never actually be used against an enemy. They also took a position against non-nuclear uses of armed force, arguing that escalation to nuclear force could be expected. Two decades later, the opposition to nuclear weapons and fear of escalation has morphed into opposition to use of force as such and prognoses of 'unforeseeable consequences' when force is being contemplated. Political thought within the liberal Protestant churches has followed similar lines.

## Vatican II

The Second Vatican Council influenced American Catholic thinking about war in three major ways. The first was in the creation of national organisations of bishops and the accompanying sense that bishops in such conferences, acting together, could speak for the church on important matters affecting religious and moral life. Vatican II had the effect of reawakening older conceptions of conciliarism as opposed to central Vatican authority. Second, Vatican II created a new sense of empowerment on the part of theologians, religious, and laity – classes of people who had been involved in various ways in the council and who sought to increase their involvement in Church affairs after the council's close. Third, the council's call for the spirituality of the religious to be extended among the laity was read by anti-war Catholics as effectively removing the old distinction by which those called to the religious life practised a pacifist non-involvement in military force as a facet of their larger withdrawal from secular life, while the just war teachings remained the moral guide for those in secular life. The effect of this change quickly manifested itself in the argument that historical Catholic teaching includes two parallel traditions, that of just war and the parallel, but different, 'Catholic peace tradition', an interpretation that appears in *The Challenge of Peace*. There the idea of a 'presumption against war' represented an effort to define the common ground between these two parallel traditions.

## Loss of historical knowledge

Affecting Catholic and Protestant thought alike, if not identically for each, has been a virtually complete loss of knowledge of the historical just war tradition. Because knowledge and use of that tradition had generally disappeared by the time Ramsey's *War and the Christian Conscience* was published in 1961, the recovery of just war thinking that this book initiated has more often than not been a reinvention of the just war idea without reference to the tradition or understanding of it. This shows in various ways in the shape of much recent church-based just war discourse, with its recasting of the purpose of just war reasoning, redefinition of the traditional categories, introduction of new utilitarian categories (giving these equal or greater importance than the traditional deontological just war criteria), jumbling of the *jus ad bellum* and *jus in bello* criteria and making the latter do service as the former, and so on.

This situation is unlikely to change. The study of just war tradition is not pursued today in American theological schools, whether Protestant or Catholic; rather, the focus of such study is within secular universities, privately funded think-tanks and the military service academies and war colleges. Without a proper grasp of this earlier Christian tradition on just war and the larger conception of just social order within which the tradition was developed, contemporary Christian thought gives up a great deal of its unique perspective in public debate with other versions of moral thought about war. The military academies and war colleges approach the idea of just war with their own context and values in mind; philosophers approach the idea of just war with their own assumptions and generally today reason as utilitarians. Ideally the churches would offer thinking rooted securely in a base of Christian tradition that provides a secure vision of the good society and the place of the use of force in securing and maintaining that good society. The inability of churches to do so is a serious loss for the moral debate.

## Inversion of the Church–sect roles

Ernst Troeltsch typologised European Christian bodies into two broad groups, the Church and the sect.[18] Among its other characteristics, wrote Troeltsch, the Church 'accepts the secular order'. It 'utilises the state and the ruling classes, and weaves these elements into her own life; she then becomes an integral part of the existing social order; from this standpoint, then, the Church both stabilises and determines the social order'. Sects, on the other hand, are connected with 'those elements in Society which are opposed to the State and to Society'; their aim is 'usually either to tolerate their presence alongside of their own body, or even to replace these social institutions by their own society'. While Troeltsch's typology was not intended to address the character of religion in the USA and never completely fitted it, certain American Protestant denominations exercised the function of Troeltsch's Church-type within American social and political life. Political and social leadership, as well as relative and absolute wealth, tended to be concentrated in these denominations. Non-members who wished to enter the ranks of such leadership or to progress econom-ically ratified the role of these denominations in society by becoming members of one or another of them. At the other end of the spectrum were many of the religious bodies and individual congregations today grouped under the heading 'evangelical'. Until recently the Catholic Church in the United States also lay at this end of the spectrum, impor-tantly because of its status as a Church of recent immigrants.

Many of these long-standing historical roles have changed. In partic-ular, prominent Protestant denominations like the United Methodist and Presbyterian churches have taken on the role of sects, identifying with 'those elements in Society which are opposed to the State and to Society'. This is a role which correlates with the involvement of the most socially and politically liberal elements of these denominations with the cause of the Civil Rights movement and the opposition to the Vietnam War. At the same time the Catholic Church, which was functionally a Troeltschian sect in most of the country and at the national level through the nine-teenth century and the first half of the twentieth century, since the Second World War has lost this character. Evangelical Protestantism, formerly the

---

[18] Ernst Troeltsch, *The Social Teaching of the Christian Churches* (New York: Harper and Brothers, 1960), pp. 331–2.

epitome of the sect-type within American society, has become more affluent and has taken on roles of social and political leadership that earlier would have been denied to persons from these religious bodies or which members of these bodies themselves would have shunned.

If one looks at who, from among American Christian bodies, has had an influential voice regarding public policy in recent decades, it is people from the evangelical movement. It is not the leading clergy of the older mainline denominations who had earlier occupied such a role. The position of the Catholic leadership in recent decades falls somewhere in between. Arguably their influence on the question of military force was at its height with *The Challenge of Peace*, when bishops on the drafting committee of that pastoral letter worked closely with representatives of the military and from the Reagan administration to formulate a position that could be taken seriously by those in positions of political and military responsibility. This influence was squandered by the position taken by the Catholic bishops' national leadership in the debate over the 1991 Gulf War. While the Catholic bishops continue to have an important metaphorical seat at the policy table in relation to public issues like abortion and the legal definition of marriage, it is not at all clear that they do so any more on questions regarding the utility of military force.

There are, of course, many exceptions to the generalities above. There are 'evangelical' elements in the Protestant denominations known for their social and political liberalism, and to a lesser extent vice versa. There are also important regional differences: being a Presbyterian or United Methodist in Texas is rather different from being one in the Northeast or Midwest. And, positions taken by denominational leadership on social issues, including war and the use of military force, may be quite different from those found in the pews. But thinking broadly in terms of Troeltsch's two ways in which a Christian body may relate to the society in which it exists nonetheless helps to explain why the diverse forms of American Christianity have come to their respective positions on the question of war as this arises in public debate.

## Do the churches make a difference in policy debates over war?

When the leadership of the American churches speak in public debates over war and the use of military force, do they have an influence? The clearest success story is that of *The Challenge of Peace*. I have noted above the significant attention given by the media and in military and policy circles to the process that produced this pastoral letter and to the statement itself in the aftermath of its being published. None of the various Protestant denominational statements drafted during this same period had a similar impact; indeed, one had to search them out deliberately to know what they said. Despite the public attention to the Catholic bishops' pastoral, though, none of the bishops' specific policy recommendations subsequently became policy. The same was true of the various Protestant statements. Nor is it at all clear that statements from the denominational leadership have much if any effect at the level of local congregations. Formal statements regarding the use of force made by denominational hierarchies do not in practice translate into the actual teaching literature promulgated by the denominations for use by member churches. Even *The Challenge of Peace* was adopted as a teaching document for their dioceses by only a handful of the US bishops.

A personal anecdote illustrates the limited impact that denominational public statements have on congregations. In 2002, as debate intensified over the question of using force against Iraq, I received a phone call from a reporter for a national newspaper in a state widely recognised as one in which religion is taken seriously. She was to write an article on what the churches in her city were saying about this question. She had called clergy in all the major churches and synagogues and had come up empty: they were simply not talking about this; they were instead treating matters closer to the faith or closer to the individual and family lives of their members. So she went to the Internet, found my contact information and called with a plea for help. I suggested she try again with the churches in her city. I told her about *The Challenge of Peace* and other statements from the US Catholic bishops; I·told her about the United Methodist bishops' *In Defense of Creation*; and, noting the very large number of Southern Baptists in her city, I told her about the letter by Richard Land and his colleagues. She had not heard of any of these, and from her earlier research, it was clear that the clergy in her city were not using them with their congregations. As this anecdote testifies, the fact that one or another statement has been issued under the auspices of a denomination's office of social justice, religion and society, or justice and peace does not translate to what goes on at the level of individual congregations. How should the denomination's national offices expect to be heard on public policy when they do not speak for their membership or when their membership does not hear them or disregards what they have to say?

In broader terms, to be sure, the recovery of the just war idea over the last four decades has clearly affected the conceptualisation, shape and direction of public reflection and argument over uses of military force. Continuing reference to just war reasoning by the churches helps to keep the idea of just war alive within the churches and in the public debates over the use of military force. Yet misusing the just war tradition does only harm. The majority of just war thinking in the USA today, in any case, takes place not in the churches but in the academic world, in the military and in some parts of the policy sphere. The success of just war thinking as a secular phenomenon raises the question of what additional value the churches' own way of thinking about just war contributes to the public debate. It seems to me to be quite mistaken, for example, for the churches to present the just war idea as if it had to do centrally with the prudential criteria of last resort, overall proportionality and reasonable hope of success. These are categories secular utilitarians can use equally well, or perhaps better. There is nothing specific to Christian values or tradition in these prudential categories, and there is nothing in the theological training or experience of denominational officials that might privilege their judgements on these matters over that of the persons in government and the military whom they are seeking to influence.

There have always been elements in the just war idea which are common to both religious and secular versions of it, as well as other elements that are rooted chiefly or uniquely in the religious or the various secular spheres which have contributed to the overall tradition. The special Christian element in the idea of just war as classically defined, however, was to place the criteria for moral judgement on the use of force within a larger, theologically informed conception of the purpose of the political community – and the network of all political communities – in history. This special element was expressed directly in how Christian just war theorists understood the meaning of sovereign authority, just cause and right intention, the classic requirements for a justified use of armed force. The churches would, in my judgement, better serve their own values by attending centrally to these concepts in their reflection on just war and by seeking to elucidate their meaning for contemporary government and international relations. By doing so they would also make a unique and valuable contribution to policy debates over the use of military force.

# PART II

Responding justly to new threats

# 6

# Humanitarian intervention

## DAVID FISHER

Is there a right of humanitarian intervention? Can a state legitimately intervene, if necessary, by military means, in the affairs of another state for humanitarian purposes? For most, if not all, of the last century there has been no international consensus that such a right exists in international law. In this chapter I shall argue that – where human rights are seriously under threat – there is a moral right to intervene for humanitarian purposes, and that there should be a corresponding legal right. International law should be amended, as required, to reflect the moral consensus that is emerging in the twenty-first century in favour of intervention. This question raises profound issues of philosophy, theology, jurisprudence and politics. But it is also an intensely practical moral issue.

## The moral challenge of Rwanda

In April 2004 world leaders commemorated the tenth anniversary of what happened in Rwanda when the international community failed to agree on humanitarian intervention. The cost of that failure had been high. Following the shooting down of a plane carrying the presidents of Rwanda and Burundi on 6 April 1994, the Hutu-dominated Rwandan military unleashed a genocidal assault on the minority Tutsis. This led to the deaths of over 800,000 Tutsis. The United Nations, which had a small military presence in Rwanda and was well aware of what was happening, did nothing. Or rather the UN did do something. Following the murder of ten Belgian soldiers, on 21 April 1994 the Security Council voted to reduce the size of the UN Assistance Mission to Rwanda to a token 270. In a report for Human Rights Watch published in spring 1999, Alison Des

The views expressed in this paper are those of the author and do not in any way constitute official policy or thinking.

Forges scathingly concluded: 'The Americans were interested in saving money, the Belgians were interested in saving face, and the French were interested in saving their ally, the genocidal government. All that took priority over saving lives.'[1] On the tenth anniversary of the genocide world leaders vowed never to allow such a tragedy to happen again. As so often, Tony Blair summed up well the prevailing international mood: 'If Rwanda happened again today as it did in 1994 when a million people were slaughtered in cold blood we would have a moral duty to act there also.'[2]

And yet even as the UN held a special ceremony to commemorate the genocide, reports were reaching New York of large-scale killings taking place in Darfur, the western province of Sudan. The civil war that had been raging for nearly twenty years in Sudan between the Muslim north and Christian south had claimed 2 million lives, but the world had ignored it. But, with the tragedy of Rwanda so fresh in the memory, surely the brutal oppression in Darfur would attract the attention and action of the world? Human rights violations had started in early 2003 when an uprising by the Muslim African population in Darfur had been violently suppressed by the Muslim Khartoum government, assisted by the notorious Janjaweed militia. By spring 2004 the scale of human rights violations had escalated dramatically. In June 2004 the African Union sent ten monitors to the region followed by a 300-strong protection force.

Throughout the autumn of 2004 the UN debated the Darfur crisis on a number of occasions. No action was, however, agreed, not even a modest proposal to impose a no-fly zone. China, a large importer of oil from Sudan, threatened its veto. The USA and UK, while expressing concern, were preoccupied with Iraq. It was not until April 2005 that the UN finally agreed a Security Council resolution – not to take military action to prevent the genocide, but to authorise prosecution of Sudanese war criminals by the International Criminal Court, with thirty-one names passed to the Court. By then an estimated 300,000 had died, a third brutally murdered and the rest dying from hunger and disease caused by the conflict. Over two million displaced persons had fled to neighbouring Chad and remain there, too frightened to return to their homes. Despite

---

[1] Quoted by William Shawcross, *Deliver Us from Evil* (London: Bloomsbury Publishing, 2000), p. 123.
[2] Prime Minister Tony Blair in a TV interview, October 2001, quoted on BBC *Panorama*, 3 July 2005.

all the glowing rhetoric on the tenth anniversary of Rwanda, the world had once more failed to intervene. As Kofi Annan summed it up on a BBC *Panorama* programme on 3 July 2005: 'We were slow, hesitant, uncaring and we had learnt nothing from Rwanda.'[3]

## The self-defence paradigm

So why is the international community so reluctant to contemplate humanitarian intervention? To answer that question we need to go back to 1648 and the Treaty of Westphalia. For the Treaty of Westphalia not only ended the Thirty Years War and the territorial aggrandising ambitions of the imperial Habsburgs, it also put an end to Pope Innocent X's grand vision of a unified Christendom. Henceforward, Europe was a continent of horizontally organised nation-states. Nation-states became the central actors on the world stage, whose rights and duties it became the role of international law to define and to defend. The doctrine of the absolute supremacy of the rights of states and the inviolability of state boundaries, however arbitrarily drawn and whatever wickedness was perpetrated behind them, gradually developed over the succeeding centuries.

This doctrine reached its apogee in the 1945 UN Charter. After two devastating global wars resulting from the intervention of great states in the affairs of lesser ones (Austria–Hungary in the affairs of Serbia, Germany in those of Czechoslovakia and Poland), the UN Charter prohibited intervention. Article 2(4) declares: 'All member states shall refrain in their international relations from the threat or use of force against the territorial integrity or political independence of any state.' Only two exceptions are allowed: 'the inherent right of individual or collective self-defence if an armed attack occurs' as provided under Article 51; and military measures authorised by the Security Council under Chapter VII in response to 'any threat to the peace, breach of the peace or act of aggression'. There is thus no legal right of humanitarian intervention recognised by the UN Charter. On the contrary, Article 2.7 specifically prohibits interventions 'in matters which are essentially within the jurisdiction of any state'.

---

[3] Kofi Annan on BBC *Panorama*, 3 July 2005.

Following two calamitous world wars, this sanctification of state borders was not without good reason. The political philosopher Michael Walzer writes:

> The boundaries that exist at any moment in time are likely to be arbitrary, poorly drawn, the products of ancient wars. The mapmakers are likely to have been ignorant, drunken, or corrupt. Nevertheless, these lines establish a habitable world. Within that world, men and women (let us assume) are safe from attack; once the lines are crossed, safety is gone ... it is only common sense, then, to attach great importance to boundaries. Rights in the world have value only if they also have dimension.[4]

Moreover, during the long years of the Cold War the doctrine of the inviolability of boundaries largely went unchallenged. Superpower rivalry meant there was little prospect of the Security Council agreeing to collective action under Chapter VII, while the risk of nuclear escalation induced a cautious prudence in inter-state behaviour. The West accordingly chose to turn deaf ears to the cries for help from Hungary (1956) and Czechoslovakia (1967), and even failed to intervene to stop the genocide of more than a million Cambodians perpetrated by the Khmer Rouge in the 1970s.

With the ending of the Cold War, the unanimous international condemnation of Saddam's invasion of Kuwait in 1990 appeared to offer hope that the UN might recover a capacity for effective action, as intended by its founding fathers. The thawing of the bipolar glacier also released ethnic rivalries and tensions leading to mayhem and massacre within Europe itself. Meanwhile, globalisation meant that news channels carried instant detailed reports of atrocities virtually wherever they occurred in the world. The moral clamour for action in the early 1990s became intense.

So how has the UN responded to such cries for action? An honest answer is that the UN response has been mixed. As crises have deepened, too often the UN has fumbled and fudged. The report of the Secretary-General's High-Level Panel on Threats, Challenges and Change concluded in December 2004: 'The Security Council so far has been neither very consistent nor very effective in dealing with these cases, very often acting

---

[4] Michael Walzer, *Just and Unjust Wars* (London: Allen Lane, 1977), pp. 57–8. Walzer has more recently argued in favour of intervention, 'I don't mean to abandon the principle of non-intervention – only to honour its exceptions': Michael Walzer, *Arguing about War* (New Haven and London: Yale University Pres, 2004), p. 18.

too late, too hesitantly or not at all.'[5] The UN, for example, intervened too little, too late from 1992 in the former Yugoslavia where the initial mandate of UNPROFOR (United Nations Protection Force) was only to protect humanitarian aid convoys and so notoriously failed to prevent the massacre of 7,000 Bosnian Muslim men at Srebrenica in 1995. Alternatively, the UN failed to intervene at all – as noted above – in Rwanda and now Darfur. By far the most successful humanitarian intervention was NATO's operation in 1999 to prevent the ethnic cleansing of Albanians in Kosovo. But this was not a UN operation nor was it authorised by the United Nations Security Council.

The reasons why the UN finds it so difficult to intervene effectively for humanitarian purposes are multifarious. But paramount amongst these are the inviolability accorded state boundaries and the consequent failure to agree any legal right of humanitarian intervention. Adam Roberts summed up the legal situation in 1996 thus: 'There is absolutely no possibility of securing general agreement among states about the legitimacy of humanitarian intervention ... humanitarian intervention will, and perhaps, should remain in a legal penumbra.'[6] Five years later in 2001 Simon Chesterton concluded his survey of humanitarian intervention and international law even more starkly: 'There is, in short, minimal state practice and virtually no *opinio juris* that supports a general right of humanitarian intervention.'[7]

## The just war revisited

Is such a pessimistic conclusion inescapable? Critics of humanitarian intervention often cite the just war tradition in support. In particular, Vitoria's claim that there is one and only one just cause for war, '*iniuria accepta*' or 'wrong done', is often quoted to support the modern view that self-defence is the sole legitimate pretext for traversing borders. In fact, Vitoria added that there were various legitimate objectives in war, chief among which are to defend the public good, to reclaim losses and

[5] *A More Secure World: Our Shared Responsibility*, Report of the Secretary-General's High-Level Panel on Threats, Challenges and Change (New York: United Nations Publications, 2004), p. 57.
[6] Adam Roberts, *Humanitarian Action in War* (Oxford: Oxford University Press, 1996), p. 30.
[7] Simon Chesterton, *Just War or Just Peace* (Oxford: Oxford University Press, 2001), p. 235.

indemnify oneself, and to punish the wrongful aggressor.[8] On that basis, not only could defensive wars be justified, but also wars of reparation and punitive wars. An example of a war of reparation might be a war of national liberation fought to restore lost political rights and freedoms (perhaps the struggle of the ANC against apartheid in South Africa). Indeed, it is a curious consequence of the self-defence paradigm, betraying its inherently conservative nature, that all the wars of national liberation fought during the twentieth century are ruled out a priori as unjust! In Vitoria's view punishment could justify wars of intervention where a society practised human sacrifice, cannibalism or tyrannical and oppressive acts.[9] Regime change – so much criticised in the current debate on Iraq – was thus authorised in the classic just war tradition not, of course, as an end in itself but as a necessary means to end oppression and tyranny.

Vitoria's sentiments are echoed by other classical just war theorists. Grotius argued that sovereigns could exact punishment from those who 'excessively violate the laws of nature or of nations in regard to any persons whatsoever'.[10] The classical just war tradition reaching its zenith in the sixteenth century – a century before the Treaty of Westphalia – had a broader and more altruistic conception of the possible aims of war than our current obsession with the self-defence paradigm. In *The Just War Revisited*, the theologian Oliver O'Donovan puts it thus: 'The attempt to privilege the defensive aim exclusively is a significant retreat from the spirit of the juridical proposal. It withdraws from the concept of an international community of rights to the antagonistic concept of mortal combat; correspondingly, it is formally egoistic, protecting the rights of self-interest while excluding those of altruistic engagement.'[11] Quite so. For what has happened in the twentieth century is that the rights of states have become paramount at the expense of individuals. The key question for the twenty-first century is whether some rebalancing is now required by the claims of morality; and, if so, whether international law needs some amendment to enable it to catch up with morality. For as O'Donovan

---

[8] 'Vitoria, De Iure', in Anthony Pagden and Jeremy Lawrance (eds.), *Political Writings* (Cambridge: Cambridge University Press, 1991), pp. 303–4.

[9] *Ibid.*, pp. 273–5, 287–8.

[10] Hugo Grotius, *De iure belli ac pacis libri tres*, in F. Kelsey (trans.), *Classics of International Law* (Oxford: Clarendon Press, 1925), p. 40.

[11] Oliver O'Donovan, *The Just War Revisited* (Cambridge: Cambridge University Press, 2003), p. 55.

again reminds us: 'International law, like all law, needs to be developed in relation to cases; but lacking the courts to develop it, it can too easily become locked into an arbitrarily doctrinaire posture.'[12]

When we consider the tragedies that have taken place in Rwanda and are now unfolding in Darfur, the moral case for such a rebalancing seems inescapable. When I argued this in the early 1990s, mine was a somewhat lonely voice.[13] But during the 1990s the moral clamour for intervention has grown, with more people no longer prepared to accept that state boundaries should represent impenetrable barriers behind which torture and genocide should be freely allowed to take place. There appeared to some to be not merely a moral right but even a duty to intervene, where we could do so, to prevent widespread abuse of human rights. The moral clamour has, moreover, elicited some important shifts in international thinking. As Frank Berman's later chapter indicates, there may still not be an international consensus amongst lawyers in favour of a humanitarian right of intervention, but there has been at least some shift in legal opinion with a readiness on the part of successive British Attorneys-General to concede a right of intervention in the face of imminent or actual humanitarian catastrophe. This doctrine, developed in response to the humanitarian catastrophe facing the Kurds in Northern Iraq in 1991, was most clearly explained in public by Baroness Symons in the context of NATO operations in Kosovo in 1999.

> There is no general doctrine of humanitarian necessity in international law. Cases have nonetheless arisen (as in northern Iraq in 1991) when in the light of all the circumstances, a limited use of force was justifiable in support of purposes laid down by the Security Council but without the Council's express authorisation when that was the only means to avert an immediate and overwhelming humanitarian catastrophe.[14]

There have also been two important reports by international commissions calling for a change in the United Nations' attitude towards humanitarian intervention.

---

[12] *Ibid.*, p. 28.
[13] David Fisher, 'The Ethics of Intervention', *Survival* (Spring 1994): 51–60. David Fisher, 'Some Corner of a Foreign Field' and 'The Ethics of Intervention and Former Yugoslavia', in Roger Williamson (ed.), *Some Corner of a Foreign Field: Intervention and World Order* (Basingstoke: Macmillan Press, 1998), pp. 28–37, 166–73.
[14] *Hansard, House of Lords*, 6 May 1999, col. 904.

The 2001 International Commission on Intervention and State Sovereignty sponsored by the Canadian Government called on the international community to recognise its 'international responsibility to protect'. This interesting and new concept was introduced thus: 'Sovereign states have a responsibility to protect their own citizens from avoidable catastrophe – from mass murder and rape, from starvation – but that when they are unwilling or unable to do so that responsibility must be borne by the broader community of states.'[15] The principle of non-intervention accordingly yields to an 'international responsibility to protect'.[16] There would be a just cause for military intervention where there is: serious and irreparable harm occurring to human beings or imminently likely to occur of the following kind: first, *large-scale loss of life*, actual or apprehended, with genocidal intent or not, which is the product of deliberate state action, or state neglect or inability to act, or a failed state situation; or second, *large-scale 'ethnic cleansing'*, actual or apprehended, whether carried out by killing, forced expulsion, acts of terror or rape.[17] These conclusions were echoed in the December 2004 report by the UN Secretary-General's High-Level Panel. This report endorsed what it called: 'the emerging norm of a responsibility to protect citizens from large-scale violence that is held, first and foremost, by national authorities. When a state fails to protect its citizens, the international community then has a further responsibility to act, through humanitarian operations, monitoring missions and diplomatic pressure – and with force, if necessary, though as a last resort.'[18] The threat must be serious involving 'genocide and other large-scale killing, ethnic cleansing or serious violations of international humanitarian law, actual or imminently apprehended'.[19]

The responsibility to protect was subsequently endorsed at the UN Summit, 14–16 September 2005. The declaration, endorsed by heads of state and government, states:

> Each individual state has the responsibility to protect its population from genocide, war crimes, ethnic cleansing and crimes against humanity ... We are prepared to take collective action, in a timely and decisive manner, through the Security Council, in accordance with the Charter, including Chapter VII, on a case-by-case basis and

---

[15] 'The Responsibility to Protect', Report of the International Commission on Intervention and State Sovereignty, December 2001, p. 4, available at http://www.iciss.ca/pdf/Commission-Report.pdf.

[16] *Ibid.*, p. 6.    [17] *Ibid.*, p. 7.    [18] *A More Secure World: Our Shared Responsibility*, p. 4.

[19] *Ibid.*, pp. 57–8.

in cooperation with relevant regional organisations as appropriate, should peaceful means be inadequate and national authorities manifestly fail to protect their populations from genocide, war crimes, ethnic cleansing and crimes against humanity.[20]

The readiness of the international community to take action remains somewhat equivocal as the heavily qualified and convoluted prose of the declaration testifies. The acceptance of a responsibility to protect is, however, clear and significant. As Tony Blair noted: 'For the first time at this summit we are agreed that states do not have the right to do what they will within their own borders.'[21] The summit declaration does, therefore, constitute an important step forwards. With the failures of Rwanda and Darfur before us, the way is perhaps finally clear for the international community to establish through its practice and precedent an unambiguous right of humanitarian intervention.

In defining what constitutes a just cause for humanitarian intervention it is important, as both these reports recognise, that we should not make it too easy for states to intervene. There are strong reasons against intervention and the principle of non-intervention should only be lifted when the threat to human rights is sufficiently dire. On the other hand, it is important to avoid a cliff-edge approach of waiting to see whether the deaths and suffering taking place in a foreign calamity really amount to a humanitarian catastrophe before contemplating intervention. If the barrier is set too high or too steep, the risk remains of any intervention being too little, too late or even not happening at all. Indeed, it is arguable that this is just what happened in Rwanda in 1994. As the days and weeks went by and only a few thousand more Tutsis were slaughtered, the international community argued amongst itself as to whether this really constituted a genocidal catastrophe requiring intervention; or whether, as the USA argued, the killings were rather attributable to renewed fighting in the civil war.[22] To avoid such deadly prevarication, the right of humanitarian intervention should be based on a clear and not too precarious a definition. For that purpose the definition offered by Adam Roberts would appear to suffice: 'Humanitarian intervention in its classic sense

---

[20] UN General Assembly, *2005 World Summit Outcome*, 15 September 2005, pars. 138–9.
[21] Tony Blair's address to the UN Summit on 14 September 2005, reported in Ian Williams, 'Annan Has Paid His Dues', *Guardian*, 20 September 2005, p. 8.
[22] Shawcross, *Deliver Us from Evil*, p. 117.

may be defined as military intervention in a state without the approval of its authorities, and with the purpose of preventing widespread suffering or death among the inhabitants.'[23] On that basis, 'the prevention of wide-spread suffering or death' taking place or imminent would constitute a just cause for intervention. Humanitarian intervention can thus justify military action.

But a new concern now arises: if we ditch the self-defence paradigm we will end up being responsible for protecting suffering people all over the world. A universal guilt sets in like that felt by Father Zossima's younger brother in *The Brothers Karamazov* that: 'everyone of us is responsible for everyone else, and I most of all'.[24] Indeed, such fear of universalism can underpin a *reductio ad absurdum* argument against humanitarian intervention: If one ought to intervene in country A, one ought to intervene in countries B, C, D, E . . . But it is impossible to intervene in A, B, C, D, E . . . One only ought to do what one can do ('ought to do' presupposes 'can do'). Therefore one ought not to intervene in A. A similar *reductio* can be used to argue against charitable giving to the Third World. Such arguments are mercifully fallacious since the key major premise is false. If we ought to intervene in country A, it does not follow that we ought to intervene in every country where there is suffering, any more than the fact that I have an obligation to save a particular starving child means that I have an obligation to save every starving child. The latter may, indeed, be impossible and so not a moral obligation, but the former is only too possible and so can very much be my moral duty. This *reductio ad absurdum* argument is fallacious.

A variant of this argument seeks to undermine the moral case for intervention by pointing to the inconsistency and mixed motivation in the behaviour of the West. The argument runs thus: You are contemplating military action in country A but you failed to intervene in countries B, C, D, E where there were equally valid grounds for intervention. So your motivation cannot just be humanitarian. Other factors must be influencing your calculations, such as oil or imperialist ambitions. So you should not intervene in country A. This is an equally fallacious argument. Human motives are very often mixed, with both an ethical and a non-ethical

---

[23] Roberts, *Humanitarian Action in War*, p. 19.

[24] Feodor Dostoyevsky, *The Brothers Karamazov*, trans. David Magarshack (London: Penguin Books, 1982).

component, but that does not automatically invalidate an ethical motive. For example, the allies' motives in intervening in Afghanistan in 2001 were undoubtedly a mixture of self-defence (reducing the terrorist threat to the USA) and humanitarian considerations (rescuing the Afghan people from the brutal oppression of the Taliban). But this complexity surely does not mean the humanitarian considerations were invalid. Moreover, our failure to intervene in Rwanda hardly requires us not to intervene a decade later in Sudan. Indeed, it could be claimed more plausibly that the reverse argument is valid: our intervention in Sudan would demonstrate that we had learnt the lesson from our previous failure to intervene in Rwanda.

Such knock-down arguments against intervention do not work. But the fear of universal responsibility that prompts them still persists. We, therefore, need some way to choose between humanitarian interventions. Part of the answer to this challenge is that, according to the just war tradition, a cause, however just, does not justify military action unless *all* the criteria set by the just war tradition are met. These criteria, fashioned over the centuries in response to human needs, are not of mere academic interest but provide very practical guidance to policy-makers. Indeed both the recent international reports on intervention – the International Commission on Intervention and State Sovereignty and the Secretary-General's High-Level Panel – faithfully reflect just war criteria in the principles for military intervention they prescribe before an intervention can be agreed (although curiously without in either case explicitly acknowledging their indebtedness).[25] Taken together, the just war criteria present further significant constraints against military action.

## The just war criteria

The just war conditions are of two kinds: first, those that have to be met before war can be engaged in – the requirements of *jus ad bellum*; and, second, those that have to be met in the conduct of the war – the *jus in bello* requirements. The *jus ad bellum* prescribes that war is permissible if

---

[25] 'The Responsibility to Protect' includes as principles for military intervention: just cause; right intention; last resort; proportional means; right authority (pp. 7–9). *A More Secure World* lists five criteria of legitimacy: seriousness of threat; proper purpose; last resort; proportional means; balance of consequences (pp. 57–8).

and only if it is waged: by a competent authority; as a last resort, no peaceful means being available to settle the dispute; for the sake of a just cause; and the harm likely to result from the war is judged not disproportionate to the likely good to be achieved, taking into account the probability of success. The *jus in bello* adds two further conditions governing the conduct of war: the harm likely to result from a particular military action should not be disproportionate to the good aimed at; and non-combatant casualties should be minimised (the principle of discrimination). So let us consider what kind of constraint is imposed by each of these criteria.

## Authority

Within the classic just war tradition the requirement of competent authority is taken to refer to governments and so to preclude bellicose actions being undertaken by private individuals. In recent years just war commentators have sought to extend this to a requirement for UN authorisation of interventions other than for self-defence. The point was well made in 1984 by Hedley Bull: 'Ultimately, we have a rule of non-intervention because unilateral intervention threatens the harmony and concord of the society of sovereign states. If, however, an intervention itself expresses the collective will of the society of states, it may be carried out without bringing that harmony and concord into jeopardy.'[26] So UN authorisation is clearly highly desirable and would be sufficient to establish competent authority. As the International Commission on Intervention and State Sovereignty noted: 'There is no better or more appropriate body than the UN Security Council to authorise military intervention for humanitarian purposes.'[27] There are, therefore, good reasons why a government contemplating military action should seek explicit authorisation from the UN for military operations. What happens, however, if the Security Council fails to reach a prompt decision even though the need for intervention is urgent?

The key question is, therefore, whether UN authorisation is always necessary. The answer, as Michael Quinlan argues in his reflection chapter, is that there may be a graduating scale, depending on the degree of international consensus and the gravity and urgency of the crisis to be

---

[26] Hedley Bull, 'Conclusion', in Hedley Bull (ed.), *Intervention in World Politics* (Oxford: Oxford University Press, 1984), pp. 187–211 at p. 195.

[27] 'The Responsibility to Protect', p. 8.

averted. At one extreme, Hitler invading Czechoslovakia to protect the Sudeten Germans was clearly acting unlawfully. Closer to the other end of the scale, NATO intervening to protect the Kosovar Albanians lacked UN authorisation but had substantial international support. The 1991 coalition operations to expel Saddam from Kuwait had both widespread international support and specific UN authorisation. There are then cases where the gravity of the crisis demands urgent action. On these I defer to the judgement of the Secretary-General of the United Nations. In an address to the UN General Assembly on 20 September 1999, Kofi Annan, recalling the events of Rwanda, asked: 'If, in those dark days and hours leading up to the 1994 genocide, a coalition of states had been prepared to act in defence of the Tutsi population but did not receive prompt Council authorisation should such a coalition have stood aside as the horror unfolded?'[28] The implication was that they should not.

## Last resort

As with authority, so with last resort this condition is the subject of much debate. Some of the discussion is confused as if the condition required that war should only be reverted to temporally last, after all other options have been tried and failed. Postponing military action until last in time may, however, be a recipe for disaster as the lapse in time may make the military situation ever more difficult. In fact, the last resort condition requires that war should be not temporally but logically last, only preferred if other options are judged unlikely to succeed. That condition can be fulfilled, particularly now that economic sanctions are no longer regarded as the panacea they were once thought to be. Our experience in Iraq and elsewhere has shown the extent of suffering among the civilian population that economic sanctions can cause, while having no impact on the decision making of a tyrant who does not have to answer any democratic test. In determining whether the last resort condition is met, much depends on what is deemed to be the cause for war and how urgent is the need for intervention. If the grounds for war are humanitarian – for example, to prevent the widespread suffering being carried out by a brutal dictator – that might suggest the need for action sooner rather than later.

[28] Quoted by Shawcross, *Deliver Us from Evil*, p. 375.

## Just cause and right intent

The next requirement is that there is a just cause for the sake of which the military action is being undertaken. I have suggested that the prevention of widespread suffering or death can constitute a just cause. It is, however, not enough for there to be a just cause. This requirement insists that the military action must be undertaken for the sake of that cause; undertaken with what the tradition sometimes terms '*right intention*'.

## Proportion

Even if a just cause exists, military action cannot be justified unless it is judged likely to bring about more good than harm, taking into account the prospects for success. In judging this we need moreover to assess not just what happens in the military action but also, as considered below, the *post-bellum* settlement. And this balancing of consequences, as the intense argument still raging over the justice or otherwise of the Iraq intervention shows, is a very hard condition to meet. For it involves difficult decisions made in conditions of uncertainty and fine judgements about the likely outcome of military action. And yet such judgements, however difficult, must be made. For military action can clearly only be justified if more good than harm is judged likely to result.

## Jus in bello

The just war tradition requires that the conditions of proportion and discrimination have to be met in the conduct of military operations. The former requires that for each military action the military force used is proportionate to the objectives to be achieved. The principle of discrimination requires that non-combatant casualties are minimised, a challenge made more achievable by the introduction of smart weapons with a highly accurate targeting capability.

## Jus post bellum

The just war tradition always recognised that it is not enough for a war to begin justly and be conducted justly but that it must also end justly. The establishment of a just *post-bellum* settlement – righting the wrong that had occasioned the war – is a key objective of 'right intention'. The *post-bellum* settlement also, as we have seen, has to be taken into account in the overall balance of consequences that has to be weighed up before war can be undertaken. It is, nonetheless, perhaps helpful to separate out *jus post bellum* as a condition in view of its importance for interventions, particularly those for humanitarian purposes. For where the international community intervenes in a failed state or to stop a government oppressing its own people, some political reconstitution, including regime change, is likely to be a necessary constituent of any *post-bellum* settlement. Without political reconstitution, the oppression that gave rise to the intervention is likely to recur.

Some interventions may take the form of a quick in-and-out rescue operation, like the UK intervention in Sierra Leone in 2000 that successfully removed the rebel threat to President Kabbah's incipient democracy. Moreover, the state that intervenes may not necessarily be the state committed to nation building since a division of labour such as that between NATO and the UN and European Union in Kosovo may be appropriate. But what is important is that the intervening state needs, in Prime Minister Tony Blair's cautionary words during the Kosovo conflict, to 'be prepared for the long term'.[29] A state contemplating intervention must include the *post-bellum* settlement in the overall balance of consequences to be assessed. It must also crucially have a carefully thought-out plan for dealing with *post-bellum* conditions to ensure that the war ends justly. The just war criteria all have to be satisfied before military action can be justified. This thus presents a powerful constraint against military action.

## Choosing between interventions

If all the just war conditions are met, there is a moral case for intervention. But to whom does it then fall to exercise that right, whether by supplying forces to the UN or undertaking the action in concert with allies under the authority of a UN resolution? The UN has no forces of its own, so who should undertake the military action? Once more we appear haunted by Father Zossima's brother's nightmare of universal guilt and responsibility.

---

[29] Prime Minister Tony Blair's Chicago speech, reported by Michael Evans, 'Conflict Opens Way to New International Community: Blair's Mission', *The Times*, 23 April 1999, p. 2.

In order to limit the demands of morality, some have suggested that there are spheres of moral responsibility. Just as the ripples caused by a pebble thrown into a pond fade and eventually disappear with distance, so too, it may be supposed, does our moral responsibility lessen the further from us the events are unfolding. On such grounds it was argued that the UK had a particular responsibility to prevent massacre and ethnic cleansing in the former Yugoslavia, a neighbouring European state. But the moral claims for action were less pressing further afield, for example in Cambodia. The doctrine of spheres of moral responsibility affords a robustly practical ethic. But it accords a moral significance to mere distance that it cannot bear. It is as wrong to kill an innocent stranger far away by an intercontinental missile as to kill someone close by with a hand gun.

If distance alone cannot provide an adequate criterion of choice, for what suffering in the world can we be held responsible? One answer is suffering that is within our control and which through our action we could prevent; and suffering of which we are fully aware so that, if we do nothing to prevent it, we have in some sense consented to its occurrence. A valid attribution requires both consent and control to be present. Consent alone will not suffice, as illustrated by the poisoner who slips arsenic into his wife's bedtime cocoa only to find she dies coincidentally of a heart attack before the fatal beverage has passed her lips. He may have consented to her death but did not control it and so cannot be held responsible for her death. Similarly, even if control is exercised, without consent an attribution of moral responsibility may be avoided. This was the basis of the excuse proffered for the US bombing of the command bunker/air-raid shelter at Amiriyah during the 1991 Gulf War. The US spokesman did not dispute that the air-raid caused the deaths but argued that they did not know nor could reasonably be expected to know that civilians were sheltering in what they believed with good reason to be a military facility. If they did not know about something then *a fortiori* they could not have consented to it. Thus, even if there is control, without consent attribution of moral responsibility may fail.

Armed with these distinctions, we can see why distance, while morally neutral in itself, may acquire moral significance. For the further afield are the events unfolding, so may the likelihood of our knowing about them decrease. And the lengthier the causal chain, the gappier may be the causal nexus and so our ability to control events may be diminished. On such grounds we may be judged to have particular responsibilities to those countries linked to us by association, whether past (for example a former colony) or present (for example an alliance) or through geographical and/ or cultural proximity (hence the role envisaged for regional organisations acting under the auspices of the UN). In such cases our control over events and consent to their occurrence may be deemed that much greater.

## Conclusion

Such considerations may provide some practical guidance to help us choose between humanitarian interventions. But the demands of ethics can still be very challenging. For suppose the scale of suffering in a distant land is very great and widely reported in the media. Suppose further that we have the capability to do something successfully to relieve that suffering. The conditions of consent and control are thus fulfilled. Let us suppose all the criteria of the just war are met. In those circumstances, it may be very difficult to resist calls for intervention in faraway countries to which our only link is shared humanity. For, as Michael Walzer asks, if the help is not provided 'by us the supposedly decent people of the world, then by whom?'[30] Indeed, as I have argued, just such a challenge to the conscience of the West is being made right now by the 2 million refugees still displaced in Chad, fleeing ethnic cleansing in the Darfur province of Sudan.

The West's alibi for failing to respond to such pleas for help has hitherto been the lack of international consensus in favour of a right of humanitarian intervention. But that alibi, as I have sought to show in this chapter, is unfounded. Ethically, there is a right of intervention, as the classic just war tradition has always recognised. Now that the UN Summit has accepted that state borders are no longer to be regarded as impermeable, there is, moreover, a unique opportunity for the international community to endorse a legal right of intervention. But UN Summit declarations and fine speeches will not suffice. What matters is the action that follows. For the injured stranger we were called upon to help in the gospel story lay on the road to Jericho. He or she could be lying now on a dust-trodden road in Darfur.

---

[30] Walzer, *Arguing about War*, p. 18.

# 7

# Terrorism

JEAN BETHKE ELSHTAIN

It is sometimes said that one person's 'freedom fighter' is another person's 'terrorist'. This chapter argues that this is not the case: there are well-accepted and clear definitions of terrorism that preclude any such reductive and simplistic equation. After having defined terrorism in a manner generally accepted among serious scholars of the subject, this chapter argues that the just war tradition – often construed as a way of thinking and adjudicating that applies only to collisions between sovereign states – can be usefully applied to conflicts between states and those non-state entities that engage in the planned and intentional destruction of innocents. For, as I have argued elsewhere, just war is not just about war: it is also a way of thinking about politics and political life more generally.[1] Sadly, much political commentary today appears to have lost a robust way in which to speak about politics of which war, in the traditional sense, is a subset. Refusing to think seriously about politics leads to such widely accepted nostrums as those that claim there are 'root causes' for terrorism and that unless these are solved or ameliorated, terrorism will flourish. This puts the cart before the horse. It is only after relative political stability, including bringing illegitimate violence to heel, is restored that social questions can be addressed meaningfully. Without a structure of political accountability there can be no meaningful tackling of social questions. The just war tradition is a way to grapple with political questions that are too often treated naïvely in contemporary commentary. This means tying just war thinking to the great tradition of Augustinian realism.

---

[1] Jean Bethke Elshtain, *Just War against Terror: The Burden of American Power in a Violent World* (New York: Basic Books, 2003).

## Contested conceptual terrain

Terrorism is a protean topic. Although there is a relatively settled definition to the term in what might loosely be called international norms (if not international law), there are those who seek to legitimate a term, and activity, that is widely condemned. Contestations about terrorism are nothing new, although they have taken new and virulent forms in an era of weapons of mass destruction of the sort that can be seized, transported and deployed by small numbers of determined agents committed to violence against non-combatants. Although this essay is not primarily a history of terrorism, some historic focus – including conceptual and intellectual history, for that is most salient to this essay – may be helpful.

'Terror' and 'terrorism' are neither new terms nor new phenomena. The terms as characterisations of political phenomena trace from the French Revolution. But there is an even older lineage to current charges that 'one man's terrorist is another's freedom fighter'. This history takes us back to the late medieval debate between realists and nominalists. The nominalists, who deny the existence of 'universals' and claim there is no such thing as an objective truth, laid the basis for later subjectivism, namely, some label it 'terrorism'; others characterise it as 'freedom fighting', and never the twain shall meet. The implication is that in naming certain actions as instances of 'terrorism', those doing this are only, in their own way, repeating what the terrorists do themselves. But they wish simply to rouse the public against those they are fighting and the label 'terrorist' is a handy mechanism. The underlying presupposition, of course, is that 'terrorism' is an entirely subjective term having no settled meaning.

Today's post-moderns did not invent this insouciance where terrorism and other political phenomena are concerned. Thomas Hobbes, with his relentless nominalism and desire to overturn, and eradicate all traces of, medieval philosophy – especially Thomism – insisted that: 'tyranny and oligarchy . . . are not the names of other forms of government, but the same forms disliked. For they that are discontented under monarchy, call it tyranny.'[2] There is really no phenomenon for which objective criteria can be mounted that, when present, add up to tyranny, as St Thomas and others in the medieval 'right of resistance' tradition contended. Rather, it is a matter of 'likes' or, as political scientists tend to say nowadays,

---

[2] Thomas Hobbes, *Leviathan* (New York: Penguin Books, 1986), p. 250.

'preferences'. It follows that designations such as 'terrorist' and 'terror-ism' are wholly arbitrary and driven by un-stated and narrow self-interest.

If one accepted this Hobbesian nominalism – and its post-modern variants – the discussion would end there. Because 'terrorism' is a word applied by some to what they 'dislike' and as a way to disguise their own violent purposes, it follows that terrorism cannot be studied so much as endorsed or condemned. Those of us involved in debating the ethics of war and peace hear this sort of reductive argument frequently, to which is often added the parry that, because one can attribute to the United States, or any other society fighting terrorism, historic crimes in the past, it follows that neither the USA nor any other society can advance a moral mandate to fight terrorism in the present. If one's own hands are dirty, one can do nothing. This is an invitation to passivity. It avoids not only the complex question of arriving at settled definitions, but also a response to contemporary terrorism.

If one is to present a coherent and consistent argument concerning terrorism, one cannot deploy the term arbitrarily. Let us approach a consistent definition by noting that terrorism is a term that describes and evaluates simultaneously. Consider the difference between a 'battle' and a 'massacre'. The term 'massacre' is employed to describe and eval-uate the slaughter of unarmed persons, or the slaughter of large numbers of armed persons incapable of mounting a credible defence. There is an unavoidably negative valence attached to the term. Obviously, a major epistemological debate lies behind this claim but, for now, I simply note that 'terrorism' is by no means a neutral term. It is a term that condemns by defining a phenomenon that warrants such condemnation.

'Terrorism' is twisted beyond recognition if we claim that it applies to anyone anywhere fighting for a cause, with labels applied whether one 'dislikes' it or not. Terrorists are those who kill unarmed people they consider their 'objective enemies', no matter what those people may or may not have done. 'Terrorist' and 'terrorism' entered ordinary language to designate a specific phenomenon: killing directed against all ideological enemies indiscriminately and often outside the context of a legal war between combatants fighting under the legitimate authority of a state. According to the logic of terrorism, those designated enemies – as Osama bin Laden calls all 'Americans, Jews and infidels', for example – can legitimately be killed no matter what they are doing, where they are, whether they are young or old, male or female, healthy or infirm. It suffices for them to be Jews, or Americans or infidels – just as it sufficed under totalitarian terror to be a Jew, a Slav, a class enemy and the like. The enemy is always depicted without nuance and includes all members of a condemned and despised category, no matter what they are doing, where they are, or whether, indeed, they do or do not bear arms or can in any way resist.

As noted above, terror first entered Western political vocabulary during the French Revolution. Those who guillotined thousands in the Place de la Concorde in Paris were pleased to speak of 'revolutionary terror' as justice. Since the French Revolution, a complex, subtle and generally accepted international language has emerged to make critical distinctions between different kinds of violent acts. Combatants are distinguished from non-combatants. A massacre is different from a battle. An ambush is different from a fire-fight. When Americans look back with sadness and shame at horrors like the My Lai massacre during the Vietnam War, that is what they have in mind. Those who called the slaughter of more than four hundred unarmed men, women and children a 'battle' were regarded as having taken leave of their senses, perhaps because they were so determined to justify anything that America did in the Vietnam War that they had lost their moral moorings.

A terrorist sows terror. Terror subjects its victims or would-be victims to paralysing fear. The political theorist Michael Walzer notes:

> Terrorism's purpose is to destroy the morale of a nation or a class, to undercut its solidarity; its method is the random murder of innocent people. Randomness is the crucial feature of terrorist activity. If one wishes fear to spread and intensify over time, it is not desirable to kill specific people identified in some particular way with a regime, a party, or a policy. Death must come by chance.[3]

Walzer develops this theme further when he writes:

> In a sense, indeed, terrorism is worse than rape or murder commonly are, for in the latter cases the victim has been chosen for a purpose; he or she is the direct object of attack, and the attack has some reason, however twisted or ugly it may be. The victims of a terrorist attack are third parties, innocent bystanders; there is no special reason for attacking them; anyone else within a large class of (unrelated) people

---

[3] Michael Walzer, *Just and Unjust Wars* (New York: Basic Books, 1977), p. 197.

will do as well. The attack is directed indiscriminately against the entire class. Terrorists are like killers on a rampage, except that their rampage is not just expressive of rage or madness; the rage is purposeful and programmatic. It aims at a general vulnerability: kill these people in order to justify those ... This, then, is the peculiar evil of terrorism – not only the killing of innocent people but also the intrusion of fear into everyday life.[4]

Terrorism is, then, the random murder of the innocent because of who they are rather than anything they have done – because they are in some way associated with, or members of, the enemy the terrorist seeks to destroy.

The reference to innocence, of course, is not to moral innocence, for none among us can claim that. It refers instead to our inability to defend ourselves from murderous attacks as we go about everyday life. In other words, civilians are not combatants. Terrorists who engage in the random slaughter of innocents are not interested in the subtleties of diplomacy or in compromise solutions to political questions. At times, targets – pizza parlours, restaurants, buses – are random, too. They are targets of convenience. Sometimes the targets are selected – the World Trade Center – but who is within them at a particular moments is a matter of indifference. Terrorists have, as political theorist Hannah Arendt argued, taken leave of politics. They have embraced what she calls the 'instrumentalities of violence' rather than the complexities of generating political power to struggle for doable social and political change.[5]

Of course it is sometimes the case that elements of movements that resort to terrorism – say, the Irish Republican Army – also develop a political arm and begin negotiating a political settlement. No political solution is possible, however, when the destruction of innocent civilians and some fantastic notion, say, of restoration of the classical caliphate, as in bin Ladenism, is the alleged aim. Thus, bin Laden, in fatwa after fatwa, calls upon the faithful to kill 'crusaders, Jews and infidels' wherever and whenever they are found. He disdains any distinction between Americans in uniform and those going about daily civilian life. His claim is that to kill all Americans anywhere is a 'duty for every Muslim ... God willing, America's end is near.'[6]

---

[4] Michael Walzer, *Arguing about War* (New Haven: Yale University Press, 2004), p. 51.
[5] Hannah Arendt, *On Violence* (New York: Harcourt Brace, 1969).
[6] *Jihad against Jews and Crusaders*, World Islamic Front Statement, available at: www.fas.org/irp/world/para/dogs/90o223-fatwa.htm.

## Terrorism is terrorism

Before turning to the context of ethical evaluation and restraint within which just war thinkers insist terrorism and measures used to combat it should be located, it is important to examine some apologies for terrorism, that remove the onus of moral criticism and condemnation from those committed to terrorist deeds. For there are some who insist now, as they have in the past, that the victims of terror somehow 'had it coming'. Others claim that those who resort to terror have no other option as they are in a state of 'rage' as well as helplessness so they must use whatever weapons they can. Then, too, there is the 'everybody does it' claim.

These lines of thought strip away a moral vocabulary of the sort required to make crucial distinctions between rule-governed war making and terrorism. One often finds rationales for terrorist acts that, in the rush to exculpate, wind up patronising those who resort to terrorism. As theologian David Yeago writes:

> To suppose that the Islamic faith, or Arab culture, or poverty and the experience of oppression somehow lead young men directly, of themselves, to be capable of flying an airliner full of passengers into a building crowded with unsuspecting civilians is deeply denigrating to Muslims, to Arabs, and to the poor and oppressed. It requires us to suppose that Muslims, or Arabs, or the poor lie almost beyond the borders of a shared humanity, that however much we pity and excuse them, we cannot rely on them simply because they are Muslims, Arabs, or oppressed to behave in humanly and morally intelligible ways. I would suggest that this is a dangerous line of thought, however humanely motivated it may initially be.[7]

This is a powerful – and controversial – argument and it warrants some unpacking.

Often arguments that take the form of 'they have no other option' are working with crude binary models of victim/victimiser or oppressor/oppressed. If the victimising is absolute on one side of the pair, it follows that victimisation is absolute. If this is so, then victims will and must resort to anything they can to undo their 'oppression'. The origins of such an approach conceptually most likely lie with Hegel's famous (or

---

[7] David S. Yeago, 'Just War Reflections from the Lutheran Tradition in a Time of Crisis', *Pro Ecclesia* 10 (2001): 401–27, p. 410.

infamous) master/slave dialogue. More recently, this argument is associ-
ating with a text that was a staple in third worldist ideological circles,
namely, Franz Fanon's *The Wretched of the Earth*.[8]

Unsurprisingly, these sorts of arguments have resurfaced with Islamist
fanaticism and terrorism. But no one has thus far made a convincing case
that 'structural' causes lie behind a resort to terrorism – like poverty and
desperation. It is, therefore, clear that we must look at terrorism not as
epiphenomenal to some underlying problem but as itself the problem.
Poverty does not breed terrorism. The vast majority of the poor never
resort to terrorism. The attackers of 9/11 were middle class and reasonably
well educated. Alan Krueger and Jitka Maleckova have explored in depth
the relationship, if any, between economic deprivation and terrorism.
They conclude that a 'careful review of the evidence provides little reason
for optimism that a reduction in poverty or an increase in educational
attainment would, by themselves, meaningfully reduce international terrorism'. The issue is important, they aver, because drawing a false causal
connection between poverty and terrorism is potentially quite dangerous.
We may be led to do nothing about terrorism, and we may also lose
interest in providing support for developing nations should the terrorism
threat wane. By 'falsely connecting terrorism to poverty', policy-makers,
analysts and commentators only 'deflect attention from the real roots of
terrorism', which are political, ideological and religious.[9] There is a huge
gap between claiming that poverty 'causes' terrorism and acknowledging
the ways in which terrorist entities exploit various conditions, including
desperation of all sorts.

The key lies in the word 'exploit'. Terrorists exploit certain conditions.
These conditions are part of the matrix out of which terrorism grows. It
does not follow that terrorism is caused by these conditions. Because
terrorists exploit certain conditions, it makes good sense for those who
are victimised by terrorism to seek to ameliorate the conditions out of
which terrorism may flow. But this gets very tricky very fast, not only for
the reasons noted above, but because a good bit of al-Qaeda terrorism of
the sort that stunned the United States and Great Britain is the act of those

---

[8] Franz Fanon, *The Wretched of the Earth* (New York: Grove Press, 1981).
[9] Alan B. Krueger and Jitka Maleckova, 'Does Poverty Cause Terrorism?', *New Republic* (24 June
2002): 27–33.

who became ideologically inflamed actors within the very bosom of the society they seek to destroy.

In light of the enormous varieties of circumstances that may yield up terrorists, those combating terrorism must in their response, first and foremost, concentrate on terrorism itself. Confronted with a serial killer, the first thing police seek to do is to stop the violence. Attempting to discern what particular concatenation of circumstances led to this particular person taking up serial killing comes later. Urgency is added to this effort if one recognises that there are always unscrupulous political leaders who are only too happy to exploit the very conditions that make terrorist recruitment easier. To alter the circumstances is to alter their own fortunes, to the extent that they have profited from the misery of their own people. Acknowledging this in no way removes responsibility from the shoulders of others, but what it does do is to alert us to a kind of sacralisation of victimhood that invites exculpation when the 'victim' commits abhorrent acts. This is itself a patronising gesture that traffics in the most demeaning sorts of cultural stereotypes.

It follows from what has been said that to collapse 'soldier' and 'terrorist' into one category effaces the distance between those who fly civilian aircraft into office buildings and those who fight other combatants by taking the risks attendant upon military forms of fighting. It is vital therefore to observe the distinction between terrorism, domestic criminality and 'normal' or 'legitimate' war fighting. The distinction helps us to assess what is happening when force is used. If we cannot distinguish the intended targeting and killing of non-combatants and the deliberate sowing of terror among civilians, from fighting under certain restraints that make all such actions illegitimate, we live in a world without political and moral bearings.

## Confronting Islamist terrorism with just war: *ad bellum* issues

The focus of this remaining chapter is contemporary Islamist ideology and terrorism. Islamist fundamentalism is a twentieth-century phenomenon that threatens the sleep of the world wherever it is established. Islamism is a totalistic ideology with structural similarities to the totalitarian ideologies of the twentieth century as described by Hannah Arendt in her classic work on the subject. But there is this added, controversial element, namely, that Islamism claims to be the only authentic version of

Islam in the world today. This chapter takes its bearings from those who insist that Islamism, far from being an ineluctable product of one strand of traditional Islam, is, instead, a dangerous perversion of a great and various religion.

Following those who resist the 'culture wars' argument in its adamant form, namely, that there is 'something' in Islam innately and intrinsically opposed to modernity and all the features of modernity, I will instead assume for my purposes the following possible analyses of what the Islamist/al-Qaeda (and al-Qaeda-like entities) threat represents: (1) Islamist terrorists are always allied with and dependent upon state sponsors. It follows that to oppose Islamism is to oppose a particular state or states; (2) Islamist terrorists comprise a tiny cohort of criminals in a vertically organised criminal syndicate with Osama bin Laden at its head. It follows that the most appropriate response is a criminal law-type approach that seeks somehow to apprehend and 'arrest' a finite number of criminals; and (3) Islamist terrorism poses a particularly challenging threat because it is horizontally structured, consisting of many cells that function largely independently of one another; because it makes use of modern technologies that are inherently difficult to control or interrupt (like the Internet and cell phones); because it makes use of pre-modern technologies that are similarly difficult to intercept (like informal, pre-modern banking and money exchange); and, finally, because it makes use of nearly any available state structure, although it flourishes best under failed state or rogue state auspices.

Al-Qaeda spin-offs also function and commit deadly acts in Western Europe, without state sponsorship and in the absence of a weak state structure. The third option is the most appropriate analytical framework for thinking through what the Islamist threat represents. It is the only one that accounts for all the distinctive features of Islamism in action. This approach means that some version of a military, not just a legal-criminal, response is not only appropriate but may be necessary – although the response need not be, indeed will surely not be, narrowly and exclusively military. Although my specific focus is the contemporary threat from fanatical Islamism, my argument applies with equal force to other forms of international terrorism.

Once a state embarks on the use of organised force, that state encounters the tenets of the just war tradition. The just war tradition is an outgrowth of Western history. It emerged in the centuries known collectively as the period of 'Christendom' in the West. But, by the time Christendom as anything like a coherent entity ceased to exist, just war norms had been absorbed within the nascent forms of international law then emerging. Over the centuries just war has been debated, argued with, amended and absorbed within the infrastructure of international law and what the late Hedley Bull called 'international society'.

There are versions of the just war tradition that would seem to place terrorism outside its purview. I refer to those accounts that privilege states and define the war that just war either justifies, or does not, and seeks to restrain as, by definition, the use of force between combatants fighting under the flag of specific states. The implication here would be that, should a war against terrorists be waged, it should take the form of assaults on a particular state that sponsors or permits terrorist organisations to flourish in its midst. I have suggested something similar, it would seem, in my definition of terrorism and critique of apologies for it. I spoke above of 'rule-governed' use of force and a command-and-control structure. Obviously, this becomes tricky if one is confronted by shadowy entities that lie outside a state structure, although they may be parasitic upon such or take advantage of a failed state.

The most common post-9/11 argument along these lines held that because Osama bin Laden and al-Qaeda are, by definition, non-state actors, we cannot really fight a war against them. It follows that because we cannot go to war against them, we cannot legitimately deploy organised coercive force to fight terrorism. Others go further and claim that UN member states cannot legitimately declare war unless they get UN approval. It follows that a state whose citizens have been the victims of terrorism becomes the unjust aggressor should it go to war against non-state actors like terrorists. In this perspective, the moral onus is put on the victims rather than the perpetrators. This approach leads to such palpably unrealistic and naïve recommendations as that the USA should deputise a posse to arrest bin Laden and bring him to the USA for a trial. Many of this persuasion in the USA are functional pacifists who claim to be trying to make 'just war honest'. In reality, they set up just war criteria in such a way that neither the USA nor any other society could ever engage in a just war to combat terrorism.

Let us suppose, instead, that one recognises that contemporary Islamist terrorists may function with or without state sponsors. On the *ad bellum* side of the ledger, there is the challenge of fighting non-state actors.

Considering the criteria for just cause – a war must be openly declared by a legitimate body; it must be a response to an act of aggression or the imminent threat of such; it must begin with the right intention; it might be waged on behalf of a third party facing a very high probability of destruction; it should be a last resort; there should be a probability of success – the complexities of fighting terrorism are set in bold relief. This complexity requires a flexible nuanced response – the ability to use criminal law when appropriate (as in the arrest of the terrorists who perpetrated the 7 July 2005 attacks in London); to attack a rogue-state sponsor (as in Afghanistan); and to pursue terrorists' networks in other countries using a variety of methods, including armed combatants.

It is important to remember that a state seeking to determine the justifiability of armed force within a just war framework must be authorised to do so. The 'enemy' must be named. Certainly the USA was the victim of aggression on 9/11, a series of violent acts that claimed the lives of 3,000 civilians. Following the attacks, the stated US intention was to stop terrorists in order that no similar massive slaughter of civilians would occur in the future – clearly a right intention. What about last resort? Probability of success? And stating the enemy with some precision? It is difficult to figure out what a 'first resort' against a terrorist campaign might be, given that terrorism does not rely on widespread public support or mobilisation. Terrorists claim they are the violent vanguard of the people, but the truth of the matter is that terrorists are a band of violent elites. For them, terrorism is most often a first resort, as Michael Walzer puts it, the first resort of fanatics who are quite prepared to 'endure, or to watch others endure, the devastations of a counter-terrorist campaign'.[10]

One cannot ponder every possible idea someone might have and never reach last resort. It is always possible for someone to claim a state that has decided on the use of force jumped the gun (so to speak) and it was not last resort. Sometimes such claims have credibility; sometimes they are tendentious, mounted by those who never believe last resort has been reached. Be that as it may, when one has sustained such an attack and has every reason to believe that further attacks are planned, one must interdict this violence – but not by any and all means whatsoever. This takes us to *in bello* considerations to which I will turn in a moment.

---

[10]  Walzer, *Arguing about War*, p. 61.

One arrives at last resort very quickly if one is the victim of terrorism. Let us look at an analogy. The Japanese attack on Pearl Harbour constituted, as President Franklin Delano Roosevelt rightly stated, 'a state of war'. From the first moment of that attack, the USA was in a war. Officially declaring such became a *de jure* recognition of a *de facto* reality. The attacks of 9/11 present an analogous situation in some important respects. The attacks were an act of war carried out by a sub-state actor then allied with and supported by a state or states. Osama bin Laden had declared war against America *de jure* – officially – and al-Qaeda had already carried out a series of deadly attacks, though not on the US homeland. That al-Qaeda is a non-state actor does not, and must not, undermine the analogy which is not to domestic criminality but to unjust massacres as a stipulated act of aggression that *de facto* begins an armed conflict. In other words, the authorisation to use force is the *de jure* recognition of a fact. If one is satisfied with this particular move, it does not resolve every issue. There is the matter of against whom should the war be fought? And what about probability of success? What counts as success? When has one prevailed in such a conflict?

Many have criticised the Bush administration for declaring a war on terror, as if this meant the USA would try to extirpate all terrorism everywhere – a clear impossibility. No doubt greater precision would have been desirable in the language deployed by administration spokespersons. The Bush administration attempted to meet it by speaking of 'terrorists of international reach' – thus incorporating al-Qaeda as well as other transnational and trans-state terrorist entities like Hezbollah. Because Afghanistan under the Taliban harboured al-Qaeda, they became an appropriate target in so far as they refused to rein him in or to turn him over. The war authorisation was clear about this. But there clarity ends.

I see no easy way around this situation given the murkiness and lack of transparency in international terrorist operations. Terrorists function outside the law, in the shadows, through the use of computers and cell phones. It is as if there is a shadow world, a kind of vicious twin of the world of states and legitimate authorities and rule-governed use of force. Still, one must do one's very best to abide by the requirements of justifiability. It would have been better if the Bush administration had targeted that 'terrorist entity or entities responsible for the attacks of 9/11, those who supported actively such entities, and those who continue to plan future such attacks'. It is important not to be completely open-ended in declaring who the enemy is.

This brings us to likelihood of success and another conundrum. How do you measure 'success' when there is no nation to surrender? President Bush is surely right – 'this is a new kind of war'. But just war requires that any war fulfil certain criteria and probability of success is one of them. How can you tell if you have achieved success if there is no clear entity to surrender, no way to stipulate terms of peace, and all the standard repertoire of war making between states? Terrorism has no terminus. It is open-ended. At one point it may fade away, but by definition it does not go out of business or surrender. Indeed, in the case of al-Qaeda's total-itarian ideology, it cannot surrender by definition, as the war against the infidel is perpetual. Given that there is no way to end such a war in the standard scenarios we are accustomed to, it nevertheless remains the case that one must articulate what 'reasonable success' looks like. No attacks on innocent civilians, certainly. Destroying the terrorist entity's ability to plan such attacks, yes. But one can never demobilise – not for the foreseeable future. One can stand down from explicit military operations, but a war continues. If war is politics by other means, in Clausewitz's famous dictum, politics can surely be war by other means. The war against terrorism must be fought on many fronts. That being the case, do *in bello* norms continue to have salience and to be relevant to the struggle at hand?

### Restrained force against unrestrained violence

A standard charge against *in bello* restraints against ruthless foes is that one is, in effect, fighting with one hand tied behind one's back. Whatever merit there may be in such a concern, one cannot back down and throw restraint and caution out the window. In *The Just Assassins*, Albert Camus tells the story of a Russian anarcho-terrorist group who have planned to assassinate an Archduke, one directly responsible (although not totally responsible, of course) for the miserable condition of the Russian peas-antry, the desperation of the urban poor, the lack of political freedom and so on. One of their number is designated to throw a bomb into the carriage as it passes by. He freezes and cannot do it. The band gathers after the failed attack. The leader of the terrorist group, one Kalialev, is furious with Stepan, he who stood down from the bomb throwing. Kalialev berates him furiously when Stepan says that, when he saw the Archduke's two children in the carriage, he could not go through with the planned violent act. Kalialev, like the Marxist extremists Camus no doubt had in his sights, proclaims that in promoting 'the revolution' there are no limits. Stepan should have thrown the bomb rather than being soft and sentimental. But Dora, another member of the group, refutes Kalialev's proclamation of limitlessness. Even in revolution, she argues, there must be limits. If the revolution starts murdering children it will be 'loathed by the human race'.

We know that radical Islamic terrorists hold no such limitation. Everyone is fair game. Within Islamist ideology, even the children who died on 9/11 were infidels. The historic just war campaign against crusading and holy wars over time bore fruit in the West. But such restraints never took hold in Islamic thinking on war and peace in such a systematic way, and this according to nearly all reputable scholars.[11] Given that the categories that dominated thinking about war, depicted war as that which takes place against religious enemies who inhabit *dar al-harb*, the House of War, the important point to underscore was just how necessary it was to extend Islam into the non-Islamic House of War and by what means. Many schools of interpretation emerged in historic Islam that had the effect of softening the binary distinction between the two 'houses' with the correlative that warfare, too, was de-emphasised as a necessary, and necessarily just, tool. It is not at all surprising that bin Ladenism calls for a holy war of extermination against infidels. Because infidels can be found everywhere on the globe, as internal infidels – Muslims who disagree with Islamism – are found in large numbers in Muslim-majority societies, it follows that there are no geographical restrictions on who is the enemy.

And, because terrorism is not bound by the laws of armed conflict nor the many protocols and treaties now in place to regulate and to terminate wars – limitations deriving from the centuries-long efforts by just war thinkers in the West – it follows that the *in bello* restraints in the just war tradition, refined for hundreds of years, find no analogue in the annals of Islamism. Philosopher Michael Baur writes:

> For the terrorist there are in principle no contexts, no conditions, no times or places, and no persons that fall under the basic rules of armed conflict. Accordingly, the terrorist may target anyone at any time . . . But the terrorist's refusal to recognise any rules of armed conflict also means something deeper than this. It means that the terrorist in

---

[11] See Bassam Tibi, 'War and Peace in Islam', in Terry Nardin (ed.), *The Ethics of War and Peace* (Princeton: Princeton University Press, 1996), pp. 128–45.

principle refuses to recognise any rule that … governs the parties' conduct during the time of conflict. Because of this the terrorist is implicitly committed to a perpetual state of war.[12]

Just war fighters, by contrast, are constrained under two broad norms: proportionality and discrimination. Proportionality often means several things, among them the need to use the level of force commensurate with the threat. You do not use a nuclear weapon to stop illegal border crossings. You do not field an entire army if a small, mobile unit of special forces can do the job. Discrimination, the best-known and most complex constraint where fighting terrorists is concerned, lays down the hard-and-fast requirement that one is not permitted to target non-combatants intentionally. Knowing that non-combatants, sooner or later, will come into harm's way in any war, the just war fighter nevertheless recognises that his and her own cause will, in some palpable way, be undermined if the army in which each fights begins to indiscriminately kill unarmed men, women and children.

That is the easy part. Far more difficult is figuring how to recognise a combatant in a war against terrorism. Terrorists do not identify themselves with uniforms or other standard insignia. Terrorism blurs the distinctions just war *in bello* norms assume and underscore. Islamists are quite prepared to see any number of their own 'people' die in a counter-terrorist effort. They are even prepared to mislead those fighting them so that civilians are mistakenly taken for combatants. This enables the terrorists to proclaim: 'See, they slaughter civilians yet they dare to condemn us!' Even were there not clear ethical requirements for the restraint of force involved, prudence, too, dictates caution. Terrorists are not distinguishable from the rest of a given population. Time and patience are necessary dimensions of discrimination in a war against terrorism, for one must make every effort to identify the terrorists correctly. Clearly, fighting terrorism within just war restraints is a multi-pronged affair: there may be occasions for ordinary warfare, as in Afghanistan; there will be occasions for infiltrating terrorist bands, if possible, in order to determine what they are planning; one must attack networks of communication and funding; it will be necessary to put pressure on states that may not be harbouring terrorists directly but are,

[12] Michael Baur, 'What is Distinctive about Terrorism', unpublished manuscript, p. 46.

in other ways, providing them support. And, surely, the frustration is that much of this will be hidden from the public and little of it, on principle, can be revealed to the public as satisfying the public's 'need to know' since that might, in fact, jeopardise that very public.

This helps to explain why a war against terrorism is so frustrating. One measures success when nothing happens. But there are other complicating dimensions as well. A counter-insurgency effort may well put pressure on liberal and democratic institutions themselves. Some might agree with this claim but wonder what, or whether, it has to do with the just war tradition. Just this: just war emerged and remained nestled within Christian theology and statecraft for centuries. Medieval theology and political philosophy made explicit and careful distinctions between legitimate rule and unjust rule which counted as no rule at all. This was the category of tyranny. Although the just war tradition underwrites no particular regime form, it surely opposes, or cannot endorse, tyranny. The reasons for this are obvious. Tyrannical regimes are those that know no restraints. They are law-less. They violate the laws of God and man alike. They usurp power and govern with an eye to private interest rather than a common good.

The distinctions concerning legitimate versus illegitimate rule that Hobbes rejects are central to the wider framework of just war. Just war is not just about war. It is a way of thinking about politics that locates justice centrally. Tyrannous regimes by definition are unjust, just as terrorism, by definition, is unjust. Terrorist means and methods are inseparable from terrorism's wider political advocacy of regimes that are repressive and oppressive. Afghanistan's misrule under the Taliban illustrates what politics al-Qaeda endorses. Bin Laden's fatwas make it clear he seeks a goal of coercive 'purity' characterised by the oppression of women, the negation of the very humanity of homosexuals, denial of religious freedom and totalitarian control over every aspect of human life in general. When one fights Islamist terrorism in today's world, one is fighting tyranny. We have seen what radical Islamism in control of a state apparatus means. But it need not exercise that sort of control, as we have also seen, to represent a deadly threat.

It is, therefore, all the more important to keep alive the characteristics of a politics of decency that terrorism would destroy. This is not to suggest that all countries attacked by terrorists are decent and based on the moral equality of persons, but it is that distinction I am highlighting in contrasting human rights-based constitutionalism with contemporary Islamism. Many have pointed out that terrorism would instil an atmosphere of systematic fear and mistrust. People would mistrust one another; mistrust their government; fear fellow citizens and foreigners alike. If trust breaks down it proves much more difficult for citizens to comply with the undeniable inconveniences of anti-terrorist measures. Hannah Arendt pointed out a number of years ago that totalitarian systems require the isolation of persons as a precondition. This isolation flows from mistrust on both the vertical and horizontal levels. When this happens, it is easier for tyranny to gain a stronghold or for terrorists to gain an advantage.

Generalised and paralysing fear is scarcely the stuff out of which decent and minimally just societies are made. As citizens become isolated and mistrustful, governments have to work harder to fight terrorism and in so doing they will be more tempted to violate the norms of a constitutional democratic order to do so. As Michael Baur puts it:

> Terrorism puts civil society in a difficult bind: terrorism challenges civil society to defend itself; but since the modern terrorist cannot be deterred by more traditional, less extreme methods, civil society's war on terror must at times resort to invasions of privacy and to pre-emptive and excessive force – precisely the kinds of techniques that cause intimidation and undermine trust – and that is just what the terrorist also aims at doing.[13]

To avoid such a worst-case scenario, the moral restraints and tragic recognitions of human fallibility and shortcomings – we cannot protect ourselves perfectly – are more exigent than ever. Just politics and just war go together: not perfect justice, of course, but regimes that respect the dignity of persons, that offer religious freedom and substantial individual freedom, that regularly hold elections or otherwise involve citizens in the tasks of governing and accountability, that do not place categories of persons in a subordinate status by virtue of accidents of birth, race or gender, and so on. Our ideal of a just society and St Thomas's are by no means identical, but there is a powerful family resemblance. Each understands that politics and ethics cannot be severed. Each understands the dangers and temptations of tyranny. Each believes law and governing aim at justice.

---

[13] Baur, 'What is Distinctive about Terrorism'.

## Conclusion

In conclusion, there are many good reasons for rich nations to assist poor ones. The challenge is always to determine how to do that most effectively. But to suppose that ameliorating certain conditions will bring an end to Islamist terrorism, or any other form of terrorism, is naïve. It may help to ameliorate and to soften those conditions terrorists exploit. But because, thus far at least, no causal link has been demonstrated between poverty and terrorism and, second, because the impetus to care for others less fortunate should not be an artifact of revocable self-interest narrowly defined, terrorism must be treated as a phenomenon in its own right, not downplayed as epiphenomenal. Terrorism must be combated covertly and overtly and by means that may skirt the edges of law and restraint, but always in recognition that that is precisely what one is doing.[14] Keeping just war robust is one way to assure this outcome.

[14] See Sanford Levinson (ed.), *Torture: A Collection* (Oxford: Oxford University Press, 2005).

# 8

# Rogue regimes, WMD and hyper-terrorism: Augustine and Aquinas meet Chemical Ali

PAUL SCHULTE

For Layla Muktar al Jassim

This essay examines how the just war tradition might be developed to provide a framework of moral political analysis to help judge when it is right to use force against 'rogue regimes' which sponsor terrorism or seek to acquire weapons of mass destruction (WMD). It seeks to define what might constitute a 'rogue regime' and looks at considerations surrounding anticipatory self-defence or preventative action and the moral hazards posed by approaching the issue of just cause from a regime-centred analysis. Finally, it suggests a checklist of moral points that might apply in situations where the international legality of intervention against a 'rogue regime' is contested.

The purpose is not to expound any particular position but to assist debate by pointing out underlying inter-linkages and dilemmas. My understanding of the just war tradition is that military conflict should be avoided unless precise and demanding conditions are satisfied. (Other contributors to this volume may disagree with such a reading.) The concerns set out here are not intended to reverse that basic presumption, but they often involve balancing considerations – many of them relatively new and historically unprecedented – that could inform right intention and give rise to just cause. Like most commentators, I shall propose no more systematic and universally applicable process than a case-by-case balancing of different factors. I will suggest that the best, and often the only, way this can be achieved is through political prudence: the considered judgement of democratic politicians accountable to their informed publics, guided by realistic diplomatic, intelligence and military assessments and, wherever it is sufficiently clear-cut, by international law.

This essay is written in a purely private and personal capacity.

I do not write from either a religious or a legal position. This chapter's basic moral stance is utilitarian and concerned with an ethics of consequences rather than an ethics of principle. It assumes that the relevant consequences are the effect of action, or inaction, upon the progressive establishment of a safe, just and prosperous world. It does not attempt to address questions about the legality of war in general or specific wars, although I note that lawyers differ between themselves on these questions. I shall confine myself therefore to pointing out that legality and morality are not identical. International law does not seem, at least at present, transcendently clear enough to serve as a simple guide for action in every situation as criminal domestic law might do. While legal norms have evolved against bombarding hospitals or torturing criminals, there is, yet, no similar certainty about the scope for humanitarian intervention, the crime of aggression or the acquisition and deployment of various WMD.

The effect that decisions to resort to military action would have upon the rule of law in the world should certainly be a consideration in reaching them. Clearly, it is a *possible* moral position to hold that no military action should ever be taken unless completely unchallengeable by international law. However, it is not the *only* moral position. Others could reasonably doubt that it would contribute to the best interests of most people on the planet. If it had been so applied then, for example, Bangladesh might never have been brought into existence, Cambodia might not have been freed of the Khmer Rouge and Serbian repression in Kosovo might continue. Moreover, without these interventions, by India, Vietnam and the NATO states, international law itself might not have moved onto its present qualified recognition of a responsibility to intervene and protect. It is of some moral importance that the future behaviour of a 'rogue regime' is unlikely to change for the better if such a regime was assured that no military action would ever be taken against it without absolute compliance with all possible legal requirements. A single, possibly self-interested, prospective veto in the Security Council would then provide an impregnable defensive protection behind which a 'rogue regime' could shelter with complete impunity. Again, it is not obvious why that would lead to a better world.

## Preconditions for peace, justice and security

The present state in the evolution of international law is just one of the historically contextual aspects of the topic. My fundamental assertion is that the modalities and unequal distribution of human progress continually create new circumstances in which judgements of justice must be made. The stakes have changed – and will change further. Accelerating human development means that more is now lost than in previous eras if stultifying tyrannies are allowed to frustrate attainable improvements in life chances. Similarly, the use of scientific technologies to create and spread new WMD could threaten many more than ever before from mass-casualty terrorism or state-engineered holocausts.

Different styles of governance and economics can now cumulatively throw up enormous and systematically different life chances for the majorities of different societies. (North and South Korea sixty years after the Japanese occupation are perhaps the most vivid current examples.) Changing the instruments of governance in poor and oppressive countries could make a huge difference to their populations. So, no doubt, might larger international aid budgets or changes in the rules of world trade. However, those are separate issues, where progress is anyway unlikely to be assisted by a deterioration of international security. And it is increasingly clear that unless governance is right, well-intentioned aid will be wasted. This is not to argue that there is no economic salvation outside the full neo-liberal dogma, but simply that some combination of functioning markets, open borders, transparency and political accountability through free and fair elections seems to be a requirement for progressive improvement in the life of millions, all of whom have a moral claim on the concern of the world community. The alternative is the prospect of innumerable needlessly impoverished, and probably oppressed and humiliated lives.

Peace and security in one region is now bound more closely than ever before with conditions in what could previously be regarded as faraway countries. This is most obvious in human security terms. Refugee flows can appear suddenly and affect the mood on the streets thousands of miles away. It was frequently pointed out during the 1990s that insecurity in Mostar, for example, changed the dynamics of Manchester. Ending situations which drove out populations in fear of their lives from the Balkans became a legitimate concern of others all over Europe, as a requirement for wider order and peace. It is imaginable that utterly immoral or feckless state-tolerated internal behaviour, which led to disastrous ecological externalities, could create analogous and severe problems in the future. Lengthening missile ranges, potentially allowing more and more states to exercise threats across continents, represents another technology-driven example of widening dangers.

To expand the argument, the ordering of change and the dynamic management of the international system is a precondition for peace, justice and security. Unlike relatively small-scale and static political and economic systems in the ancient and medieval worlds, decision-makers now need to consider how best to ensure that their choices to intervene, or not, will have good outcomes globally and in fast-evolving circumstances. The ramifications of unopposed aggression, uncontrolled technology or weakened international order need to be predicted and rectified as far as this is intellectually possible. Bad precedents can be expected to widen out and ought, accordingly, to be prevented. Some states will be able to do more to achieve this ordering and management function than others, including through the possibility of interventionary force.

## International terrorism and the costs and risks of weapons proliferation

Technologically empowered and lethally ambitious terrorism is one of those perils overhanging the future that cannot be responsibly ignored. State-sponsored terrorism hijacked much of the course of the last century. It is easy to forget that the First World War was started in Sarajevo by state-sponsored suicide terrorists. The first war of the twenty-first century also resulted from the belief that those who flew into the World Trade Center and Pentagon were at least tolerated by the Taliban. Terrorists have always been able to kill senior and symbolic political figures. With developing WMD technologies, it becomes increasingly possible that groups committed to 'megalomaniacal hyper-terrorism' will use scientific options that could destroy entire cities and so change the political face of our world. The attacks of 9/11 did not only change American judgements about the acceptability of risks from potential terrorist action. Vigorous concerted responses by the wider international community have together inflicted significant losses on al-Qaeda, but it is not at all clear when, if ever, the threat from that group and possible messianic successors will have shrunk so far that its imperatives can be downgraded. It is unlikely that states which assist, sponsor or tolerate terrorists will soon be tolerated by others whose populations are at real risk of mass-casualty terrorist attacks.

The cumulative risk of deliberate transfer or eventual uncontrolled leakage of WMD materials to terrorists is only one reason to believe that opposing WMD proliferation would be a right intention – though one which would have to be balanced against others. Unchecked and expanding proliferation among states would have very serious direct and indirect human costs. In certain unstable regions, like the Middle East or South Asia, they could be spectacularly high. Nuclear, biological and chemical capabilities differ enormously in their potential destructiveness. Biological and chemical agents have come close to being universally outlawed following disarmament treaties that call for total bans on possession. By contrast, possession of nuclear weapons is legal for five specified Nuclear Weapon States under the Nuclear Non-Proliferation Treaty. Those states are also Permanent Members of the Security Council (P5). There exist outside the treaty a small number of nuclear-capable states, generally thought to be India, Pakistan and Israel. North Korea has stated recently that it has withdrawn from the treaty but that it might be induced to rejoin.

The normal international public assumption is that the spread of WMD is intrinsically undesirable. These weapons are expensive to produce, hard to use discriminatingly and would multiply the human, and particularly the civilian, costs of any conflict. When weaponised, in a form that could fit on to missiles, they can be prepared and delivered with little warning. Therefore, their spread increases the risk of war by hasty mistake or misunderstanding. Once states achieve WMD capabilities – even if clandestine or denied but credibly suspected – they begin to exert a new, permanent and often fearful influence on the strategic calculations and fears of others. These calculations will often produce knock-on effects and chains of further proliferation, with additional diversions of public resources at each point. Indeed, historically, the true overall costs of WMD research, production, ownership, maintenance and eventual clean-up have seldom been accurately estimated or openly debated. It is therefore intellectually inadequate to concentrate only on the imminent threat of WMD *use*. There should remain a strong international policy imperative to prevent the spread of possession of these weapons and to prohibit transfer of the technologies necessary to build them.

There is, however, disagreement about the justification of efforts, especially forceful efforts, to prevent or reverse WMD proliferation. Many critics assert that their purpose is simply to maintain the military advantage enjoyed by the five Nuclear Weapon States and so has little moral force until those states themselves disarm. Responses tend to be that the P5 are critical stabilising pillars of the current international order who have refrained from nuclear coercion or attack on non-nuclear states since 1945, and that each has reaffirmed its commitment under the Nuclear Non-Proliferation Treaty to achieve eventual total nuclear disarmament. However, this process will be slow, difficult and hard to imagine without wider changes in the way that force is used or threatened in the world. In the meantime, every new or potential WMD proliferant makes it more difficult to bring about the disarmament of existing nuclear states. It creates an additional obstacle that would have to be overcome if a nuclear (and chemical and biological) weapon-free world is ever to be achieved.

A broad source of scepticism about the price worth paying to avoid proliferation is that of the neorealist school of international relations. The underlying argument is that that WMD technologies will inevitably spread anyway, that deterrence and containment work well enough, and that nuclear weapons may even encourage political stability by inducing general caution in the international system. From this perspective, force-ful action to oppose their spread is unlikely to be worth taking. However, the numbers of actual nuclear-proliferating states have in fact been held down far below the anxious projections of past decades. And the grim, 'realist', alternative prospect of eternal, inescapable, WMD-backed com-petition between great and, given time, smaller powers has not achieved widespread appeal as an acceptable future.

New nuclear-capable states might well be outgunned in nuclear capa-bility by supporters of the status quo, but inadequate intelligence, poor judgement or more fanatical commitment to the outcome of a crisis could still lead them to miscalculate, fatally, their chances of 'winning' any heightened confrontation. One implication of the 2003 Iraq War is that at least some risk-taking regimes will knowingly gamble on their own destruction, rather than be seen to relinquish symbolically important WMD capabilities that they no longer have, or possess only vestigially. This does not bode well for their indefinite containment through the creation of rationally dissuasive balances of military power.

## 'Rogue regimes'

'Rogue regimes', at their worst, represent the particular form of the nation-state most likely to block progress and increase peril in the foreseeable future. Since the term 'rogue state' itself is so imprecise, I shall scrupulously refer instead to 'regimes' and enclose the term within inverted commas. It is generally used as a rhetorical label rather than a precise descriptor. Its usefulness as an analytical category has been frequently challenged. For the thought experiments required for moral argumentation in this sphere, I shall propose it as a Weberian Ideal Type, against which real circumstances and configurations can be judged. This essay is not an exercise in name calling and I do not imply that particular, actually existing states fit the type in all dimensions. Nor will 'rogue regimes' always inevitably pose the most pressing security problems. However, the categorisation is neither entirely fictitious nor trivial. Cambodia under the Khmer Rouge, Iraq under Saddam and Afghanistan under the Taliban approached the Ideal Type in various ways. The pathology may recur.

I take a 'rogue regime' to be an authoritarian political system that, for political reasons, proves itself indifferent or hostile to the welfare and democratic preferences of its people and the legitimate security interests of other political communities. Such regimes stand out increasingly clearly in rejecting developing international standards in human rights, trade, economic behaviour and good governance. Their populations will consequently be kept poorer and more oppressed than in other systems. Typically, they will be obstructed from free travel, trade and communication with the rest of the world. Their neighbours will tend to feel threatened by their behaviour because it threatens covert or overt aggression. These regimes lack checks on human wickedness and corruption. They are intentionally and self-declaredly closed to fundamental reform. Even when internally quiescent, they are better seen as in a state of continuous repression rather than at real peace. This repression can range from frozen mass fear to campaigns of active suppression of particularly distrusted or restive groups. Social capital and moral restraint are eroded. So, when oppressive control is removed, for whatever internal or external reasons, there can be long-term legacies of violent, vengeful discord (especially from resentful formerly favoured groups), anarchic lack of order and diminished human concern or restraint.

Regimes of this type tend to be attracted to WMD technologies to increase their international status, their military potential and thus their capacity for intimidation beyond the levels that their structurally inefficient economies could otherwise afford. The more 'rogue regimes' emerge and the greater their freedom of action, the less chance that the twenty-first century will develop peacefully. At their worst, 'rogue regimes' call into question the original moral justification for the nation-state, which legitimised the concentration of power in the hands of the sovereign, to reduce violence and protect innocent lives. 'Rogue regimes' are themselves indifferent or hostile to just war considerations, although they use sovereignty to sanctify their frontiers and hinder outside intervention against their crimes. At the extreme, their oppression of their own people can turn into genocide. Their aggression and hegemonic drive can trigger cross-border invasions. It is then relatively easy in legal and moral terms to calculate the case for intervening to reverse external aggression. Nevertheless, the obligations on the outside world to respond are less clear in response to internal misbehaviour.

Talk of 'rogue regimes', therefore, carries with it the assumption of a package of unjust future behaviours with serious internal and external consequences. This should facilitate examination in terms of the just war tradition, which is about future consequences rather than past evils. In this century, 'rogue regimes' may characteristically generate at least three kinds of injustice:

### Tyrannical behaviour against their own people

Murder, mass imprisonment, torture and random widespread oppression were not rare in previous centuries. Tyrannical behaviour today, however, is often characterised by technological options such as helicopter gunships and organophosphate chemical weapons, both employed and threatened against dissident groups in Saddam's Iraq. I shall later return to a particularly proficient and unapologetic proponent of these modern state possibilities.

### Frustration of modern economic possibilities available for their own people

Immiseration to varying degrees seems common, sometimes mitigated by hydrocarbon or other rents, but often leading directly to malnutrition or to starvation for unfavoured groups. Resources are frequently wasted on grandiose military projects, spectacular palace building and wider networks of regime corruption. Infrastructure, which could support take-off into collective economic opportunity, is never built, or allowed to run down. When combined with high birth-rates, the consequences will be even grimmer for future generations. This slow and avoidable suffering, like brutal behaviour within prisons and interrogation centres, is frequently intangible, taken for granted, purposely invisible or un-photogenic. It may therefore not lodge in the world's imagination as vividly as the human costs of conflict, which might be necessary to bring it to an end.

### Enhanced peril for their own people and for others

Warlike behaviour and an aggressive, uncompromising or messianic style increase the direct risks of bloody military conflict and force others to divert more resources to defence. In the worst cases, there may be deliberate cross-border campaigns of conquest. Indirect threats to more distant states and peoples are also likely, creating refugee crises and economically destabilising diasporas. In addition, international terrorists may be fostered, sponsored or at least tolerated and permitted to operate. Nuclear, biological or chemical materials and delivery systems may be acquired and perhaps sold on to other would-be proliferators, deliberately or with indifference to the consequences. Intransigent attitudes, or obvious cheating, would undermine disarmament or non-proliferation regimes. At the extreme, there may be outright defiance of strict international disarmament obligations, which calls the whole structure of international efforts to control these technologies, or the general enforceability of international resolutions, into question. Consistent refusal of strong obligations to prove compliance is likely to mean that, whether or not the 'rogue regime' retains prohibited weapons or materials, it will be believed to possess them by other concerned governments, whatever statements they choose to make publicly. This pattern amounts to the destruction of international social capital because successful and sustained bad behaviour by some diminishes general confidence that order will hold.

Potentially, many of the above tendencies associated with 'rogue regimes' ought in principle to be resisted. Therefore, assistance to those, inside or outside the country, who were already resisting them might often constitute a right intention. However, the specificities of the regime would matter very much in judging how far opposition should be taken towards conflict. An irredeemably reckless 'rogue regime' might be expected to continue its malign set of behaviours whenever it gambled that it was sufficiently safe to do so, until it guessed wrong and was forcibly overthrown or collapsed. Less malignant types might be susceptible to containment, deterrence, diplomatic and economic engagement and, eventually, reconciliation. Containment of the Soviet Union eventually succeeded in this way. But of course, regime dynamics may go the other way. Notoriously, Chamberlain was incapable of noticing that Hitler's regime could not be satisfied through compromise and that it was growing more reckless as the 1930s wore on.

Despite their vivid defining characteristics, an unbalanced regime-centred analysis of a case for just war with a 'rogue regime' would entail moral hazards. These could include demonisation through culturally determined distaste and unjustifiably righteous superiority. Regime attitude and ideology may be too far from ours to make us want to coexist. Yet, as John Stuart Mill observed: 'It is as little justified to force our ideas on other people as to compel them to submit to our will in other respects.' Certainly, the mendacious style, grandiosity, brutal hypocrisy and deceit of these systems will often be hard to accept. Their claims for their own sweeping legitimacy and ambition can hypnotise opponents as well as supporters. Their obsession with state secrecy can make it genuinely difficult to discern actual capabilities, activities and motives. Anger at their deeds could obsess outsiders who became preoccupied with them, whether as policy specialists, diplomats, reporters, aid workers, intelligence experts, human rights advocates or refugees, outweighing considerations that could help to put their significance in context. Errors of this kind might include overlooking how far 'rogue' behaviour was a defensive reaction to plausibly threatening regional rivals or to perceived Western ambitions. They might involve exaggerating the country's relative importance and real capabilities, excessive optimism about what might follow the regime and blindness to signs that it might carry within itself the seeds of change and improvement.

Naturally, the moral hazards of misjudgement do not run only one way. Faced with an intransigent regime that cannot be expected to back down without the dangerous and distasteful threat of violence, we should not ignore temptations to underestimate how bad it is, and to overestimate the collateral risks of its overthrow. Whatever the unfolding evidence, even the threat of armed conflict could be too emotionally distasteful – or politically and economically inconvenient – to be accepted as a lesser evil. This is a very humanly understandable distortion of perception. However, at the extreme, it is legitimately labelled appeasement.

## Unavoidable assessments

In considering what constitutes a 'just' policy towards a 'rogue regime', much would depend upon the reliability of intelligence on what was actually happening inside the regime, and what that implied for the future. Fateful assessments have to be made and then continuously and rigorously revised. How permanently and dangerously hostile is the regime to which other states? Are there any signs of softening and accommodation amongst prospective successors within the regime, especially in neo-dynastic systems? How widespread and intensified is repression? Does it amount to ethnic cleansing or genocide? Are illicit weapons being acquired or maintained? Are new technologies being developed with an underlying military rather than economic purpose? When will they reach completion? Are terrorists actually being assisted, and, if so, how serious a threat do they represent and against which countries? Might WMD be deployed? Is there any reliable way of defending one's citizens or allies against these threats?

Intelligence information, as far as it was available, often in relation to closed societies, would be essential to deciding the degree and kinds of future threat posed by 'rogue regimes' and whether war was the essential last resort to prevent it. But it would have to be supplemented by openly available and publicly debated diplomatic and media reporting. Resultant forecasts of actual 'rogue regime' behaviour under different conditions and incentives (as opposed to regime promises and propaganda) might be inherently difficult and publicly disputed. Even so, predictions of some kind could not be avoided, by anxious neighbours, and by other states with wide international interests and the willingness to play a responsible role in managing threats to justice and world order. As in private life, in order to coexist with those we cannot trust to maintain moral or legal constraints, it may be morally and prudentially important not to be driven to violent panic, but irresponsible not to try to foresee and mitigate what they may do to us or others in the future.

## Export controls and sanctions

There will be a strong case to restrict international sales of weapons and associated technologies and materials to such states. It will usually also be necessary to consider how amenable these regimes might be to various wider economic pressures. The record is mixed. In South Africa, prolonged international sanctions seem to have played an important part in ending the apartheid state and securing majority rule. However, following other experiences, most recently and notably Iraq, there has been some loss of confidence in the ability of sanctions to influence the behaviour of 'rogue regimes'. The problem is the indifference of the ruling group, in seriously tyrannical states, to the welfare of the general population. They may simply not care about overall economic hardship – or even hope to exacerbate and publicise it to gain world sympathy. Even the most tightly regulated sanctions policy will be susceptible to some degree of leakage. Worse still, sanctions may actually achieve perverse results by strengthening the internal hold of a ruling group, which can control and selectively dispense whatever resources remain available to its supporters. On the other hand, sanctions may still fulfil an indispensable warning and signalling function as a precondition for further international action.

## Last resort

In a crisis caused by their aggression, 'rogue regimes' may be exceptionally dexterous in playing for time, wearing out opponents' determination and counting on their transgressions turning into accepted facts. It has been asserted, for example, that Saddam's strategy in 1990 was based on contempt for the UN and international legal processes: that he had essentially wagered that if he could get the Iraq–Kuwait issue thrown into the UN system, then he could have twenty years in Kuwait. Where, as in 1990–1, concessions and the infinitely tempting possibility of a negotiated outcome emerge only after the deployment of superior forces, it is reasonable to doubt that they would be sustained if those forces withdraw. However, no one can expect outside armies to remain deployed indefinitely at enormous political and economic expense. In some way, the 'rogue' must be put under realistic pressure and yet the possibilities of peace cannot be ignored. Mediators might help but may be cynically manipulated to buy time. Choices have to be made, which again revolve around predictions of 'rogue-regime' intent, often having to rely on un-publishable intelligence, but needing explanations that will sustain public debate and examination.

## Geopolitical realities, strategic cultures and national choices

At present, the number of political leaders in the world likely to be involved in critical decisions about just war in relation to 'rogue regimes' is small. There is no UN army and few states have the ability to conduct high-intensity military expeditions over long distances. Most countries have not chosen or been able to pay the 'entry costs' for this style of warfare. The USA is the great exception, and America's vast cumulative investments let it support junior alliance or coalition partners. France and Britain are probably the only other countries with significant trans-continental deployment capacities. The general international scarcity of such strategic actors is partly because of cost and technical difficulty. Nevertheless, the more critical determinant seems to be national self-definition. Some countries define themselves as prepared to undertake optional high-intensity interventions. Others do not. Their choice is influenced by national historical experiences of applying military force, as with the attitudes and capabilities of Germany and Japan. No government confronts questions of peace or war unaffected by national strategic and political culture. However, even when public opinion permits entry into a discretionary conflict, the choices confronting most national leaders will seldom be wide-ranging or unconstrained. There may only be a question of whether to support an alliance strategy or to join a coalition or not, and resort to military operations if the major partner or partners were prepared to do so. Nevertheless, although the incremental military contribution of additional countries wishing to join a coalition may be small, the political benefit of giving wider active support cannot be ignored. That would imply another moral obligation.

## Public opinion as a decisive factor

There is a huge imbalance in technology and military training between modern expeditionary forces and local opponents such as 'rogue regimes'. The gap may be widening. However, the politics that are likely to determine the outcome, and therefore the start, of possibly justified wars are much less favourable to intervention. We are very far from the nineteenth century's indifference to human losses and unabashed appetite for the annexation of territory. Countries with interventionary capability spend immense amounts of time and money ensuring that their forces can precisely discriminate between military and non-military targets. Even so, there is now an enormous public concern to avoid casualties – among enemy civilians as well as friendly forces, and increasingly, even enemy combatant losses and the destruction of infrastructure. The 2003 Iraq War has now created considerable apprehension about insurgent resistance after even the most brilliant conventional military victories.

Taken together, these concerns create a new non-physical vulnerability, a historically novel Clausewitzian centre of strategic gravity. Favourable public opinion is critical for the successful conclusion of any intervention. In an important sense, therefore, these campaigns are, as much as military conflicts, international contests of will, mediated through television coverage. Interventions against 'rogue regimes' would usually make no demands for physical risk or sacrifice from the electorates in whose name they were launched, yet they do imply serious domestic political dispute about their justice and prudence. The terms of these controversies will usually be grounded in just war argumentation.

## Prudence and the responsibilities of democratic leadership

Critical choices about resort to conflict with 'rogue regimes' are therefore, in foreseeable circumstances, most likely to be taken by a small number of governments in advanced democratic countries on a case-by-case basis. They will combine military assessments of probable outcomes, legal analyses, and diplomatic and intelligence assessments. They will be weighed against internal political judgements about obtaining and sustaining necessary support for military action under different conditions, and the expectation of having to answer rigorous public questioning. The overall ethic for this will be 'prudential'. This does not necessarily mean timidity. However, conflicts that could not be won, because the will to sustain them was absent, could not prudently or justly be embarked upon. What then are the likely types of military conflict with 'rogue regimes' and how will their implications vary morally?

## Pre-emption

The public terminology of debate has become confused. True pre-emption would be an anticipatory attack on enemy forces which are about to launch an attack themselves, in order to prevent them from doing so, or at least to limit the damage they could inflict. It would therefore be a form of self-defence or, conceivably, the defence of an ally. The test classically formulated after the famous Caroline Incident in 1837 was one of necessity that was 'instant, overwhelming, and leaving no choice of means, and no moment for deliberation' – or, presumably, for obtaining international legal authorisation. Such cases are historically rare.

The example that best approaches the ideal type is the start of the 1967 war. Israel mounted a decisive surprise air-strike on numerically superior surrounding forces in a period of deliberately heightened tension. It had reason to fear that the alternative would have been the destruction of the Israeli state in a successful but unjust attack by its avowed enemies. Even so, this has certainly not avoided controversy about whether the attack was a true last resort in a crisis, which might, at least theoretically, have been resolved diplomatically. In much of the Arab world, at least, it has been consistently denounced as a thinly concealed war of aggression.

If the anticipated attack, which might justify pre-emption, were being prepared with WMD, it is likely to be much harder to detect, and subsequently prove, than the preparations for a mass conventional assault. Intelligence uncertainties could produce exquisite dilemmas. The moral and cognitive hazard of assuming worst-case offensive intentions from a regime which one has labelled 'rogue' would have to be confronted. However, decisions could not be avoided and might have to be immediate. How much does one owe a previously reckless antagonist the benefit of the doubt, if forbearance could lead to the deaths of many more of one's own citizens? Yet, in a situation of reciprocal deterrence, if the enemy can still retaliate, even partially, after pre-emption, many on one's own side will still die – and all the deaths will have been needless if an attack were not actually intended. Working through those questions in a worst-case modern military crisis might not allow for extended consideration of principle.

## Preventative war

The slower timescale of preventative war makes it even more controversial. Here there is no instant and overwhelming necessity, only a judgement that the threat represented by an opponent is so great and inevitable that it is best met early on. Preventative wars have had a bad reputation ever since Bismarck is supposed to have said that they amounted to committing suicide for fear of death. Arguably, that was exactly what his country did in 1914 for those historians who believe that there was a decisive intention to defeat rising Russian power, rather than tragic unplanned entanglement, behind Germany's entry into the First World War. Conversely, the criticism made of the British and French political classes in the late 1930s centres around their disastrously prolonged refusal to contemplate preventative war against the rapidly rearming Third Reich.

A limited preventative response to technological proliferation is the example of Israel's air-strike on Iraq's Osirak nuclear reactor in 1981. This action was precise and discriminating. It forestalled the acquisition by Saddam of a nuclear capability that would have posed a direct, continuing existential threat to Israel and hindered, or perhaps entirely deterred, effective international responses to his aggression against other neighbours. However, Israel's action was also illegal. It was denounced worldwide at the time as destructive to international legal controls, and a further source of bitterness to the Arab world. In retrospect, it has been increasingly reinterpreted, especially in the USA, as a justifiable and even laudable preventative act when faced by a regime like Saddam's Iraq. While weapons technologies for precision strikes have advanced since the 1980s, appropriate targets for limited prevention would almost certainly be better concealed, dispersed or defended. It cannot be assumed that there will be many conveniently surgical preventative options to counter proliferation in the future.

## Moral luck and preventative war

Certain standard arguments about the morality of action in conditions of radical uncertainty emerge repetitively in discussions of preventative war. Should a violent and morally controversial action be taken to avert the worst potential consequences of an unfolding and disputed situation? The history of Western confrontation with the Soviet Union provides epic illustrations on a global scale, with the additional dimension of a profound ideological division. After adjusting for the scale of the potential risks, it illustrates the dilemmas that could arise in the handling of 'rogue regimes' at a regional level.

The new Soviet regime was regarded by the West as a prototypical 'rogue': ideologically intoxicated, internally tyrannical and violently subversive of existing world order. It was opposed by many – perhaps

most – Russians in a violent civil war. Outside powers attempted ineffec-
tive interventions during 1919–20. Counterfactually, if they had succeeded,
the disaster of the Soviet experiment would never have been revealed.
It would have appeared a lost romantic enterprise unjustly terminated
by self-interested outsiders, which should be attempted repeatedly.
Retrospectively, it is now possible to argue that allowing the infant
Soviet Communist Party to consolidate its power, misrule Russia, then
expand through much of Eurasia, and assist the fateful creation of another
huge communist state in China, was a human catastrophe. What actually
occurred would lead to tens of millions of unjust deaths in famines,
purges, punishment camps and territorial annexations. Its consequences
are still being lived out in impoverished, corrupt and demoralised economies and societies from the former inner German border eastwards.

The question of what should have been done becomes even more
complex when weapons technology enters the picture. By the late 1940s,
there were calls, including by Bertrand Russell, for US preventative
nuclear attack, or at least nuclear blackmail, to force the Soviet Union
to relinquish its own nuclear option and the dreadful possibility of an
indefinite and unstable nuclear confrontation. Retrospectively again, it is
very easy to be thankful that America refrained from what would have
been denounced as an appalling historic crime involving, at the minimum, thousands of Russian deaths, and to assume that containment,
which was in fact the American strategy adopted, was an inevitably safer
and more humane long-term alternative. This conclusion is comforting
because we have seen the Soviet regime mellow, liberalise and eventually
crumble away.

Nevertheless, it was not inevitable that confrontation with the Soviet
bloc would end peacefully. History could have been hideously different.
By 1962, Russia's nuclear capability had grown immensely. To improve
further the balance, the Soviet leadership made a reckless move within
the contemporary rules of the Cold War by clandestinely introducing
medium-range missiles into, and with the consent of, the sovereign state
of Cuba. The subsequent missile crisis, so often re-examined as a triumph
of statecraft, was not spurred by the need to *pre-empt* any immediate risk of
Soviet attack. The world was brought to the brink of unprecedented
destruction as President Kennedy's administration judged that Russia's
attempted horizontal proliferation was an unacceptably destabilising
development that would lead to even worse crises. The historical consensus

seems to be that this assessment was accurate. The crisis was resolved largely through the successful threat of an overwhelming preventative American conventional air and ground assault on Cuba.

This has been called the most dangerous moment in human history. The risks of resultant escalation into total nuclear exchange seem to have been very high. The destruction within North America, Western Europe and the Soviet bloc would have been enormous. Western, and perhaps even Russian, survivors of that catastrophe would have looked back on the earlier decisions to refrain from decisive preventative action in 1919 and the late 1940s very differently. US administrations at each juncture therefore enjoyed enormous *moral luck*, the notion that the perceived morality of a moral agent's actions sometimes depends on luck or chance. Or, as Thomas Nagel writes: 'Where a significant aspect of what someone does depends on factors beyond his control, yet we continue to treat him in that respect as an object of moral judgment.'

We live in a world that has been generally morally fortunate in its handling of proliferation and terrorism. There is no evidently rational basis to assume that such luck will hold indefinitely. It is the professional responsibility of those diplomats, military officers, intelligence professionals and civil servants working in the national security community to minimise the extent to which their governments would have to hope for moral luck in even the most difficult and complex strategic calculations. This requires 'doing everything one can to anticipate the possibility of unintended consequences in a complex environment of autonomous actors'.[1] Yet, even so, an irreducible minimum of uncertainty will certainly remain. There are two tendencies of response to this aspect of the human predicament.

On the one hand, there are those who believe that military action must sometimes be taken in situations of radical uncertainty about future consequences. They argue that hard choices are unavoidable when dealing with 'rogue regimes' and responsible leaders should not flinch from acting forcefully on the best available long-term predictions. They see no intrinsic reason to believe that moral luck would be absent from 'the right application of power and will'. Even if things then go wrong, they would emphasise that miscalculation is not the same as moral error, and that interventionary decisions could be taken conscientiously, in good faith,

---

[1] Owen Harries, 'Power and Morals', *Prospect Magazine* (April 2005): 29.

with just intent. Sometimes, however, unpredictability, inherent in all human affairs but magnified in war, simply prove too great.

The opposite tendency is to insist it is hubristic or even blasphemous to attempt to calculate indirect positive consequences measured in decades against the certainty that large numbers of human lives will end violently in the short term. In this view, it is always and inevitably arrogantly wrong to gamble on future outcomes resulting from discretionary military action. The strongest proponents of this position would therefore consistently have opposed, even with hindsight, all the actual or potential actions touched on here: preventative action against the Russian Empire in 1914, the USSR in 1919–20, Nazi Germany in the late 1930s, Soviet vertical nuclear proliferation in the late 1940s, intervention to reverse North Korea's invasion of the South in 1950, the explicit threat of preventative war against Soviet horizontal nuclear proliferation in 1962, Israel's (probably) pre-emptive attack in 1967 and preventative strike in 1981, international military interventions over Kuwait in 1991 and Kosovo in 1999, and the invasions of Afghanistan in 2001 and Iraq in 2003.

If we assume that neither side in fact will have a permanent monopoly of moral luck (and it is not apparent that an inflexible commitment to either approach could be rationally justified, and therefore, in the utilitarian terms of this article, moral), how could claims to justice and the possibility of consensus be maximised in situations of disputed legitimacy?

## Conclusion: considerations for difficult scenarios

Analysing the arguments which have swirled around the 'rogue regime' problem, military action conducted without formal international authorisation would appear more obviously justified to the extent they approximated 'wars of enforcement' of evidently desirable world-ordering principles. A provisional checklist for this might include the following:

1. They are waged for clear and compelling principles – the clearest is liberation of aggressively occupied territories, as South Korea and Kuwait were freed by US-led international military forces (against retrospectively surprising political opposition). In future, these principles might be effectively extended to prevention of illegal proliferation, support for terrorism or ethnic oppression at levels approaching genocide.

2. These general principles are developed, shared and restated by as many countries as possible to provide Red Lines which 'rogue regimes' cannot overlook or inadvertently ignore.

3. As the character – and therefore the likely future conduct – of the 'rogue regime' becomes adequately demonstrated, concerted international efforts are attempted to influence its actions, dissuade it from further reckless behaviour and prevent it from securing proliferation-sensitive materials.

4. Legal considerations are followed as closely and frequently as possible, although they may be complicated by unreasonable vetoes threatened for what could be disputed as self-interested motivations.

5. The consequences both of action and inaction are rigorously evaluated and as far as possible publicly debated. This means resisting the temptations to fall into unrealistic judgements of easy victories and rapturous welcomes or, on the other hand, total regional conflagration or unspecified apocalyptic terrorist retaliation. It also means resisting or rebutting the fallaciously universalist argument that, since not every otherwise possibly just intervention would be prudent and sustainable, none should ever be undertaken. Similarly, debates on the justice and prudence of military action must take a long and steady view, avoiding rapid fluctuations between despair and triumphalism caused by excessive preoccupation with the trajectory of current events.

6. The specific precipitating reasons that would lead to military action are clearly stated well in advance to give an opportunity for the 'rogue regime' concerned to change its behaviour in order to avoid conflict.

7. A composite moral and political reasoning is allowed which takes into account the 'rogue regime's' behaviour both inside its own borders and beyond and the threats they can both together reasonably be predicted to cause to peace, security and justice.

8. Where the case for military action is prompted by evidence of severe levels of humanitarian abuse, arguments for a long delay to ensure last resort are accepted to have less salience.

9. Those conducting military operations need to make clear in advance that they do not seek to make permanent seizures of territory or gain unfair economic advantages for themselves.

10. When states feel obliged to change a 'rogue regime', they should plan from the start for early elections to allow the people concerned to take control of their own destiny as soon as possible.

11. When obliged to occupy, they help rebuild and stabilise and stay the course in the interests of the population, whatever costs and losses occur, including those from terrorists and insurgents. In such cases, the justice of the war may not be fully established until its aftermath had been constructively carried through, in a *jus post bellum*.

## Chemical Ali

I conclude with a quote from an emblematic personality in this discussion: Ali Hassan Majid, Saddam's cousin, allegedly responsible for gassing the Kurds of Halabja, and later military governor of Kuwait. It is widely reported that he was recorded, probably in 1987, saying to his subordinates: '*That evening I went ... and hit them with the special ammunition. We continued the deportations ... I will kill them all with chemical weapons! Who is going to say anything? The international community? Fuck them! The international community and those who listen to them.*' His utterance neatly brings together WMD acquisition and use, and violent internal repression as twin systematic temptations for 'rogue regimes'. His language also gives some impression of the man and his regime and their contempt for moral factors. It should be a lastingly instructive exercise to consider what the founding fathers of the just war tradition would make of him and all the circumstances in which he did finally have to fear what at least some of the international community would do.

# 9

## Moral versus legal imperatives

FRANK BERMAN

It is now some forty years since H. L. A. Hart famously made his careful delineation between law and morality.[1] When he did so, it was not to denigrate the status of either, nor to elevate one over the other, but to draw attention to the different sense in which legal and moral rules can be said to be binding. So far as international law was concerned, Hart's reasoning marked an analytical break with a natural law tradition that had waxed and waned over the previous three centuries: at times in a jurisprudential effort to locate the binding origins of international law, and at other times in a more normative effort to isolate the content of the fundamental rules of international behaviour.

It is not the purpose of this essay to revisit that old issue, or to trace its recent recurrence in surprising new clothing. The paper adopts instead a different angle of approach, one which corresponds to the greater pre-occupation latterly with the linked questions of compliance and enforce-ment, rather than with the ultimate origins of international law as such. In any society, the correlation between *compliance* and *enforcement* is funda-mental to the functioning quality of its system of legal rules. Faced with the truism, however, that the international legal system lacks any general machinery to sanction breaches of its rules, the vital significance of patterns of voluntary compliance becomes immediately apparent. Moreover, given that enforcement (in the literal sense of overbearing the non-complier) is such a rare occurrence on the international plane, special attention must necessarily be given to the appropriate circumstances for it to happen, and whether there is any quality in certain rules that suits them to enforcement, or vice versa.

---

[1] H. L. A. Hart, *The Concept of Law* (Oxford: Clarendon Press, 1961, 2nd edn, 1994), and esp. pp. 221–6.

## Law and its enforcement: enforcement and values

Enforcement by compulsion is a problem of a special kind in the field of international law. There is, however, a further problem, which is not as frequently noted, namely the relationship between a rule's enforceability and the solidity of its acceptance. Once again, the difficulty is especially obvious in the case of international law, in as much as the rules of international law are subject to processes of change both more subtle and more continuous than law based on Statute (or Scripture). This derives from the fact that the two main sources of international law are custom, which depends on the continued assent of states (and is constantly developing), and treaties, which similarly draw their binding force from the consent of the parties.

The relationship between customary law and treaty law is not a straightforward one and defies simplistic description. Particular elements in the relationship include the following: treaty prescriptions may reflect established custom, or may have a generating effect, helping to create new custom (even amongst states not themselves bound by the treaty in question); treaty obligations, as between parties, are to be interpreted taking account of any relevant customary rules applicable in the relations between them: a treaty may in theory become otiose as a consequence of its abandonment in the practice of the parties to it, nevertheless, a specific treaty obligation would normally prevail (as *lex specialis*) over a rule of general customary law; some rules of customary law are, however, claimed to have the special status of *jus cogens*, so that they may not be overridden by treaty (and would render any inconsistent treaty invalid); *per contra*, a limited number of treaties may be regarded as having a special status such that they prevail over other rules (including later treaties).[2]

A further question enters in here, namely what influence *does* righteous indignation or moral outrage have on the content itself of the rules of international law? Starting from the premise (as one must) that international law is not a branch of natural law but is a system of positive law, the answer is obvious: moral considerations of humanity or right conduct can act as drivers for the formation or creation of new law, either treaty law or custom, but cannot have the quality of generating axioms from which legal rules can be *deduced*. Human rights treaties, which are such a feature of our era, are the best possible example of the creation of law in the

---

[2] The class is quite possibly limited to the sole case of the UN Charter (see its Article 103).

service of morality – irrespective of whether the law-creation involved is at the same time also in the service of principles other than 'pure' morality.

None of the preceding discussion is to say that rules of international law are any less binding than rules of national law, only that there is more room for argument in particular cases over what the rules are, and what they require or allow; at the same time, the means for settling these questions are less readily to hand, and that that, in turn, has an important effect on attitudes towards the legitimacy of some rules when it comes to their enforcement. Be that as it may, both of these elements conduce strongly towards laying a substantial premium on voluntary compliance through widespread assent, rather than unwilling compliance through external enforcement. In short, therefore, the question of enforcement is inextricably joined to that of the acceptability of the values underpinning the rules to be enforced. Law, in other words, is a system of codified morality; short of this, its enforceability falls into doubt, and never more so than in the case of international law.

An excursus is in place at this point into a jurisprudential question that lies at the heart of thinking about the nature of legal rules, and in particular their comparison or contrast with precepts of morality. The conventional analysis is that law is a matter of rights and duties, or rights and obligations, which are correlative: a 'right' implies the existence of an 'obligation' owed to the holder of the right, allowing the latter to vindicate his right against its actual or threatened breach. In that latter sense, 'rights' properly so called are organically linked to remedies, an axiom particularly strongly advanced in the common law tradition. Legal usage tends, moreover, to treat 'obligation' and 'duty' as synonymous with one another; there is no practical distinction between a 'legal obligation' and a 'legal duty'. This is in contrast to some political and moral thinking, where 'duty' can be used in a looser and broader sense, to include also what is due from the individual to the group, or to society, or even to mankind as a whole – or indeed to include duties owed by a group to other groups, or to a wider group of which it itself forms part. In that sense, 'obligation' would distinguish itself from 'duty', and the germ of the distinction would lie precisely in the area of enforceability. A 'duty', so called, which did *not* have a remedy attached to it would be termed one 'of imperfect obligation'.

On closer examination, however, these analytical distinctions turn out to be less than watertight. It is clear, for example, that in particular cases 'duty' and 'obligation', even in this differentiated sense, can readily coincide: the same action (or forbearance) can be owed by one individual to another individual and simultaneously to the group and can be exacted from the one individual by the other, even if not by the group; moreover, duties owed from group to group can in most instances easily be broken down into parcels of obligations owed by individuals to one another. And, on the strictly legal level, within the social structure of any given society the criminal law can without difficulty be seen as a collection of rules which are, literally, enforceable by the group. There are many powerfully analogous examples in international practice, too: a particularly good example being in the field of human rights, in the tension between 'first-generation' human rights, which are characterised by a hard-edged specificity suiting them to enforcement at the instance of the individual against the state, and 'third-generation' human rights which, as collective rights, resist the derivation of concrete 'remedies' of a kind that can meaningfully be ordered against specific defendants.

This discussion of right/duty/obligation/enforcement takes on a particular interest and importance in the context of armed intervention on humanitarian grounds discussed below. Much of the public discussion has taken place at the superficial level of 'Is there a right to intervene (or not)?', often translated into the alternative form of 'Is humanitarian intervention permitted by international law (or not)?' In both forms, however, the question is at best of only limited help, at worst positively misleading. The reasons for saying so require some explanation.

Looked at in its 'rights' form, the question opens itself to the obvious objection (in the light of the analysis just given) that, if we are genuinely in the presence of a 'right' – which in context would have to be a 'legal right' – where is the correlative obligation, and who has the legal quality to enforce it? A rigorous analysis would suggest the converse of what the question implies; it would suggest namely that the holder of the *right* is in fact the people or group being oppressed, so that the rescuer is not the right-holder but rather the *obligee*; moreover, the putative holder of the right is, by definition, not the state, and therefore is not in any normal sense the holder of rights under international law, and most of all is not endowed with the capacity to enforce respect for an 'obligation' owed to it. Furthermore, to reorient the analysis this way produces the converse of what the would-be rescuers seek to assert. Their claim is to be able to *choose* to intervene in cases which they deem suitable, and this is indeed the language of 'rights', on the basis that it is always a matter for the right-holder to decide whether or not to exercise (assert) his rights. So it would seem that we are not in the presence of a 'right', but at the most of an 'entitlement'[3] which the holder is free to make use of or not, without compulsion.[4] It then becomes clear, however, that the question as put conceals the *real* question, which is partly a matter of where the 'entitlement' comes from, but most of all a matter of what the rules are that enable us to identify *who* is entitled? Both of these aspects will be discussed further below. It is simply worth observing at this point how, when subjected to rigorous analysis, the realpolitik has become detached from the considerations of morality alleged to be its basis, for the moral calculus must necessarily end up with the identification of duties to act (and who bears them) and cannot have as its concluding point no more than a discretionary entitlement.[5]

No lengthy analysis is needed to show that to put the question in its alternative form ('Is humanitarian intervention permitted by international law?') turns out to be no more satisfactory, in that it fails even to address the question of *who* is entitled. This element in the discussion raises the important question of values in the international law context: What are they? Who determines them? How do they influence the content of the legal rules? It is easy to assume, from the standpoint of a Western observer in the twenty-first century, that the moral values underpinning international law are those touching the welfare of the human individual, or even that that is what they must be. The viewpoint is, however, both ahistorical and too narrow. The values in question must encompass – must

---

[3] A synonym or alternative for 'entitlement' in this context is, of course, 'power' – setting up a resonance of a different kind altogether.

[4] The notable exception is the International Commission on Intervention and State Sovereignty, which, by choosing the term 'responsibility' in place of 'right', consciously shifted into the area of duties or obligations; yet its report (see footnote 22 below) maintains a studied vagueness over the *location* of the duty, which in the last analysis is to fall on 'the broader community of states', an expression without legal content. The UN Secretary-General's High-Level Panel on Challenges and Threats is in absolutely no doubt in locating it in the Security Council (paragraph 203 of its report).

[5] It should be noted that this dilemma was recognised by those around the foundation of *Médecins sans frontières*, who grasped that their advocacy of a *droit d'ingérence* led inexorably to a *devoir d'ingérence*. It should also be noted, though, that their demand, as originally formulated, was capable of being presented in the language of rights, i.e. as a right not to be held back at the frontier when bringing purely humanitarian succour to those in need of it. See Mario Bettati and Bernard Kouchner, *Le devoir d'ingérence* (Paris: Denöel, 1987).

indeed originate with – those regarded as essential for the functioning of international society as such. The primary concern with the functioning of international society is one which (it hardly needs to be demonstrated) ante-dates by a considerable margin international law's direct concern for the individual. This is not, however, to say that the two sets of values are antithetical to one another. On the contrary, it can be said that international law's modern focus on the individual is a product of the recognition that, under contemporary conditions, the treatment of individuals within national boundaries has at least a mediate impact on the maintenance of normal international relations.

## Who decides? Peace and self-determination: sovereignty and welfare

The outlawing of war as an instrument of national policy was the cardinal development in international law in the twentieth century. As a necessary corollary came the prohibition on the use of force as a lawful means of settling international disputes. This in turn inevitably carried within it a momentum towards the establishment of institutional means for media-ting international differences, to take the place of forcible self-help. Thus Article 2(3) of the UN Charter includes, as one of the basic principles of the organisation, the settlement of international disputes in such a matter that 'international peace and security, and justice' are not 'endangered'. Both the choice of words, and even the punctuation, evidences the ten-sions at play. These developments elevated *peace* into a supreme value. That cannot, however, be thought to have happened for its own sake; it must rather be presupposed on the underlying notion that peace is a necessary precondition for human welfare.

The development of *self-determination* into a cardinal principle carry-ing commensurate weight came much later, as the wrangling over the drafting of the UN Charter and the early practice of the organisation show. But the principle possesses a different kind of moral quality, in as much as it propounds an *inherent* endowment of each people with the right to determine its own welfare without external interference, even at a stage of development preceding the acquisition of formal 'sovereignty'; indeed self-determination now provides one of the validating tests for the emergence into full statehood. The underlying theme of this devel-opment is thus welfare. But the increasing recent concern with setting *international* standards for both individual welfare and group welfare creates a tension with the inherent quality of the self-determination principle. The tension is particularly marked at the group level, given that standards for the welfare of the group as such are not at all self-evident. This poses a profound challenge to the international legal system, a challenge that is as yet far from being resolved. Is peace now regarded as the necessary precondition for human rights, or respect for human rights as the necessary precondition for peace?

This inner tension is often described as one between sovereignty and justice, or sovereignty and welfare, as, for example, in Kofi Annan's much-repeated remark that we cannot allow the last prerogative of sovereignty to become the right to oppress one's own people.[6] It is doubtful, though, whether the tension between sovereignty and welfare is the real dichotomy. At the deep level the systemic question is rather one of the distribution of legitimate authority. The question presents itself in the first instance in the form: who determines what constitutes 'justice' or 'welfare' in general? Who, in other words, sets the international standard? The answer may seem relatively straightforward at that level of high generality – though even there the furious disputes over certain aspects of human rights, over democratisation, or over methods of trade and production of certain goods, should serve to warn us off facile conclusions.

In the second instance, however, the question presents itself differently: even granted the existence of a generally agreed international standard, who determines whether its requirements are duly met in the circumstances of particular cases? This represents an altogether more difficult, and also more acute, problem. The problem is compounded by the fact that many of the accepted international standards require relativistic judgements, balancing one interest or value against another, and by the fact that some standards are recognised in some systems as yielding, at least to some extent, to the demands of 'national emergencies' (two further candidates for the exercise of relativistic judgement).[7] The problem needs no further elaboration.

---

[6] See, for example, speech delivered in The Hague, 18 May 1999 (published in *Speeches at the Ceremonial Opening of the Centennial of the First International Peace Conference*, by the City of The Hague).

[7] To take as the example the International Covenant on Civil and Political Rights 1966, relativised rights can be found in Articles 6, 8, 9, 10, 12, 13, 14, 15, 17, 18, 19, 21, 22 and 25,

If international standards, even on cardinal principles of justice or welfare, are not self-executing, the fact has inescapably important consequences as well for any question of enforcement, i.e. by external compulsion. Enforcement by external compulsion is in itself, and by definition, incompatible with the *self-determination* principle. Likewise, if the external compulsion takes the form of the application of armed force, it is incompatible with the *peace* principle. These contradictions presuppose important value judgements as between valid competing principles and place heavy demands on the identification of legitimate authority to make them, and thence equally heavy demands on the process by which any such judgement is made.

## A just response to new threats?

That general background analysis allows one to approach the question of what would constitute a 'just' (in the legal sense) response to new threats? First, however, the 'new threats' themselves: under current circumstances, these have to be understood to be large-scale human oppression, terrorism and acquisition of weapons of mass destruction (WMD). Whether these – or indeed any of them – genuinely merit the epithet 'new' remains to be shown; but they are at least contemporary preoccupations. And the use of the substantive 'threat' begs a key element in the legal analysis. In any case, each of the catch-phrases is a shorthand, which has to be elaborated or qualified in order to make sense of the question, particularly the last two: 'terrorism' – where? by whom? and against whom?; 'acquisition of WMD' – in what quantities? and by whom?

To tease out the necessary elaborations and qualifications would be beyond the scope of this paper. Some comment has suggested that what is in fact new is the actual or potential combination of all three.[8] Even in this form, the proposition is factually dubious, as well as analytically unsatisfactory: it is difficult to see how adding legal categories together can result in a 'super-category' free of the legal restraints that attach to the

---

even without the general safeguard provision in Article 5, or the possibility of derogation under Article 4.

[8] See, for example, the proposal by Anne-Marie Slaughter for a Security Council resolution to weld all three into a portmanteau justification for the use of force: *Washington Post*, 13 April 2003. It is not, however, clear whether this proposal was for a self-definition by the Security Council of the situations in which it would itself act, or for a general validation by the Security Council of unilateral or joint action by UN member states. See also footnote 22 below.

component parts.[9] The rest of the discussion in this chapter accordingly concentrates on the first of the three, the relief of large-scale human oppression, and on the basis that what is 'new' is not the large-scale oppression itself, but the presence of at least a conditional willingness to do something about it.

It is proposed that, if international law is to move towards a policy of forcible intervention under a humanitarian banner, answers will have to be found on five points, here referred to as *altruism, authority, purposes, means* and *consequences*. Although this list shows a striking similarity to the likely list of moral touchstones, they are here proposed as specifically legal criteria. Given the introduction to this chapter, the degree of congruence between the legal and moral criteria should not be a source of surprise.

## *Altruism*

Altruism is self-evident; it is inherent in – or necessarily implied by – the fact that the justification for resorting to force is a humanitarian one. From a legal point of view, the altruism criterion serves the vital function of marking out the distinction between intervention on humanitarian grounds and self-interested intervention, the prime example of which is self-defence. The external intervener has in some important sense to be above the fray, not a partisan for one side or the other in an internal conflict. This means, amongst other things, that an extended model of collective self-defence is not available, in which the intervener comes to the rescue of a beleaguered minority – or indeed majority – at the latter's request. There is a long-standing international prohibition on external intervention in civil war, even in support of the government side, the policy reasons for which remain obvious. But asserting the claim of disinterest will not be enough; it has somehow to be established, against a counter-swell of anticipated international suspicion. The claim will

---

[9] It is worth noting how all three of the 'new threats' became jumbled together in the political rhetoric surrounding the intervention in Iraq, and how, as the factual foundations for 'terrorism' and 'WMD' faded away, the argument has concentrated more and more on 'humanitarianism', as if that in itself self-evidently provided a good justification. Though it may also be noted that 'terrorism' has made a latter-day comeback, applied now to internal strife and resistance against occupation, thus in a way which seriously engages the qualifying questions posed in the preceding paragraph.

without doubt be challenged, so that the challenge has to be met. But it is not easy to see how a claim of *pure* disinterest can ever be convincingly established, against the presumed need for the intervener to justify to its domestic audience at least the expenditure of money and the risk to life involved.

## Authority

The part played by the notion of authority should be equally plain. It derives from the discussion above. It has, however, a much wider aspect than that canvassed earlier of setting standards and determining whether they have been breached. If the claim to act is that it is not in pursuit of a national interest (however legitimate), then it seems obvious that an entitlement to act in vindication of a general international interest requires some further validation in order for it to be legitimately asserted. It is possible that overwhelming emergency might be accepted as displacing this requirement in law as well as in morals, and it is noteworthy that that was the crucial element in the official justifications offered for the Safe Havens in Northern Iraq in 1991 and for the Kosovo intervention in 1999. But this validating element would, at best, only be available in a very small number of true emergencies, and even then controversy would remain over what constituted an emergency and over the reliability of the facts of the particular case. So an emergency exception hardly seems apt to cover the general case, and one is left with the basic proposition that a claim to act in the capacity of agent for the international community as a whole necessarily presupposes a form of authority conferred on the agent by the principle. It therefore seems inescapable that some process of international authorisation has to be foreseen – which is not to say that the authorisation need in all cases be *ante factum*. Though that would be the normal course, it is perfectly possible to conceive of the authorisation coming in, if not strictly *ex post facto*, then at least after urgent action had already begun. Nor need that be seen as contrary to either moral or legal principle – but on the basis that, up to that point, the agent was operating at his own legal risk.[10]

---

[10] The Security Council has, on three occasions at least, given some form of retrospective approval to non-authorised interventions (Sierra Leone 1997 onwards; Kosovo 1999; Iraq 2003), though never directly. An authorisation would of itself cover the situation from then

A process of international authorisation fulfils the further function of bridging the gap, identified under the rubric of altruism, between the protestation of absence of self-interest and the way it is likely to be received internationally. The problem is rather the practical or institutional one that international law has no system by which authorisation of this kind can be given – short, that is, of the UN Security Council. But the powers of the Security Council are formally linked, under the Charter, to *peace* not to *welfare*, and the forays by the Security Council over the last decade in extending the reach of the *peace* principle have had mixed results both in their practical outcomes and in the degree of their international acceptance. Moreover, even while being the only available authoritative international institution, the Security Council embodies a further problem, in the inevitable grubbiness of its own decision-making processes; the way in which decisions are taken will be subjected to ethical criticism, and the criticism is bound to rub off on the content of the decisions themselves.[11] Nevertheless, utilising (or expanding) the potentialities of the Security Council is clearly where the current concentration of effort lies; the report of the UN High-Level Panel on Threats, Challenges and Change[12] and the large-scale endorsement of its recommendations by the Secretary-General are significant events, the reception of which by the UN membership in general is on the point of being tested as this chapter goes to press.[13]

There is no room, within the scope of this chapter, to explore the issue whether authorisation procured from some other collective body might stand in the place of an authorisation by the Security Council. All that can be said is that the Security Council's overriding powers rest on the unanimous consent of the member states given in advance on becoming

on; whether it would have retroactive effect would depend, amongst other things, on its terms.

[11] There is no reason to believe that the current discussion on the 'reform' of the Security Council would have any positive impact on this question; it is essentially a numbers game, going to the 'representativity' of the Council, but it is difficult to see why a larger Council would conduct itself in a more high-minded way than a smaller one.

[12] UN Document A/59/565 of 2 December 2004, available at http://www.un.org/secureworld/report.pdf.

[13] The prophet Jeremiah would, however, warn that the record of the Security Council (like that of other 'sovereign' bodies) in binding itself to future action is not impressive, and there is even room to question whether full liberty of appreciation from case to case is not an integral part of the institutional intentions of the UN's founding fathers. This is not, however, to decry the value of the effort, or to deny the shaping effect it might have for the future on the applicable legal framework, in line with the discussion earlier in this chapter.

party to the UN Charter (including, therefore, the malefactor state itself), a key factor that was absent, say, for the NATO intervention in Kosovo. It might, conversely, be present in the case of an intervention *within* a regional organisation or alliance, but it should be remarked that the UN Charter nevertheless requires, under its Chapter VIII, that all 'enforcement action' taken by a regional agency or arrangement receive Security Council approval.[14] That aside, the question would remain as to *why* authority had not been obtained from the one body with the undoubted overriding competence to give it; nor would the decision-making processes in other bodies necessarily appear as having greater integrity than those of the Security Council, especially in those cases where the malefactor is not within the membership group.

One final observation might be in place under this head. There is a tendency in much of the commentary to assume that the legitimacy (not to say lawfulness) of the Kosovo intervention is established by the simple fact that it took place. The fallacy of that way of thinking – when applied, for example, to the situation in Iraq current at the time of writing – is obvious. It is therefore worth remarking that the legality of the Kosovo intervention was indeed challenged in the International Court of Justice, and, although the challenge never proceeded to final judgement, it went far enough to reveal some unease on the part of the judges.[15] The Foreign Affairs Select Committee of the UK House of Commons, for its part, while clearly sympathetic to the intervention in view of their finding that it averted a pending humanitarian catastrophe, was prepared to go no further in its conclusions than that 'NATO's military action, if of dubious legality in the current state of international law, was justified on moral grounds.'[16] In doing so, the Committee appears to have taken the view that the intervention was unlawful but nevertheless justifiable. The undesirability of opening up a gap between the two should, however, be plain. The official British justification for the 'Safe Havens' in Northern Iraq in

---

[14] See further Frank Berman, 'The Authorization Model: Resolution 678 and Its Effects', in David M. Malone (ed.), *The UN Security Council: From the Cold War to the Twenty-First Century* (Boulder: Lynne Rienner, 2004), pp. 153–66. Without the control introduced by Chapter VIII, the international community might have been hard put to reject the Soviet Union's repeated 'fraternal interventions' in its Warsaw Pact allies.

[15] Decision of 2 June 1999 on the Request for an Indication of Provisional Measures, available at http://www.icj-cij.org/icjwww/idocket/iyuk/iyukframe.htm.

[16] Report No. HC 28-I of 7 June 2000, paragraph 138, available at http://www.publications. parliament.uk/pa/cm199900/cmselect/cmfaff/28/2802.htm.

the aftermath of the first Gulf War in 1991, and later extended to the rather different circumstances in Kosovo, was balanced with exquisite care between asserting that overwhelming humanitarian need justified temporarily *setting aside* the applicable legal rules and claiming that an emergency response to overwhelming humanitarian need was *allowed for* in the applicable legal rules themselves.[17]

## Purposes

There remains, furthermore, yet another side to the need for authorisation in some form. This is that an external intervention needs to be justified as to its purposes, not simply as to the circumstances or events that legitimately give rise to it. This is to some extent an aspect of the altruism criterion discussed above, but the question is of sufficient importance to justify elevating it into an independent criterion. This is partly because of the sheer importance of the question in its own right, but also as an essential check on a right or power of intervention becoming a pretext for ulterior purposes. The argument would seem obvious. Yet it is an aspect of the debate which has been damagingly neglected.

The point can be usefully illustrated by reference to the two interventions in Iraq, in 1991 and 2003. On the first occasion, the authorising resolution of the Security Council contained a statement of purposes which included, alongside the aim of compelling compliance with the security Council's decisions, 'the restoration of international peace and security in the area'. On the second occasion, an intervention justified as a response to breaches of subsequent resolutions requiring Iraq to disarm mutated, without any very evident explanation or argument, into a war of outright conquest and occupation. Yet on the first occasion, when the Security Council's authorisation was unarguably still in full play, it was surely one of the elements leading to the decision not to 'push on to Baghdad', that to do so could not readily be brought within even an extended interpretation of the purposes for which the authorisation had been given. There can be no clearer indication that the specification of the purposes of an intervention has a primary significance that is every bit as important as the entitlement to intervene in the first place. It follows that,

---

[17] See the Government's Response to the Foreign Affairs Committee's Report, Cm 4825, August 2000, pp. 7–8, available at http://www.fco.gov.uk/Files/kfile/FACresponse049900,0.pdf.

if it seems likely to be a crucial component of a developed doctrine of humanitarian intervention that the authority to intervene should be internationalised, then by the same token the purposes pursued by an intervention themselves need international validation.

That may, however, be a proposition that is easier to state than to make good in practice. The enunciation of the purposes of a humanitarian action can be bafflingly difficult. Self-evidently, some purposes are potentially lawful, whereas others *a fortiori* would not be. Idiot examples are easy to find: the annexation of a tyrannical state by a democratic neighbour might certainly suffice to remove the threat the former poses to international peace and justice, but could not under any circumstances be a lawful aim. The debate over 'war aims' is a familiar historical subject, and the problems are well known, even in a classic case where both the purpose and justification for the resort to war is a direct (and unlawful) threat to the (lawful) interests of the responding state. Given, however, that a humanitarian intervention is, by definition, not against a state but against its rulers for the time being, or against their policies, there are huge questions about the achievement of authorised purposes which are simply not present in the case of conflict over territory or over specific threats to the adversary state.

It follows from what has been said above that the interveners, acting in some agency capacity for the international community, cannot be permitted the final say, let alone the exclusive right, to determine the purposes of an intervention. If so, then it follows equally that they cannot be the sole or final judges, either, of whether the purposes of the intervention have been achieved (or sufficiently achieved) so that no occasion remains for the intervention to continue. All the same, the difficulties of arriving at collective international determinations of this kind are formidable. The experience within a body like the Security Council, of expressing itself both in broadly general terms and in minutely detailed terms, shows that international decisions can never realistically be expected to have the quality of semi-automatic enforceability; they may (in the best cases) share the lapidary quality of scriptural or ethical pronouncements but cannot do without the continuing process of exegesis and interpretation needed to put them into effect. To revert to the two Iraq cases mentioned above, what were the standards by which to judge whether there was still, or is no longer, a 'threat to international peace and security in the area', or even whether all Iraq's weapons of mass destruction had or had not been destroyed? How, then, is one to cope with even perfectly legitimate differences of opinion on these questions?

## Means

This concentration on the *why* and the *when* of humanitarian actions does not foreclose a separate debate on the *how*. Just as (contrary to the apparent view of some international leaders) ends cannot lawfully justify means, so also the fact that a humanitarian action is axiomatically well intentioned does not accord *carte blanche* for the means chosen to pursue it. The law regulating the use of force in self-defence has formed itself, in the era of the UN Charter, around the twin pillars of necessity and proportionality, both of these being concepts which, once again, are familiar features of the moral and ethical debate as well. Their presence as limiting criteria is at the same time a continuation of a longer tradition under which the structure of the legal rules regulating formal armed conflict recognises the simultaneous existence of a *jus ad bellum* and a *jus in bello*: the entitlement in principle to resort to force is a question entirely independent of whether the particular force used is excessive in extent or wrong in kind, and thus unlawful. Moreover the rules apply reciprocally; the purpose of the *jus in bello* (to moderate the effects of warfare and protect, so far as can be done, its victims) requires, as a matter of implacable logic, that the rules defining what kinds of force may or may not lawfully be used apply equally to both contesting parties, irrespective of the fact that one of them may have been wrongful in its resort to force in the first place. Nor is this conclusion simply a derivation from abstract logic; the logic of experience also demonstrates that any attempt to differentiate between the combatants, in the attribution of acceptable methods and means of warfare, leads to disrespect for the rules, and thence to lessening the effectiveness of the protection which the rules offer to their intended beneficiaries.

This inescapable state of affairs poses particular problems for determining the *jus in bello* of humanitarian interventions. On the one hand, there is a deep paradox involved in the claim to a right to kill foreign citizens and destroy their property in order to rescue them from oppression. On the other hand, the principle of the equal application of a *jus in bello* unavoidably carries the implication of an entitlement to resist. Specifically, it would seem to imply a *right* on the part of the oppressor

to resist, by force, the force being brought to bear by the righteous
intervener. This second paradox has led some writers latterly to question
whether disinterested interventions on humanitarian grounds permit the
maintenance of a clear separation between *jus ad bellum* and *jus in bello* –
without, however, any suggestion having come forth as to what device
could take its place as a mechanism for stimulating the observance of
humanitarian rules of restraint.[18]

At the more mundane level, though, the question remains of determining *what* rules of combat apply to a humanitarian intervention. The
tendency has been simply to assume that the normal laws of war apply –
subject no doubt to some implicit *mutatis mutandis* codicil. The problem
is, however, that the normal laws of war have developed around a concept of war as a struggle for control and occupation of territory, and for
authority over populations. Engrafted on that is the principle of distinction, which seeks to maintain a clear separation between armed forces and
military objectives, on the one hand, and civilians and civilian objects on
the other, in order that warfare can be confined to attacks on the former
while sparing, so far as possible, the latter. The difficulty resides in the fact
that for humanitarian interventions the concept no longer fits; the intervener is not contending for control over the territory of the 'enemy' (or
expulsion of the 'enemy' from home territory); nor is the intervener's
purpose to gain or regain control over a population that follows from
mastery over territory, but rather to discourage or deter the 'enemy' from
certain forms of conduct, within its own territory and jurisdiction, over its
own population.

It follows that – unless the intervener's purpose is in fact the overthrow
and replacement of the adversary's government – there are deeply troublesome problems over deciding what are legitimate targets for attack, and
what the principle is that legitimates them.[19] Moreover, if the impugned
conduct which provoked the intervention is maltreatment by the adversary of its own population (therefore by definition civilians), it becomes
extraordinarily troublesome to devise methods of attack (linked, for
example, to actual acts of oppression) which do not themselves implicate

---

[18] For example, Rein Müllerson, *Ordering Anarchy: International Law in International Society*
(The Hague: Martinus Nijhoff, 2000), pp. 316–29.
[19] For example, if not all parts of the adversary's armed forces or governmental structures are
subject to attack, which ones are and which ones are not? And (in both cases) why?

those very civilian victims. What standard should, for example, apply to delimit the acceptability of collateral damage to civilian persons or objects? The laws of conventional war define the standard in proportion to 'the concrete and direct military advantage anticipated' from the attack, but what meaning can be given to that in relation to attacks whose purpose is to change a course of policy? Even the very underlying concept of legitimate attack is conceived in terms of the target's 'effective contribution to military action' or to the 'definite military advantage' to be expected from its destruction or capture, neither of which makes great sense in the circumstances under contemplation here.[20]

## Consequences

The last factor for consideration is that of consequences. It wears both an empirical and a qualitative aspect. Empirically, it is clear that the intervener cannot simply walk in and then walk out again regardless of what follows; by intervening he takes on himself a responsibility for what follows the intervention, which has been a potent factor against a policy of intervention in numerous cases. To abandon the process incomplete undermines retrospectively the main arguments discussed above, but to leave in circumstances that expose the beneficiaries of the intervention to further or worse abuses is radically incompatible with the animating rationale for the original claim of entitlement to intervene. The logic that impelled the intervention may therefore suck the intervener into purposes or means beyond those initially bargained for.

The qualitative aspect is equally important though harder to pin down. It resides in the fact that, if – on the way in – the argument for an entitlement to act at all is one derived from human welfare, so – on the way out – the justification for having acted has to be a marked improvement brought about in human welfare. It may be objected that there is something unappealingly retrospective in this proposition, but that is not in fact an objection of substance, since the law is very accustomed to the thought that its standards are applied after the event to arrive at a judgement as to legality. The approach is in any case of the essence of accountability for the exercise of public powers. The important point is rather to

---

[20] The passages quoted are drawn from Articles 57 and 53 of Additional Protocol I to the Geneva Conventions.

note that the criterion is put forward in its negative form: not (illegitimately) that doubtful means can be justified by a good end, but that, without a good end, the particular means cannot in any circumstances be entitled to approval. And if issue is taken with that, on the basis that it loads the scales too heavily, the answer is surely that armed intervention is so extreme a step that it demands a high threshold of justification.[21] In short, a humanitarian action must, by definition, stand or fall by the improvement it actually produces in the situation it professed to remedy. In less abstract terms, the taking of life and the destruction of property requires valid legal justification and, if the justification does not reside in the specific circumstances of the individual, or of individual property, but becomes instead a form of individual sacrifice for the general public good, then only a clear and convincing demonstration of sufficient public benefit will suffice.

## An interim balance sheet

Is it possible to draw conclusions from the above? Not easily; an interim balance sheet has to suffice. To begin with, the establishment of a list of criteria as a framework for the development of a legal doctrine to govern the employment of military force in pursuit of humanitarian purposes cannot qualify other than as work in progress, in an area that is the subject of intense current attention. Various lists of criteria have been put forward, none of them greeted with instant acceptance. Those of an essentially political character have been criticised as setting the law to one side – or as being devices to put a gloss of acceptability on fundamentally unlawful practices. Those of an essentially legal character have been accused of repeating a static and outdated view, which takes insufficient account of changes in the realities of international relations.

The present study tries to be less pragmatic than the first but less prescriptive than the second. It attempts to put forward, looking from within the legal regime as broadly understood and accepted in the era of the UN Charter, a set of criteria (or problem areas, or obstacles) that would have to be addressed satisfactorily in any effort to create a new doctrine of humanitarian intervention. The organising principle has been

---

[21] Which is presumably the reason in turn why, in the political polemic, leaders seek so often to reverse the situation, by calling on their opponents to justify a failure to intervene.

to ask the question, What issues would have to be dealt with in order to establish a regime that would enable the distinction to be drawn, efficiently and convincingly, between desirable interventions and those the international community would want to disapprove of? To achieve this, the criteria have had to span the 'after', as well as the 'before' and the 'during'.

In the second place, it emerges clearly even from so tentative an analysis that any imaginable set of criteria will prove difficult to fulfil in particular cases. That is, however, no great surprise, since on any analysis forcible interventions of this kind will be rare exceptions, so that the expectation must be that the criteria for action will be exacting. That should serve, at one and the same time, both to keep the exceptions exceptional, and to help offer criteria for *not* acting – which manifestly will be more readily justified if based on principle, rather than on capricious political choice. Exacting as they are, some of these criteria will be easier to meet in the case of humanitarian actions launched by collective decision, and carried out collectively, though that is not true of all of them. Conversely, some of the criteria will be very difficult indeed to meet in the case of an action launched by unilateral decision, even if carried out quasi-collectively.[22]

Finally, it is worth remarking how the legal questions calling for answer turn out to be strikingly similar to those that arise on a moral analysis. The recognition is in itself not unwelcome, in that it tends to validate the nature of the enquiry; unfortunately, though, it offers only limited assistance in providing answers to the questions themselves. The moral calculus can far more easily generate a duty to act, out of a gross offence against common humanity, than is possible on a strictly legal level. So the

---

[22] One of the texts most frequently cited in this connection is the speech by the British Prime Minister in Chicago at the height of the Kosovo Crisis in 1999 (speech by the Rt. Hon. Tony Blair to the Economic Club of Chicago, 22 April 1999, available at http://www.globalpolicy. org/globaliz/politics/blair.htm). Revisited today, however, this text reads more like a challenge to the UN, and the Security Council in particular, to live up to its responsibilities, than an incitement to unilateral action by member states individually or in groups. This latter is also the approach taken, deliberately and explicitly, by the International Commission on Intervention and State Sovereignty in its report ('The Responsibility to Protect', 30 September 2001, available at http://www.iciss.ca/pdf/Commission-Report.pdf). Whatever its other merits, this report makes little contribution to the legal debate: the 'responsibility' it advocates is an uncertain quantity, which may perhaps have been consciously chosen to sidestep some of the legal difficulties discussed earlier in this chapter. The terminology does, however, at least resonate with the 'primary responsibility' conferred on the Security Council by the member states in Article 24 of the UN Charter.

concluding remark to the present chapter must be a reminder that the essay undertaken in it is a deliberately neutral one from the moral point of view. The attempt was to see what would in principle be required in order to create a viable legal regime. By 'viable' is meant in this context a regime that would not simply prove to be workable as a justificatory mechanism for dealing with the current outrage of the moment, but would equally be proof against the conflicting pressures to which it would certainly be subjected in practice. Specifically, the regime would have to be proof against its abusive invocation in bad faith and for unwelcome purposes. The assessment is that the prospects of a viable regime in that sense are poor. That is not in itself grounds for gloom – merely a salutary recognition that 'sovereignty' is not the only cloak behind which wrong can hide; self-anointment can serve just as well, even if in the latter case the ill consequences may be less consciously willed than in the former. The saving grace must thus lie in collective international authority, and more particularly in building up its regularity, predictability and modes of operation, and most of all its accountability.

# PART III

## Fighting wars justly

# 10

# The ethics of 'effects-based' warfare: the crowding out of *jus in bello*?

PAUL CORNISH

## Introduction

The resort to armed force against Saddam Hussein's regime in 2003 was, and remains, deeply controversial. International organisations, national governments and public opinion around the world all divided over the diplomatic, political, legal and moral circumstances of the intervention, and its consequences. Was the use of armed force necessary, and had all other, non-military avenues been tried? Was the intervention legal? What were the real motives behind the intervention? Does the apparent absence of weapons of mass destruction (WMD) in Iraq constitute a fatal flaw in the case for the intervention? Under what circumstances or at what date should coalition forces be removed from Iraq? Has the international order, and with it the framework of international law, been undermined? Is the Middle East a more stable, or more volatile region as a result? Are the Iraqi people better off?

The conduct of military operations in Iraq has, similarly, been examined closely, and from a variety of perspectives. The operations of the US-led coalition were reported in great detail, on a day-to-day basis by journalists 'embedded' with coalition troops. The campaign was a vivid display of the extraordinary capabilities of Western armed forces, and their weapons and equipment featured prominently in media coverage. Operational and tactical differences between US troops and their allies (particularly the British) provoked interest from the earliest days of the conflict. Through 'lessons learned' processes, those armed forces involved in the intervention have also reviewed the campaign in fine detail, identifying the need for better tactical communications and personal protection, the need for greater clarity in rules of engagement and better understanding of individual obligations under the laws of armed conflict, and the inescapable requirement for full-scale preparation for post-conflict stabilisation operations. From the perspective of military planners and analysts, the campaign was also a demonstration of the potential (and the limitations) of a new style of Western strategic thought and practice – 'effects-based' warfare or operations.

Among a number of definitions and interpretations available, the US Joint Forces Command presents the 'effects-based' idea in the following way:

> Effects-based operations (EBO) is a process for obtaining a desired strategic outcome, or effect, on the enemy through the synergistic and cumulative application of the full range of military and non-military capabilities at the tactical, operational, and strategic levels. Effects-based thinking focuses upon the linkage of actions to effects to objectives.[1]

For its advocates, effects-based warfare or operations (EBW or EBO) represents a fundamental change, not only in the way in which warfare is to be prosecuted, but also in the closeness of the relationship between the conduct of warfare on the one hand, and the political rationale for the use of armed force on the other. The argument of the 'effects-based' school would be that recently developed technologies in communications, target acquisition, target attack and so forth have all combined to ensure that the conduct of warfare can be more focused and thus more purposive than ever before, and that the goals of warfare can be pursued more immediately than in the past, by military and other means (diplomatic, economic and psychological, for example), and simultaneously. The over-all aim of EBW/EBO is to tighten the decision-making circle[2] so considerably that an opponent would immediately perceive himself to be overwhelmed, would capitulate at the first opportunity, or – better still – would be deterred from fighting in the first place. The effects-based approach does, however, have its critics, who argue that the concepts it embodies are not new (in some cases, as I will show, they are well over two thousand years old), that it is too reliant on technology at the expense of the 'human factor' and that it creates divisions among allies (on the grounds that the effects-based approach of the United States, with its

---

[1] D. A. Macgregor, *Transformation under Fire: Revolutionizing How America Fights* (London: Praeger, 2003), p. 65.

[2] In military parlance, the decision-making circle is often described by the term 'OODA loop', an acronym for 'Observation, Orientation, Decision and Action'.

emphasis on technologically advanced communications and weapons systems, is far beyond the capacity of even its closest allies).

Critics might also be concerned about the ethical dimensions of the effects-based approach. Where the use of armed force is concerned, the normative preferences of liberal democratic societies are well established and are threefold: first, that organised military activity should be the exclusive privilege of legitimate, accountable government; second, that the choice to use armed force should always be rationalised and justified by an overarching liberal political *end* (rather than descend into self-serving and self-justifying militarism); and third, that military activity – the *means* used in warfare – should itself be subject to, and constrained by, moral and political oversight. Particularly for those approaching the subject of armed force and warfare from the just war tradition, the second and third of these preferences will be especially important; the just war tradition provides a single framework within which warfare can be evaluated not only in terms of its rationale and the ends to be sought (*jus ad bellum*), but also in terms of the means to be employed (*jus in bello*). The just war tradition also insists that these two lines of enquiry and assessment cannot be dissociated. But the tradition does not insist – nor even merely allow – that *jus ad bellum* and *jus in bello* should in some way be fused into one, and it is at this point that the tradition's compatibility with the effects-based approach to warfare comes into question. In the just war tradition, the purpose and the activity of warfare each offers a different set of ethical challenges; both are necessary, but neither provides sufficient grounds upon which to judge the moral quality of the organised use of violence. Yet the effects-based approach to warfare, I have suggested, implies precisely that fusion of ends and means which the just war tradition tries to avoid. Effects-based warfare reduces the distance (conceptually, geographically and temporally) between strategic ends and tactical means, making the effect/end of warfare the principal focus for politician, military strategist and individual combatant alike. In the process, intellectual and hierarchical demarcations soften, the means of warfare become less of an ethical concern in their own right, and the role of the individual combatant soldier as the moral agent for *jus in bello* loses its relevance and urgency.

This chapter is not an essay on the just war tradition, or on ethics more widely, but it is an essay on the *possibility* of ethics in the complex and still-evolving environment of effects-based warfare. Whatever the technological complexity of this supposed revolution in the nature of warfare, it is still warfare, in which men and women confront the starkest of moral challenges: to kill some but to protect others; to discriminate; to survive. With the effects-based approach sharpening the emphasis on goals and ends, and with communications technology making long-distance micro-management of military operations ever more possible, this paper asks whether there is a risk of the *jus in bello* principles of proportionality and discrimination being crowded out of the framework for moral reflection and decision making in war? This crowding-out, as I describe it, could happen in one of two ways. In the first place, the requirement to exercise proportionality and discrimination in the conduct of warfare might simply have been overtaken by events and superseded by a new, overarching framework for the comprehensive evaluation of all aspects of the use of armed force. The second problem is more to do with agency; it might no longer be possible – or indeed thought necessary – for there to be individuals (that is to say, combatants) who can be charged with the specific moral responsibility of implementing the *jus in bello*. The chapter asks, essentially, who in the era of effects-based armed conflict should 'own' the implementation of *jus in bello*, and whether this pillar of the just war tradition has so conclusively lost its discrete significance that 'ownership' of it is now a matter of passing interest at best. The chapter begins with a brief summary of the military campaign in Iraq in 2003, using this narrative as the basis for an explanation of the effects-based approach to warfare. The final section of the chapter gauges the implications of the effects-based approach for *jus in bello* and, therefore, for the just war tradition as a whole.

## Iraq 2003

In testimony to the US Congress in July 2003, US Secretary of Defense Donald Rumsfeld described the plan for Operation Iraqi Freedom[3] as 'an unprecedented combination of speed, precision, surprise, and flexibility'.[4] The campaign was indeed executed at a remarkably fast pace, by closely integrated forces, using the most sophisticated military technology. With

---

[3] National contingents chose their own operational title: 'Operation Iraqi Freedom' was the US term; British forces used 'Operation Telic'; Australian forces used 'Operation Falconer'.

[4] D. Rumsfeld, testimony to US Congress, 9 July 2003, quoted in A. H. Cordesman, *The Iraq War: Strategy, Tactics and Military Lessons* (Westport, CT: Praeger Publishers, 2003), p. 1.

key bridges having been secured on their behalf, the US 3rd Infantry Division advanced some three hundred miles in just four days to a position fifty miles south of Baghdad, incurring only two casualties along the way.[5] Coalition casualties were kept to a minimum throughout the conflict: between 20 March and 1 May 2003, when President George Bush announced the end of combat activity, the United States had lost 138 troops, 114 from combat, while their British allies had lost 42, 23 from combat. US and allied armed forces were more closely integrated into one fighting force than ever before, with all contingents conforming to a 'common operating picture': 'The United States and Britain [fought] a kind of joint warfare different from any previous conflict. [...] air and missile power, rapid and focused armoured manoeuvre, the creative use of Special Forces and air mobile forces, and sea power were combined to inflict a massive and sudden defeat on a large traditional army.'

Coalition troops had highly sophisticated and effective equipment at their disposal, which Iraqi forces simply could not match. Vast computing power enabled close co-ordination of every aspect of the campaign. Coalition naval forces achieved complete dominance, with the USA, UK and Australia between them deploying fifty-four major surface warships, thirteen submarines and a host of support ships. On the ground, coalition forces deployed advanced personal weaponry, highly mobile armoured vehicles, precision artillery and short-range missile systems. The coalition quickly established control of the air over Iraq. At the peak of operations, coalition air forces mustered 1,800 combat aircraft of various types, plus helicopters. Over 40,000 fixed-wing sorties were launched, 20,000 of which were strike sorties. There was no Iraqi air response. No coalition aircraft were lost to Iraqi airpower, although there were losses (fewer than 10) to Iraqi ground-based air defences. Coalition forces launched almost 20,000 precision-guided munitions against Iraqi targets and dropped a further 9,000 unguided weapons. Whereas during the Gulf War of 1991, some 7 per cent of munitions had been precision-guided (PGM), in Iraq in 2003 that percentage had increased almost by a factor of ten. The network of US military satellites was used for communications and intelligence gathering. Command and control of coalition forces was improved by airborne command and control aircraft kept on station by air-to-air refuelling. 'Unmanned aerial vehicles' (UAV) also provided

5 Macgregor, *Transformation under Fire*, p. 237.

vital intelligence. A short-range, tactical UAV could be carried, assembled and launched in ten minutes by a team of two. At the opposite end of the spectrum, *Global Hawk* aircraft, flown from an airfield in the United Arab Emirates and controlled from California, provided real-time surveillance and reconnaissance over Iraq for every day of the campaign. Importantly, coalition commanders were able to make use of these new capabilities concurrently, rather than serially. Rather than wait for the conclusion of a lengthy bombing campaign (as in the Gulf War of 1991), unusually the ground attack on Iraq began *before* the air campaign, with coalition special forces being deployed to Western Iraq and the Kurdish region to secure airfields and attack other objectives.

## Effects-based warfare

The US-led campaign in Iraq was the culmination of a programme of development in military doctrine and equipment, known since the early 1990s as the 'Revolution in Military Affairs' (RMA).[6] Latterly, RMA has given way to yet more jargon, such as 'defence transformation', 'network centric warfare' (NCW) in the United States, and 'network enabled capability' (NEC) in the United Kingdom. In the words of one defence analyst:

> The idea of NCW is to collect intelligence for rapid processing, analysis, and interpretation and to share timely battlespace informa- tion between decision-makers at all command levels and the indivi- dual warfighter. NCW promises superiority in weapons systems' efficacy through the rapid distribution of information to each posi- tion within a theatre of operation. This is being achieved by distri- buting intelligence which is gathered by a multiplicity of highly advanced sensors carried by various platforms.[7]

---

[6] See, for example, D. Jablonsky, *The Owl of Minerva Flies at Twilight: Doctrinal Change and Continuity and the Revolution in Military Affairs* (US Army War College, Strategic Studies Institute, May 1994); M. J. Mazarr, *The Revolution in Military Affairs: A Framework for Defense Planning* (US Army War College, Strategic Studies Institute, June 1994); and for a broader view, C. Gray, *Modern Strategy* (Oxford: Oxford University Press, 1999), pp. 200–5, 243–54.

[7] S. Nitschke, 'Network-Centric Warfare – The European Initiatives', *Military Technology* 28 (March 2004), 18. See also J. Williams, 'Network-Enabled Capability – The Concept', *World Defence Systems* 7/1 (Spring 2004): 6–7.

At its simplest, the transformation of the vast, armour-heavy, largely static armed forces of the Cold War, into the lighter and more responsive forces deployed to Afghanistan and Iraq, has been made possible by innovations in three areas of military technology: communications and computing; target sensing and identification; and target acquisition and attack. Thus, military command and control and intelligence gathering have become faster and more responsive, as well as better informed through real-time communications links. Modern weapon platforms not only provide greater mobility and stealth, longer range, improved accuracy and ever more destructive impact on the target, but are also closely connected to improved command-and-control systems and to a range of sensors, thus ensuring timely and decisive effect. Military transformation also draws upon new ideas and possibilities in systems integration and network theory. In the past, individual systems and capabilities would be designed to achieve a specific task and would often be deployed in isolation from other systems. This 'platform-centric' approach has been abandoned in favour of a new, dynamic network of military activity. The key components of any military operation, ranging from the command and control organisation through to the intelligence gatherers, the logistics providers and the combat elements, are all to be integrated to an unprecedented degree. At the heart of this 'sensor-shooter' network, the various components interact 'without prescription', enabling weapon and communications platforms 'to exploit each other's capabilities rapidly and flexibly in ways not originally envisaged when designed'.[8]

But the new Western style of warfare amounts to more than the sum of recent advances in military communications and weaponry. Just as important is the operational and strategic framework which both is enabled by these new technologies, and in turn enables modern military technology to be exploited to the full. 'Manoeuvre' and 'mission command' are key aspects of this framework. For as long as there has been the organised use of armed force to achieve a political goal, so commanders have sought to find the weak spot in the enemy's posture and to out-manoeuvre him. Manoeuvre is often misunderstood to mean simply movement on the battlefield, but for Western armed forces manoeuvre involves the most imaginative use of whatever appropriate means might be available, whether directly against the enemy's positions

---

[8] Williams, 'Network-Enabled Capability': 6.

or indirectly against his supporting infrastructure, in order to demoralise and defeat him. Military writing on the subject of manoeuvre often defers to the words of Winston Churchill:

> There are many kinds of manoeuvre in war . . . some only of which take place on [or near] the battlefield. There are manoeuvres to the flank or rear. There are manoeuvres in time, in diplomacy, in mechanics, in psychology; all of which are removed from the battlefield, but react often decisively upon it, and the object of all is to find easier ways, other than sheer slaughter, of achieving the main purpose.[9]

In other words, manoeuvre in war is much more than movement; manoeuvrism calls for breadth and speed of operations, and for imagination and intelligence on the part of commanders. And of particular importance, 'manoeuvre warfare' need not be exclusively military: political, diplomatic, economic and psychological measures can all contribute to success over an enemy.

The central idea of 'mission command' is that subordinates should be issued with a *mission* (setting out the commander's intent), rather than a *task* or set of tasks (where the commander's intent remains best known to himself). In short, subordinates should be instructed on what to *achieve* and why, rather than what to *do* and how. Although mission command was not formally adopted by the British Army until the late 1980s, the idea has a lengthy pedigree. In contrast to the traditional and more restrictive style of *Befehlstaktik* (loosely translated as 'task-oriented tactics'), the 1930s German notion of *Auftragstaktik* ('mission-oriented tactics') is widely understood to be the source of contemporary mission-command thinking:

> *Auftragstaktik*, the concept praised by advocates of manoeuvre warfare, was not so much a tactical doctrine, as many mistakenly believe, it was a cultural *weltanschauung* (worldview). Through *Auftragstaktik*, the Germans were able to establish a paradoxical framework in which the martial virtues of discipline and obedience could coexist with independence and initiative. The commander's intent – what he wanted to accomplish – was the unifying force in tactical and operational decision making. Within this framework, the subordinate commanders were expected to use their initiative and judgement to fulfil the commander's

---

[9] W. S. Churchill, *The World Crisis* (1923), quoted in DG Joint Doctrine and Concepts, *Joint Operations* (UK Joint Warfare Publication 3-00, 30 March 2000), par. 109.

intent and act independently when their initial orders no longer reflected the reality of a changed situation – as long as their actions operated within the framework of the commander's intent.[10]

Mission command therefore amounts to well-trained field officers and soldiers being encouraged to use their own judgement, intelligence and initiative in pursuit of their commander's overall goal.

Manoeuvrism and mission command come together in effects-based warfare. The opponent is understood as a system, made up of many elements: political, military, cultural, psychological, economic and moral. Rather than focus exclusively on the military threat to be resisted or defeated, and rather than seek numerical or qualitative superiority over an opponent's equipment and force capabilities, the effects-based approach calls for political and military leaders to identify clearly the effects on the opponent that will bring about the desired result, whether that would be deterrence of future activity, a return to negotiation, the collapse of domestic political legitimacy or a military defeat. Operations against the enemy are then conceived in a similarly 'systemic' way. Political leaders and military commanders will select the means best suited to achieve the desired effect(s), at whatever point on the politico-military spectrum, in whatever combination and at whatever time, seeking what one analyst has termed 'the optimum complementarity between attacks on the will and attacks on capability'.[11]

From a military perspective, EBW is essentially a modern restatement of a goal that military commanders have pursued for millennia: the ability to defeat an enemy cleverly and swiftly, and, ideally, as painlessly as possible.[12] To the extent that EBW can be said to be revolutionary, it is simply that these very old ideas have now become more achievable, as a result of communications, processing and weapon technology of the sort seen in Iraq in 2003. Another term closely associated with EBW is 'knowledge-based warfare', whereby advanced, high-speed communications permit an unprecedented level of battlefield and operational knowledge, more or less instantaneously, on the part of more elements in the command chain than ever before. But within EBW a premium is also placed upon

---

[10] C. Kolenda, 'Technology, Leadership and Effectiveness', *Military Review* (July–August 2000): 88.

[11] C. Bellamy, 'Cause or Effect?', *Defence Director* 6 (Spring 2004): 55.

[12] The ancient Chinese general and philosopher of war Sun Tzu is often quoted in this regard: 'To win one hundred victories in one hundred battles is not the acme of skill. To subdue the enemy without fighting is the acme of skill.' Sun Tzu, *The Art of War*, trans. S. B. Griffith (Oxford: Oxford University Press, 1963), p. 77.

'strategic knowledge': a close understanding of the opponent and a clear judgement as to which effects will bring about the desired result. This full spectrum of tactical, operational and strategic knowledge combines with new surveillance, target acquisition and weapon technologies to enable a more precise, focused application of military force simultaneously on a variety of targets. EBW therefore offers unprecedented concurrency or effort, or 'parallel warfare' as it is often described. Rather than fight a sequential or 'linear' war, typically with suppression of enemy air defence systems being the first requirement, enabling subsequent attacks against enemy air and ground forces, 'parallel warfare' allows for all the different phases of a military campaign to be fought in great detail, at once, in order to bring about the desired result as rapidly as possible.

In summary, effects-based warfare uses modern communications and military technology in order to realise traditional – if not ancient – military goals. But the effects-based approach represents much more than the collective impact of recent military technological innovation. Effects-based thinking and practice also place military means in a purposive framework that is shaped, more explicitly and more closely than ever before, by the overall strategic and politico-military rationale. Effects-based warfare, in other words, arguably prioritises ends over means. The normative significance of this observation should be apparent to all those familiar with the work of Clausewitz, the nineteenth-century Prussian military thinker, who observed that 'war is not a mere act of policy but a true political instrument, a continuation of political activity by other means'.[13] The real significance of the effects-based approach, therefore, is that it makes it possible for military activity to be 'more Clausewitzian', as some advocates of EBW have realised:

> Instead of a traditional attritional approach in terms of listing a series of targets and then go bombing them, or finding where the enemy is and killing all of them, we came to the conclusion that what we really wanted to do was to achieve some sort of policy objective, and that you could, in fact, craft military objectives to better achieve those policy objectives in a more efficient and effective manner.[14]

[13] C. von Clausewitz, *On War*, ed. and trans. M. Howard and P. Paret (Princeton, NJ: Princeton University Press, 1976), p. 87.

[14] G. L. Crowder, 'Effects-Based Operations: The Impact of Precision Strike Weapons on Air Warfare Doctrines', *Military Technology* (June 2003): 16.

The ethical challenge posed by the effects-based approach to warfare can now be set out more clearly. To the extent that the effects-based approach binds warfare more tightly into consideration of the political goals ('effects') being sought, it seems compatible with the Clausewitzian idea outlined above. I have argued elsewhere that while Clausewitz has often been dismissed or condemned as the ideational underpinning of the brutal mass warfare of the modern industrial era, his politico-military framework can actually be said, if not to *be* ethical then at least to be an enabling device for the political rationalisation and ethical constraining of the use of armed force.[15] As might be expected, something of this 'ethical Clausewitzianism' can indeed be found in the effects-based approach: in the insistence that there are always means other than military force by which to resolve disputes, or to achieve the desired 'effect'; and in observation of the norm that the use of armed force should always be the last resort. And when military force is nevertheless to be used, the effects-based approach, with all its technological sophistication, also promises more precise targeting, less associated death, destruction and damage, and a quicker conclusion to the conflict. By this view, there would seem to be sufficient grounds to suppose that the effects-based approach to warfare would be functionally and substantially compatible with the just war tradition. The contention of this paper, however, is that in spite of any technological, strategic and political merits, and in spite even of certain moral advantages that could be associated with it, effects-based warfare could in the end have a disabling effect on the application of the just war tradition in modern military operations, by crowding out one indispensable feature of that tradition – the *jus in bello*.

## The crowding out of *jus in bello*

Effects-based warfare is a fusion of traditional military ideas and aspirations with new technology and weapons. The result is a radical shift, in the style and tempo, and perhaps even in the rationale for warfare. By bringing means and ends into a tighter and closer relationship, the effects-based approach makes the Western way of warfare, at all levels, more purposive than ever before. There are many dimensions to EBW – technological,

---

[15] I develop this idea more fully in P. Cornish, 'Clausewitz and the Ethics of Armed Force: Five Propositions', *Journal of Military Ethics* 2/3 (2003): 218–27.

tactical, operational, strategic and political – several of which have been
discussed above. There is also (or should be) a moral dimension to the
debate, where EBW is examined for its compatibility with efforts to
constrain warfare on ethical grounds, as in the just war tradition. New
thinking and practice in warfare should always be subjected to an ethical
appraisal of this sort. But for those sympathetic to the just war tradition,
there is a more compelling, epistemological reason for doing so where
effects-based warfare is concerned, with its compression, if not homogenisation of means and ends.

The just war tradition combines 'a theory of ends and a theory of
means'.[16] In his seminal *Just and Unjust Wars*, Michael Walzer noted
'the dualism of *jus ad bellum* and *jus in bello*' and observed that justice
of war (*jus ad bellum*) and justice in war (*jus in bello*) are 'logically
independent'.[17] While it would certainly be possible in war to satisfy
just one or other set of criteria – by fighting an unjust war according to
the rules of *jus in bello*, or by satisfying *jus ad bellum* but then fighting
disproportionately and without discrimination – to qualify as a *just* war,
both sets of standards must be observed. Compliance with just one set of
criteria should not be allowed to compensate for failure in the other. 'The
just war tradition', noted Anthony Coates, 'upholds the moral determination of both the recourse to war and the conduct of war: the *jus ad
bellum* and the *jus in bello* carry equal weight in that tradition'.[18] But if
moral reflection on warfare cannot be fully represented in either dimension, to the exclusion of the other, it might also be asked whether the just
war tradition can function as a unitary framework, with one dimension
having effectively absorbed the other.

Effects-based warfare challenges the coherence of the just war tradition
both quantitatively and qualitatively. The first of these challenges is that
in EBW there could simply be too much going on, in terms of scope,
intensity and pace, for troops to be able to keep pace with events and
make appropriate decisions. The 'three-block war' concept, originating
in the United States, is one much-quoted summary of the challenges
of modern warfare, whereby troops 'may be confronted by the entire

---

[16] J. McMahan, 'War and Peace', in P. Singer (ed.), *A Companion to Ethics* (Oxford: Blackwell,
1994), p. 386.
[17] M. Walzer, *Just and Unjust Wars: A Moral Argument with Historical Illustrations*, 3rd edn
(New York: Basic Books, 2000), p. 21.
[18] A. J. Coates, *The Ethics of War* (Manchester: Manchester University Press, 1997), p. 98.

spectrum of tactical challenges in the span of a few hours and within the space of three city blocks'.[19] NATO uses similar terminology, albeit with broader scope: 'The most complex scenario is the 3 Block War. One in which high-end warfighting, peacekeeping and humanitarian aid occur within the same area at the same time.'[20] Even the best-trained soldier might find it difficult to identify and adjust to new circumstances as he or she moves from one city block to another, and from one type of military operation to another. Rules of engagement might shift, and aspects of the international law of armed conflict applying in one situation might not apply (or be so significant) in another. The soldier might then find it difficult to ensure that his or her actions, as well as being militarily effective and efficient, are also appropriate in terms of proportionality and discrimination, the central demands of *jus in bello*. The emphasis on rapid change also has relevance here. Terms such as 'agility', 'flexibility', 'adaptability' and 'proactivity' all feature prominently in writing on effects-based warfare. Armed forces are expected to 'adapt rapidly to changing circumstances with great agility – in terms of posture, profile and presence',[21] and to 'generate change rather than respond to it'.[22] The challenge for armed forces, in other words, is not simply that they should be trained and prepared to act effectively in very different circumstances, but that they should also be trained to make the transition from one type of operation to another (and back again) very quickly.

The scope and varied intensity of military operations and the requirement to change rapidly from one type of operation to another (and, indeed, to anticipate such a requirement) could be borne out in various ways. First, it could be that these quantitative challenges will be met, by intelligent, well-trained soldiers in the field. Considered decisions could be made, at the appropriate moment, military action could be discriminate and proportionate to the circumstances, and *jus in bello* could be applied properly and fully. On the other hand, individual soldiers could perceive themselves to be overwhelmed, could become intimidated and risk-averse and could fail to make decisions of a military, moral or any

---

[19] C. C. Krulak, 'Strategic Corporal: Leadership in the Three Block War', *Marines: Official Magazine of the Marine Corps* (January 1999): 32.

[20] I. Forbes, 'NATO Transformation', *World Defence Systems* 7/1 (Spring 2004): 18.

[21] R. Lane, 'The Challenges of Expeditionary Operations for NATO', *World Defence Systems* 7/1 (Spring 2004): 59.

[22] Forbes, 'NATO Transformation': 15.

kind. As far as the unit as a whole is concerned, sensitivity to the legal and ethical demands of each, very different set of circumstances could become a weakness to be exploited by an adversary, particularly one willing and able to act asymmetrically and unexpectedly by, for example, attacking a party of soldiers involved in distributing food and water to civilians: 'The legal framework under which we will be required to operate has become so complex that some writers have identified a new phenomenon, "lawfare" – the use of law as a virtual weapon, and one which otherwise weaker opponents will seek to exploit.'[23] In circumstances of individual or unit overwhelming, as self-confidence erodes and judgement clouds, it is conceivable that the moral reflection and action required in *jus in bello* could become more difficult.

This concern becomes more vivid when considering the qualitative challenges offered by EBW, where questions of authority and account-ability come to the fore. In spite of its aspiration to bring decision, action and effect into closer proximity, effects-based warfare could undermine the organisation and authority of the political-military hierarchy, in a number of ways. In the first place, manoeuvrism could remove structures and boundaries: vertically between the various functions and responsi-bilities of government (diplomatic, economic, military and so on); and horizontally, between what have traditionally been known as the 'levels of war'. The levels of war amount to a graduated framework designed to convey the connection between the highest level of political decision making and the lowest level of military action. In this traditional model, the application of armed force was understood in hierarchical terms. At the apex of the hierarchy would be found grand strategy or political strategy, beneath it military strategy, then military operations and finally, the basis of the entire effort, tactical and individual effort. In the tradi-tional view, war was also considered in temporal terms to be a linear activity, in which time would serve the organisational hierarchy. Thus, instructions and objectives would be passed from the top to the bottom of the hierarchy, with objectives at each level being allocated a certain amount of time. A tactical commander would use the time available to ensure that objectives were met, enabling operational objectives to be achieved on time, and so on. It is easy to see that without the levels of

---

[23] J. Bailey, 'Land Warfare: A Contemporary Perspective', in C. Finn (ed.), *Effects-Based Warfare* (London: Stationery Office, 2002), p. 45.

war, or some similar framework, the civilian management of military operations – itself an ethical goal – could become far more complex and perhaps less effective.

Within the military structure, the dogged pursuit of ever higher standards of integration and interoperability could have a similar effect. National armed forces, naval, ground and air, are all now expected to act as one 'joint' force. High standards of interoperability are also now expected of forces working in an alliance or coalition operation. In the spirit of EBW, with its sophisticated information networks and all-informed decision making, the flattened organisational structure which results could offer benefits in efficiency and synergy. But, taken together, the homogenising process entailed by manoeuvrism and integration could result in the strategic equivalent of 'grey goo', with organisation, decision, command and control becoming all but impossible. The coherence of the politico-military hierarchy could be undermined in other ways. The pace of change sought at the tactical level could result in a disconnection between the lower, action-oriented levels of the hierarchy, and the more bureaucratised upper echelons, which could prove slower to adapt. A similar disconnection might occur if a tactical commander acts promptly upon the wealth of operational and strategic information he receives: such 'fatal displays of initiative by subordinates' could be entirely inappropriate from an operational or strategic perspective.[24]

Another challenge to authority for the application and direction of armed force comes in the form (or, at least, the possibility) of micro-management of military operations. To a considerable extent, EBW is all about micro-management, in that one of its goals is to 'provide an audit trail all the way from policy to individual tactical act'.[25] Micro-management is not a new phenomenon. During the American War of Independence, the British Governor-General of Canada wrote to General 'Gentleman Johnny' Burgoyne, after the latter's surrender at Saratoga in October 1777:

> This unfortunate event, it is to be hoped, will in future prevent ministers from pretending to direct operations of war in a country at 3,000 miles distance, of which they have so little knowledge as not to be able to distinguish between good, bad, or interested advices, or to give positive orders in matters which from their nature are ever

---

[24] Bailey, 'Land Warfare', p. 50.
[25] C. Finn, 'Air Power and Effects-Based Warfare', *World Defence Systems* 7/1 (Spring 2004): 70.

upon the change: so that the expediency or propriety of a measure at one moment may be totally inexpedient or improper at the next.[26]

More recently, General Rupert Smith, British commander of the UN Protection Force (UNPROFOR) in Bosnia from 1995, voiced a colourful complaint against the tendency to intrusive supervision and micro-management:

> We are conducting operations now as though we are on a stage, in an amphitheatre or Roman arena; there are at least two producers and directors working in opposition to each other; the players, each with their own idea of the script, are more often than not mixed up with the stage hands, ticket collectors and ice cream vendors, while a factional audience, its attention focused on that part of the auditorium where it is noisiest, views and gains an understanding of events by peering down the drinking straws of their soft drink packs.[27]

By one account, the US Army was also afflicted by micro-management during its operations in Iraq, with adverse consequences for mission command:

> Whilst the US Army may espouse mission command, in Iraq it did not practise it [...] Commanders and staff at all levels were strikingly conscious of their duty, but rarely if ever questioned authority, and were reluctant to deviate from precise instructions. Staunch loyalty upward and conformity to one's superior were noticeable traits. Each commander had his own style, but if there was a common trend it was for micro-management, with many hours devoted to daily briefings and updates. Planning tended to be staff driven and focused on process rather than end effect. The net effect was highly centralized-making which [...] tended to discourage lower level initiative and adaptability.[28]

Micro-management has a number of components: technological, political, legal and humanitarian. The technological component suggests that advances in communications, and intelligence gathering and collation, have changed the political–military relationship fundamentally. A real-time

---

[26] R. Harvey, *A Few Bloody Noses: The American War of Independence* (London: John Murray, 2001), p. 278.

[27] R. Smith, 'Wars in Our Time: A Survey of Recent and Continuing Conflicts', *World Defence Systems* 3/2 (2001): 4–5.

[28] N. Aylwin-Foster, 'Changing the Army for Counterinsurgency Operations', *Military Review* (November–December 2005): 6–7.

data link between a surveillance aircraft and a national capital not only provides strategic-level political and military leaders with high-quality intelligence, but also invites comment and instruction, which can return to the operational theatre from the capital just as rapidly.

In north-east Afghanistan in late 2001, for example, satellite communications proved invaluable tactically and operationally, as a means with which to co-ordinate the various anti-Taliban factions. The same devices also served a strategic purpose, in briefing Western capitals on the progress of the campaign and in enabling instructions to be passed back quickly into the theatre of operations. At the very least, therefore, it can be said that, technologically, political leaders increasingly have the opportunity to comment upon and direct military activity.[29] Technology in another guise – precision-guided munitions – has also led to what might be termed structural micro-management, in the form of the political and public expectation that deaths and injuries to innocent bystanders (sometimes euphemistically referred to as 'collateral damage') can and must be minimised if not excluded altogether.[30]

The political impulse to micro-manage stems from the well-documented and almost overwhelming presence in conflict situations of the international media (accredited and otherwise) with very sophisticated, real-time means of communication. The presence of the media does not merely enable political involvement in the conduct of the campaign but insists upon it.[31] The president of ABC News has gone so far as to describe the role of his company as 'giving people the information they need to know in deciding whether to go to war and how we execute a war ... because ultimately it's up to the people to decide'.[32] The legal component of micro-management refers to the involvement of legal advisers further

---

[29] The relative ease with which governments can now monitor and control the operations of their troops, even at very great distance, can also undermine any other, subsidiary chain of command under which the troops have been deployed, such as the UN; M. Goulding, *Peacemonger* (London: John Murray, 2002), pp. 77, 329.

[30] 'Forces Want Funds for "Safer" Weapons', *The Times*, 16 July 2001. For a broader discussion of the possibility that modern remote, precise and automated weapons technology might see a 'disengagement' from the 'horrible nature of war', see D. K. Shurtleff, 'Deleting the Human Factor: an Ethical Inquiry into Armed Unmanned Vehicles', *World Defence Systems* (December 2002): 10–11.

[31] It has been said that when the 10,000-strong NATO-led Kosovo Force (KFOR) moved across the border into Kosovo in June 1999, it was accompanied by 2,500 accredited media representatives, a soldier/media ratio of 4:1.

[32] D. Westin, quoted in Bailey, 'Land Warfare', p. 46.

and further down the military command chain, even to the extent that in the Balkans NATO foot patrols (of around thirty men) were on occasion reportedly accompanied by a military lawyer.

Finally, the humanitarian dimension of micro-management reflects political unease with the prospect of a military operation being seen vividly and immediately to have caused the so-called 'collateral damage' referred to above. A humanitarian intervention which results in the death and injury of the innocent on whose behalf the intervention might have been ordered would come uncomfortably close to one of the more celebrated travesties of the Vietnam War, whereby a village was destroyed in order that it might be 'saved'. But there is a second strand to humanitarianism that is not always compatible with the first; governments also feel obliged to minimise the risk of death and suffering to their own combatant troops – an impulse reinforced by the US experience in Somalia in 1993. The effects of risk- and casualty-aversion on the conduct (military and moral) of humanitarian operations are a subject of growing interest,[33] not least because an operation which shifts the risk of death and injury largely onto non-combatants can scarcely be called humanitarian: 'High-tech warfare is governed by two constraints – avoiding civilian casualties and avoiding risks to pilots – that are in direct contradiction. To target effectively you have to fly low. If you fly low you lose pilots. Fly high and you get civilians.'[34]

As the management of organised armed force becomes increasingly compressed and homogenised, so it becomes important to ask whether the much-vaunted doctrine of mission command can remain relevant in EBW-style military operations. What, precisely, is mission command for, when the effect of military action can be calculated by others far away from the battlefield, who have the technical means to indulge in command and control at the tactical level? Is mission command giving way to 'submission command', with decisions being 'pushed upwards' (and perhaps also pulled) for approval?[35] To the extent that the doctrine of mission command could be said to be under threat from EBW, what could also be undermined is the willingness on the part of local commanders

[33] See F. Harbour and P. Cornish, 'Planning for Casualties: Insights from World War II and Kosovo', paper presented to the International Studies Association, Chicago, February 2001.
[34] M. Ignatieff, *Virtual War: Kosovo and Beyond* (London: Chatto and Windus, 2000), p. 62.
[35] Lane, 'The Challenges of Expeditionary Operations for NATO', 59–60.

and even individual soldiers to make complex judgements quickly, and to accept responsibility for the consequences of their decisions and actions. Since these qualities – self-confidence in judgement and decision, and a sense of accountability – are also essential to the exercise of *jus in bello*, it is clear that there could be ethical risks associated with effects-based warfare.

The risk is not simply that *jus in bello* is made more difficult in the context of EBW, but that it might be regarded as unnecessary. Effects-based warfare offers political and military leaders, at the highest levels, the opportunity to make what amount to *jus in bello*-style judgements from the strategic level where, previously, the preoccupation would principally have been with issues of *jus ad bellum*, the ending of conflict at the appropriate point, and the management of its aftermath. In military terms, micro-management of this sort is described as 'reach-down'. At one level, 'ethical reach-down' could challenge the expectation in *jus in bello* that there should be moral agents (i.e., soldiers) 'on the ground' able to make ethical decisions. But 'ethical reach-down' could have a yet more destructive effect on the just war tradition. If and when politicians and military commanders at the strategic level forbear from taking tactical control and making tactical judgements (including on aspects of the implementation of *jus in bello*), then a vacuum could be created which no one in the politico-military system will have the inclination or training to fill. If troops are not encouraged and empowered to act as responsible, individual moral agents, then serious errors could be made by and within the military structure. No matter how lucid, articulate and persuasive the requirement for discrimination between military and civilian target, the ethic of discrimination is part idea and part act. Only the person who is acting at the moment of contact with the enemy can judge whether a particular action would satisfy the standards set by *jus in bello*. Institutions – military and otherwise – which fail to encourage individuals to ask searching questions risk unknowingly (but avoidably) committing wrongful acts.[36]

Of course it would be reasonable to suppose, however far away from the battlefield they might be, that political leaders and military commanders,

---

[36] P. Cornish and F. V. Harbour, 'NATO and the Individual Soldier as Moral Agents with Reciprocal Duties: Imbalance in the Kosovo Campaign', in T. Erskine (ed.), *Can Institutions Have Responsibilities: Collective Moral Agency and International Relations* (London: Palgrave, 2003), p. 134.

together with all those involved in preparing and delivering, say, an attack by a remotely controlled unmanned aerial vehicle such as the US *Predator*, would be no more or less morally competent than soldiers on the ground.[37] The concern here is that 'ethical reach-down' could amount to a strategic-level, arms-length version of decisions which have traditionally been made, and still ought to be made immediately, with no intervening agency, by soldiers in the field. Almost perversely, *jus in bello* requires that those who make moral decisions in warfare should themselves be exposed to the immense vulnerability and personal risk of combat. It is amidst the heat and horror of warfare, effects-based or otherwise, that the soldier 'must bear the burden of deciding the right and of choosing the true'.[38] Otherwise, alternative (and perhaps morally preferable) courses of action, only apparent to those in the immediate vicinity, might not be considered, and mistakes might be made.

## Conclusion

It is useful to understand effects-based warfare as a device to compress – conceptually, spatially and temporally – the relationship between means and ends in warfare. As such, EBW seeks explicitly to lock military activity into a political framework, an outcome that would be recognised and welcomed by military philosophers from Sun Tzu to Clausewitz. Although he warned of the dangers of political meddling in the conduct of military operations, Sun Tzu nevertheless saw that successful strategy required the sovereign and his generals to be bound in a politico-military contract: 'In general, the system of employing troops is that the commander receives his mandate from the sovereign to mobilise the people and assemble the army'; 'It is said that enlightened rulers deliberate upon the plans, and good generals execute them.'[39] Clausewitz was clearer on this point: 'The political object is the goal, war is the means of reaching it, and means can never be considered in isolation from their purpose.'[40]

---

[37] A US *Predator* UAV was used to kill suspected al-Qaeda personnel in Yemen in November 2002. Reportedly, close surveillance of the targets, for as long as one week, made it possible to postpone the attack until 'the target was safely out of a densely populated civilian area'. See M. Vesely, 'A Different Kind of War', *Middle East* (February 2003): 8.

[38] J. H. Toner, *Military Ethics: Dr Jekyll and Mr Hyde* (US Air Force Academy, Joseph A. Reich Lectures on War, Morality and the Military Profession, 9 November 1999).

[39] Sun Tzu, *Art of War*, pp. 111, 142.    [40] Clausewitz, *On War*, p. 87.

Elsewhere in *On War*, Clausewitz cautioned, in terms that continue to resonate powerfully today, that the conduct of war must always be proportionate to politics: 'The degree of force that must be used against the enemy depends on the scale of political demands on either side.' If, for whatever reason, the 'political demands' were not expressed with sufficient clarity or firmness, the result could be either too little military effort, or too much. It would seem to be the latter possibility which concerned Clausewitz most; in the event of a 'a maximum of effort', 'all proportion between action and political demands would be lost: means would cease to be commensurate with ends'.[41]

Under the enduring influence of Sun Tzu, Clausewitz and others, in Western strategic thought warfare is understood as a balanced relationship between means and ends, with neither one nor the other taking precedence. Military means can have no value in themselves. Equally, it would be fatuous to conceive of warfare as the setting and pursuit of certain political goals, without acknowledging the significance of the means to be employed. But the question now arises, what happens when means and ends in warfare are brought too closely together, when the otherwise laudable 'compression' of the effects-based approach begins to suggest that means and ends are, somehow, to be homogenised? For the military practitioner, it could become harder to function in such a fluid and relatively unstructured environment, with no (or less) distinction between 'strategic', 'operational' and 'tactical' levels of war, and it could prove more difficult to attribute responsibility for decisions, actions and consequences among commanders and combatants. The relevance and implementation of *jus in bello* could also become more difficult, at the same moment and for much the same reasons. Walzer's insistence that soldiers should be 'responsible for what they do' is of course vital if *jus in bello* (and, hence, just war thinking more broadly) is not to be overlooked *in extremis*.[42] But the soldier is not only the object of war morality, in the sense that he must be held responsible for crimes and errors in warfare. The soldier is also, properly, an instrument of war morality: it is only soldiers who, as moral agents, can grasp the ethical framework of *jus in bello* and apply it – as best they can – to the reality only they face, using their own judgement. All this presupposes that soldiers should be in a position where their judgement matters, and where they are able to make

[41] *Ibid.*, p. 585.    [42] Walzer, *Just and Unjust Wars*, p. 40.

and effect appropriate decisions (military and moral) on an empirical basis. If soldiers fail in this – perhaps because they have become part of a system which is unable to permit such professional and moral autonomy, or which considers that military and moral tactics can be decided remotely – then the moral project to contain the means by which war is fought could fail with them.

The just war tradition, as currently practised, requires its two components – *jus ad bellum* and *jus in bello* – each to be coherent and fully functioning. Weapons, military technology and warfare are all morally problematic. The conviction driving the just war tradition, however, has so far been that these moral problems are not insurmountable, and that enough of the purpose, activity and means of warfare can be set in a conceptual framework providing enough moral constraint. Effects-based warfare challenges the implementation of the just war tradition, not by bringing new, morally questionable weapons and military means to the battlefield (after all, in certain cases these new means of warfare offer fewer, more precise attacks and could result in a swifter conclusion to conflict), but by making individual judgement and decision making more difficult (or simply less necessary) at the tactical level. Whatever its strategic, technological and military merits, and even though democratic oversight and political control of military activity is to be preferred on ethical grounds, if effects-based warfare makes it difficult to act tactically, both militarily and morally, then it presents a structural challenge to the just war tradition: by hampering the implementation of *jus in bello*, the just war approach as a whole is undermined. In order that effects-based warfare and the just war tradition do not become fundamentally and finally estranged, some effort is required so that the traditional, bicameral just war tradition is fully understood and can be implemented by properly trained soldiers empowered to use their judgement. Alternatively, perhaps it could be that with effects-based warfare the moment has now arrived to devise a new, unicameral variant of the just war approach, in which authority and responsibility are also clearly understood and can be distributed appropriately as circumstances change.

# 11

# The just conduct of war against radical Islamic terror and insurgencies

TERRENCE K. KELLY

The moral challenges of using force against enemies who hide amongst innocent populations is as old as warfare itself, though reshaped some-what by modern technology and militaries. This chapter explores this modern challenge from the perspective of the traditional ethical frame-work of Western society bequeathed to it by Christianity, namely the just war tradition. It argues that justice, in a broad sense, is required to defeat insurgencies, and this extends beyond the battle itself to the development of what St Augustine called *tranquillitas ordinis*, or a justly ordered society. Modern just war requires considerations beyond those present in the traditional just war theory structure; just policies for war. These policies include not only those that shape armies and guide their use, but also those for establishing a justly ordered society.

Classical just war theory operates from a 'will to peace' and is tradi-tionally divided into the ethical considerations of just recourse to war (*jus ad bellum*) and just conduct in war (*jus in bello*). This chapter is primarily concerned with the latter and only then from the viewpoint of how to combat radical Islamic terrorism and insurgencies. The chapter proceeds by considering the 'moral calculus' of the ethical decisions in war, then briefly presents information specific to fighting terrorists and insurgents in the twenty-first century. In discussing what this means for policies, analysis considers justice from the eyes of the people among whom terrorists and insurgents hide.

This paper is the author's and does not reflect a position or research of the RAND Corporation.

## Terrorism and the challenge to just war

According to the Christian, or Western, just war tradition, *jus in bello* actions are those that are discriminate and proportionate. 'Discrimination' means that destructive actions are aimed at those who we are fighting and in particular that non-combatants and the innocent are not targeted. 'Proportionate' means that the effect of our destructive actions are not out of proportion with the end we seek to achieve. Justice, therefore, does not exist in a vacuum. Justice, discrimination and proportionality have meaning only with respect to that which threatens peace and makes decisions about war necessary.

The gravity and magnitude of the evil against which we fight, both in terms of our actions and the consequences of inaction, make up the context in which decisions about discrimination and proportionality are made and have meaning. For example, in *Just and Unjust Wars* Michael Walzer poses the question of the 'supreme emergency' and in considering the British decision to bomb German population centres asks: 'Should I wager this determinate crime (the killing of innocent people) against that immeasurable evil (Nazi triumph)?' He concludes that in the limited circumstances defined by the real threat of defeat at the hands of 'immeasurable' evil and the lack of other means to strike back, the decision to bomb German cities early in the Second World War was just.[1] In the context of nuclear war with the Soviet Union, John Courtney Murray juxtaposes the victory of injustice with annihilation (of ourselves or the Soviets), and because both are unacceptable he proposes that solutions between these extremes based on 'a reasonable moral calculus of proportionate moral costs' must be sought 'at the cost of every effort, in every field, that the spirit of man can put forth'.[2] In other words, to give meaning to real-life considerations of proportionality and discrimination we must understand who we are fighting and what is at stake.

A comprehensive description of the radical Islamic organisations in the global jihadist movement is beyond the scope of this paper. However, the characterisations of them current in public and some academic circles

---

[1] Michael Walzer, *Just and Unjust Wars* (New York: Basic Books, 1977), pp. 259–61. It should be noted that Walzer's argument applies only to the early period of the war before other means of striking the Nazis were available. He does not condone bombing population centres in general.

[2] John Courtney Murray, *We Hold These Truths: Catholic Reflections on the American Proposition* (New York: Sheed and Ward, 1960), p. 268.

suffer from an unwillingness or inability to understand the importance of the theological framework through which they view the world. Their core members are motivated by what they believe to be the will of God, and by their ideas of the spiritual and eternal. They are not motivated by the same things as is the secular West, and they view what they perceive as the West's secular motivations as corrupt. The core members of radical Islamist movements are in fact very devout, but the good of authentic devotion should not be confused with the evil of their actions. Their goal is to bring into being a Taliban-like Islamic state through violence in what is called *defensive jihad*. Bernard Lewis tells us that, '[a]ccording to the jurists, the natural and permanent relationship between the world of Islam and the world of the unbelievers was one of open or latent war'.[3] If they succeed, logic, history and tradition tell us that they would then export their brand of Islam to the rest of the world, by force if necessary.

This is not new. Historically, Islam has conducted *offensive jihad* to expand the *dar-al-Islam* (realm of Islam) and while many modern Muslims no longer believe in this approach, radical Islamists do. Western scholars and analysts see the Middle East and parts of north Africa; central, south and south-east Asia; and southern Europe as a set of countries, where radical Islamists see artificial boundaries created by unbelievers who split up what was once the Islamic caliphate. In their minds, they are fighting what amounts to a pan-Islamic insurgency to recreate this caliphate. They insist that it is the duty of all Muslims to take part in this *defensive jihad* in order to bring this state of affairs to fruition. They believe that what they are doing reflects God's will and if killed they will be richly rewarded. It is imperative to understand the nature of this fight if governments are to succeed in defeating it.

Radical Islamists believe that such concepts as the freedom to choose good or evil, that no human can completely understand God's will and that there is some element of truth in most religions are contrary to God's will. Some believe that those holding these beliefs deserve death (for failing to accept their version of Islam as the complete revelation of God's will). Their perception of divine mission coupled with their total rejection of Western ethical and moral concepts creates a situation that is at once difficult for us to understand and very dangerous. One need only look to

---

[3] Bernard Lewis, *The Political Language of Islam* (Chicago: University Of Chicago Press, 1988), p. 78.

Sudan's on-going civil war, Afghanistan under the Taliban or Algeria in the 1990s to see this danger manifest in practice. Clearly we should not confuse genuine devotion to God with good actions, but there is another error to be guarded against that is more likely in Western secular nations; viewing all religious perspectives as morally equivalent. This is a fatal error. There should be no doubt that what we face is genuinely evil (in the theological as well as the rhetorical sense), and that should we fail to face it squarely we will be making a moral choice with dire consequences.[4]

Statements about the goals, motivations and character of radical Islamists should not be interpreted as pertaining to Islam. There is neither no common ground between the world-view of radical Islamic terrorists and more moderate Muslims, nor are the majority of Muslims likely to accept a world-view based on violent jihad. What is probably true, however, is that while most Muslims admire Osama bin Laden and other radical Islamists for standing up to the West and for their genuine devotion to God, they are not ready to follow them down the path of violence. This means that we face a precarious situation. Our actions must consider the high regard in which millions hold Osama bin Laden and those like him, weigh the likelihood that our actions will cause more to follow him and present the Muslim world with more attractive paths. This understanding is important when discussing counter-insurgency efforts and the centrality of justice to such actions.

Consider the following scenario: Islamic terrorists detonate a crude 12-kiloton-equivalent nuclear device near the Smithsonian in Washington, DC.[5] The blast 'destroys everything from the White House to the lawn of the Capitol building; everything from the Supreme Court to the FDR memorial would be left in rubble; uncontrollable fires would reach all the way out to the Pentagon'.[6] It causes radiation poisoning in many thousands in the area outside of ground zero, and it will cause many cancer

---

[4] For an excellent exposition of this point, see Jean Bethke Elshtain's *Just War against Terror: The Burden of American Power in a Violent World* (New York: Basic Books, 2003).

[5] On 21 May 2003, Sheikh Naser bin Hamad al-Fahd issued a fatwa that granted the jihadists religious cover for using weapons of mass destruction to kill up to 10,000,000 Americans. See Reuven Paz, 'Yes to WMD: The First Islamist Fatwah on the Use of Weapons of Mass Destruction', *Global Research in International Affairs (GLORIA) Centre, The Project for the Research of Islamist Movements (PRISM) Special Dispatches* (2003): 16–35.

[6] Graham Allison, *Nuclear Terrorism: The Ultimate Preventable Catastrophe* (New York: Time Books, 2004), p. 5. Allison believes there is a good chance of terrorists using nuclear weapons sometime in the next decade.

deaths and birth defects in the years to come. Next, Osama bin Laden appears on a tape provided to Al-Jazeera, stating that al-Qaeda is responsible for the explosion and has other such weapons. These, he states, will be detonated by the 'lions of Islam' in other cities unless: the USA and all imperial powers abandon Muslim lands and stop persecuting Islam; the USA stops supporting the Zionist entity; the USA stops supporting the apostate monarchies in Islamic lands; and all regions previously under Islamic rule agree to return to Islam (i.e. the historical *caliphate* is to be restored).[7]

This apocalyptic scenario may be far-fetched, though this depends on the likelihood of al-Qaeda, or one of its affiliates, acquiring and being able to employ nuclear weapons, not on any doubts that they would do so if the opportunity arose. Bin Laden has repeatedly made his goals clear during the last decade. This scenario clearly illustrates what is at stake in the struggle between radical Islam and the civilised world, which, it should be stressed, includes much of the Islamic world. The clarity of radical Islam's intentions and the likely availability of biological, if not nuclear, weapons in the near future are sobering indeed. Yet it is important to realise that the threat comes not from a state, as in conventional wars, but from an enemy intermingled among Muslim and non-Muslim populations – people who are in a real sense innocent.

The political and physical realities of this conflict, as well as the Islamic terrorist perspective on what (in the metaphysical sense) they are, as well as their relationship to God and what is demanded of and permitted to them in their fight, creates a set of asymmetries that need to be taken into consideration when developing a just response. These Islamic terrorists hold *asymmetric national status*. As the armed bodies of subnational or transnational organisations, they feel little responsibility for the civilian populations amongst whom they live. Even if they do feel some responsibility, it is overridden by the demands of jihad. They also possess *asymmetric capabilities*. Unable to match Western armies on the battlefield, they will fight where the strengths of Western forces cannot be applied without killing non-combatants or damaging civilian infrastructure (which furthers their cause). If they can, they will use weapons of

---

[7] These demands are primarily derived from, though not identical to, bin Laden's policy goals as stated by Anonymous, in *Imperial Hubris: Why the West is Losing the War on Terror* (Washington, DC: Brassey's, Inc., 2004), p. 210.

mass destruction to level the strategic playing field. It follows from this that they are willing to engage in *asymmetric targeting* since they will not hesitate to target civilians if it furthers their cause, branding all who assist their enemies as unbelievers or apostates, thus making it legal (under their interpretation of Islamic law) to kill them.[8] The final asymmetry is that of *asymmetric ethical restraint*, since Islamic terrorists will not be bound by Western considerations of proportionality and discrimination – indeed, disproportionate and indiscriminate methods may be their methods of choice. Some hold a literal eye-for-an-eye philosophy and believe they may kill up to 10 million US citizens (the number of Muslims they believe the USA has killed) without further justification (a different concept of proportionality).

## How to defeat an insurgency

There are three primary players in insurgencies – friendly governments and military forces; the insurgents; and the general population. One can defeat an insurgency in two ways – by using massive levels of violence (an option I believe not available to Western countries) or, in Gerald Templar's phrase, by winning the 'hearts and minds' of the people. For either approach to be successful it is important that such approaches are designed to combat terrorists and insurgents, not the people amongst whom they live, even if they are sympathetic to the insurgents.[9] Since the violence used against insurgents will often be used amidst innocent people, counter-insurgency operations must separate the insurgents from the population and, by isolating the insurgents, deny them what they need to survive. At the same time it is necessary to convince the population that the government's way is better than the insurgents' (winning hearts) and that they are better off siding with the government (winning minds). Providing security allows the wider population to give information about the insurgents without fear of reprisal, thus enabling government forces to defeat the

---

[8] As used here, 'assistance' could be as weak as belonging to a democratic nation whose policies are viewed by radical Islamists as anti-Islamic.

[9] Non-combatants are immune from military strikes – see, for example, the Department of the Army, *Law of Land Warfare, US Army Field Manual 27–10*, Washington, DC, 1956, which derives its restrictions from the various Geneva Conventions, the Hague Convention, the Roerich Pact (Treaty for the Protection of Artistic and Scientific Institutions and Historic Monuments) and tradition.

insurgents' 'political' infrastructure (the most important effort) as well as their armed factions.

As noted earlier, only a minority of Muslims currently agree with the extreme positions of radical Islam. Recent polls, however, show that an overwhelming majority of Muslims object to US actions throughout the world, and trends are unfavourable.[10] If in order to avoid Samuel Huntington's clash of cultures it is necessary to win the hearts and minds of Muslims, then it is crucial to address three questions: What level of force, if any, is acceptable, and against whom should it be applied? What level of force will lead to success? What else besides force is needed?

It has been established that the enemy we face is not deterrable and is willing to pursue its goals through objectively evil means (e.g., killing 10 million civilians). In their own statements, radical Islamic leaders indicate that they would force their brand of Islam first on the *dar-al-Islam* after a successful *defensive jihad*. Afterwards, it seems likely that they would seek to impose their beliefs on the rest of the world through an *offensive jihad*. It is neither illogical nor far-fetched to argue that we are faced with a conflict as morally consequential as those with the Nazis or the Soviets, and one that cannot be lost. This would imply that governments may use all force necessary to win this struggle.

Few would deny that governments should use all necessary force against terrorists and insurgents, but governments are not fighting all Muslims, all Arabs, or all of any people, and they must use force only in ways that do not exceed the bounds set by Murray's 'moral calculus'. Those terrorists the civilised world is fighting live amongst what are largely *innocent* populations and, under normal circumstances, are indistinguishable from non-combatants in places like Iraq and Afghanistan. Extreme care must be exercised. Indeed, one could argue, as indeed Mary Kaldor does in her later chapter, that proportionality in its truest sense would preclude any 'collateral damage' in the case of a truly innocent population, just as such damage is not permitted in police actions in peaceful countries.[11]

Since it is unacceptable to kill massive numbers to quell an insurgency, it is imperative to win the hearts and minds of the people. To do this it is

[10] Christopher M. Blanchard, 'Al-Qaeda: Statements and Evolving Ideologies', *CRS Report for Congress*, RL32759, p. 10.

[11] This is not meant to imply that a law enforcement paradigm is appropriate for this situation, but rather to illustrate the centrality of justice in questions of force.

necessary to create the political, social and security situation that will free the people from insurgent intimidation and encourage them to work with government efforts to defeat the insurgents. Conversely, this means that such a policy cannot succeed if a government regularly kills innocents and destroys the homes of the very people it needs to win over. In a just war, discriminate and proportionate means are all that is allowed to governments – such force targets the true enemies and does not cause excessive 'collateral damage' (an unfortunate, bloodless term). These are very difficult hurdles to overcome, as we demonstrate in the next section.

One final concept is needed to make our argument. If Christian theologians and philosophers are right about *what* humans are, then 'man has in his heart a law written by God' – an intrinsic understanding of what is just and unjust (what theologians call the natural law).[12] This means that disproportionate and indiscriminate actions will be viewed as unjust by the people who suffer them, and work against our efforts to win their hearts and minds. This is not to say that there is universal human agreement on the difficult decisions that are made during conflicts. Perspective, culture, propaganda and many other factors are important. But indiscriminate and disproportionate force will be recognised as such, and will make it likely that though a government might win on the physical battlefield, it will lose on the moral and psychological one. Similarly, just actions will, for the most part, be recognised as such despite all propaganda to the contrary.

## Bridging the gap between theory and practice

The trouble comes in that *jus in bello* guidelines dictate that how an army fights must be tailored to the circumstances of the situation in which it finds itself, but military doctrine and culture do not always fit the circumstances of a conflict. In particular, American military doctrine and culture have historically not been well attuned to the demands of counter-insurgencies, a case in point being the concept of 'overwhelming' combat power. While bringing 'overwhelming' combat power to bear on an enemy is a good thing in the abstract, it is problematic in any conflict short of total war. 'Overwhelming' is, by definition, unbounded. It is

---

[12] Walter, Abbott S. J., *The Documents of Vatican II*: *Gaudium et Spes* (Baltimore: Geoffrey Chapman, 1966), p. 213.

resistant to concerns for proportionality, and so also to the psychological, political, economic and moral considerations needed in a counter-insurgency.

The modern American military was developed to fight the next world war on the plains of Europe against a massive armoured Soviet army. The legacy of the great wars of the twentieth century caused the USA to create a military culture, and military organisations, training regimes and doctrine that reflected its experience – namely, that wars are won by destroying the enemy's will to fight, and this is done by bringing overwhelming combat power to bear on the enemy.[13] This thinking is exemplified by the Powell Doctrine, which states (in part) that the USA should not engage in any conflict unless it brings overwhelming force.[14] John Nagl makes the point well in his insightful work on the British and American military's ability to adapt to counter-insurgency warfare. 'The demands of conventional and unconventional warfare differ so greatly that an organization optimized to succeed in one will have a great difficulty in fighting the other. It will likely also be unsuccessful in efforts to adapt itself to meet changing requirements in the course of the type of conflict for which it was not originally designed and trained.'[15] The great majority of the US military is optimised for large-scale conventional warfare and it is through these lenses that it viewed and to some extent continues to view conflict.[16] This very fault is what caused America to fail in Vietnam. The experiences of the British Army in Malaya (and, indeed, in the entire post-Second World War period in British military operations in Kenya and Northern Ireland) point out that it is not until this exclusive perspective is put aside to permit a more flexible response tailored to the circumstances that success may be possible.

In short, militaries fight wars as they are organised, trained and equipped to fight, guided by a military culture and perspective that causes them

---

[13] For a discussion that traces this development through the Vietnam War see Russell F. Weigley, *The American Way of War* (Bloomington: Indiana University Press, 1973).

[14] To the extent that the Powell doctrine was derived from the lessons Secretary Powell drew from his experiences as a young officer in Vietnam, he, and the US Army, arguably reached the wrong conclusion – that the USA lost that war due to a lack of military wherewithal. John Nagl argues convincingly that America lost in Vietnam because it attempted to fight a counter-insurgency as a conventional war. John Nagl, *Counterinsurgency Lessons from Malaya and Vietnam: Learning to Eat Soup with a Knife* (New York: Praeger, 2002).

[15] Nagl, *Counterinsurgency Lessons from Malaya and Vietnam*, p. 219.

[16] Bradley Graham points out that the Pentagon may now be moving away from the traditional and rigid focus on large conventional warfare. Bradley Graham, 'Pentagon Prepares to Rethink Focus on Conventional Warfare', *Washington Post*, 26 January 2005, p. 5.

to see the use of force in specific ways. The US military is a tool designed to do specific things, but not everything. Furthermore, the military is not an infinitely flexible organisation that can quickly change 'tactics, techniques and procedures'.[17] The US military achieved its great efficiency by training to do certain things very well in prescribed ways. Unfortunately, success at doing certain things well makes it difficult to understand that new situations require doing things differently, and changing ingrained habits – particularly habits that have been acquired through great effort and expense, and which are essential in large wars – is a difficult task.

Because the American military is trained to fight other armies rather than insurgents, it hits very hard and this may mean disproportionately in counter-insurgencies. For example, dropping a 500 lb bomb on a house in which insurgents are thought to be located will no doubt destroy that house and kill those terrorists, but it is highly likely that it will also destroy much of that neighbourhood, killing innocents and damaging property unrelated to insurgent activities.[18] This is not to say that American military planners make no attempt to ensure that their actions are proportionate, but it does seem that far too often when it comes down to putting soldiers or non-combatants in danger, or killing a legitimate target even though non-combatants will also die, it is the safety of the soldier or the importance of a mission that wins out.

Many seem to convolve the concept of precision, made possible by advanced technologies, with proportionality and discrimination. Precision weapons are good at hitting what they are aimed at, but what one aims at should be what one intends to hit. Due care must be exercised to ensure this is the case. Examples of failures in this regard abound from Kosovo, Afghanistan and Iraq. Notorious among these are the bombing of a refuge caravan on the Djakovica-Decane Road in Kosovo on 14 April 1999, as well as the toll taken by the use of cluster bombs in this and other bombing raids, unnecessary deaths that are attributable to the policy that required

---

[17] Organisational flexibility is, indeed, a characteristic of the US military. However, the flexibility needed here is more than the ability to form units with specific functional characteristics. It also requires the ability to employ them consistently in appropriate ways, a characteristic that is at least as dependent on doctrine, training and culture as on organisational structure.

[18] The 500 lb bomb was the smallest in the inventory at the start of the Iraq War. According to the US Army's Field Manual, troops who are lying flat on the ground in combat gear closer than 200 metres from the detonation point of a 500 lb bomb are 'danger close'. Department of the Army, *Field Manual 3.09-32: J-Fires* (Washington, DC, November 2002).

all aircraft to stay above 10,000 feet, thus making target identification difficult. Also relevant here are the Tarnak Farms incident on the Afghan border in which American aircraft mistakenly bombed a Canadian training exercise; and the bombing and subsequent ground attack on an Iraqi wedding celebration in the town of Makr al-Deep on 23 May 2004, in which over forty Iraqi wedding guests were mistakenly killed.

In practice civilised nations face a paradox. They must defeat implacable enemies intent on destroying their very way of life (or the way of life of those they seeks to protect), and so great force, properly applied, is justified. But armies trained to fight other armies rather than insurgents may produce effects in counter-insurgencies that the population will view as unjust, and so counterproductive to the goal of winning the hearts and minds of the people. In other words, such efforts may very well fail. Under the classical just war framework, if *in bello* decisions are just and the outcome unjust, then the moral error must lie at the feet of the statesman who decided to pursue the conflict in the first place (explicitly, we cannot claim a high likelihood of success). If the West cannot succeed with the military it has, then the decision to go to war seems ethically fatal.

In reality, the situation is never so clear-cut. It is real people who make moral decisions, at specific times, based on what they think they know. For the statesman making the decision to go to war, much will be unclear at the time decisions must be made. It is quite possible that a president or prime minister would be certain of success based on an incorrect understanding of his or her country's military capabilities. The gulf between what statesmen understand to be their military capabilities and what those capabilities are is often quite wide. Based on his or her mistaken understanding of a situation, a statesman could make a morally correct though objectively incorrect decision that a just cause for recourse to war exists; and similarly a military commander could make a morally correct decision about the application of the military force under his or her command within the context of the situation he or she perceives; and for the outcome to be unjust (as has arguably been the case in Iraq). This indicates a problem with the traditional framework of just war theory.

## Developing just policies for war

The gap in our understanding of situations and capabilities, which is all but inevitable in systems as large and complex as modern states and militaries, is mirrored in our use of just war theory. Specifically, the *ad bellum* and *in bello* categories are insufficient for modern-day governments and militaries. When Augustine, Aquinas and others wrote about just war there was no bureaucratic middle ground between the regent who made the decision to go to war and the commander who conducted that war. Often, the prince was the principal player in both, as regent and commander, and generals could see all of their soldiers on the battlefield. Even when this was not the case, political systems and militaries were simpler. Looking back over the military developments across the centuries, it is possible to identify, even as late as the eighteenth century, Napoleon as both Emperor and Captain. By the end of the Napoleonic period this figure no longer existed, as the size of armies and the bureaucracies that supported them grew larger, more complicated and technologically dependent. In August 1914 the die was irrevocably cast for war by the inertia of the mobilised and moving German army, before the Kaiser had quite made his final *ad bellum* decision – in effect making this decision for him. Subsequently, large government bureaucracies were created in the USA and other countries during the Second World War to manage huge militaries. For the most part they remained in place after the war, further separating heads of state from a working knowledge of their armies.[19]

Today it is possible to see something very like the physical inertia of the moving German armies of 1914, but now it is an organisational inertia that affects *in bello* considerations. In the conflicts for which the American military was created, an enemy army and support structures would be relatively easy to recognise, and decisions to strike them relatively clear-cut. This perspective, created by a military culture focused on large wars, greatly facilitates accomplishing large conventional war goals while blinding one to the demands of other situations for which it is ill-suited. Decisions made while looking through the lenses of a military culture may appear just from that perspective, and indeed might be entirely appropriate for the situations that army was designed to face, but may lead in circumstances outside its peripheral vision to injustices and, in

---

[19] For an exposition of the impact of bureaucracies on armies, and vice versa, see Bruce D. Porter, *War and the Rise of the State: The Military Foundations of Modern Politics* (London: Free Press, 1994).

counter-insurgency warfare, to its attendant failure.[20] In short, a gap now separates *ad bellum* and *in bello* considerations, creating situations in which all players could make moral decisions that result in unjust outcomes.

Governments have a moral responsibility to reconnect *ad bellum* and *in bello* considerations. This means creating militaries, indeed, entire governmental structures, that can justly win the conflicts they anticipate joining. Governments create militaries through policies that describe desired capabilities and programmes that execute those policies – in other words, by conscious decision and effort. This implies another aspect of justice – what might be called 'just policies for war' – that reconnects the *ad bellum* and *in bello* components of our just war framework. These are those decisions that determine, before a conflict is joined, what tools, knowledge and skills the statesman and soldier will have in order to craft a good political and military outcome. They guard against the myopia of the statesman and the tunnel vision of the commander.

An analogy illustrates the situation well. Suppose you are to remove a screw from a piece of machinery but all that you have in your tool kit is a hammer. If it is necessary that you remove the screw (*ad bellum* decision), you will attempt the job using the hammer (*in bello* decisions), and in so doing you may end up destroying the piece of machinery. This raises a number of questions not least of which is, could you have reasonably anticipated needing a screwdriver? If so, why did you only have a hammer in your toolkit? It is precisely this analogous policy question that makes up just policies for war. What types of conflicts does one anticipate, and what capabilities does one need to engage in them justly? A country that answers the first but fails to meet the requirements of the second cannot claim a reasonable hope for success, and arguably cannot justify going to war.

Clearly no nation can anticipate all future contingencies, nor afford to have a military tailor-made for every possible circumstance. Furthermore, some countries must address a spectrum of military challenges, and their militaries cannot be specialised in only one type of engagement. However, given foreseeable circumstances in which military force would be needed, at least one of two things must be done to provide the military connective

---

[20] Fighting insurgencies at home may not be avoidable. For a discussion of guerrilla warfare see Walzer, *Just and Unjust Wars*, pp. 176–96.

tissue of just policies for war: either military capabilities must be created to win in these foreseeable circumstances, or sufficient flexibility must be fostered in the military to permit it to adapt quickly to new circumstances. Ideally, both will occur.

## Concluding observations

If Clausewitz's observation, that war is policy carried out by other means, is accepted then the *ad bellum* requirement of having a reasonable hope of success before going to war implies having a reasonable hope of achieving these policy goals; otherwise the war, though militarily successful, will be lost (as was the case in Vietnam) and the scales of our 'moral calculus' will not tip in our favour. Insurgencies are different from conventional wars. To win a conventional war one must destroy the enemy's ability or will to fight, usually by destroying his army or government, and so realise national goals. The main effort is military. However, in counter-insurgencies one must win the battle for the people – the hearts and minds – and this involves achieving political goals almost never gained by destroying the enemy's armed elements alone. The main effort is political rather than military. Addressing conventional war, 'Essentials of a Good Peace', a statement of the American Catholic Episcopate issued in November 1943, states that, 'unless we have the vision of a good peace and the will to demand it, victory can be an empty and even a tragic thing'.[21]

For counter-insurgencies it is possible to take this statement a step further. Unless there is the vision of a just peace and the will and capabilities to achieve it, there will be no victory. Other tools besides militaries are needed to succeed at this, covering a spectrum of capabilities aimed at improving the political, social and economic state of the population – all those things needed to create the conditions in which a justly ordered society can come into being and flourish. Although Mary Kaldor, Gwyn Prins and John Langan will present their views on this matter in the latter sections of this book, nonetheless, we should observe here that much of this is not the domain of armies. If, however, Clausewitz and Augustine are to be believed, then logic dictates that we be reasonably certain of our ability to win the war and establish the foundations of *tranquillitas*

---

[21] As quoted by George Weigel, *Tranquillitas Ordinis: The Present Failure and Future Promise of American Catholic Thought on War and Peace* (Oxford: Oxford University Press, 1987), p. 58.

*ordinis* before the conflict is taken on. To do this, what are currently called 'stability and reconstruction' capabilities are needed. These capabilities need to be part of a more holistic effort to defeat enemy insurgents while bettering the lives of the innocent people among whom they live and fight. Policies that create these capabilities as well as commit the resources needed for this holistic effort are essential elements of just wars against insurgents.

The requirements discussed above have significant implications for the way modern states organise, train and equip military forces, and prepare stability and reconstruction capabilities. They also have significant implications for the way governments look at justice in the coming decades, and for whether or not they will succeed in securing a *tranquillitas ordinis* by force. If they are to both defeat radical Islamic insurgents and live up to what for almost two millennia has been viewed as the ethical requirements of a state when it uses military power, these challenges need to be understood and addressed.

# PART IV

Securing peace justly

# 12

# Justice after war and the international common good

JOHN LANGAN

While it is true according to Dr Johnson that nothing concentrates the mind so much as the prospect of being hanged, the prospect of being shot by a sniper or hit by a mortar or blown apart by a bomb will probably do just as well in bringing certain issues to the fore with an urgency and vigour which they do not customarily have. For this reason, the parts of just war theory which fall under the headings of *jus ad bellum* (the right to enter into hostilities) and *jus in bello* (the right to be observed in the conduct of hostilities) have drawn more concentrated and more sustained attention than the moral issues which cluster around the end of hostilities and the return of peace, a cluster which there is now an increasing tendency to speak of as *jus post bellum* (the right to be established after hostilities). At this point, politicians, diplomats and lawyers return to the centre of the stage; a complex process of negotiations brings us closer to the resumption of politics as usual. The territory is less well charted, and its features are less arresting and less ominous than the precipitous and craggy landscape of war.

This chapter is not primarily concerned with the events which terminate hostilities, but with the altered network of relationships between combatants and among nations which arises at the end of hostilities and with different ways of conceiving this network. This chapter begins by laying out four approaches to thinking about a morally acceptable order after the conclusion of hostilities and examines the attractions and drawbacks of each. The approaches are: first, the endorsement by John XXIII in *Pacem in Terris* of an international political authority to promote the international common good; second, the concept of a democratic peace with its promise of eliminating violent conflicts among democracies; third, the demands of the US National Security Strategy Statement of

2002; and fourth, the contrast in Islamic thought between the *dar-al-harb* and the *dar-al-Islam*.

Justice after war is shown to be dependent on meeting the conditions of just cause, probability of success and proportionality in *jus ad bellum* in the war which is to be terminated and on preventing the emergence of conditions which would justify a war in the future. This chapter traces some of the difficulties of the American and British position in Iraq to the failure to meet the conditions of *jus ad bellum* and to the American persistence in linking the war in Iraq to an ill-defined 'war' on terrorism. The chapter then reviews the tension between a conception of peace involving a rich and robust moral order and a minimalist conception of peace and raises the question of the extent to which the fuller conception of peace can justify the continuing use of force. It concludes by arguing for a syncretistic conception of the international common good which is sensitive to the basic demands made in the four approaches considered at the beginning of this chapter.

## Catholic institutional internationalism

The first way of thinking about a morally acceptable order after the conclusion of hostilities is to be found in *Pacem in Terris*. *Pacem in Terris* is the widely influential encyclical which John XXIII issued shortly before his death in 1963. Angelo Roncalli had lived through the First World War as a chaplain in the Italian army and through the Second World War as a Vatican diplomat in the Balkans. He had witnessed personally the catastrophic failures in the nation-state system that had brought to an end European economic and political colonial domination of many parts of the world. It is not surprising, given that he was writing after the Cuban missile crisis of 1962, that John XXIII reached this somewhat negative conclusion: 'Therefore, under the present circumstances of human society, both the structure and form of governments as well as the power which public authority wields in all the nations of the world must be considered inadequate to promote the universal common good.'[1] He then puts the matter more positively:

---

[1] John XXIII, 'Pacem in Terris', in David J. O'Brien and Thomas Shannon (eds.), *Catholic Social Thought: The Documentary Heritage* (Maryknoll, NY: Orbis Books, 1992), p. 135.

Today the universal common good poses problems of worldwide dimensions, which cannot be adequately tackled or solved except by the efforts of public authority endowed with a wideness of powers, structure and means of the same proportions: that is, of public authority which is in a position to operate in an effective manner on a worldwide basis. The moral order itself, therefore, demands that such a form of public authority be established.[2]

He quickly points out, however, that such a public authority entrusted with the promotion of the universal common good must not be imposed by force, but needs to be established by the consent of both more and less powerful states.

In both his positive and his negative conclusions, John XXIII was venturing into new territory for the tradition of Catholic social thought. Previously, Catholic social thought had focused on the nation-state (or at least on a single political community), and on the requirement that the laws and policies of the state must serve the good of all the members of that community. This is a requirement which Thomas Aquinas builds into his definition of law in the *Summa Theologiae*. The 'common good' is an inherently inclusive concept, though it also has to be seen as realised in particular forms of social organisation and co-operation. As John XXIII had argued earlier in the encyclical: 'The very nature of the common good requires that all members of the state be entitled to share in it, although in different ways according to each one's tasks, merits, and circumstances.'[3] In a manner which anticipates the later development of what came to be called 'the preferential option for the poor', he observes: 'Considerations of justice and equity, however, can at times demand that those involved in civil government give more attention to the less fortunate members of the community, since they are less able to defend their rights and to assert their legitimate claims.'[4]

John XXIII's case for interpreting the common good in an inclusive manner applies not merely to the economically deprived, but to minority groups of all sorts. As Jacques Maritain saw when he was confronted with the rise of totalitarian regimes in traditionally Catholic or Christian countries, the inclusive interpretation of the common good brings with it both

---

[2] *Ibid.*, p. 137.    [3] O'Brien and Shannon, *Catholic Social Thought*, p. 56.

[4] For an account of the development of the option for the poor in Catholic social teaching over the last century, see Donal Dorr, *Option for the Poor: One Hundred Years of Vatican Social Teaching* (Maryknoll, NY: Orbis Books, 1992).

an affirmation of the human rights of minorities, and a basis for criticising the excessive concentration of power in the state.[5] The papal approach also draws on the wisdom of the Anglo-American constitutional and diplomatic traditions in promoting a world in which power will be separated rather than concentrated in the hands of one state and its leadership.

This first conception of the international common good looks both backward and forward. Retrospectively, the occurrence of war shows a failure of the nation-state system to ensure the international common good. Prospectively, the just order of the future includes an international political authority which can effectively achieve that common good and which will take as one of its central tasks the prevention and limitation of war. Neither the common good, which is the goal and which provides the primary criterion for assessing the post-war situation, nor the proposed authority, regardless of its precise shape, is to be equated with the well-being or the power of one particular state, no matter how well intentioned or technologically advanced that state may be. Rather, John XXIII had in mind the development of an institutional framework which would be comprehensive in its scope and which would draw on a widely based consensus. It would provide just procedures for the resolution of disputes between states. Although the Vatican has been generally supportive of the UN, despite serious disagreements in recent years on issues of sexual morality and family life, he did not necessarily identify this institutional framework with the United Nations as it developed after 1945.

Even though the Cold War involved a broad ideological conflict as well as more sharply defined disputes between states and even though the Vatican was clearly aligned with one side of the great ideological conflict both in its social teaching and in its diplomatic practice, papal teaching continued to affirm the relevance and the attainability of an international common good. If we think about the shape of such an international common good in the 1960s, we can readily see that it would have to be a very imperfect good, given the serious systematic defects in many of the key actors in the international system of that time, notably the Soviet Union and Communist China, and given the profound disagreements in the governing moral and political philosophies of the two sides. Seen from this particular context, the international common good would exemplify

[5] Jacques Maritain, *Rights of Man and Natural Law*, trans. Doris Anson (New York: Scribner's Sons, 1943), pp. 1–17.

what John Rawls discusses as a *modus vivendi* rather than a shared conception of a comprehensive good.[6]

Is it possible to characterise this good in more positive terms? Three elements stand out as possible candidates. The first is the avoidance of war. The resort to force can sometimes contribute to the achievement of the common good; but even if war is initially justified, situations are very likely to arise in which continuing the war will produce grievous harm to the international common good as well as to the national common goods of the contending parties. One need only think of both the First and Second World Wars to see this point. The second element is the development of international instruments of co-operation, which states and other parties can use to achieve a wide range of goods as well as to prevent significant harms. Maintenance of diplomatic relations, membership in international organisations, ratification and observance of treaties can all be important ways of contributing to the international common good. The international common good is not a simple good to be straightforwardly attained; rather, it is a complex set of goals subject to change and development and requiring sensitive and imaginative adjustment. These instruments of co-operation can be used in relations between states which are competitive or even hostile. Renouncing or invalidating them is one way in which states signal the increasing tension in their relations; enhancing or joining them conveys a desire for closer relations. There is, and should be, a considerable overlap between the pursuit of the international common good and the normal progress of international relations as states work to resolve their problems with each other and as they attempt to meet the needs and protect the interests of their people.

The third element is the opening to others, to states and groups which have previously been at the margins of the global political process, or have even been deliberately excluded from the scope of the international common good. This opening takes the notion of common good beyond adversarial contexts and requires that we think in terms of human solidarity across the various boundaries, political, economic, ethnic, linguistic, religious, within which we normally transact our affairs. The international common good cannot be fully achieved within the structure of alliances and coalitions, since these are customarily directed against some adversary, or, as

---

[6] John Rawls, 'The Idea of an Overlapping Consensus', in Samuel Freedman (ed.), *Collected Papers* (Cambridge, MA: Harvard University Press, 1999), pp. 432–44.

Mary Kaldor argues later in the book, to the maintenance of a friend–enemy distinction. The international common good must be in principle all-inclusive. This universal openness applies both to the processes and institutions by which the international common good is to be achieved, and to the distribution of benefits from these processes and institutions. This is a claim which, I would argue, follows from the notion of the international common good itself. It also provides a basis for moral criticism of the performance of those processes and institutions which profess to shape and regulate the international order. Thus a failure to offer opportunities for participation in and benefits to groups and states always counts as a negative consideration. This need not be decisive, of course, and may be outweighed by other considerations.

The notion of the international common good does not provide us with an institutional blueprint or with substantive policies for realising the international common good. For this reason it should not be surprising that the endorsement of international political authority in the teaching of John XXIII is vague and generic and cast in largely negative terms (e.g. not imposed by coercion, not violating human rights, not replacing the authority of individual states). This was a conception proposed for a world divided into ideological blocs which were in economic and military competition with each other. It may well seem to realists that this understanding of the international common good has a moralistic and even utopian flavour. In both theory and practice, however, it is best taken as a reformist proposal which assumes that greater efforts are to be made for protecting and achieving the international common good within the limits allowed by existing political structures. It does not presuppose the prior transformation of states into morally or ideologically purified entities. Rather, it commends the establishment of an authority capable of adjudicating disputes among states and of enforcing its decisions. This, of course, brings in the classic difficulty which stands in the way of securing acceptance for an effective international political authority, namely, the limitation of sovereignty which is required if such an authority is to be truly effective.

On a more positive note, these three elements do give us starting points for the task of defining and realising the international common good. They also correspond to three pressing tasks: of preventing war; maintaining the international patterns of co-operation which are necessary for security and economic activity; and responding to the needs and moral demands of those who are at risk in the present form of the state system whether these be Sudanese in Darfur, Tutsis in Rwanda, Somalis and Kurds in Iraq or Chechens in Russia.

## Three alternative conceptions of international order

So far, this chapter has reflected on the conception of an international common good to be realised by an effective but far from omnipotent international political authority as this was articulated by John XXIII in the early 1960s. This may seem to be a somewhat parochial and dated conception, but it represents a way of thinking about the global predicament in the aftermath of the First World War and the Second World War and in the period before the actual performance of the United Nations revealed a whole series of flaws and vulnerabilities which diminished confidence in it without destroying it completely. Despite the political context in which it was written, the international common good still remains the basic conception with which most people begin, when recognition of the need for an international political authority is overtaken by the realisation that the straightforward move to the construction of a world government is not politically feasible. Its distinctiveness, as well as some of its attractions and limitations, can be seen more readily if we compare it briefly with some alternatives.

### Democratic peace

One alternative to John XXIII's international common good is the concept of democratic peace, which has its roots in the moral philosophy of Immanuel Kant. It has been presented in a more empirical form over the last fifteen years by Bruce Russett.[7] The starting point for this view is the thesis that democratic states do not wage wars against each other. They clearly wage defensive wars against aggression and threats by non-democratic states, but the claim is that they do not choose to attack each other. Now, on one level, this is an interesting empirical claim, which can be established or refuted by looking at the various wars which democratic states undertake. It can be protected by suitable analytical refinements

---

[7] Bruce Russett, *Grasping the Democratic Peace* (Princeton, NJ: Princeton University Press, 1993).

which will handle apparent counter-examples. But it also serves as a powerful reason for a moral judgement affirming the superiority of democratic governments. But the idea of democratic peace can also be the germ of an ambitious policy for the transformation of states.

This chapter leaves the assessment of the empirical claim to the historians and political scientists. But on the normative and policy levels it should be noted that the concept of democratic peace in its strongest form seems to allow for the imposition of democratic regimes (as in Germany and Japan after 1945) and perhaps even to require the conversion of states with non-democratic regimes. In this respect it sets the bar for the attainment of the international common good higher than does the Catholic institutional theory articulated by John XXIII. Now there is good reason to think that an international order structured around the idea of democratic peace will match the three constitutive elements mentioned in our discussion of the Catholic idea of the international common good. Peace will be achieved, co-operative relations will develop and the system will be open to all comers. In fact, in the word of Scripture which St Augustine used to justify coercion in religious matters, 'Compel them to come in' (Luke 14).[8] Thus envisioned, the democratic peace has a missionary character. But in this ambitious form, it also has a crusading character. The outsiders will be persuaded to enter the system and will be encouraged to enjoy its benefits; but, if persuasion fails, there will be justification and perhaps even the desire for forcing them in. But, of course, there is a paradox present here, since peace is then to be achieved through war, an ideologically driven war at that.

The democratic peace is like a sunlit plateau marked by an attractive serenity, but which is to be approached only by a steep and dangerous path. One can wax enthusiastic about the benefits that can be expected on the plateau and commend the plateau as an ultimate goal for policy, and one can dismiss the pains and risks of the ascent as merely temporary. It is likely that the policy leading towards a democratic peace, especially if resistance is extensive and is rooted in cultures which we understand only imperfectly, will be both sanguinary and utopian. It is interesting that

---

[8] This verse, which comes from the parable of the wedding feast in Luke 14, was used by Augustine late in his life to justify the coercion of the Donatists in North Africa. See Perez Zagorin, *How the Idea of Religious Toleration Came to the West* (Princeton, NJ: Princeton University Press, 2003), pp. 29–30; and Peter Brown, *Augustine of Hippo* (Berkeley, CA: University of California Press, 1967), pp. 234–43.

such proposals have been entertained by those who think that the military forces used to bring about democratic peace will have an overwhelming advantage and will suffer few casualties. It is also noteworthy that the debate over democratic peace began in earnest when the United States was no longer confronted with a heavily armed and undemocratic adversary, but dealing with intractable and elusive adversaries who could challenge American power only on a hit-and-run basis.

The prospect of establishing a system of democratic peace throughout the Middle East from Islamabad to Cairo and Istanbul is indeed attractive, but the costs and uncertainties of such a project over time seem to stretch well beyond the bounds of prudent statesmanship. In the absence of such a system, the democratisation of individual states in a highly contentious region marked by religious, ethnic, linguistic, economic and ideological divisions may or may not reduce the frequency and intensity of violent conflict. The reason for this is that, as advocates of the democratic peace thesis admit, democracies do wage war against non-democracies and vice versa.[9] Given the multitude of conflicting interests in the region and the many forces resisting democratisation, the likelihood that such wars would arise in the Middle East seems fairly high. But it has to be granted that the democratic peace in its Kantian and more recent forms offers the brightest view of the future, since the evil and destructive forces would not have significant political power and their military capability would be limited. But this happy outcome is achieved by stipulation rather than by deep social transformation.

## The 2002 US National Security Strategy

The second alternative conception of the international common good shares some features with the democratic peace. Its core is the notion of US hegemony as asserted in the National Security Strategy Statement of 2002.[10] In this remarkable document, the United States positions itself as the supreme arbiter and primary enforcer of security in the international system. It claims the right to launch both pre-emptive and preventive wars. The United States will forestall any other nation from assembling

---

[9] Russett, *Grasping the Democratic Peace*, p. 32.
[10] Executive Office of the President, *The National Security Strategy of the United States of America*, 17 September 2002 (hereinafter, *NSS-2002*).

and deploying forces which could inflict significant harm on the United States and its interests. While this document is merely a broad statement of the current policy objectives of one state, the pre-eminent power and the central role of the United States in so many areas of global life require that this statement and similar documents be taken quite seriously.

George Weigel is correct to argue earlier in this collection of essays that there is a great deal of talk in the statement about international co-operation and about the importance of freedom. Yet regardless of Weigel's efforts to rewrite the *NSS-2002*, there is a darker side to this document in which the assumptions come much closer to classical, even Hobbesian, realism. Not merely are the intentions of potentially hostile states to be altered; their capabilities are to be restricted so that no effective challenge to the security and the interests of the United States is possible. The framework for this way of conceiving international order and the international common good is emphatically not egalitarian. It gives much greater importance to adversarial situations and possible hostilities than does the concept of democratic peace, which tends to dismiss these as temporary and local barriers to the implementation of the ultimate pacific vision.

The *NSS-2002* also assumes the steadfast benevolence of the United States toward co-operative powers. It holds out the prospect of numerous benefits for them. But its focus is understandably more on the short term and on the responses to present crises of terrorism and the (real or imaginary) proliferation of weapons of mass destruction, and not so much on the ideal benefits which may follow from the democratic peace. It is naturally of more immediate concern both to policy-makers and to critics of American foreign policy. It does not attempt to argue for its conclusions on the basis of what would make for a fair agreement among the various powers of the world, or of what reasonable persons would agree to accept as universally normative.

Contrary to Weigel's analysis, it is therefore difficult to show the world in general that the goals that the *NSS-2002* proposes can be derived from a universalist moral theory or from the principles of Christianity. The world is to be made safe for American democracy. The international common good is determined by one pre-eminent power, and it consists very largely in maintaining the security of that same power. A principal difference between the national security conception and the democratic peace conception is that the national security conception is more explicit in considering the difficulties of the uphill approach to the promised land of the sunlit plateau.

## *Holy war*

The third alternative conception of international common good comes from a more starkly and profoundly adversarial view of the international order. It takes as fundamental the distinction between the community of believers and the community of unbelievers. It can be found not merely in the Islamic contrast between the *dar-al-Islam* and the *dar-al-harb*, where Islamic law either governs the community or is rejected, but also in the Augustinian contrast between 'the city of God' and 'the city of man'.[11] It is of particular importance that we do not identify this sort of contrast as being characteristic of or confined to the Islamic world, though we find significant examples of it there. In this approach, the fulfilment of humanity ordained by God is found on only one side of the great and fundamental division of society along religious lines. Only incidentally or in passing is the common good shared by those persons and communities which are on the wrong side of the line. When the great divide between believers and unbelievers is seen as prior to all other morally significant divisions, what results is an exclusionary conception of the common good, a position which the Catholic tradition has explicitly renounced since Vatican II. An exclusionary conception of the common good fits well with the attitudes and practices characteristic of the crusade and the holy war. The crucial thing is that the forces of good prevail over the forces of evil. Moral questions about the acceptability of the means are treated as secondary; the primary demand is that the means be effective in defeating the adversary and in ensuring the triumph of good over evil.

The constituent elements of the Catholic conception of the international common good – the insistence on avoiding war, on building relationships and on opening out to other parties – are lacking in this purely adversarial conception. A significant implication of the language used in 'the war against terrorism' conducted by the American Government and its allies is that it leads us to conceive the other side in purely negative terms. We are not to think of 'the terrorists' as fighting for a political cause with certain possibly

---

[11] Augustine, in a famous passage in *The City of God*, Book XIV, c. 28, contrasts the two cities as motivated by the love of God and the love of self. This is clearly a religious contrast which it would not be appropriate to translate directly into political terms. But the temptation to do this has been recurrent in Christian history. See Frederick Russell, *The Just War in the Middle Ages* (Cambridge: Cambridge University Press, 1975), pp. 16–39, for an overview of the tensions in early medieval thought.

just claims, or as defending a community of values, but purely in terms of the morally unacceptable tactics which they have decided to employ. Since the relationship of the terrorists to particular states (which have complex histories and significant internal divisions) is opaque at best, and since the terrorists routinely put their case in ways which do not encourage outsiders to respond sympathetically, or even to want to understand, it is easy for their opponents to paint them in highly reductive terms.

This yields a conception of the adversary which is emotionally satisfying but intellectually crude and which is likely to be politically disastrous. One instance of this is our development of a remarkably insensitive casuistry which asserts that we can justifiably deny persons whom we have captured and whom we suspect of links with terrorism the protections of American law, of the Geneva Conventions and of human rights law. It should be noted, however, that this casuistry is not the application of a general theoretical perspective, which devalues the other side, so much as it is the rationalisation of bad practice. The goal in this sort of adversarial situation is not the defeat of the adversary, the recovery of lost territory or honour, the defence of one's own country and its allies. Rather, it is the elimination or conversion of the adversary. This starkly and uncompromisingly adversarial conception, however, is not inherently genocidal. The possibility is open to the other side, the servants of darkness, to accept God's grace and to be converted from their evil ways. A pagan can become a Christian, a *harbi* can become a Muslim. Furthermore, while it will be difficult to ensure that the limits prescribed by the just war tradition are observed in this situation, there is no logical necessity that these limits will be violated. Both Muslims and Christians have stories of salvation in which it is God who effects a definitive separation of the good and the evil (who, however, are not to be identified with the members or non-members of a particular religious group).

Warriors and their political leaders in these traditions can decide to anticipate the divine verdict; or they may defer the matter to the ultimate judge. In any case, the satisfactory outcome for the use of force is a situation in which the adversaries of God are either eliminated altogether or are completely segregated from the realm of the good and the elect. The destruction or the unconditional surrender of the adversary is the only morally satisfactory outcome. Here the adversarial conception comes close to the theory of democratic peace, for the final condition is one of tranquillity and agreement, since those who promote conflict and dissent will have been eliminated. In comparison, both papally approved internationalism and American hegemony are modest in their goals and familiar in the expectations which they encourage.

## Back to *jus ad bellum* and *jus in bello*

How are we to assess the various conceptions of international order which could be actualised at the end of a war? How are these end conditions related to the traditionally recognised norms of just war theory? This chapter can do no more than offer some plausible criteria which would be widely accepted as relevant, if not decisive. The four criteria likely to guide public reflection and decision are: first, the benefits achieved in a particular conception and the distribution of these benefits and of related harms; second, the fairness of the process by which the conception is realised; third, probability that the benefits will actually be realised and that related harms will be reduced; fourth, the political attractiveness of the conception, especially, but not exclusively, in the United States.

The Catholic institutional conception offers the prospect of moderate benefits with a reasonable likelihood of their being realised in a familiar distributional pattern. Since it relies on a plurality of distinct nation-states agreeing together, its chances of being perceived as fair are greater than a conception which relies on unilateral decisions or on exclusivist coalitions. Its political attractiveness is likely to be higher outside than inside the United States. These points follow from the fact that this conception is at bottom a meliorist, incrementalist interpretation of the internationalist project attempted in the United Nations. The democratic peace conception offers very high benefits which can be shared on a universal basis. The perceived fairness of the process will vary greatly depending on the extent to which democratisation is consensual or coerced. The probability of achieving the benefits in a world as divided as our own is not high. The political attractiveness of the conception is quite variable, depending on whether it is seen as the universalisation of American and democratic values, or whether it is interpreted as an intrusive and aggressive utopianism.

The *NSS-2002* conception, which is marked by a durable American hegemony, offers high benefits for some, most notably the USA and its allies, and very little for opponents. This raises questions about fairness and about its sustainability over the long term, even after one grants that the overwhelming military power of the USA somehow ensures that significant benefits are achievable at the beginning of the new peace. The political attractiveness of such an approach is highest in times of threat and emergency and would be considerably diminished by prolonged resistance. The fourth conception, religious or ideological adversarialism, also proposes a starkly uneven distribution of benefits and harms. Not surprisingly it raises similar problems about fairness. While it presupposes a sharp divide between opposing forces and civilisations, it need not aim at the elimination of the other side which is enshrined in democratic peace. In the interminable struggle with evil and unbelief, it can accept partial successes and periods of truce. The probability of limited success then goes up. As the stories of Muslim–Christian conflict and of the Cold War manifest in different ways, religious and ideological adversarialism draws on powerful emotions, a fact which confirms its political attractiveness and usefulness.

The result of this brief comparative evaluation is that no one conception emerges as clearly superior on all criteria. We should expect all of them to have appeal to participants in public debate who will be tempted to slide from one conception to another in an opportunistic fashion. Each of them raises problems in the interpretation of the generally recognised just war criteria. The way in which judgements of proportionality are made and contested depends on the kinds of benefits being aimed at, their distribution and their attainability as well as on the extent to which concomitant evils are thought to be tolerable or avoidable or not. Each of the conceptions shapes the proportionality discussion in a different way.

But each of them also raises more specific questions about the other criteria. Catholic institutionalism seems to jeopardise the likelihood of success, because of its reliance on multilateral procedures which are likely to be frustrated by acute conflicts. Democratic peace includes a definite idea of proper authority, namely, the democratic state. Ironically, democratic societies now confront debates about whether the crises of contemporary warfare require a less democratic way of exercising authority and whether the desires of military and political leaders for secrecy and flexibility are really compatible with democratic institutions. The *NSS-2002* approach has particularly questioned the traditional just war requirement of last resort and includes an explicit argument for allowing preventive war. This is likely to make peace less stable and to undercut negotiating processes in critical situations. Religious or ideological adversarialism is likely to assume that its preferred side easily meets the criteria of just cause, proper authority and right intention; it is likely to interpret proportionality in ways which play down the losses of its foes and overvalue benefits for its own side; and finally, it is constantly tempted to replace the constraints of just war with the unfettered commitment of a Holy War or a crusade.

The immense technological advantage which the United States enjoys in comparison with other powers, and the willingness which it shows to spend resources for its military objectives, suggest war termination scenarios in which the enemies of democracy and of American power are to be coercively converted, re-educated, reorganised and co-ordinated into a new and more perfect order of the ages. The principal plausible alternative scenario (and one which may be impending in Iraq) is one in which American power is worn down by terrorist attrition and by politically unsustainable costs.

The preponderance of American power enables the proponents of comprehensive American interventionism to express their confidence that enormous good can be achieved through the use of military force and that devastating evils can be averted, at least for the Americans and their allies, though not for their adversaries. The consequence of this is that judgements about proportionality in the use of force by the manifestly superior power are systematically skewed in favour of active reliance on force. Once the constraints arising from uncertainty about the issue of a war and from potentially excessive losses in soldiers and resources are removed, we should not be surprised that analysts arise who will point to the enormous goods which can be achieved by the low-cost use of overwhelming power.

Furthermore, the more perfect the promised final condition, the more apparent justification there is not merely for launching a war, but also for escalating the use of force and for expanding the political agenda in a maximalist direction. My own suspicion is that expanding the agenda beyond the modest goals envisioned in the moral justification of essentially defensive conflicts, such as the Gulf War of 1990–1, and the equally modest goals proposed in the papal version of international common good and international political authority, will commit the United States and its friends to an unrealisable programme which can be characterised either as world liberation or as world domination, depending on your location in the conflict. In the present situation, when goals of more than imperial ambition have been set for US foreign policy and when the characteristically American temptations of technological utopianism have come to seduce the national security establishment, as well as significant portions of the intellectual world, it may be a salutary outcome for the costs and sufferings produced by the acting out of our current moralistic and quasi-apocalyptic fantasies to be sufficiently high to persuade us that aiming at less lofty goals than universal democratisation, perpetual hegemony and the eradication of the forces of evil and darkness may actually make the flight of our arrow less costly and more sustainable, more reliable and ultimately more just.

Proposing grandiose projects of international transformation as the justifying goals of military action, as the peace to be realised *post bellum* and as the basis of national strategy is parallel to using printing presses and bond salesmen to finance wars. The initial result is inflation (in several senses); the long-term result is the loss of credit and credibility. Formulating strategies for the future which envision a permanently privileged place for the United States renders suspect the moral character of that which is proposed and the motives of the proponent. These are attitudes which will make the long-term contribution of the United States and its allies to the peace and security of the world, a contribution which is extremely important, even indispensable, more difficult to carry out, more open to criticism and more likely to provoke resistance. The post-conflict situation in Iraq should help to convince us that the path of moral responsibility and the path of prudent realism converge in the pursuit of limited and specific objectives in the post-war world.

## Concluding reflections

The desirable post-war situation will itself remain a contested reality, since it includes different ways of organising the world and conceiving the international common good, which have support from diverse constituencies and which cannot be integrated into one conception. The United States and other participants in international conflict as well as contending politicians within these nations will be drawn to significantly different conceptions of the *post-bellum* situation and of the goods which are to be attained in it. Just war theory will remain indeterminate and will support different final judgements on the morality of particular instances of war, but it will also provide the outlines of a framework for linking these different views of the end to our moral judgements about what makes for a right decision to go to war, or to wage war in one way rather than another. But achieving greater clarity about the post-war situation, and about the character and scope of the end which is being sought, makes an important contribution to the shaping of policies which will be more than wishful thinking or ideological fantasies, and which will not be crippled by internal inconsistencies and increasingly manifest contradictions with social, political and religious reality.

# 13

# Conditions for *jus in pace* in the face of the future

GWYN PRINS

## Introduction: surfacing submerged assumptions

For the theory and practice of just war, is it the end of the matter when the fighting ends? Does the quality of the peace matter? Does it matter who made the peace and how? This chapter will suggest that it is not the end of the matter and that they both do, respectively.

Rousseau observed that the axiomatic question in all politics is what produces legitimate authority. Statesmen who have reflected on the matter subsequently have agreed with him. What then shall be the moral and the practical basis for judgement of legitimacy in the governance arrangements which follow a war? Post-war moments are often fraught and contested. The legitimation of the peace in fraught circumstances is less often a dogmatic judgement than a question of choosing the lesser evil. Michael Ignatieff has re-stated the case for the simultaneous centrality and unavoidability of this type of moral choice in war-related contexts in his essay on the subject.[1] Choosing the lesser evil is, like Rousseau's question, one of the oldest questions in politics and one of the hardest to answer. So the nurturing of legitimacy in post-conflict situations, and adoption of the lesser evil within them as a foundation for the consequent construction of public good, provide the moral calibrators for this essay.

Are the issues of legitimacy and of adjudicating between greater and lesser evils affected by just war criteria? Can they affect those criteria? Are they different following a war with a just cause, justly fought, from one entered for just cause but conducted unjustly? This latter is one of Michael Walzer's questions in *Just and Unjust Wars*. It prompts the converse question. Can just peace building after war repair resentment? Can it

---

[1] Michael Ignatieff, *The Lesser Evil: Political Ethics in an Age of Terror* (Edinburgh: Edinburgh University Press, 2005).

right a wrong? Some philosophers say no.[2] I am not so sure; and this chapter will explain why.

With a topic of this nature we must be fastidious about our assumptions, especially our hidden assumptions. I notice four, which I list in reverse order of seriousness. The less consequential, but nonetheless widely encountered, pair are tied to the conviction that consensual processes are prerequisite to just peace. The first states that unilateral actions are less likely to result in just peace than multilateral ones. The second states that a war in which one community conquers another and forces changes in its values after unconditional surrender is less likely to result in just peace than negotiated settlement.

Such positions are predicated upon social and moral relativism. This relativism stands upon a stated ground of liberal toleration. Culturally it forms a residual part of the background glow from the 1960s Big Bang of *marxisante* political theory in the minds of the age cohort of 'sixty-eighters'. Looking at recent debates within the churches, the 1960s seem to have left a particular mark in the contemporary clerical mind. But this position has been thrown into profound confusion both by jihadist consequences from the failure of its social project, and also by the arrival in strength of restated and by definition universal human rights. In its more extended form, social and moral relativism combined with the Left's natural instinct to subordinate liberty to levelling, can quickly destroy fundamental freedom and introduce reverse discrimination. But in its less extreme and more widely pervasive presence, it already affects the terms of the debate about securing just peace by entering criteria of consensuality, negotiation and compromise in judging the justice of the peace. Are these correct and useful criteria?

The third assumption to be examined is that, by definition, imperial rule cannot give just peace. Contemporary circumstances make it especially important to interrogate this assumption. It is tied to the fourth and the most commonly encountered submerged assumption. This thinks that the answer to the core question of the deep sources of legitimacy is to be found in structural and institutional evidence. I, like Ignatieff, am sceptical about that. I propose a process-based criterion. So we begin here and then work back up the list: that is the form of the second part of this chapter. However, before I surface these four assumptions, in

---

[2] Jeff McMahan, 'Just Cause for Just War', *Ethics and International Affairs* 19 (2005): 1–21.

honesty within a charged discussion, I must first expose four implied arguments within my own approach so that, aware of them, the reader can more accurately weigh his or her opinion of my case.

## Working in a charged discussion

The first implied argument is that we conduct this discussion at no normal moment in international affairs. We discuss this during a period of remission after the arrival of jihadist violence in Manhattan. When the remission ends, a more profound direct transformation in relations between the victim and the perpetrator is to be expected. So far the full successor to 9/11 has not occurred. Neither Madrid, nor the two Bali bombings, nor Ankara nor the London Tube bombings of 7 July 2005, nor Abu Musab al-Zarqawi's bombing of a Jordanian wedding in November 2005, were that. The defining characteristic of the remission-ending attack will be success in shaking the Western psyche to its core with the psychological and semeiotic brilliance that the design of 9/11 achieved.

So while I suggest that, conservatively, the free world may have to endure a generation-long struggle with jihadists, there is a degree of urgency to settle our moral compass. Otherwise, when the remission ends we risk having to cause potentially grave rupture of many peoples' civil rights and liberties without having forged that mental armour of understanding both why and how we choose the lesser evil. As we walk the precarious line between the overreaction of false necessity which could ravage our internal landscape of toleration and justice, and the moral perfectionism that would preserve maximal civil liberties, we all ask, with Ignatieff, 'what lesser evils may a society commit when it believes it faces the greater evil of its own destruction?'[3]

My second implied argument is that I identify a bundle of four deep secular trends as the first General Crisis in modern history since that of the late eighteenth century gave us the terms of engagement for the 'long twentieth century': the period from the beginning of the French Revolution to the end of the Soviet and 'European Union' federal experiments. I shall mention two of these trends in discussing the first assumption, below. These are the accelerating erosion of the post-colonial state settlement especially in sub-Saharan Africa and in west Asia and the

---

[3] Ignatieff, *The Lesser Evil*, p. 1.

Pacific archipelago and the simultaneous draining of much power from all the post-1945 multilateral institutions, respectively. I shall mention the other two in discussing the assumption about imperial projects. They are, first, that the return to a world with a dominant imperial hegemon is a return to business as usual, in the thousand-year-long view. The second is that with the lifting of the general nuclear threat and the arrival of effects-based warfare, the morally harnessed use of armed force again becomes conceivable.

The third implied argument is practical. The cosmopolitan constitutional instincts and black letter law of today's American hegemon, combined with effects-based capabilities within the Anglosphere and a willingness still to try to direct the impetus to use force pre-emptively through the United Nations Security Council (UNSC), has produced a liberal imperial project that should not be ashamed to speak its name.

The fourth implied argument is the ethical sequel of the last sentence. Such enterprises are not merely not necessarily bad but can, if conducted competently, open the door to just peace. Evidence is accumulating to this effect. The relationships between arguments and conduct *in bello*, *ad pacem* and *in pace* both can be, and are, reflexive. While I agree with Jeff McMahan in distancing myself from the traditional view that just cause and just conduct are logically independent, and therefore that without a just cause, it is hard to see how just conduct or just post-war reconstruction can remedy that deficit, I do believe that the articulation of goals of just peace are insufficiently prominent in the *ad bellum* discussion. They can provide useful guidance.[4] This is a systematically different position from that to be found in some other chapters in this book and represents a different judgement on the balance between greater and lesser evils.

## The first assumption surfaced: about institutions and structures

When a cultural identity exists, it is, by definition, shared. A shared cultural identity underpins a culture of consent; and a culture of consent is the prerequisite to a rooted democracy. The proposition is most easily illustrated by its opposite.

---

[4] McMahan, 'Just Cause for Just War', 4–5. My reasons for the necessary linkage are not as systemic as his. I draw them from the fact that the mission of humanitarian intervention cannot be divorced from a view of the peace without risking moral implosion.

The fifty-year-long attempt to equate a 'European identity' with the proliferation of self-generated bureaucracy and associated *soi-disant* representative structural entities like the European Union's 'Parliament' should warn of the danger of misunderstanding the sources of legitimacy. In the absence of a spontaneous up-welling, but under the accelerating pressures of its promoters to crystallise the federal settlement in a currency and a constitution, the death blow struck by the Dutch voters on 1 June 2005 was predictable in principle although surprising in its decisive scale and timing.

The impending death of the European Union is matched by another feature of the contemporary general crisis, namely the rapid erosion of post-colonial state structures that were similarly parachuted in on top of pre-existing arrangements. Both are a salutary warning as we choose our analytic categories. The prerequisites for success of the American federal venture, de Tocqueville noticed when he examined what made democracy real in the United States of America in 1831, were four: the habit of local self-government; a common language that becomes a first language from the second generation of immigration; an open political class dominated by common law lawyers; and some shared moral beliefs. When Larry Seidentop applied these tests to Europe he found them wanting.[5]

Although social scientists may be expected to bridle at what is a historian's test, judging the *capacity to deliver a social contract*, rather than the *characteristic of the regime that does it*, may be a more fruitful route to follow in the quest for legitimate authority upon which just peace is perched. This process-based criterion is particularly apt at a volatile moment when, for the first time since the Napoleonic Wars, governments of all descriptions are simultaneously in the process of recasting fundamentally their contracts with their subjects.

The assumption that one or another structural form of government is by definition likely to be more just than another is simply, if uncomfortably, unsafe. Intolerant, tyrannical and divisive exercise of democratic power can happen – is happening now – in unexpected places. Astonishingly and sadly for such an old country, contemporary England provides a case in point. Without prior notice of intent, but presented wrapped in a cloak of 'modernisation', the internal balances in England's unwritten constitution are being unhinged and removed. The motives for doing this are

---

[5] Larry Seidentop, *Democracy in Europe* (London: Penguin, 2001).

various, but the effect is certainly congruent with the strategy of forming an executive federal European state of administrative regions that subvert sovereign arrangements.

The measure of legitimacy in a just peace is to be gauged not by the presence of structures but by the health of the relationship between stated rights and performed obligations. To do this, we require two measures: one of activity, the other of scale. What do rulers and subjects do to and for each other? A basic test is who willingly pays taxes to whom, for what. How complete is the hierarchy of rights that the subject can expect to be underwritten by the just sovereign in return for a duty of obedience? How broad or narrow is the dispensation of toleration? What is the lowest common denominator, either of activity or of scale, that is present? Conversely, how and to what extent do rulers discriminate against, exploit, persecute or kill sectors of their own populations? To what degree, in countervailing response to discrimination, is legitimacy withheld?

That reciprocal spectrum of means of expressing disapproval runs from the voting abstention now commonplace in low-trust democracies to tax avoidance to mute and cold non-co-operation to acts of non-violent, then of violent resistance, to Lockean righteous rebellion, to utter rejection, by revolution, of the legitimacy of groups of people and of ideologies to rule. A valuable if queasily demanding consequence of this choice to look at performance rather than at structure is that we can take rather little for granted, analytically, in these modern times. What we can take for granted with increasing certainty is the creeping conditionality of state sovereignty.

Life, liberty and the pursuit of happiness come in this order in the American Declaration of Independence for reasons of logical and moral priority. The third is predicated upon the presence of the second which is predicated upon the presence of the first. It is an indication of the degree to which the post-colonial settlement has eroded in many places, principally in sub-Saharan Africa, that the driving force of international peace building has come to reside in a powerful reiteration of the most fundamental human rights to life before all else via the doctrine of the responsibility to protect individuals at risk from their own pathological governments. We are driven back to first principles in the face of a circumstance that was not in the minds of the generation that contemplated impending decolonisation and its benefit. That benefit was taken for granted, especially with the liberation rhetoric of De Gaulle, the Free

French and the other occupied, recently liberated Europeans, ringing in their ears. 'Seek ye first the political kingdom,' cried Kwame Nkrumah, first leader of the first British colony to gain independence in Africa, in a biblically inspired flourish, 'and all else shall come to you!' But the lesson of the next generation was that it did not.

During the Cold War, the mad, bad and dangerous rulers such as Bokassa or Mobutu were tolerated, supplied and used in the proxy wars of the superpowers or of the French. They were permitted to hide behind the screen of sovereign immunity. However, the remarkable rise in prominence of human rights since the Cold War ended has meant that while Robert Mugabe has not yet been halted, the trend of the times is against him. The responsibility to protect fundamental rights has become the central motif in the two most important restatements of general responsibilities in international politics of recent times: the International Commission on Intervention and State Sovereignty in 2001 and the report issued by the UN Secretary-General's High-Level Panel on Threats, Challenges and Change in December 2004. This concept was singled out by Kofi Annan's March 2005 report to the Millennium Summit entitled 'In Larger Freedom'. It was one of the only pieces to be rescued from the train-wreck that was the UN's 60th anniversary summit in September 2005. The UN emerged from the summit with only the agreement to endorse the principle of the right to protect and a watered-down statement on terrorism as cold comfort. The global South reneged on the implicit grand bargain that had been carefully constructed during the middle months of 2005. Its leaders wanted free money from development aid promises and presumed added power from enlargement of the Security Council. They were not in the end willing to give the North what it wanted in the struggle with unconditional terrorists in particular. So they got neither. It was not the Americans or their allies who were the deal-breakers.

### The second assumption surfaced: about the inherent injustice of imperial rule

Is imperial rule inherently unjust so that an imperial peace can never meet minimum performance criteria for *jus in pace* after a war of conquest? Frankly, it would be surprising if it were a general rule, for imperial rule has been mankind's norm. The Melian dialogue remains its basic interpretative text. When, during the Peloponnesian Wars, the Athenians presented the Melians with the choice to submit and pay tribute or to be killed and enslaved, the Athenians observed to them that they should not take the situation personally. The powerful do what they wish, and the weak put up with what they must. It might feel bad, but that is just the way things were. The question is whether it actually *is* bad. The Athenians submitted that their rule was light and their tribute not unreasonable. Does this make a difference?

It is – of course – the case that disproportionality in hard and often of soft power, and the presence of armed force, is a defining characteristic of an imperial situation. But against that background gradient, history reveals a range of imperial situations. The historian of Empire, Anthony Low, captured the dynamic counterpoint of consent and legitimacy precisely, in an overarching spectrum.[6] Power runs from influence to sway to predominance to control. Influence is when the exercise of power is barely felt. Control is gun-boats and Maxim guns. He compared the power of the first two categories to that of a magician whose illusion is only fully successful if there is empathy between performer and audience. He may be armed, but force is in the deep background. The power of the last two lies in domination, founded increasingly upon the kinetic effect of the gun.

So if we apply performance criteria, the question of whether or not imperial rule is just rule will be seen to be a relative not an absolute judgement. It may well be a choice of greater and lesser evils. It depends, in short, upon the relationship between applied moral conditions and arrangements for the exercise of suzerain power. We must assess the motives of the suzerain by external criteria. While neither relationship is prescriptive, only indicative, as *jus ad bellum* conditions *jus in bello* so *jus ad pacem* conditions *jus in pace*. Cases can show suzerains' intention and the degree to which imperial power is accepted as legitimate by subjects. The balance of 'hard' and 'soft' power that is achievable in consequence of the interaction of the previous two criteria is then struck. As just noticed, we are only likely to find just peace in areas with much soft power, much magician's art. In particular, we should check these criteria against evidence in the present situation when, after an intermission of two generations, historically more usual service in power politics is being resumed.

---

[6] Anthony Low, *Lion Rampant: Essays in the Study of British Imperialism* (London: Cass, 1973), pp. 30–3.

That resumption is witnessed in several ways. In one, Kofi Annan placed the principle of the 'two sovereignties' firmly at the centre of the international stage, in now-celebrated words from his essay in *The Economist* of 18 September 1999:

> State sovereignty, in its most basic sense, is being redefined . . . States are now widely understood to be instruments at the service of their peoples and not vice versa. At the same time, individual sovereignty – by which I mean the fundamental freedom of each individual, enshrined in the Charter of the United Nations and subsequent international treaties – has been enhanced by a renewed and spreading consciousness of individual rights. When we read the Charter today, we are more than ever conscious that its aim is to protect individual human rights, not to protect those who abuse them.[7]

It was prompted by the rancorously contentious use of force by the international community to protect the Kosovar Albanians from the Milosevics' attack. Earlier that year, and under the same prompting, on 22 April in Chicago, Tony Blair had delivered an intellectually substantial speech on these matters. Blair recognised that there might well be a rising demand for humanitarian intervention and he wanted to establish a morally defensible filtering methodology by which to choose in which cases to act and in which not. He did this by coupling traditional just war criteria of right motive, of last resort, of feasibility, of discrimination and proportionality with the meliorative criterion (that after force has been employed the result should be better than after the best efforts of not using force) to a cosmopolitan criterion last widely current two hundred years ago, before the French Revolution. This states that saving strangers is integral to the safety of the realm. That innovation prefigured the much more extended investigation underpinning the norm of the responsibility to protect. It also sets a high and narrow threshold to justify breaching state sovereignty in defence of individual sovereignty.

Blair's Chicago speech and Annan's 'two sovereignties' can, if used dispassionately, be construed as the moral calibrators of a new exercise of liberal imperial power in which the strong and willing take actions on behalf of the weak and prostrate. Looking back to 1999 from 2005, the restorative effects of democratic opportunities have been remarkable. They have been displayed in the Balkans before and after Slobodan

---

[7] Kofi Annan, 'Two Sovereignties', *The Economist*, 18 September 1999, p. 8.

Milosevic departed to The Hague. In west Africa, a much smaller combined services strategic raid by 6,500 British armed forces saved Sierra Leone from another bout of amputations and massacres by the Revolutionary United Front. Operation Palliser is a classic example of a mode of warfare which has been described as 'war among the people'.[8] This is not a new sort of war – new wars were the industrial slaughterings of the European Civil War 1914–45. Effects-based operations are a modernised form of an old sort of war: in principle, a return to nineteenth-century imperial strategic raiding.[9]

The intoxicating political effects of a democratic chance were also displayed by Afghan women kicking down doors of closed polling booths in their eagerness to vote after the banishment of the Taliban. Then, in January 2005, 9 million Iraqis voted their views in fraught circumstances. Eye-witnesses, from the United Nations women's organisation, UNIFEM, reported the mobilising role of Muslim women in their previously oppressed societies. Early to the polls in the most insecure areas where insurgents were active, they returned home to fearful menfolk with their forefingers defiantly stained purple to prove that they had voted safely.

In both Afghanistan and Iraq, a technically brilliant employment of the psychological leading edge was made possible by modern military capability. Repugnant regimes were evicted with levels of casualties on both sides that were inconceivably lower, relative to the scale of the political outcome achieved, than could have occurred in the twentieth-century exercise of mass industrial military power. In the just war calculation, the more obnoxious, totalitarian and unreformable an enemy is, the clearer is *jus ad bellum* and the higher the butcher's bill that will be tolerated to remove that evil enemy under the principle of proportionality. The recent liberations score high marks in this grisly arithmetic.

But in each case, a glittering victory was sullied by various errors in the management of the immediate post-conflict situation. Nonetheless, in both cases, I believe that the evidence is straightforward on two counts: first, that these wars were conducted well within the *jus in bello* criteria – dramatically so in the Afghan case; second, that bungled short-term exploitation of victory by the liberators meant that they were only rescued

---

[8] Rupert Smith, *The Utility of Force: The Art of War in the Modern World* (London: Penguin/ Allan Lane, 2005), pp. 267–306.

[9] This argument is spelled out in Gwyn Prins, *The Heart of War: On Power, Conflict and Responsibility in the Twenty-First Century* (London: Routledge, 2002).

politically from spoiling the victory by the liberated peoples' own courage
and actions: the rescuers rescued by the rescued. So we must come next
to a judgement on the assumption of inherent injustice in episodes of
imperial peace.

The underlying reason why *jus in pace* was imperilled in these cases was
the deep American reluctance to recognise that it is an imperial actor.
Rather the illusion was entertained that America's job is to liberate and
then to depart. The reluctance is not hard to fathom. The birth of the
nation was, after all, the modern world's most carefully expressed withdrawal of consent from a sovereign by the people. The lesson – hard and
simple in Washington – is that in the face of the twenty-first century,
America has no choice about whether to be an imperial power or not. That
is prescribed by circumstance. The choice is between doing the job competently or incompetently. The arrangements for suzerain exercise of
power that offer the best chance to realise noble motives in peace building
after war are facilitated, firstly, by frank acknowledgement of the nature
of the mission. Secondly, historical experience shows that ideological
agenda, openly driven, are brittle and usually shatter; often in violence.
The better road to take is the indirect one; and there is an ample stock of
past experience upon which to draw for guidance in that purpose.[10]

New recruits in the generation of officers in the Indian Civil Service
who entered service during the last quarter of the nineteenth century were
taught one central lesson by the preceding cohort: do not push the natives
too far. From the meticulous micro-historical researches of Eric Stokes
and the Cambridge School of Indianists, we now know that the Indian
Mutiny of 1857 was neither a proto-nationalist uprising against British
rule, nor a millenarian yearning for the return of Mughal rule; nor was
it really a mutiny. It was, in fact, a more broadly based social protest
driven by resentment in poorer regions at perceived relative deprivation.
Uprisings flared, for example, among Jats in lightly taxed areas where the
British had not extended drainage and irrigation systems, adjacent
to those where British rule weighed heavier, where they had.[11] But to
contemporary imperial eyes, those primarily to blame for the chaos were

---

[10] E.g. Kimberly Marten, *Enforcing the Peace: Learning from the Imperial Past* (New York: Columbia
University Press, 2004) although coming to rather different conclusions from mine.

[11] Eric Stokes, *The Peasant and the Raj: Studies in Agrarian Society and Peasant Rebellion*
(Cambridge: Cambridge University Press, 1978).

enthusiasts. The ending of the Napoleonic Wars was followed by waves of evangelical Protestant missionaries fanning out from Britain and from Europe across the imperial world. In India, as is famously known, military chaplains tried to convert sepoys to Christianity; and that, contemporaries believed, had been the cardinal mistake.

Therefore when Frederick (later Lord) Lugard transferred from India to Northern Nigeria, he prepared political memoranda to guide colonial officers in the first years of the new century, published first in 1906 with a further edition in 1919, incorporating the lessons of the skeleton staffing of the wartime years.[12] Lugard's advice was to go with, not against the grain: to learn the language and the culture of those to be ruled; to identify natural leaders and make them allies; to keep the aura of the magician by using force as little as possible, but then to act decisively; and not to forget the awful lesson of the Indian Mutiny. Indirect rule was philosophically opposed to the alternative approach of cultural assimilation within overseas regions of the motherland, in francophone west Africa. In stratified British colonial Africa, no one pretended to be other than who they were.

Which is the greater and which the lesser evil? The balance sheet of indirect rule carries in one column the Melian fact of imposed rule. In the other stand the achievements of colonial medicine in raised life expectancy, the amelioration of mass famine by the application of the Indian Famine Codes and the absence of major famine for sixty years in Africa. By definition, imperial rule also banished civil war; and the last decade before Independence, during which the principles of the Colonial Development and Welfare Act of 1940 were in effect – manifestly a statement of right intention at the height of the Battle of Britain – gave rural British Africa its best period of settled and impartial government and administration in modern history. These were the produce of sway and influence and they yielded soft power. While it was hard to admit during the early decades of Independence, the Raj and the African Empire were shared, not imposed, social constructions even at a time when political power was exercised exclusively. Only now, when the erosion of the post-colonial Political Kingdom is so visibly extensive, does this valuable truth again dare to speak its name.

---

[12] Frederick Lugard, *Political Memoranda: Revision of Instructions to Political Officers on Subjects Chiefly Political and Administrative, 1913–18* (London: Cass, 1970).

Nor were the principles of indirect rule alien to Americans. What else was the rescue of defeated Europe under the Marshall Plan or the economic and political reconstruction of Japan after the atomic bombs? The just peace that was obtained in both cases from these investments was not the result of negotiated terms. General Lucius Clay in Germany and General MacArthur in Japan were pro-consuls and ruled as such.

The mistake of viewing a place and people in it initially through ideologically tinted spectacles was made by the Americans in Vietnam. That much is in common with the way that modern neo-conservatives have recently viewed the Middle East, although there the similarity ends. The difference was that in Vietnam, sufficient physical and destructive power was applied to convert the pre-existing reality – whatever it was – for a time into a crude imitation of what the Domino Theory said the Vietnamese should be. Unjustly fought war could not be converted into just peace within the gunman's frame of mind; only defeat of the invaders could do this, and, as a visit to Vietnam today confirms, has done so. And Vietnam is unhelpful to our present purpose for another reason. It was an episode in the twentieth century's Wars of Religion. It was not intended to be and was not cast in the same mould as the modern imperial humanitarian interventions. The mismanagement of the liberation of Iraq as a consequence of the neo-conservative preference for categories over process may prove to be as formative a lesson for the American imperial moment as the Indian Mutiny was for the British one.

I have sought to sketch how and where there are ways in which right intention can be translated into conducive arrangements for just peace after imperial war. I have suggested that a brilliantly achieved liberation is not a sufficient foundation for *jus in pace*. This requires an intelligent learning of and application of the lessons of indirect rule and an open acceptance of the nature of the commitment. However, this may be difficult to do because of American reluctance to accept the implications of an imperial mantle, against which so much in the American experience rebels.

The situation surrounding *jus ad bellum* in the case of the liberation of Iraq was once incandescently contested and confused and is still, if less so as the rescued peoples put facts on the ground. Insight is injured by the festering disagreements over motives. They persist because Mr Blair failed to argue consistently from the outset for action in Iraq in the terms of his Chicago speech, which were always available to him and probably were what he really believed. Instead he was persuaded to trifle with his electorate and to mistrust its capacity to think generously; so he sought to frighten it into support with the promise of real and present danger of attack rather than speaking of the moral duty that was redoubled (especially for the USA) by the betrayal of those who had answered Bush the Elder's call to rise in rebellion in 1991.

In each of the recent cases, starting with the Balkans and successively in case after case, opposition to the use of American-led force became louder and the constituencies expressing it, broader. This was especially true in Western Europe where the issue became inextricably Melian in nature, bound up with anger at and resentment of American power and hatred of George Bush Jr and his administration. At the time, I participated in a debate at the LSE with students opposed to the use of force in Iraq and was sobered to realise that most viewed George Bush as a greater threat to world peace than Saddam Hussein. Quiet discussion of the best interests of Iraqis, informed by Iraqis, has become virtually impossible.

However, in each of these uses of American-led force, it is now increasingly hard for critics to argue that the key relative criteria of discrimination and proportionality *in bello* and the meliorative criterion *in pace* were not met, even if not yet definitively in Iraq. Nor can the demonstration effect in the wider Middle East be easily dismissed. It started with Colonel Gaddafi's decision to come inside the tent rather than to be pulled out of a hole like Saddam Hussein. Obviously there were many motives for his decision. The point is that it is reasonable to see this as one. Turning Gaddafi was probably the biggest boost to global security of the past decade. It broke open the A. Q. Khan nuclear network and gave pause for thought to other Muslim aspirants to nuclear weapons. It has had further ramifications outside the area, such as the financial destabilisation of Mugabe's clique in Zimbabwe of which Gaddafi had been a key guarantor. It remains to be seen whether President Ahmadinejad's Iranian ambitions to obtain nuclear weapons can be deterred or will have to be pre-empted by force; but the deterrent threat to his regime owes an important (if unquantifiable) element of its credibility to the past record. The point at issue is that the purpose of major intervention is not to do more of them, but fewer. The pattern of recent history shows why and with what effect.

With all their many and deep imperfections in recent execution, the string of modern imperial wars of liberation has opened the way to possibilities of just peace. They have displayed a pattern of arrangement for suzerain power that can give effect to noble intentions and that has worked. They were lesser evils which have provided the basis for the subsequent construction of public good. Equally they have suggested what not to do.

## The third assumption surfaced: about the restoration of community

If a war has been entered for just reasons and has been conducted justly, with the amazing lightness of casualties relative to ends that modern techniques now permit and produce, how do victors on the battlefield use their just victories to promote the international common good? Victors, after all, take the spoils. They have won the right to dictate terms. In uncontroversially just wars, such as that against fascism or, by contemporary extension, that against unconditional jihadist terrorists, the moral nature of the *jus ad bellum* case combines with overwhelming social assent and total war effort to require that terms are dictated unconditionally. Because the defeat of Hitler was a victory of one community over another, was it rendered unjust for that reason? I think not.

If the victors believe in the Universal Declaration of Human Rights, plainly *jus in pace* is established by insisting upon that particularistic agenda, and any facilitating political arrangements. The defeated party has to mend its ways and rise to the victor's standards. This is what happened in Germany and Japan. Terms were initially imposed but quickly led to the creation of a new and morally superior form of community of values, both domestically and internationally, which in turn assisted the emergence of a stronger West. As a previous German foreign minister, Joschka Fischer, once observed, the two parents of modern Germany were Hitler and the Americans.

We have already seen how a botched immediate post-conflict situation can imperil the fruits of a justly fought war to the point where the rescued have to rescue their liberators. The Vietnam case showed what the gunman's mentality could not do. Now Walzer's other type of case must be reviewed. Can the effects of unjustly fought wars ever be corrected by just peace? In the recent Iraq War, the American army had to reconstruct itself physically and psychologically in the course of the operations because the army which entered the campaign was not designed for its later demands.

Just the same thing had happened to British imperial forces built on the template of the Cardwell military reforms, after 1899. The Boer War, Kipling observed, taught the British 'no end of a lesson'. The forces with which Redvers Buller landed at Cape Town on 31 October went through the wringer of the battles in Natal leading to the relief of the siege of Ladysmith – notably that at Colenso on 15 December which prefigured in miniature the new warfare of trenches soon to be scaled-up on the Somme. The red coats had already been replaced with khaki after the Zulu Wars of 1879; now the close order infantry columns and heavy horse artillery were replaced with Kitchener's counter-guerrilla block-houses, stop lines and drives of 1901–2, accompanied by the segregation, suffering and death from disease of Boer women and children in concentration camps. On 7 August 1901, Kitchener amplified his explicit rejection of discrimination and proportionality in the conduct of his campaign. He declared that any Boer leaders found fighting after 15 September would be banished. Food stockpiles were deliberately destroyed.

Indiscriminate war had its effect within six months. The Boer leaders, pressured by Generals Botha and Jan Smuts, signed the Peace of Vereeniging on 31 May 1902. But the terms invited re-engagement. While the Boer republics were abolished, Kitchener's terms included amnesty, financial help for reconstruction and the prospect of (white) self-government, which came in 1906. (What it did not include, of course, was any element of black liberation.) The British strategic aim was Sun Tzu's: to give the enemy a golden bridge across which to withdraw and to identify allies among former enemies. The example is given to illustrate process only. Jan Smuts moved from being a guerrilla leader to being a member of the Imperial General Staff, who drafted the concept paper for the creation of the Royal Air Force, within twenty years. The lesson appears to be that the rebuilding of community is undermined if the offer is made too early.

A remorseless war like Kitchener's follows a different moral logic from that of just war theory. It is the logic of General Sherman in his letter to General Hood, demanding the evacuation of Atlanta. He justified applying the maximum horror in the hell of war, the more quickly to end it. He also explicitly shifted all moral responsibility for his actions onto the shoulders of 'you who, in the midst of peace and prosperity, have plunged a nation into war'. That is a moral argument in war. The Boer War example taken here is offered for its practical evidence of a route back from conflict to community, though a generous settlement in the making of the peace. And whose decisions drove that?

## The fourth assumption surfaced: about unilateral action

The final assumption is often encountered and is of the least consequence. Are moral judgements in these cases best keyed by identification of the 'unilateralist' or 'multilateralist' character of actors' actions? Not at all. This would be a facile category mistake, using a lower-order categoriser inappropriately, for grounds earlier rehearsed. Furthermore it shackles the argument hostage to accuracy in description of specific circumstances. Although this argument is extensively ventilated, there is little point or need in rehearsing much more in refutation; for the point just made is sufficient.

Recent events provide a case in point. The assertion is commonly made among critics of recent uses of American power, that it has been politically, intentionally, even truculently 'unilateralist' and, therefore, implicitly bad because in breach of the criterion of consensuality. In fact the negotiating history of the Iraq UNSC resolution (1441) does not support the widely canvassed opinion that the coalition did not seek a competent mandate.[13] A slogan repeated does not thereby become a statement grounded in evidence. What American action has reaffirmed since 9/11 are the three truths demonstrated during the closing phase of the Cold War – that a 'unilateralist' lead is the most efficient stimulant to 'multilateralist' response, that an ounce of prevention is worth a pound of cure and that selfishly motivated co-operation is the most efficient. The situation with unilateralism and the pursuit of just peace is therefore close to the reverse of this assumption.

These truths were well digested by Kofi Annan's High-Level Panel of December 2004. Its central proposals of a Peace-building Commission, sustained by a Peace-building Support Office in the Secretariat – fragments of which may come about despite the loss of all the other main proposals of the Panel – were predicated upon recognition that the responsibility to protect is indivisible. Chapter VII mandates must henceforth contain a

---

[13] Margaret Crahan, John Goering and Thomas G. Weiss (eds.), *Wars on Terrorism and Iraq: The US and the World* (London: Routledge, 2004).

full spectrum of intention and of promised funding: from initial opposed military intervention to withdrawal after successful reanimation of humane political and civil society according to the basic universal values. That is a practical expression of my underlying argument that the relationship of *jus ad pacem* and *in pace* is reflexively linked to just conduct and, differently, to just cause. Can these return the world's principal – and probably last – formal multilateral political forum to utility in constructing *jus in pace* in a world order that, fortunately for just war criteria, is currently conducted by the forces of liberal capitalism and the values of the US Declaration of Independence? Time will tell. The disappointment of the 2005 summit was very grave, but the case is not yet hopeless. In fact, just as with roses, hard pruning back to a viable core in all the mid-twentieth-century multilateral institutions may look drastic at the time but is essential to stimulate new growth that is not sappy and over-extended.

## Conclusion

This chapter has argued against the tide of much left-wing and soft liberal opinion in the West today which swirls and eddies around the issue of just war and just peace in Melian resentment of American power and action. In conclusion I wish to insist upon the superior liberal credentials – liberal in the strict sense of a respect for freedom and the rights of the individual, not in the colloquial sense – of the case advanced above.

The four submerged assumptions which anchor the popular case have all been found to be defective. Structural criteria have been found to be brittle and unilluminating. A process criterion has been proposed to have better success. Contrary to the reflex assumption of the illegitimacy of imperial rule, a case has been made to defend both the morality and the efficacy of modern liberal imperial power in which the strong and willing take actions on behalf of the weak and prostrate. This can be a lesser evil as a basis for the construction of public good in the same way that formal imperial rule historically underpinned much that secured life and the pursuit of happiness for colonised peoples at the cost of constraints on degrees of liberty. Neither the assumption about the importance of consensuality, nor the utility of a unilateral/multilateral distinction, were found to bear much weight. Both were remnants from a superannuated set of criteria formed in the 1960s. Ways were illustrated of how a just war botched by an incompetent post-conflict settlement might be saved, and of how just peace building might rectify – indeed might complement – the effects of a Shermanite conduct of war.

The case advanced here is presented as an exercise in applied cosmo-politanism, giving grip to principles of universal human rights and a privileging of the sovereignty of the individual in dynamic tension with that of the state. It follows that the state becomes more conditional upon its performance which is measured against criteria that may well be external to its own values. It has been suggested that only such tough-minded criteria can bear the strain that ethics in an age of global terrorism will apply. Only if that line can be held can toleration – which is not the same as saying that anything goes – be preserved; and that in turn is prerequisite to the legitimation of suzerain power after war. But legitima-tion is no structural 'given'. It has to prove itself again each new day.

# 14

## From just war to just peace

MARY KALDOR

In one of its modes, just war theory would also abolish war by the (theoretically) simple method of calling unjust wars 'crimes' and just wars 'police actions'. We have here a nice example of what the Chinese call 'the rectification of names', but it presupposes in practice a thoroughgoing transformation of international society.[1]

In this essay, I argue that just such a thoroughgoing transformation in international society is taking place even though it does not amount to the establishment of a global state, which is what Walzer implied. Just war theory is difficult to apply in the context of those changes we lump together under the rubric of globalisation. A new ethical approach is needed, and one that is grounded in the notion that the rights of individuals supersede the rights of states and that, therefore, international law that applies to individuals overrides the laws of war. In other words, *jus in pace* cannot be suspended in wartime in favour of *jus ad bellum* or *jus in bello*.

There is still a role for legitimate military force, but the way it is used is more akin to domestic law enforcement than war fighting. I use the term 'human security' to refer to the defence of individuals as opposed to 'state security'. Of course, some of the just war principles are relevant to law enforcement, as is much of the content of humanitarian law, but a change in the language is important. Just war theory does offer a framework for thinking about the justifiable use of force, but that is different from a 'just' war. In particular, crucial differences with just war theory are the reconceptualisation of aggression as a gross violation of human rights, the shift in the authorisation of force from the nation-state to a multilateral set of arrangements, and a rejection of notions like 'collateral damage', 'proportionality', 'double effect' or 'unintentionality'.

[1] Michael Walzer, *Just and Unjust Wars: A Moral Argument with Historical Illustrations* (New York: Basic Books, 1977), p. xxii.

## The global context

'Globalisation' refers to many different phenomena. Nevertheless, its widespread use reflects an awareness of some kind of fundamental change in world order, with specific consequences for the character of state sovereignty. The most common factor that helps to explain these different phenomena is technology, especially but not only the spread of communications and information technology. In what follows, I describe various elements of this fundamental change we call globalisation, with particular emphasis on the implications for state sovereignty.

### Human consciousness, human rights, and democracy

One interpretation of globalisation is that we have become conscious of a single human community. Immanuel Kant's argument, made in 1795, that the world community has shrunk to the point where 'a right violated in one part of the world is felt everywhere' is becoming a reality. This growing human consciousness is reflected in the development of human rights and norms in the period since the end of the Second World War. The 1948 Declaration on Human Rights and the various Covenants and, more recently, the Tribunals for the former Yugoslavia and Rwanda and the establishment of the International Criminal Court have created a body of international law that applies to individuals and not states. This law has been strengthened by an emerging human rights lobby, composed of civil society groups and sympathetic governments. Growing global consciousness means that it is harder to sustain closed authoritarian states. Even in Saddam Hussein's Iraq, there were subversive bloggers and underground opposition groups with links to the outside world. The so-called third wave of democratisation in Latin America, Africa, Asia and Eastern Europe was, it can be argued, an outcome of globalisation – the links that were made between opposition groups and the outside world and the recourse to international human rights law. We seem to be on the brink of a fourth wave, with civil society revolutions of various colours in Serbia, Georgia, Ukraine and Kyrgyzstan, and pressures for democratisation elsewhere especially in the Middle East. These developments imply that state sovereignty is increasingly 'conditional' – dependent both on domestic behaviour and on the consent of the outside world.

## Travel and migration

The last decades of the twentieth century witnessed a new wave of migration. Because of the ease of communication and travel, however, the new migrants, unlike the great waves of migration at the end of the nineteenth century, remain in touch with their homeland. The notion of a diaspora, which earlier applied only to the Jews, has become widespread. The emergence of transnational communities based on ethnicities and religion has implications for state sovereignty since the notion of a vertically organised, territorially based community congruent to the state is greatly weakened. It is often argued that the cohesion of states depends on the idea of the 'other' – what Carl Schmitt called the friend–enemy distinction.[2] Yet nowadays, citizens have multiple loyalties: to the state, to their community – which may no longer be congruent with the state. Friend–enemy distinctions, as between Israel and Palestine or Serbia and Croatia, are often reproduced within the global cities of the advanced industrial world.

## Interconnectedness

In the social sciences, globalisation is often defined as interconnectedness in all fields – economic, political, cultural and social. Decisions that affect everyday lives are often taken far away by multinational corporations and international institutions. Some authors talk about a 'hollow state' in which civil servants are more often in communication with their counterparts in other countries than their domestic constituencies. The task of political leaders is less to rule than to manage complex relationships with international institutions, other states, international companies and NGOs, as well as domestic interests and the wider public. In extreme cases, the difficulty of reconciling all these pressures leads to state failure or collapse. Today's risks or threats are less likely to come from authoritarian states but from failing states, although the latter are usually a combination of authoritarianism and state failure.

## The changing character of warfare

In the twentieth century, military technology became more destructive, more accurate and more widely available. Symmetric war, war between

---

[2]  Carl Schmitt, *The Concept of the Political* (Chicago: University of Chicago Press, 1990), p. 33.

two similarly armed opponents, has simply become too destructive to be fought. The destructiveness of symmetric warfare does not, of course, mean an end to war. But the new types of war are asymmetric, that is to say violence is primarily directed against unarmed and unprotected civilians rather than against other warring parties; in other words, the increasing use of terror. What I call 'new wars' are wars that have evolved from guerrilla warfare and 'low-intensity wars' as ways of getting around concentrations of conventional force. The warring parties try to control territory politically through fear rather than through militarily attacking an enemy. These wars involve a mixture of warfare (political violence), human rights violations and violations of the laws of war (violence against non-combatants, genocide, massacres, torture and atrocities, mass rape) and ordinary crime (loot, pillage, smuggling and other illegal forms of war finance). They involve state and non-state actors and they blur classic distinctions between combatant and non-combatant, competent political authority and lack of authority, international and external. George Weigel argues earlier in this book that advanced military technology is capable of much greater precision than ever before, so that wars can be more proportionate and discriminate. It is true that contemporary wars that make use of precision weapons greatly reduce collateral damage in comparison with the wars of the twentieth century. Nevertheless, as I shall argue below, such damage is often relatively high from the perspective of human rights partly because of the difficulty of distinguishing between combatants and non-combatants.

### Global governance

These combined changes can be said to amount to a 'thoroughgoing transformation of international society'. States remain the juridical repository of sovereignty; international institutions derive their legal foundation from treaties agreed among states. But in practice, states are hemmed in by a system of global governance, in which they remain key actors, but along with international institutions, regional organisations like the European Union or the African Union, transnational corporations, NGOs and civil society and even individuals. Their capacity to act as autonomous agents is greatly circumscribed and, in particular, the recourse to war as an instrument of policy is now prohibited. A system of global governance is not the same as a 'global state with a monopoly on the legitimate use of force' and indeed, such a state is probably not desirable since it would have great potential for tyranny.[3] But it is quite different from a world where states act as individuals pursuing their national interests to which just war theory, at least in its Westphalian guise, is supposed to apply. Walzer says that the rights of states derive from the social contract within states in which individual rights are transmuted into state rights in exchange for protection against external encroachment and life and liberty at home. The Great Divide, as it is known in International Relations literature, between the domestic civil society peopled by individuals, norms, law and politics and an external state of nature peopled by states that pursue their self-interest, is an expression of this conception of the rights of states. The social contract within states is being increasingly supplemented by a social contract at a global level. Rules and laws that apply to individuals, as well as to states, are being negotiated among the family of individuals, groups and institutions that constitute what we call global governance. It is possible now to talk about a blurring of the distinction between inside and outside, domestic and external. The Great Divide has not disappeared but it is no longer so clear-cut. The inside can no longer be insulated from an outside of terror, organised crime or ethnic and religious conflict. The outside is increasingly a world where individual as well as state rights apply and where states no longer have the same autonomy to pursue their interests. This is the context in which to rethink the applicability of the precepts of just war.

## The awkwardness of just war

James der Derian uses the term 'virtuous war' to describe the combination of 'virtual war', that is war at long distance that we only experience through our television screens, and just war. He talks about the capacity of 'virtuous war' to 'commute death' not only to keep death out of sight but also to legitimate death.[4] There is a fine line between legitimate killing and murder, between soldiers as criminals and soldiers as heroes. Just war is about managing that fine line. This is why rules of warfare have always

---

[3] Michael Walzer, *Arguing about War* (New Haven: Yale University Press, 2004), p. xiv.
[4] James der Derian, *Virtuous War: Mapping the Military-Industrial-Media-Entertainment Network* (Boulder, CO: Westview Press, 2001).

been so important. But it also means that just war thinking can be used to legitimate war and evade responsibility rather than to elucidate what is permissible and what is not, especially in the case of long-distance wars. This argument applies to both branches of just war doctrine.

## Jus ad bellum

Nowadays, the most common cause for using military forces is human-itarian intervention, which has been renamed by the United Nations Secretary-General's High-Level Panel on Threats, Challenges and Change as the 'responsibility to protect'.[5] This proposal, originating in the Canadian-sponsored International Commission on Intervention and Sovereignty, was debated by the United Nations Millennium Review Summit in September 2005. Yet in most contemporary accounts of just war theory, humanitarian intervention is an exception, a footnote in discussions of just cause. In the third edition of his seminal work on just war theory, Walzer says that this is the one 'large and momentous shift' that has taken place since he first wrote on this matter. 'The issues that I discussed under the name "interventions" which were peripheral to the main concerns of the book have moved dramatically to the centre ... [T]he chief dilemma of international politics is whether people in danger should be rescued by military forces from outside.'[6]

In the twentieth century and in most contemporary accounts of just war doctrine, just cause is seen as constituting self-defence in the event of external aggression. This follows from the prohibitions against war intro-duced as a result of the two world wars. It was not always so. St Augustine, the father of just war theory, was primarily concerned about restoration of the moral order. In Christian teachings on just war, the notion of neigh-bourly love, the protection of others, was an important element. War was necessary, according to St Augustine, in order to 'curb licentious passions by destroying those vices which should have been rooted out and sup-pressed by the rightful government'.[7] This 'punitive' concept of war overrides self-defence. For St Augustine, war can be authorised only by

---

[5]  *A More Secure World: Our Shared Responsibility*, United Nations, December 2004, A/59/56.

[6]  Michael Walzer, *Just and Unjust Wars, A Moral Argument with Historical Illustrations*, 3rd edn (New York, Basic Books, 2000), p. xii.

[7]  Quoted in John Langan, 'The Elements of St Augustine's Just War Theory', *Journal of Religious Ethics* 12/1 (1984): 19–38.

a public authority for public purposes – it is about the protection of others. Obedience to a rightful authority is central to his thinking, and individuals, even if they reject temporal rulings, have no right to resist.

Following St Augustine, medieval scholars, particularly Aquinas, viewed just cause as righting an injury or a fault caused by others. Just war was distinguished from holy war, in that it was authorised by secular authorities and recognised certain *in bello* restraints. Holy war, by contrast, could be authorised by religious authorities and could be waged against non-Christians. In the transition to modernity, scholars like Vitoria and Grotius were responsible for the 'dethroning of religion'. Following the Treaty of Westphalia, war came to be regarded 'as a means – and a highly imperfect one at that – of settling disputes between two sovereigns who recognised no common judge'.[8] The total wars of the twentieth century, however, called into question the legitimacy of reasons of state, with the result that the current international consensus holds that only wars of self-defence are legitimate.

So strong is the insistence that self-defence is the only just cause and that the principle of non-intervention should not be violated, that many interventions actually undertaken for humanitarian purposes have been forced into the straitjacket of self-defence. But in a world where the difference between internal and external and between state and non-state is blurred, what is the difference between aggression and humanitarian catastrophe? In theory, one is an attack by a foreign state and the other is inflicted on a people by their own state or non-state actors. But in 'new wars', where states are disintegrating and where the warring parties involve paramilitary groups, foreign mercenaries, Mujahadeen and the like, this distinction is more difficult to apply.

The war in Bosnia Herzegovina well illustrates these dilemmas. The war was fought by a combination of remnants of the Yugoslav army and territorial defence forces and paramilitary groups composed of local and foreign volunteers, both criminal and fanatic. Those who favoured international intervention claimed that this was a war of aggression by Serbia and Croatia against Bosnia Herzegovina. Those who were against intervention claimed that this was a civil war among Serbs, Croats and Muslims. Yet the case for intervention derived surely from the rights of

---

[8] François Bugnion, 'Just Wars, Wars of Aggression and International Humanitarian Law', *International Review of the Red Cross* 84 (2002): 523–46.

the victims. This was a war of ethnic cleansing, involving massacres, large-scale population displacement, detention camps and widespread atrocities including mass rape. Did it matter whether these violations of human rights were inflicted by Serbs from Serbia or Bosnian Serbs, by regular forces or paramilitary groups, or whether Bosnia Herzegovina was an independent state or part of Yugoslavia?

The attacks of 11 September 2005 represent an even more telling case. This was an act that 'shocked the conscience of mankind'. President Bush chose to define it as an act of aggression and drew the parallel with the Japanese attack on Pearl Harbor that brought the United States into the Second World War. By so doing, he used the phrase the 'war on terror' to justify the attacks on Afghanistan and Iraq. But this was not an attack by a foreign state. It was an attack by a group of individuals. Supposing the attack had been carried out by Christian fundamentalists like Timothy McVeigh, who attacked the Federal Building in Oklahoma, or Muslim fundamentalists who were also American citizens, could President Bush have declared war? As Michael Walzer explained in an op-ed article soon after September 11, 'the word "war" is unobjectionable as long as those who use it understand what a metaphor is.' But 'there is right now, no enemy state, no battlefield'.[9] What happened in Bosnia Herzegovina and on 11 September 2001 were humanitarian catastrophes. The attackers were criminals rather than enemies; they could have been any nationality. There might well be a case for military action in a foreign country to apprehend the criminals but the nature of that action would be different from war.

Why do terms matter? There are two key differences between war and humanitarian intervention. One has to do with right authority and the other concerns the way military force is used. In medieval times, *bellum*, the use of force for public ends, was distinguished from *duellum*, the use of force for private ends. Just war theory spelled out the criteria for justifying the use of force for public ends – the use of force for private ends was considered illegitimate. Only secular authorities, who knew no temporal superior, could declare war. Nowadays, it is national wars that are becoming illegitimate. National interest can be considered a sort of private interest as opposed to the global public interest. The important distinction, nowadays, is between the use of force for humanitarian ends and the use of force for national ends.

---

[9]  Michael Walzer, 'First, Define the Battlefield', *New York Times*, 21 September 2001, p. 8.

Both President Bush and Prime Minister Blair insist that their concern in Iraq is humanitarian rather than national. But if the concern is humanitarian, it cannot be authorised unilaterally by a government that represents a particular group of citizens; it requires some multilateral authority. Although Article 2.7 of the UN Charter allows states to unilaterally authorise the use of force in self-defence in the event of foreign aggression, all other uses of military force, including humanitarian intervention, can only be authorised by the UN Security Council under Chapter VII of the Charter. Undoubtedly, this needs to be augmented by a set of rules that allow for situations where the Security Council is blocked as a consequence of power politics, but the principle of multilateral authorisation for all uses of military force other than self-defence is critical.

## Jus in bello

The second difference between war and humanitarian intervention has to do with means. In the Middle Ages, a just war was one that was fought among European princes and other political authorities; it did not apply to internal violence or to wars against non-Christians such as the Crusades. James Turner Johnson describes several instances where internal rebellions were put down with great brutality, apparently with religious approval. Thus, for example, Luther approved of the suppression of the German peasant rebellion in the sixteenth century, on the grounds of right authority, even without restraint. Likewise, restraints that were practised in wars within Europe in the nineteenth century did not apply in colonial interventions, which were never described as wars, rather as rebellions, insurrections and so forth. Attempts by Francis Lieber, who drew up the code of behaviour to be observed by both sides in the American Civil War, to define 'guerrilla parties' and the notion of 'armed conflict', involving volunteer corps or paramilitary groups have been incorporated into international law. Nevertheless, the legal status of such groups is unclear within the framework of the Laws of War.

In most contemporary wars, the various warring parties have a nebulous status. They often do not fit the criteria, drawn up by Lieber and others, for being treated as a proto-state, a sort of legitimate authority in waiting. Nor should they. To treat rebels or terrorists as potential authorities or as legitimate enemies would confer on them an undesirable degree of legitimacy. On the other hand, to act without restraint and to ignore the

framework of international law can only exacerbate tension and undermine the legitimacy of actual authorities. 'Who will believe your cause
when your behaviours are so unjust?' wrote the French Calvinists in
relation to the Wars of Religion.[10]

This is why the language of law enforcement may be more appropriate
than the language of just war. Humanitarian intervention usually refers to
intervention in a foreign country to protect civilians. Often humanitarian
intervention is seen as war because it is the state that is responsible for
violations of human rights. But in situations where violations of human
rights are inflicted by both state and non-state actors, both domestic and
foreign, the term 'war' may not easily apply and it may be preferable to
treat the situation as akin to domestic disorder. Rather than treating this
kind of intervention as war, or allowing the rules to be lost in the murky
environment of peasant rebellions or colonial insurrections, it would be
better to extend domestic rules and apply a minimum human rights
framework. As Walzer writes: 'Humanitarian intervention comes closer
than any other kind of intervention to what we commonly regard, in
domestic society, as law enforcement and police work.'[11] The task in all
these cases is the protection of civilians and the arrest of criminals rather
than the defeat of enemy states.

The difficulties of applying the principles of *jus in bello* arise from this
blurring of the difference between internal and external or friend and
enemy, and between state and non-state, combatant and non-combatant.
The central assumption underlying *jus in bello* is the immunity of non-
combatants or combatants who are wounded or taken prisoner. They
should be spared, where possible, the effects of war. Nowadays, it is
often argued that the notion of non-combatant immunity reflects an
assumption about the equality of human beings and a notion of respect
for enemy populations that earlier only applied within Europe. However,
the very concept of war implies a friend–enemy distinction in which
enemy lives are less valuable than the lives of our own side. This contradiction between the friend–enemy distinction and respect for non-
combatant immunity is expressed in different concepts variously known
as 'proportionality', 'double effect' and, in contemporary jargon, 'collateral

---

[10] James Turner Johnson, *Just War Tradition and the Restraint of War: A Moral and Historical Enquiry* (Princeton, NJ: Princeton University Press, 1981), p. 234.
[11] Walzer, *Just and Unjust Wars*, p. 106.

damage'. These concepts hold that killing or harming enemy civilians can be justifiable if it is a side effect of an attack on a military target, which is necessary in order to win the war, if it is unintentional and if the harm done is proportional to the harm that might be done if victory was not achieved.

The concepts of 'necessity' and 'proportionality' are, of course, notoriously hard to define and allow for considerable leeway. If, as the Bush administration claims, the recent wars in Afghanistan or Iraq are designed to prevent a terrorist from releasing a hideous weapon of mass destruction in a Western city, for instance, surely no amount of destruction would be permissible? But leaving aside, for the moment, the problem of definition, what these concepts effectively do is to create a hierarchy of lives. Of course, all of us do have an implicit hierarchy of lives although nowadays, this hierarchy is not necessarily defined in territorial terms. Our communities, to whom we feel loyal, may cross borders and be defined in terms of family, ethnicity, religion, class or politics.

There is no question that contemporary armies try to use new weapon technology to minimise civilian casualties. By historical standards, 'collateral damage' in Kosovo, Afghanistan or Iraq has been relatively low, but what is low by the standards of war is high by the standards of human rights. In Iraq, the best estimate of civilian casualties both during and after the invasion up to November 2004 is probably at least 24,000, of which the majority was the consequence of American attacks. This estimate is based on the figures provided in a careful study reported in the British medical journal the *Lancet*.[12] The problem is the changing perception of war. What appears to the USA as relatively low collateral damage in a just war can equally be presented as large-scale human rights violations. From the point of view of the victims, does it make any difference whether they were killed in a war or as a result of repression, or whether the killing was intentional or unintentional?

The high civilian casualty figures in Iraq underscore the difficulty nowadays of distinguishing combatants and non-combatants. When insurgents hide in cities, how is it possible to attack them without killing civilians? The American attacks on Fallujah resulted in 150,000 displaced

---

[12] Les Roberts, Riyadh Lafta, Richard Garfield, Jamal Khudhairi and Gilbert Burnham, 'Mortality before and after the 2003 Invasion of Iraq: Cluster Sample Survey', *Lancet* 364/9448 (29 October 2004): 1857–64, http://image.thelancet.com/extras/04art10342web.pdf.

persons as well as large numbers (unknown) of civilian casualties. The difficulty of distinguishing combatants from non-combatants was the central problem the United States faced in Vietnam. Walzer makes the case that where it is not possible to distinguish civilians from combatants, *jus in bello* and *jus ad bellum* come together and the war should not even be fought.

> The war cannot be won and it should not be won. It cannot be won because the only available strategy involves a war against civilians, because the degree of civilian support that rules out alternative strategies also makes the guerrillas the legitimate rulers of the country. The struggle against them is an unjust struggle as well as one that can only be carried on unjustly. Fought by foreigners, it is a war of aggression; if by a local regime alone, it is an act of tyranny.[13]

But this difficulty, of distinguishing combatants and non-combatants, is characteristic of most 'new wars'. Does that not call into question whether we can even continue to talk about just war?

## Just peace

The blurring of the distinction between external and internal, state and non-state, combatant and non-combatant also implies the blurring of the distinction between war and peace. 'New wars' do not have decisive beginnings or endings. Nor are they clearly delineated in geographical space; they spread through refugees and displaced persons, organised crime, diaspora groups and so on. The growing body of human rights law cannot be suspended in wartime in the way that domestic laws, which apply to individual rights, have often been disregarded in the name of national security. That is why it is so important to develop the concept of 'just peace' and its concomitant, the Laws of Peace, which apply at an international level.[14] Anthony Burke proposes a system of ethical peace that declares the '*illegality*' of avoidable harm'.[15]

---

[13] Walzer, *Just and Unjust Wars*, p. 196.

[14] Christine Chinkin, 'An International Law Framework for a European Security Strategy', in Marlies Glasius and Mary Kaldor (eds.), *A Human Security Doctrine for Europe: Project; Principles; Practicalities* (Oxford: Routledge, forthcoming).

[15] Anthony Burke, 'Just War or Ethical Peace? Moral Discourses of Strategic Violence After 9/11', *International Affairs* 80 (2004): 239–353.

There is a role in such a framework for the use of military force, but the principles of legitimacy derive from individual rights rather than the rights of states. This is why I favour the term 'human security'. The term was first coined in the 1994 *Human Development Report* published by the United Nations Development Programme (UNDP) and has since been elaborated in a commission chaired by Sadako Ogata and Amartya Sen.[16] The concept has been promoted by the Canadian Government, which has established a network of governments that favour the concept. Human security combines human rights and human development, both freedom from fear and freedom from want. In much of the literature on human security, the emphasis is placed on 'freedom from want', but in what follows I emphasise 'freedom from fear' and the role that military forces might play in human-security operations.

## Towards an understanding of human security

In a system of just peace, military forces are, of course, under the control of competent authorities, at present states. States remain the only author-ities capable of upholding the legitimate use of force, but their use of force is much more circumscribed than earlier by international rules and norms. The legitimate use of military force by states would need to be approved by the United Nations or to conform to a clear set of criteria that are agreed internationally. A set of criteria has been defined by the United Nations High-Level Panel under the rubric of 'responsibility to protect'. These are drawn from just war approaches and cover the criteria for right authority, in particular the right to intervene in cases of large-scale loss of life and/or large-scale 'ethnic cleansing' and the importance of multi-lateral authorisation. However, they would need to be supplemented by more elaborated criteria for the ways in which force should be applied, which distinguish the methods to be adopted for the protection of indi-viduals from war-fighting methods. If such criteria were to be elaborated and adopted, then this would cover the case of external aggression. Instead of making human rights fit rather uneasily within the just war framework, aggression can be fitted into the 'responsibility to protect'. Aggression is not just against a state, but against the individual citizens that compose

---

[16] Sadako Ogata *et al.*, *Human Security Now: Final Report of the Commission on Human Security* (New York: United Nations Publications, 2003).

the state. States can use military force under the auspices of the United Nations, within a multilateral framework and according to criteria that have been agreed. It is to be used for the protection of civilians in conjunction with international police forces and civilian experts; indeed, in the future human-security forces may combine military, police and civil elements and operate rather differently from traditional armies.[17]

Using military forces in a human-security role is thus quite different from either classic war fighting or peace-keeping. Both types of operation are defined in terms of a war between collective enemies. The job of peace-keepers is to separate warring parties, monitor cease-fires or collect weapons; in the past, peace-keepers have often been unable to prevent violations of human rights. The job of war fighting is about defeating enemies and even though counter-insurgency operations sometimes adopted a 'hearts and minds' approach, the task of protecting civilians is secondary to the task of defeating the enemy. The gap in recent operations has been public security; thus the NATO operation in Kosovo failed to prevent ethnic cleansing first of Albanians and then of Serbs, even though it did succeed in liberating Kosovo and enabling the Albanians to return to their homes. The 2003 Iraq War failed to prevent looting as well as widespread human rights violations. How this is to be achieved has received much less attention than the circumstances in which military means might be used. It is as though the use of military force were a black box to be applied as a neutral instrument.

Three principles demonstrate the difference between a *human-security* and a *jus in bello* approach. First, the primary task of human-security operations is the protection of civilians. Killing is never permissible except in self-defence or to save a third party. Thus the killing of an aggressor is permissible only if it is necessary to save civilian lives. Of course, it could be argued that this also allows for war-fighting actions that may risk civilian lives. However, there is a difference between active protection and war fighting. In 'new wars', the warring parties do try to avoid battle because the growing symmetry of military technology makes the outcome dangerous and uncertain. One should not, of course, dismiss the risk of escalation or of an unconstrained extension of violence; in the confusion and emotion surrounding all wars, warring parties do not behave as

---

[17] *A Human Security Doctrine for Europe: Report of the Barcelona Study Group on Europe's Security Capabilities* (Barcelona: Study Group on Europe's Security Capabilities, 15 September 2003).

expected and an extremist logic often takes over. But the starting point, in ethical and operational terms, is protection rather than defeat of an enemy.

Second, protection can be achieved through stabilisation rather than victory. If the aim is public security then this can only be done through the establishment of legitimate political authority. The rule of law and a well-functioning system of justice are essential to guarantee the safety of individuals and communities. Legitimate political authority does not necessarily need to mean a state, it could consist of local government or regional or international political arrangements like trusteeships, protectorates or transitional administrations. Since state failure is often the primary cause of conflict, the reasons for state failure have to be taken into account in reconstructing legitimate political authority.[18]

A legitimate political authority can only be established on the basis of a political process recognised as legitimate by the local population. The local support and consent for human-security missions is critical to their success. It also means that the role of the military in a human-security operation is, therefore, to stabilise the situation so that space can be created for a political process. This is more important than winning through military means. Of course, it can be argued that military victory is an effective method of stabilisation. But, in some cases, military victory may simply be beyond reach – every excessive use of force further inflames the situation. In other cases, short-term military victory can be achieved but the cost, in terms of both casualties and political legitimacy, is too high. Military victory may mean that stability can be sustained only through massive repression and coercion.

Third, those who violate human rights are individual criminals rather than collective enemies. Human-security forces are responsible for arresting criminals and bringing them to justice. Thus British forces operating in Sierra Leone chose to arrest members of the 'West Side Boys' engaged in looting and pillaging a village rather than engaging them in a fire-fight. This greatly diminished their stature and correspondingly raised the credibility of the British forces. This approach is not, of course, easy; there is often a tension between what counts as political and what counts as criminal. In some cases, it is important to outlaw those who have

---

[18] See Herbert Wulf, 'The Challenges of Re-establishing a Public Monopoly of Violence', in Glasius and Kaldor, *A Human Security Doctrine for Europe.*

committed terrible crimes in order to establish a legitimate political process. This is the case in the former Yugoslavia, where, in principle, excluding indicted criminals creates space for more moderate politics.

## Northern Ireland – a case study in human security

The experience of the British Army in Northern Ireland could be considered a good model for human-security operations. It also illustrates some of the difficulties. Northern Ireland was a learning process for the British Government because it was effectively a 'new war' on British territory. When the army was first deployed in Northern Ireland in 1969, the difference between Aden and Northern Ireland, or between 'Borneo and Belfast' as one soldier put it, was not sufficiently appreciated. The army relied heavily on the existing civil authority, which was itself a party to the conflict; it failed to protect the nationalist community from house burnings and expulsions, which stimulated the militarisation of the IRA; it used interrogation and intelligence techniques developed in colonial wars, later ruled illegitimate by the European Court of Human Rights; and it used excessive force, most notoriously in breaking up IRA-established 'No-Go' areas.[19] Between 1969 and 1974, the bloodiest period of the conflict, some 188 people were killed by security forces and 65 per cent of the deaths were unarmed civilians.[20]

The failure to maintain peace and security led to a new policy known as 'normalisation', 'criminalisation' or Ulsterisation. The emphasis was placed on police primacy in dealing with insurgents. Captured terrorists were to be tried and given the same status in prison as ordinary criminals. The job of the armed forces was to support the police. Army bases were often co-located with police stations, which allowed proper sharing of information and joint tactical planning. This approach lasted until the Good Friday Agreement, in April 1997, which largely ended the violence. This approach succeeded in containing violence – over the period as a whole, 1969–1997, some 4,000 people were killed, 350 by security forces.

This strategy had its weaknesses. There was never a clear legal framework, and the procedures used to deal with captured insurgents

---

[19] Peter Pringle and Philip Jacobson (eds.), *Those Are Real Bullets, Aren't They?* (London: Fourth Estate, 2000).

[20] Fionnuala Ní Aoláin, *The Politics of Force: Conflict Management and State Violence in Northern Ireland* (Belfast: Blackstaff Press, 2000).

represented a considerable modification of normal law. The notorious 'Diplock' Courts did away with juries and allowed confessional-based evidence, which accounted for the majority of convictions. The IRA always insisted that they were political rather than criminal, and the hunger-strikes in 1981 to achieve political status in prison mobilised considerable political support for the IRA. The authorities themselves were often ambiguous using 'war' arguments when needed to justify certain actions. Moreover, in the 1980s, undercover operations by the SAS and other special forces led to the killing of many IRA activists. It is sometimes argued that this strategy of attrition did lead to a situation where neither side could win and a recognition that a political agreement was the solution. But it is also the case that this behaviour contributed to the polarisation of Northern Irish society so that the extremist groups on both sides became the dominant political forces.

What made Northern Ireland different was the fact that the conflict took place on British territory. Bombing Belfast was not an option. It could be also argued that the different response of American authorities to the Oklahoma bombing as opposed to 9/11 can be explained partly by the fact that this was a domestic rather than an international incident. The assumption, however, that underlies a 'just peace' is that it is no longer possible, or relevant from the point of view of the victims, to distinguish between foreigners and citizens or between the domestic and the international. Although the state has primary responsibility for dealing with domestic violence, there are external situations, where the local state itself is the cause of violence or where it is incapable of dealing with violence, where international forces intervene but through methods that are not so very different from the methods that might be used in a domestic setting. This reflects both the changed sensibilities of society, where concerns about people far away have become more urgent as a result of global communications and transnational communities, and an emerging global social contract whereby the international community adopts the 'responsibility to protect' and recognises individual rights and not just state rights.

Elements of these principles can also be found in just war thinking, particularly in the pre-Westphalian era. Thus the emphasis on the protection of citizens is very much in keeping with notions of charity, humanitarianism and civilisation that have run through the just war literature. The need for legitimate political authority and the priority of stabilisation or peace, rather than victory, could be considered an Augustinian principle. The notion that the enemy is an individual was central to the thinking of Vitoria. Moreover, any attempt to codify the Laws of Peace would need to incorporate humanitarian law but alongside human rights law; it is, above all, human rights and the notion of global public authority that marks this approach off from contemporary just war approaches.

## Conclusion

George Weigel, in his chapter, suggests that the 'new things' in the world today, particularly failing states and rogue states, explain the need for a new kind of just war, in which individual states take responsibility for 'regime change'. His argument is reflected in the 2002 US National Security Strategy. William Wallace, in his chapter, describes Europe as a 'zone of peace' that uses 'soft power' – trade, aid, dialogue – in its external relations. I agree with Weigel that in our interconnected world, rogue states and failing states are unacceptable. But I remain sceptical about the use of war fighting as a way of bringing about 'regime change'. The wars in Iraq and Afghanistan have not created legitimate political authorities – they have speeded up the process of state failure, contributing to an environment in which various armed groups can operate. They have accentuated a friend–enemy distinction that attracts disaffected people to extremist causes. However discriminate and proportionate these wars appear from a Western perspective, the civilian victims, even if not numerous by the traditions of twentieth-century wars, perceive these actions very differently as do members of linked transnational communities across the world, especially Muslims.

The 'soft power' approach of the European Union is insufficient to deal with those who live in conditions of intolerable insecurity. In the 'new war' zones, whose borders are permeable and undefined, in places like the Middle East, the Balkans, west and central Africa, central Asia, or the Caucasus, individuals and communities live in daily fear of being killed, robbed or kidnapped, losing their homes, or being tortured or raped. Neither current security arrangements, based on traditional state-based assumptions about the nature of war and the role of military forces, nor the 'soft' approaches of international and regional organisations seem able to address these everyday risks.

I have proposed that those who wrestle with the problem of what constitutes the legitimate use of military force should adopt a human-security approach rather than try to adapt more traditional just war thinking, even though some of the insights drawn from the notion of just war may be relevant. A human-security approach is more straight-forwardly applicable to the real security problems we face today. Human security is sometimes considered a soft security approach, relegated to the aftermath of conflicts when police and development experts are supposed to 'mop up'. Human security, however, should be regarded as a hard security policy aimed at protecting individuals rather than states. A human-security operation is actually more risky than current war-fighting operations. The human-security officer risks his or her life to save others, rather as police and fire-fighters are expected to do in domes-tic situations. But in 'new wars', the risks are likely to be greater. It is often argued that politicians would be unwilling to take such risks and this is why, in many international missions, force protection receives higher priority than the protection of civilians. Given the growing consciousness of humanity as a single community, Western publics, however, may be more willing to take such risks than politicians assume.

# PART V

## Concluding reflections

# 15

# A US political perspective

MICHAEL O. WHEELER

War, as Carl von Clausewitz taught us, is political in nature.[1] War, as Sir Michael Howard reminds us, is the norm in international politics, not the exception.[2] War is ancient, inevitably brutal and will not go away. It must be dealt with in political terms and deserves our constant reappraisal. 'Politics will, to the end of history, be an area where conscience and power meet,' wrote the theologian Reinhold Niebuhr in 1932, 'where the ethical and coercive factors of human life will interpenetrate and work out their tentative and uneasy compromises.'[3] War and peace decisions are among the most important choices facing politicians in a democracy.

The just war tradition, as George Weigel discusses in this volume, is a way of thinking about war and peace that must be understood within a wider theory of responsible statesmanship. It has found its applications in the past, as James Turner Johnson argues in this volume and elsewhere, not only in the theological seminaries and ethics classrooms but in international law and in the behaviour of armed forces. To reflect on the just war tradition is to reflect on the use of power in the world. This reflective chapter poses the question, What does that tradition suggest for the twenty-first century?

## Historical lessons

In answering the above question we must be careful to dwell neither exclusively nor excessively on today's headlines. Had we asked the question in 1905, the news would have featured dispatches on the Russo-Japanese

---

[1] See Carl von Clausewitz, *On War*, ed. and trans. Michael Howard and Peter Paret (Princeton, NJ: Princeton University Press, 1976), p. 87.

[2] Michael Howard, *The Invention of Peace* (New Haven: Yale University Press, 2000), p. 1.

[3] Reinhold Niebuhr, *Moral Man and Immoral Society* (Louisville, KY: Westminster Knox Press, 1960), p. 4.

War, a struggle that had many of the features that would reappear a decade later in the brutal trench warfare of the First World War. The Russo-Japanese War was 'a terrible war, unprecedented in the world's history', or so said Baroness Bertha Sophie Felicita von Suttner, the 1905 recipient of the Nobel Peace Prize, in her Nobel lecture on 18 April 1906.[4] But worse was to come.

The First World War redrew the geopolitical map as European coalitions fought their first major conflict since 1815. Four years of battlefield carnage killed or maimed an entire generation in Europe. Over 9 million young combatants died. The war seriously challenged Enlightenment assumptions concerning the inevitability of progress in history and eroded over a century of confidence in the power of reason to shape human affairs. In the United States the war 'shook the intellectual foundations of those Americans who cared deeply about international law'.[5] The experience of the First World War virtually brought to an end the promising movement towards international arbitration of disputes. The war was a watershed – it set the tone for a century of war.

The dominant image of what Europeans remember as 'the Great War' was static trench combat. This was an image that haunted strategists seeking to avoid the massive battlefield slaughter should another war occur. The search to apply new technologies and to adapt them to new military doctrines so as to avoid static warfare intensified. The Second World War began with a co-ordinated land–air blitzkrieg, morphed into a global clash including widespread strategic air bombardment of cities. It ended in Europe after Hitler committed suicide in a bunker in Berlin and in Asia in the ashes of Hiroshima and Nagasaki. Close to 5 million civilians had perished in the First World War, mainly in Europe. The figure for the Second World War was closer to 50 to 60 million worldwide, including the 6 million who were murdered because they were Jewish. As Nigel Biggar points out in his contribution to this volume, the psychic scars of the war remain with us six decades later as do their effects on politics in symbolic places such as Tokyo's Yasukuni Shrine.

---

[4] Bertha von Suttner, 'Nobel Lecture', http://nobelprize.org/peace/laureates/1905/suttner-lecture.html, p. 3.

[5] Mark Weston Janis, *The American Tradition of International Law: Great Expectations, 1789–1914* (Oxford: Clarendon Press, 2004), p. 156.

The fog of the Cold War that settled over international politics from the 1940s onwards contained within it the threat of a nuclear collision that could lead to Armageddon. War did not disappear as some thought might happen, but it evolved and resurfaced in other forms – in proxy conflicts, civil wars, wars of national liberation, sponsorship of terrorism and the like. Many of the regional flashpoints – Palestine, Korea, Kashmir, Taiwan – remain sources of instability today. History will record with some amazement how relatively peacefully the Cold War ended. The fall of the Berlin Wall on 9 November 1989 will be one of the leading iconic images.

The end of the Cold War brought new conflict to Europe as suppressed nationalism in the Balkans, freed from the restraining hand of superpower competition, erupted into brutal ethnic cleansing. The end of the Cold War also saw the invasion of Kuwait and the American-led Gulf War to evict Saddam Hussein's forces from Kuwaiti territory. Revelations after the Gulf War about how far along the Iraqi regime had been towards covertly acquiring nuclear weapons planted the seeds for the controversial American decision after 9/11 to carry the fight against al-Qaeda beyond Afghanistan into Iraq in March 2003, on what now are widely acknowledged to be mistaken assumptions.

The end of the Cold War coincided with accelerating advances in the application of technologies that not only helped create modern globalisation but also expanded proliferation of weapons of mass destruction. These advances have taken place in a much more heavily populated world, with increasing urbanisation, diminishing natural resources, severe strains on the environment and much of the global population living in severe poverty. The challenges are daunting. Modern geopolitics appears to have lost its footings in the post-Cold War era. 'The new century', Robert Cooper argues, 'risks being overrun by both anarchy and technology. The two great destroyers of history reinforce each other. And there is enough material left over from previous centuries in the shape of national, ideological and religious fanaticisms to provide motives for the destruction.'[6]

Notwithstanding those sentiments with which one can agree, we are entering also a time when, as Richard Haas argues, 'history has given us . . . a rare, precious, fragile opportunity to usher in an age of considerable

---

[6] Robert Cooper, *The Breaking of Nations: Order and Chaos in the Twenty-First Century* (New York: Grove Press, 2003), p. viii.

peace, prosperity, and freedom'.[7] Haas is part of what might be termed the 'loyal American opposition'. His argument is that Iraq and other intense disagreements notwithstanding, American power can be tolerated if not accepted by much of the world community (at least not opposed reflex-ively). He holds that if the United States now uses its power wisely to encourage greater global integration, accepts some restraints on its free-dom of action and concentrates on building international consensus on the principles and rules to govern international politics, then an era of peace and security can follow.[8]

Part of the opportunity today resides in the legacy of the last two centuries. This legacy is not entirely negative when it comes to war and peace issues. The nineteenth century, for instance, saw the codification of laws of war regarding treatment of the wounded and prisoners of war. The twentieth century retained and expanded this body of international law and extended it to protecting civilians and their property in wartime and during military occupations. The notion of crimes against humanity was created, the range of what the international community would accept as just causes for going to war was narrowed and a growing body of interna-tional humanitarian law addressed the protection of human rights. The phrase 'genocide' was coined and the practice of genocide was agreed by the world community to be an international crime. International tribu-nals came into existence to try war criminals.

The twentieth century institutionalised the concept of collective secur-ity, however imperfectly, in bodies like the UN Security Council. It also witnessed the development of a peaceful political community encompass-ing much of Europe, the birth of modern arms control, the development of a complex and ever-growing web of international negotiations and diplomacy, and a steady expansion of worldwide networks of government officials below the level of heads of government addressing common problems of global governance, what Anne-Marie Slaughter convincingly describes as 'a key [albeit underappreciated] feature of world order in the twenty-first century'.[9]

---

[7] Richard N. Haas, *The Opportunity: America's Moment to Alter History's Course* (New York: Public Affairs, 2005), p. ix.

[8] *Ibid.*, pp. 7–23.

[9] Anne-Marie Slaughter, *A New World Order* (Princeton, NJ: Princeton University Press, 2004), p. 1.

## Understanding American foreign policy

What lies ahead for this century? A significant part of that story depends on how American power is exercised and how others react to that power. American behaviour, today as always, is a complicated blend of morality and pragmatism. In speculating about the future use of American power, it is useful to review some of its precedents. George Washington left office toward the end of the eighteenth century admonishing his countrymen to steer clear of permanent alliances so that the nation might build strength to defend itself and 'may choose peace or war, as our interest, guided by justice, shall counsel'.[10] This admonition helped shape the American tradition of unilateralism, perhaps the oldest tradition in American foreign policy. It also highlights another dimension of the American political ethos, the principle that policy should be just, which leads to the questions of what justice requires and how those requirements are to be translated into practice in the political realm.

American political thought offers some hints. In Federalist 10, James Madison expressed the view that: 'No man is allowed to be a judge in his own cause; because his interest would certainly bias his judgment, and, not improbably, corrupt his integrity.'[11] In Federalist 3, John Jay argued: 'Among the many objects to which a wise and free people find it necessary to direct their attention, that of providing for their safety seems to be first. The safety of the people doubtless has relation to a great variety of circumstances and considerations, and consequently affords great latitude to those who wish to define it precisely and comprehensively.'[12] Thomas Jefferson famously included in the Declaration of Independence reference to 'a deep respect to the opinions of mankind' – a passage connoting not only a sentiment of political philosophy but also the pragmatic recognition of what was needed to secure the support of other European states in the bid for independence.[13]

These principles – appreciation of the limits of self-interested behaviour, recognition of the inevitable differences of perspective on what is

---

[10] George Washington, 'Farewell Address', http://usinfo.state.gov/usa/infousa/facts/democrac/49.htm, p. 7.

[11] Jacob E. Cooke (ed.), *The Federalist* (Middletown, CT: Wesleyan University Press, 1961), p. 59.

[12] *Ibid.*, pp. 14–15.

[13] See Thomas Jefferson's description of the debate on the Declaration in *Thomas Jefferson: Writings* (New York: Library of America, 1984), p. 16.

required for public security, respect for public opinion, pragmatic recognition of the need for foreign support to achieve America's goals – are part of a political tradition in America. So is a deep commitment to the role of a free press in scrutinising political activities and in contributing to the public debate, and to faith in the rule of law. The late Eugene V. Rostow put it succinctly:

> American statesmen, like most of their fellow citizens, are possessed by one of the strongest passions of the American culture, its commitment to the role of law in the social process. . . . Law is unintelligible outside its social matrix, and the restraint of mores – that is, of customs having the force of law – limits the behavior of states even when the society of nations is in a condition of near-anarchy. The abiding question of policy, in my view, is not whether international society is governed by international law – by definition, it is and must be – but whether that law is or can be made just law and generally fulfilled.[14]

On 6 January 1941, President Franklin Delano Roosevelt (hereafter, FDR) delivered his annual message to Congress. Since his first term as president, he had guided an American foreign policy that walked a fine line in remaining formally neutral while favouring the forces committed to fighting fascism around the world. In his January 1941 message to Congress, FDR began by noting that American security was threatened from abroad as never before, since what was at stake was not merely the fate of foreign countries, but the future of the democracy itself. The USA might be reasonably secure he agreed, at least in the short run, from invasion, but the United States could not be indifferent to freedom's future.

FDR used this speech to spell out what he called the 'Four Freedoms'. This was, in effect, America's vision for a post-war world that would nurture freedom of speech and expression and worship, freedom from want and from fear. He also used the speech to explain that while actions he had undertaken short of war were decried by Hitler as a breach of international law, this might be technically correct but merely highlighted the need to reshape international law to the time, to oppose what he termed Nazi interest 'in a new one-way international law, which lacks

---

[14] Eugene V. Rostow, *Toward Managed Peace: The National Security Interests of the United States, 1759 to the Present* (New Haven: Yale University Press, 1993), p. 6.

mutuality in its observance, and therefore, becomes an instrument of oppression'.[15] He concluded that the United States had always stood for constructive change, adjusting itself to changing conditions in the world, seeking a world order in which free countries could work together 'in a friendly, civilized [international] society'.[16]

A full year would pass with America still officially at peace. It took the Japanese invasion of Pearl Harbor on 7 December 1944 finally to bring the United States into the war. In his joint address to Congress the following day, requesting a declaration of war against Japan, FDR declared: 'I believe that I interpret the will of the Congress and of the people when I assert that we will not only defend ourselves to the uttermost but will make it certain that this form of treachery shall never again endanger us.'[17] This theme of going to war to secure an enduring peace – one in which not only is the aggressor defeated and removed but the social order is recast to remove the causes of the war – echoed Woodrow Wilson's message to Congress on 8 January 1918 when he enunciated his fourteen points, his vision of the basic premises of a just and lasting peace. It was at the heart of FDR's messages to Congress in January and December 1941. And it remains a proactive theme in American foreign policy, as reflected in the 2002 US National Security Strategy and in subsequent statements by the President.

## Law and the invention of peace

This brings us back to international law. 'At the deepest level,' Eugene Rostow argues, 'we believe – correctly – that peace is the highest and most vital security interest of the United States. And we have learned from our history with peculiar vividness that the notion of peace is a legal concept which can be summed up in the much-abused phrase "the rule of law".'[18] "We are haunted', argued Robert H. Jackson in early 1941, 'by the greatest unfinished task of civilisation, which is to create a just and peaceful international order. If such a relationship between states can be realised,

---

[15] Annual Message to Congress (6 January 1941), http://www.fdrlibrary.marist.edu/4free. html, p. 5.

[16] *Ibid.*, p. 7.

[17] Joint Address to Congress (8 December 1941), http://www.fdrlibrary.marist.edu/dec71941. html, p. 1.

[18] Rostow, *Toward Managed Peace*, p. 6.

we know its foundations will be laid in law, because legal process is the only practical alternative to force.'[19]

A century earlier, the British jurist Sir Henry Maine had argued that peace was a modern invention. Michael Howard picks up on that theme in his essay *The Invention of Peace*, expanding upon the plenary lecture he had delivered in July 2000 to inaugurate the Anglo-American Conference on War and Peace. 'Peace', Howard writes, 'may or may not be a modern invention but it is certainly a far more complex affair than war ... [and] implies a social and political ordering of society that is generally accepted to be just. The creation of such an order', he argues, 'may take generations to achieve, and social dynamics may then destroy it within a few decades. Paradoxically, war may be an intrinsic part of that order.'[20] Law and ethics are not the same thing, as Franklin Berman correctly reminds us in his chapter in this volume. But neither are they entirely separate. What is taken to be just in a moral sense informs and frequently helps shape what is considered to be desirable in a legal sense. Morality and legality both contribute to social judgments on legitimacy, and, as Michael Howard argues, 'Legitimised order produces domestic peace, and also legitimises the conduct of war.'[21] Just order, just war and just peace are all part of the same continuum.

The debates will continue for some time about the great contemporary political and legal issues related to *jus ad bellum* principles. These include the locus of public authority for deciding on war, questions of anticipatory self-defence and preventative war, limits on sovereign rights when it comes to violations of human rights, humanitarian intervention, sincere intentions of political leaders on war and peace questions, and the like. Likewise there are important and unresolved issues related to *jus in bello* principles, e.g. who is to be considered a legal combatant, rights of prisoners of war, limits on the actions of paramilitary intelligence forces and contract security forces, and so forth. But potentially the most important task is to develop rules and principles, build consensus and expand the body of international sentiment, practice and law related to

---

[19] Robert H. Jackson, *International Order* (Havana, 27 March 1941), http://www.roberhjackson. org/theman2-7-6-2.asp, p. 1. Jackson at the time was FDR's Attorney-General. He went on to be a US Supreme Court associate justice and was America's chief prosecutor at the Nuremberg tribunal for Nazi war crimes.

[20] Howard, *The Invention of Peace*, pp. 1–2.    [21] *Ibid.*, p. 3.

*jus in pace* – reconstruction and reconciliation following conflict, in a way conducive to keeping the peace.

In 1971, with the Vietnam War still raging, Fred Charles Iklé published *Every War Must End*. His thesis was that it is much easier to plan and prepare for waging war than it is to relate the means to the ends, to plan and prepare for the post-war peace. Iklé's book was well received in the United States and was reissued in a first revised edition (1991) after the Gulf War and in a second revised edition (2005) to take account mainly of the current situation in Iraq.[22] Iklé is critical of many of the Bush administration actions in Iraq, but his argument is broader than that. 'It is crucial', he concludes in the preface to the 2005 edition, 'that the United States and its friends relearn the rules for ending a war with strategic foresight and skill so that the hard-won military victory will purchase a lasting political success.'[23] Before we can relearn the rules we must first agree on the rules – a work still in progress.

## Conclusion

War is a political activity, inevitably brutal and unlikely to go away. War and peace decisions are among the most important choices politicians make in a democracy. Just war thinking is reflected in the domestic debates on going to war, in international law, and in the practice of armed forces during and after wars. This means that peace and legitimised order are inseparable. While historians may someday look back on the twenty-first century and measure the changes in just war thinking on issues relating to *jus ad bellum* and *jus in bello*, the area where history may remember the twenty-first century for its most profound contributions is in thinking through the issues of *jus in pace*, the fabric of peace itself.

---

[22] Fred Charles Iklé, *Every War Must End*, 2nd rev. edn. (New York: Columbia University Press, 2005).
[23] *Ibid.*, p. xv.

# 16

# A British political perspective

MICHAEL QUINLAN

This essay does not attempt to summarise the chapters in this volume, still less to set out conclusions collectively reached. That would be presumptuous and indeed infeasible, since this exercise is not a negotiation to achieve agreed outcomes but a shared and wide-ranging effort in dialogue to deepen comprehension and tease out issues. What follows here is merely a limited personal miscellany, nowhere near exhaustive, of ideas stimulated or refined by preceding chapters.

## The nature of the tradition

The occasional description of the just war tradition as a 'doctrine' is not ideal, given that – at least for the non-theologian – that word may carry overtones both of handing down from above, and of a fixed corpus of analysis or prescription. Just war thinking fits neither of those models. It is crucially indebted to great thinkers from the past, and the utterances of such figures as Thomas Aquinas are entitled to our profound respect and most careful attention – but not to uncritical reverence going beyond that. The tradition is moreover a living and evolving one, undergoing modification and enriched by addition as understanding broadens under the impact of changing circumstances, challenging debate and collective learning from varied new experience.

This view of the tradition – as being open, and based upon practical reason informed by humanity-wide values, not upon institutional or scripture-type authority – is the more necessary if Christians desire that the tradition should be more than just a system for their own moral guidance. It should surely be their aim that its merits and force be accepted as fully as possible, worldwide, even by those who do not bring to its appraisal a conscious framework of Christian assumptions. The tradition has, as a matter of historical fact, been developed by Christians, and Christians can take legitimate pride in it (if not always in their practical faithfulness to it) as the most thoroughly developed account of moral discipline governing the use of armed force. It is, however, in no way an exclusive spiritual or intellectual property which others cannot embrace and apply.

Nothing in the just war tradition need be alien or repugnant to Muslims or Jews, or to those of other faiths, or indeed to non-believers in religion who accept the special status of individual human life. This came close to being recognised, albeit understandably without explicit acknowledgement, in the 2004 report of the diversely composed High-Level Panel set up by the United Nations Secretary-General to review threats, challenges and change in world security. The guidelines it put forward for the legitimate use of force closely paralleled the *ad bellum* criteria of just war thinking. The broader the acceptance of the principles drawn from the thriving tradition, the greater the legitimacy which their observance in practical situations will confer. The diverse experience of the post-Cold War era has already underlined the importance of international legitimacy in the achievement of stable success from the use of armed force. In Plato's 'Republic', Socrates patiently dismantles the claim by Thrasymachus to equate 'justice' simply with the convenience of the strong. It is humanly inescapable that suspicion should sometimes be voiced that the military actions of the West, centred around the unique power of the United States, are driven ultimately by a Thrasymachean ethic – by cynical calculations of material interest. It is accordingly all the more necessary that a framework of disciplining principle should gain the widest possible acceptance throughout the international system, and that the corollary be accepted that constraints may result upon the preferences of the powerful. It is thereafter equally necessary, for legitimacy, that judgements on how to apply the framework in practice – inevitably often requiring contestable evaluations amid complexity and uncertainty – should also not appear to be the prerogative solely of the powerful, even though the fact that executive responsibility may have to rest with them has to command a measure of special respect.

## The 'presumption against war'

Another ostensibly linguistic issue – generating a degree of divergence within this volume – concerns the claim that the just war tradition embodies (which is not necessarily to say starts from) 'a presumption against war'. European contributors mostly seem to find this phrase an unexceptionable shorthand for referring to a structure of evaluation which, recognising that war inevitably entails the intrinsically grave evil of taking life by violence, makes its undertaking subject to the satisfaction of a substantial array of stringent conditions. But some American contributors fear that, whatever linguistic purism might assert, within American debates on war in recent years the phrase has become corrupted as the slogan of an un-admitted but *de facto* pacifism that has found reasons for rejecting as illegitimate every real-life example of the external use of military force. Any such pacifism – whether grounded in a claim that one or another of the classical criteria is not met or in a belief that the classical apparatus has ceased entirely to be apt for modern conditions – has a duty, if it claims a serious entitlement to be heard in advice to those in public authority, to answer tough questions about alternatives. What practicable steps with genuine likelihood of timely success should have been taken about Saddam Hussein's seizure of Kuwait, Slobodan Milosevic's brutal expulsion of the Albanian Kosovars or the Taliban's harbouring of al-Qaeda? Or should these ultimately have been acquiesced in?

There is sometimes a reluctance – notably perhaps within some countries of Europe with either especially painful memories of war or especially long habituation to peace – to acknowledge that the satisfaction of the *ad bellum* criteria of the just war tradition may establish that the use of armed force is not merely morally allowable but morally imperative. The honest confrontation of painful choices amid conflicting considerations – a task inseparable from the responsibility of any government – has always been at the heart of moral thinking about war, whether in the just war or any other ethical tradition.

The choices need, however, to be grounded in a consistent ethic; and the demands of that grounding become more complex as candidate situations for the use of armed force move away – as they mostly have in recent years, at least for the developed West – from the simplifying imperatives *ad bellum* of defence against attack by other states, and *in bello* of avoiding military defeat. Three aspects of the complexity, cast into high relief both by the wrenching episode of the 2003 invasion of Iraq and by the course of debate in this volume, concern proportion and the management of uncertainty; right authority; and right intention.

## Proportionality

Proportionality in the decision to resort to armed force – an honest judgement, thoroughly and conscientiously considered, that even after account is taken of the bitter toll of war more good or less harm is likely to result from this resort than from refraining – is an essential criterion in *jus ad bellum*. It is, however, in several dimensions more complicated to apply than is sometimes recognised. It is a curiously common error to suppose or imply that the comparison to be made is between the situation before the war and the expected situation after it. But a moment's reflection surely corrects this. The condition of Europe was certainly worse in almost all respects in 1945 than it had been in 1939, but that scarcely rendered the decision to fight Hitler's Nazism unjust. The relevant comparison has to be between the expected situation if we fight the war and the expected situation if we do not. And a further refinement is needed: the comparison is not between fighting the war and doing nothing; it is between fighting the war and doing whatever is, in the circumstances, the best that we can by other means.

The accusation is recurrently made against this calculus of proportion that it turns ultimately upon forecasts of alternative futures, that such forecasts are enormously fallible (who in 1939 could have hoped to discern the reality of 1945?) and that it is unconscionably arrogant to undertake large-scale hazard of lives on projections so precarious. But the entire business of human living continually demands that choices be made without assured knowledge of consequences, and with some danger that estimation of these may be influenced, consciously or not, by prior inclination or interest. That cannot cease to be the case even when, as over war, the stakes may be appallingly high, though that undoubtedly imposes a special duty of care and intellectual humility. And where action is possible inaction is itself a choice, with its own consequences, its own responsibility and its own problems of unsure prediction. Abstention from or opposition to engagement in Kosovo in 1999 – or in Rwanda in 1994 – was not a cost-free moral option.

The problem of forecasting does, however, have an additional aspect in settings like the Iraq invasion. This concerns the management of risk. The assessment of proportion *ad bellum* entails more than just the comparison of alternative futures more or less clearly (albeit fallibly) delineated. It has to weigh what may be widely different probabilities for the outcomes being imagined, and to factor these into the evaluation of whether to go to war. It is undoubtedly wrong to oppose military action by portraying its outcome solely on a worst-case basis, but that error can be committed in more places than one; it may be no less wrong to depict the consequences of not taking action in the most lurid terms possible. Outcome A, from not going to war, may be plainly far graver than Outcome B from doing so; but a deep issue lies in that 'may be'. This issue has underlain the vigorous debate since 2002 on whether, in a world where the dangers of 'weapons of mass destruction' (WMD) are thought to loom larger than in the past, there is a new or enhanced case for the concept of preventative as distinct from truly pre-emptive military action.

To construct an artificially simplified example, the decision-takers in the anti-Saddam coalition could not, before the invasion, utterly disprove a speculation that terrorists using Saddam-provided WMD might one day perpetrate an outrage costing 1,000,000 lives. Against that, they had a duty to consider the potential cost of the invasion and its aftermath in lives on both sides, military and civilian; let us posit, for that, a possible forecast toll of 20,000 lives. If this had been at the heart of the 'proportionality' assessment, the case for invasion would not have been a simple matter of noting that 1,000,000 is more than 20,000. The 20,000, or some number in that order, was on any serious reckoning highly likely; the 1,000,000 would have depended on a chain of hypotheses the combined probability of which could not possibly have been so characterised.

In conditions of uncertainty commercial business appraisal sometimes employs a concept of 'expected value', factoring potential levels of profit or loss with the assessed probability of their achievement; indeed, the whole concept of insurance rests upon such an idea. On such a model, the 'expected cost' of (say) an 80 per cent probability of 20,000 killed is markedly greater than that of a 1 per cent probability of 1,000,000 killed. This may sound arid to the point of unreality; it is not to be supposed that in 1940 Winston Churchill, judging that it would be better to fight on against the odds than to negotiate a deal with Hitler, went through any conscious process of such reasoning. But once more the probability-weighing model, whether or not explicitly recognised or applied, is implicit in any rational decision making. I cannot be absolutely certain of not being knocked down and killed as I cross the road on my way to the village shop, and that would be much worse than having to go without the loaf of bread I seek; but it is not irrational for me to go to the shop.

A yet further complication arises in the war appraisal. Are all lives to be rated equally? In classical war, plainly not; if I am resisting wicked aggression I am fully entitled to kill 1,000 enemy soldiers in order to defend 100 of my own. But suppose that my opponent did not seek or start the war? – the cost in the lives of his soldiers, even if it be not fully equated with mine, surely cannot be dismissed entirely from the moral evaluation. And how should I rate the lives of civilians in my opponent's country against those in my own? The fact that in normal circumstances I have greater responsibility for the latter than the former scarcely establishes a case for differential evaluation if the war is undertaken at my and not my opponent's choice. A number of the chapters in this volume touch briefly on this question of relative value and duty, but without reaching any clear conclusion.

Experience in Iraq and elsewhere has brought home difficult aspects of relative value and duty, and their significance in handling risk, not only in the *ad bellum* context but also in respect of *in bello* and *post bellum*. How should armed forces, amid uncertainty, weigh considerations of their own protection against the risks that mistaken targeting or imprecision in delivery (neither of which can be precluded by technological advance) may kill innocents? This is an increasing problem as situations less and less like neat army-versus-army encounter multiply. Self-protection is a natural and legitimate concern, both for personal survival and for mission accomplishment. The striking fact that in the 1999 Kosovo operation not one NATO combatant was killed in action is in itself matter for satisfaction, not disquiet; modern war is not a game in which one should give the other side a sporting chance.

But again judgement of probability is an inescapable dimension of just decision. If the last three vehicles that failed to stop at checkpoints proved to be carrying suicide bombers, it is reasonable to shoot at a fourth before it gets too close; if the last hundred proved innocuous, the case is different. In practice the decision making may be hugely difficult; rules of engagement have to be framed in terms that make usable practical sense not in a courtroom or an academic seminar, but to a young soldier in a dangerous setting at night with ten seconds to decide about the use of lethal force upon sketchy information. But there still have to be rules (as well as relevant organisation, equipment and training beforehand) and the rules, if they are to be just, cannot automatically load all possible risk exclusively onto the 'other' side. The just war tradition enjoins proportionality *in bello* as well as *ad bellum*, and that has to include proportionality of risk.

## Legitimate authority

The United Nations Charter, which all UN members have accepted, lays down that the use of military force other than in self-defence (including in that the defence of allies) is subject to the agreement of the Security Council. The fact that the practice of nations has not consistently respected that requirement cannot, however, be a matter for surprise or complaint amid the complexities of the world and the shortcomings of the UN system, especially the composition of the Security Council and the working of veto powers within it. For example, collective armed resistance to the North Korean assault on South Korea in 1950 received Security Council endorsement only through the accident of the Soviet Union's having absented itself at the time when the vote was taken; but few would maintain that without that accident a near-certain Soviet prohibition of the resistance should have prevailed. But the fact that UN imperfections make it unrealistic and indeed undesirable to insist on absolute conformity with what the Charter purported to require does not mean that beyond clear self-defence there are no international rules or reasonable expectations – that those with the power of armed intervention are entitled to make their own unfettered decision on its use. The criterion of 'right authority' does not collapse into national decision alone, even where the internal process is democratic.

One might postulate a vertical spectrum of possible authority for military action, with explicit prior Security Council approval at the top and purely unilateral decision at the foot. The characteristics of intermediate points on the spectrum would be a blend of factors like the scale of multilateral consensus (and of any multilateral opposition going beyond abstention), in particular consensus or opposition among those most closely affected regionally or otherwise. On such a spectrum the authority for the 1999 Kosovo operation, for instance, might be rated fairly close to the top.

It is not possible, even if such an analytical tool be accepted, to determine in the abstract just how far up the spectrum the backing for particular sorts of military intervention should have to be rated – what would constitute a reasonable in-the-circumstances approximation to Hedley Bull's 'collective will of the society of states' – in order to qualify it as having adequate 'right authority'; that would have to be assessed in specific instances. If, however, the judgement is not to be purely arbitrary, or no more than cover for the inclinations of those wielding the power to act, it should take into account the scale, certainty and immediacy of the evils to be ended or averted, the history and prospects of efforts to remedy them by other means and perhaps the relevant standing of those who are contemplating taking or supporting (or opposing) military action – what is the nature of their concerns? How close are they to the problems? How deeply is their proper interest and responsibility engaged?

The imprecision and subjectivity of an approach of this kind make its limitations plain, both for appraising legitimacy and for securing general acceptance of that. The development of a more satisfactory account of and international structure for 'right authority', as a crucial component of the just war concept, is something which adherents of the tradition should surely desire and encourage. There is an obligation upon governments – not least upon those which most vigorously criticise the imperfections of the current UN system – to work constructively and realistically (that is, not holding improvement hostage to utopian demands) towards a better and more systematically rooted framework of legitimation. That will need to be partnered by a recognition that constraints on national choice will result, and that compromises with the views of others, modifying unilateral preferences, will sometimes have to be accepted. Such a pattern may not be found universally congenial, but an honest striving for it is a matter both of long-term interest and of moral duty.

## Right intention

Public discussion of 'right intention' (whether or not directly so described) is occasionally disfigured by confusion between motives and reasons. Debate about the invasion of Iraq in March 2003 saw widespread imputations – sometimes purely conjectural, sometimes citing utterances by individuals thought to be involved in or close to decision-taking – of 'real' motives different from the reasons for action adduced from time to time (not always consistently, but that is not the issue here) by coalition governments. For example, it was variously alleged that the driving force was an urge to complete action regarded as having been left culpably undone after the 1991 liberation of Kuwait; a desire to avenge the 1993 attempt on the life of the US President's father; a perceived need to secure an alternative source of oil against a day (whether feared or hoped for) when the Saudi Arabian regime might implode into chaos threatening the reliability of its exports; a determination to disable one of the few neighbours thought capable of doing serious harm to Israel; or an aspiration to establish in Iraq a US military infrastructure to facilitate domination of the region. Comparable allegations of ulterior purpose were heard anew as the sixtieth anniversary of the use of nuclear weapons against Japan in 1945 re-energise dispute about the justifiability of that enormous action. Was it driven by scientific curiosity, or a wish to demonstrate technological prowess? To send a warning message to the Soviet Union in anticipation of the Cold War? To end the Second World War before the Soviet Union's late intervention against Japan could seize a stronger forward position in East Asia?

It is neither possible nor necessary to prove that none of these thoughts, whether about Iraq or Hiroshima and Nagasaki, ever entered any responsibility-bearing mind. In any large collective human enterprise – even in protest movements – there will be diverse standpoints among participants, and some will see in the enterprise advantages not perceived or not welcomed by others, and not adequate or ethically appropriate to bear the weight of decision. It may well be prudent, where the range or power of such motives appears very marked, to examine proffered reasoning rigorously and, in a strict sense, sceptically; but their presence, even should it be demonstrated, does not invalidate the enterprise if it is warranted by legitimate reasons genuinely at the forefront of decision-makers' concerns. Justification stands or falls by the merits of such reasons.

## Concluding thoughts

Perhaps the strongest impression that the preceding chapters leave on this commentator is of the depth and richness of the tradition, and its cogent relevance to a wide and demanding array of practical questions facing governments and citizens as well as churches in the modern world. There is a powerful case that the legitimate use of armed force now deserves a collective intellectual effort no less intensive and widespread than that devoted so strikingly to the significance and problems of nuclear weapons during the Cold War. The living endowment of just war thinking should be a massive contribution to that.

# 17

# An American military ethicist's perspective

SHANNON E. FRENCH

Lance Corporal Gregory MacDonald of the US Marine Corps never believed there were weapons of mass destruction in Iraq. Armed with a master's degree in philosophy and well-versed in the just war tradition, he rejected the claim that Operation Iraqi Freedom was launched as a last resort to check Saddam's aggression. Before deploying to Kuwait with his light armoured vehicle (LAV) unit, Greg participated (out of uniform) in an anti-war rally in Washington, DC, and gave an anonymous radio interview expressing his mistrust of the motives of the Bush administration.

Greg was killed on 25 June 2003, near the town of al Hillah, Iraq, as his LAV raced to assist another Marine unit that had been ambushed by Saddam loyalists. I learned of his death three days later, shortly after my wedding reception. The night before, at the rehearsal dinner, my maid of honour had read a toast Greg wrote in the desert for my husband and me. Its theme was a Muslim greeting he had heard in Iraq: '*a Salam a lakum*', which may be translated, 'Peace be with you', or 'God grant you peace.' Greg explained that the greeting is 'not just a blessing for the absence of conflict, but also for compassion, repose, calm; it implies a desire for an understanding of the self and for the humanity of the other; it signifies a willingness both to trust and to accept the trust of another; it is an offering for what is just, what is fair.' In a well-intentioned effort to console me, an acquaintance who had not known Greg very well made the fatuous remark, 'At least he died doing what he loved.' Greg did not love war. Greg was a soul moved by human suffering who dreamed of being a guardian to those unable to protect themselves. And he loved his fellow Marines, which is why Greg felt he had a duty to accompany them to Iraq, despite his misgivings about the justice of the conflict.

Asked to 'picture a United States Marine', few serious academics would conjure up anyone remotely like Greg. Indeed, the majority of academics are uncomfortable with the military. In the minds of many, the archetypes of the scholar and the warrior are naturally at odds – Athens versus Sparta. Scholarly examinations of the just war tradition tend to focus on the decisions of political leaders and policy-makers. The central question is when, if ever, it is just to take a nation to war. The men and women who do the actual fighting and who pledge in advance to 'fight all wars, foreign and domestic' are seldom discussed, and when they are it is usually in the context of trying to rein them in to prevent *jus in bello* violations. Warriors are too often spoken of as if they were unstable beasts that might at any moment turn upon their handlers and maul the innocent, or even as intractable enemies of peace who fan the flames of conflict to justify their own existence.

Scholarly detachment from conduct of war issues is by no means a modern phenomenon. In Book V of *The Republic*, Plato outlines suggestions for appropriate *jus in bello* restraints when Greeks fight other Greeks, and both Aristotle and Cicero explore the issue of whether there should be consistent laws of war irrespective of the nature of the conflict or the enemy.[1] However, when the just war tradition moved out of the Greco-Roman era and fell under the influence of Christianity, rigorous examinations of just and unjust means to wage war became few and far between. In the fourth century CE, arguments by St Ambrose and St Augustine convinced the Church that Christian commitments did not demand strict pacifism, and the concepts of *jus ad bellum* and *jus in bello* were reborn. Still, details of the latter were left sketchy, as if gazing too closely at the face of war remained something Church leaders preferred to avoid.[2]

From medieval oaths of chivalry to modern ROEs (rules of engagement), warriors have, for the most part, been left to sort out the nuts and bolts of their codes of conduct themselves. This cannot be ascribed entirely to professional courtesy, since scholars have not hesitated to meddle in the affairs of other professions. For example, the study of medical ethics is well established and respected in academia, and the study of business ethics has been on the rise in recent decades. This disparity is curious, given that doctors and business professionals do not usually act as our direct representatives, as members of our militaries do. Perhaps there is an unspoken belief that doctors and business

---

[1]  See Fred D. Miller, Jr, *Nature, Justice and Rights in Aristotle's Politics* (Oxford: Clarendon Press, 1995) and David J. Bederman, *International Law in Antiquity* (Cambridge: Cambridge University Press, 2001).

[2]  For an excellent in-depth analysis of these and other tensions and threads of discourse in the history of the just war tradition, see Alex Bellamy, *Just Wars* (Cambridge: Polity Press, 2006).

professionals are by and large educated, rational individuals who can be expected to welcome (or at least tolerate) any insights into the complex ethical issues they encounter; warriors, however, might be less receptive to the musings that philosophers, theologians, social scientists and legal experts might offer them.

My own experience from teaching military ethics at the United States Naval Academy is that many modern warriors are eager to discuss the ethical dilemmas faced by members of their profession, and that they appreciate the opportunity to benefit from views developed outside their unique culture. Modern warriors recognise that hearing fresh perspectives might prevent them from overlooking inconsistencies between their principles and their actions, clinging to dangerously outdated paradigms, and failing to consider viable alternatives. Most are more than willing to submit their codes to rigorous ethical examination, while reserving the right to reject some conclusions as untenably idealistic, just as doctors and business professionals do. At the same time, one must acknowledge that comparisons between military ethics and medical or business ethics can only go so far. Medical decisions are frequently matters of life and death, as are even some decisions in the business world, but the lives at stake are rarely those of the decision-makers. As Paul Cornish points out in his contribution to this volume, there can arise peculiarly daunting problems concerning how to motivate ethical behaviour in the context of war, when doing the right thing can quite easily get both the decision-maker and his or her closest comrades killed.

In his critical analysis of the problem of motivating ethical behaviour among combat troops, *Obeying Orders: Atrocity, Military Discipline and the Law of War*, Mark Osiel tells the story of a young enlisted Marine in the Vietnam War whose judgement concerning the distinction between combatants and non-combatants was compromised after he had seen one too many of his colleagues killed.[3] An officer found the youth 'with his rifle at the head of a Vietnamese woman', about to kill a non-combatant in cold blood. The officer had only seconds to decide how to defuse this situation.[4] What are the arguments a military ethicist might give for

---

[3] See Shannon E. French, *The Code of the Warrior: Exploring Warrior Values, Past and Present* (Lanham and New York: Rowman and Littlefield Publishers, 2003), pp. 14–16.

[4] Mark Osiel, *Obeying Orders: Atrocity, Military Discipline, and the Law of War* (New Brunswick and London: Transaction Publishers, 1999), p. 23.

upholding the rules of war and not shooting the villager? There are several that spring to mind. One could argue that she is an innocent person who does not deserve to die. But could the young Marine be persuaded to see her as innocent in that moment? And would he care about someone 'deserving to die' or not? Did his friends, killed in the same conflict, all deserve to die? Was there ever a war in which innocents did not die?

It might be tempting to make an argument based on reciprocity with the enemy. The two sides in a conflict agree to accept certain restraints because if those boundaries are maintained, both sides will benefit. We want our enemies to respect the immunity of our non-combatants, so we agree to respect theirs. However, this tit-for-tat rationale is disturbingly conditional. It implies a fragile contract that can be unilaterally nullified. The young Marine may not believe that his enemies are keeping up their end of the bargain and he may have little faith that correct actions on his part will go any way towards reforming his enemy's behaviour. He may feel that 'all bets are off', and it is 'kill or be killed'. Arguments based on reciprocity are also dangerous to the degree that they suggest the code by which warriors should fight is entirely dependent on the code of their enemies.

When both sides in a conflict abandon all restraint, another casualty is the hope for peace. When atrocities escalate and conflicts devolve into personal hatreds, cycles of violence can span generations. If each side's violations are answered by reprisals, bringing both sides to the table to discuss terms to end the conflict becomes more and more difficult. One could argue that by shooting the villager, the young Marine would only be prolonging the conflict he has come to despise. While this may be true, it seems unlikely that the Marine would be able to focus his vision on a faint hope for peace somewhere in the hazy future and see that prospect clearly enough for it to cut through the raw reality of ugly war all around him. The Marine may even accept the remorseless logic of General Sherman that Gwyn Prins highlights in his chapter: make the war as unbearably brutal as possible, in order to end it more quickly.

One might argue that murdering a civilian could turn international opinion against the side associated with the atrocity or even undermine support for the war at home. If public support for a conflict is required in order to sustain funding for it, and if that support depends on the perception that the war is being conducted in an honourable manner, then concern about sustaining that support may encourage strict observation of conduct of war rules. On the other hand, concern about international or domestic opinion may do no more than inspire members of the military to cover up any actions that might be condemned by the general public. It certainly has nothing to do with a sincere commitment to upholding certain values. And there is something ridiculous about the prospect of the officer saying to the young Marine, 'Don't shoot, son – think about how it will play back home, or in the international court of opinion!'

Thankfully, the officer tried a different tack. He simply said in a calm voice, 'Marines don't do that.' Jarred out of his berserk state and recalled to his place in a long-standing warrior tradition, the Marine stepped back and lowered his weapon.[5] Why were those four words so effective? They appealed directly to the young Marine's chosen identity as a *warrior*, not a murderer. As Jean Bethke Elshtain argues in this volume, the distinction between warriors and murderers – or between freedom-fighters and terrorists – is not merely a matter of subjective opinion. The young Marine knew he was about to commit an act that would betray the legacy of his warrior community. Even in that moment, he cared above all else about being a Marine, and that to him meant holding on to some measure of control and not allowing his participation in the violence to fully extinguish his humanity. 'I am a Marine. Not a killer, or an animal. A Marine. And Marines don't do that.'

Osiel notes, 'By taking seriously such internal conceptions of martial honour, we may be able to impose higher standards on professional soldiers than the law has traditionally done, in the knowledge that good soldiers already impose these standards upon themselves.'[6] It is vital for our warriors to have a consistent, compelling code of honour that requires them to exercise restraint. Without such a code, they run a greater risk of slipping over the thin but critical line that separates them from murderers and sadists, torturers and rapists. If they cross that line, they will suffer along with their victims. The men and women who represent us in combat risk becoming not only physical casualties, but moral and psychological casualties. As psychiatrist Jonathan Shay, author of *Achilles in Vietnam: Combat Trauma and the Undoing of Character*, laments, 'The painful paradox is that fighting for one's country can render one unfit to be its citizen.'[7]

---

[5] *Ibid.*   [6] *Ibid.*

[7] Jonathan Shay, *Achilles in Vietnam: Combat Trauma and the Undoing of Character* (New York: Simon and Schuster, 1994), p. xx.

Just as it is a nation's solemn responsibility not to commit its troops to an unnecessary and immoral war, it is also a nation's moral duty not to harm the ability of those troops to maintain a consistent code of conduct by degrading the values at the heart of that code. The Abu Ghraib scandal was disturbing not only for the actual prisoner abuses that occurred but also because those actions seemed to have been approved at least conceptually if not literally through the chain of command from the highest levels of US national leadership (which also helped feed the rising tide of anti-Americanism that Nigel Biggar analyses in his chapter). The principle 'It is wrong to torture enemy prisoners' should be a component of a meaningful warrior's code. If the nation the warriors serve no longer endorses that principle, the warrior's code is corroded.

For a statement like 'Marines don't do that' to motivate the exercise of restraint, Marines must have good reason to believe that there are in fact things that honourable Marines do not do, regardless of the nature of the conflict or the enemy. There is little motivational force remaining in hedged statements such as 'Generally speaking, Marines don't do that, unless expediency demands it, or the enemy deserves it, or . . .'. If we care about the moral and psychological welfare of our troops, we must not permit the view to flourish that *jus in bello* rules morph into something fundamentally different when fighting terrorists.

Without question, the asymmetric nature of the global war on terror has put a strain on traditional *jus in bello* principles, particularly discrimination. Terrorists might not only refuse to discriminate between combatants and non-combatants or even to acknowledge the existence of the latter category; they might also use our troops' rules of discrimination against them (e.g. by employing human shields, hiding among the civilian population, and disguising themselves as civilians either to gain a tactical advantage or to manipulate public opinion by tricking our troops into killing non-combatants). However, these bitter truths must be presented to our troops as serious challenges to the application of the principle of discrimination, not as grounds to abandon the principle itself. If we allow our basic commitment to the principle of discrimination to erode because we are fighting terrorists, we also erode the very distinction between terrorists and warriors upon which the moral and psychological health of our troops depends. There is enough moral ambiguity in the choices presented to those who are sent to fight our battles for us without policy-makers back home undermining bedrock principles.

Colonel Michael Campbell, another US Marine, was commanding a tank unit in Somalia when he was ordered to destroy three tanks that the enemy had deployed on the outskirts of an impoverished civilian community. When Colonel Campbell's unit, which included both armour and infantry, came into range, the turrets of the enemy tanks turned towards the approaching American troops. The colonel's subordinates in the US tanks urgently requested permission to fire first, to defend themselves and the infantrymen all around them. However, something made the colonel hesitate. Perhaps it was just instinct, or perhaps there was something slightly wrong about the way the enemy turrets turned to bear upon the Americans that set off alarm bells in the colonel's subconscious. For whatever reason, and with both his superiors on the radio and his subordinates all around him shouting for him to order the attack, the colonel refused to fire at the tanks. Just then, the hatches on top of the enemy tanks popped open, and Somali children began to crawl out and run back to their homes. The tanks had been abandoned in the middle of the night, and the children had been playing in them.[8]

In hindsight, we admire the colonel's restraint and are grateful that he avoided a tragic mistake. If he had destroyed the tanks immediately, as he had been ordered to do, he would have caused the deaths of innocents, traumatised himself and his troops and given a gift to anti-American propagandists. Imagine reading the headline 'US Marines Kill Thirty Somali Children Playing in Abandoned Tanks'. Yet it could just as easily have been the case that the colonel's hunch was mistaken, and his delay in ordering fire could have led to the death of many Marines. Colonel Campbell risked his life and the lives of his men to uphold the principle of discrimination. Still there are those who attempt to justify *jus in bello* violations such as blanket internment, torture, extraordinary rendition and reprisals on the grounds that these measures are necessary to safeguard our troops. They seem to forget that our troops volunteered to defend and potentially give their lives for values such as the preservation of justice and natural rights, the protection of innocent life and respect for human dignity. How tragically absurd that those *not* putting their lives on

---

[8] I am grateful to Colonel Campbell for sharing this story with me – which he did with great modesty only after I heard it from another source. The conclusions I have drawn from it are entirely my own.

the line should take it upon themselves to eviscerate these very values, 'for the sake of our troops'.

What our troops need is to be able to trust that what they are asked to fight for is truly worth killing and dying for. The medieval concept of 'trial by combat', where victory is granted only to the side whose cause is just, lingers in their psyches. There is no more bitter fate for a warrior than to be tricked into defending an unworthy cause. Yet not all warriors have timely access to enough information to judge for themselves that a conflict is unjust with sufficient certainty to refuse to participate in it. And, for the most part, we want our military men and women to fight when and where we tell them to, because we cherish civilian control of the military. The United States military, for example, does not allow selective conscientious objection. Those who cannot swear to fight all of their nation's wars cannot serve at all. Thus we hear modern echoes of the sentiments expressed by the soldiers in Shakespeare's *Henry V*:

> KING HENRY:  [M]ethinks, I could not die
> any where so contented, as in the King's company;
> his cause being just, and his quarrel honourable.
> WILLIAMS:  That's more than we know.
> BATES:  Ay, or more than we should seek after;
> for we know enough, if we know we are the
> King's subjects: if his cause be wrong, our obedience
> to the King wipes the crime of it out of us.[9]

Even those who do question the justice of a conflict may feel called upon to play a part in it. Lance Corporal Greg MacDonald was a warrior who wanted peace and thought he could help promote peace by being a humanitarian voice in the midst of the horrors of war. For this, he paid the ultimate price. The best way for scholars probing *The Price of Peace* to honour the sacrifices of our troops is to continue asking hard questions about the ethics of war and to concern ourselves not only with *why* wars are fought, but also with *how* they are fought. The effort to do so is evident throughout this text.

In the global 'trial by combat' from which we seem unable to disengage ourselves, our troops play the role of our champions. If we employ them

---

[9]  William Shakespeare, *King Henry the Fifth*, Act IV, Scene I, in *The Globe Illustrated Shakespeare* (New York: Greenwich House, 1986 edition), p. 845.

unjustly or give them inadequate guidance on how to act on our behalf, we will rightly be judged for it. As Shakespeare's King Henry warned:

> [T]ake heed how you impawn our person,
> How you awake our sleeping sword of war;
> We charge you in the name of God, take heed:
> For never two such kingdoms did contend,
> Without much fall of blood, whose guiltless drops
> Are every one a woe, a sore complaint
> 'Gainst him, whose wrongs give edge unto the swords
> That make such waste in brief mortality.[10]

[10]  *Ibid.*, Act I, Scene II, p. 817.

# 18

# A British theological perspective

RICHARD HARRIES

The just war criteria remain an indispensable tool of intellectual analysis for anyone thinking about the morality of military action. If people make a judgement that a particular war is immoral, leaving aside absolute pacifists who reject all resort to force in principle, they will do so on the basis of one or more of the just war criteria, whether or not they consciously appeal to these. It is interesting that the 2004 UN High-Level Panel in discussing the morality of military intervention restates, in almost traditional terms, these traditional just war criteria as being a necessary.[1] Even if force is to be used primarily or solely for human security to protect civilians, as Mary Kaldor argues, it will be necessary to decide who should authorise this force, when it should be used and how its use should be weighed against other considerations.

The use of the just war tradition by Catholic bishops in America and by other Christian denominations there has been criticised for understanding this as a 'presumption against war', particularly by George Weigel. Rather, it is, as the late Paul Ramsey used to emphasise, a tool of statecraft primarily for statesmen. It assumes that force must sometimes be used in order to establish international order. There is certainly no absolute presumption against war in it. However, there is an assumption against war in the sense that it must be a last resort and all other options for resolving a conflict peacefully must first have been tried and found wanting. It also sets out other criteria which must be met.

Just war thinking is to be distinguished from a crusade mentality. A crusade mentality works on the assumption that one side, wholly righteous, is fighting a war on God's side against God's enemies. Just war thinking proceeds on the assumption that though war may be morally

---

[1] *A More Secure World: Our Shared Responsibility*, Report of the High-Level Panel on Threats, Challenges and Change, December 2004, p. 3.

justified in particular circumstances, it is still a tragic necessity. It is well characterised in the remark of the Duke of Wellington after the Battle of Waterloo that 'there is only one thing sadder than winning a battle and that is losing it'. There is a worry in some circles, particularly European ones, that the concept of being a 'righteous nation' has heavily influenced present US policy. Certainly the influence of fundamentalist, particularly millenarian, evangelicals appears strong in the country as a whole. Whether this has influenced or is actually influencing US policy is open to question, but just war thinkers will want to keep alive a Niebuhrian perspective on the world, in which one is as conscious of the illusions, deceptions and grandiose ambitions in one's own projects as one is of any faults in the opposing ideologies or regimes.[2] This does not necessarily and certainly should not lead to moral relativism. Moral judgements have to be made. Some things are better than others, but all are flawed.

The first criterion of the just war tradition is that for a military action to be morally justified, it must be authorised by legitimate authority. Within the tradition this has ruled out disputes being solved by private duels, because private citizens have a higher authority to whom they can appeal to arbitrate. Until recently there was no international authority to arbitrate between states, so legitimate authority was vested in the government of each state. However, the creation of the UN represents in principle a move towards that higher authority. Many are highly critical of the UN as it exists at the moment. However, whatever its faults anyone standing in the just war tradition needs to strive ardently for something better, not its abolishment. The fact that the UN is now and always will be to some extent a forum in which there are competing national interests should not be regarded as somehow depriving UN decisions of authority. The UN has never pretended to exist above the area of competition and clash. Rather, through such competition and clash, the serious hope is that agreements which are truly in the interests of the international common good, rather than simply the good of the particular state, can emerge.

The debate about where lawful authority resides for authorising military action in the modern world brings out an important difference between what might be judged to be the highest legal authority and the wider concept of authority desired by the just war tradition. In other

---

[2] As argued by Arthur Schlesinger, Jr, 'Forgetting Reinhold Niebuhr', *New York Times*, 18 September 2005, p. 10.

terms, it raises a debate about legality and legitimacy. Many would argue that the military action in Kosovo, though it was not authorised by the UN Security Council, was morally legitimate. It might also be argued, conversely, that though a case could be made out for the legality of the 2003 Gulf War, it was not in fact legitimate, because it was quite clear from the failure to obtain a second UN resolution, that there was no real international consensus behind the action. So some would argue that the Kosovo action was legitimate, most notably Michael Quinlan, but the 2003 Gulf War, even if a case could be made for its legality, was illegitimate. But the debate itself highlights two points, first that we should strive by every means possible to obtain appropriate UN backing, and secondly, there may be extreme circumstances when such UN backing is lacking but a military action authorised by a coalition of states might in fact be both highly necessary and legitimate. A related issue is that between the desirability of the United States, as the one world superpower capable of imposing international order, being encouraged to take unilateral decisions about military action as Gwyn Prins has argued and the importance of multilateral decisions with a coherent European capacity for decision and action as William Wallace has emphasised. Those stressing the latter will almost always also press for the building up of international institutions of co-operation and strengthening the possibility of a truly international political authority as John Langan does: linked to the latter is a stress on the importance of international law as the fundamental basis for order in the modern world, the particular concern of Frank Berman.

Modern thinking about warfare has tended to emphasise the right of self-defence, which the UN Charter reserves to each individual nation. However, just war thinking allows a much wider rationale for war, most generally, righting a wrong. This means that the possibility of wars of intervention, to protect people from massive human rights violations, should very much be on our present-day agenda. Connected with this is a breaking down of the idea that there is an absolute prohibition against intervening inside the borders of another country, as described by David Fisher. All this is not only congruous with just war thinking but could be said to be required by it. At the same time it must be recognised that this way of thinking multiplies the possibility of causes for war and could make the world even more dangerous.

A key debate in recent conflicts and, indeed, in the world at the moment is the moral legitimacy of pre-emptive military action. The so-called

Anne-Marie Slaughter principles for this, the presence of WMD or the desire to obtain them, proven severe human rights abuses within its own border and aggressive policies towards neighbours are all right as general considerations even if very difficult to apply in relation to particular situations.[3] As far as the presence of WMD is concerned, because these are getting ever smaller it may not in fact prove possible to find any on the ground. It may be better to ascertain whether a particular regime is, for example, willing to allow all its scientists and other people potentially involved to be interviewed. Everyone would agree that in the modern world having a just cause does not depend upon an attack actually having taken place. There are circumstances in which pre-emptive military action, which is in fact anticipatory self-defence, might be absolutely necessary and is morally justified. But many people would want to distinguish between this, when the threat is serious and imminent, and preventive war, where the threat is long-term and distant.

Right intention is the most nebulous of traditional just war criteria. At the least it means intervening in order to achieve a true peace, as opposed to an apparent order based on invasion, occupation and the suppression of opposition. So this true peace includes all that we mean by justice, as well as order. But order is certainly a major consideration in the tradition and the moral imperative arising from this is that proper forethought and planning needs to be given to the immediate aftermath of military action and the medium-term policies. The vast majority of informed people believe that this was not adequately taken into account in relation to the 2003 Gulf War. Indeed, some critics accuse the USA of wrong intent in relation to both the 1991 and the 2003 Gulf wars. They claim that the first was undertaken in order to secure its oil supplies from Kuwait and the second, in a similar way, to ensure the stability of future oil supplies from Iraq, on the grounds that those from Saudi Arabia are less secure than they once were. There are two issues raised by such criticisms. The first is about the legitimacy of national interest as part of the intention, and what might distinguish legitimate from illegitimate national interest as Nigel Biggar discusses. Some would argue that a state not only does in fact always act in its own interest but ought to do so, even if that interest is set out in long- rather than short-term ways, and that interest is conceived in terms of the values for which it stands, as well as its immediate material interests.

---

[3] Anne-Marie Slaughter, 'A Chance to Reshape the UN', *Washington Post*, 13 April 2003, p. B7.

Secondly, it is unlikely that a nation will have a single intent in what it does. There may be a mixture of reasons why military action is undertaken. In relation to the 1991 Gulf War, for example, it may be that oil was a consideration in those who decided to use military action, but from the standpoint of those guided by the just war tradition, the crucial question was whether that action conformed or did not conform to the conditions set out in the tradition. For the vast majority of just war thinkers, it did. The question of oil may or may not have been a factor in the 2003 Gulf War. But again, the crucial question was whether or not the action met the traditional criteria. On this, opinion was divided but that was the crucial moral issue which needed to be discussed, not whether it was all really about oil.

The condition that military action must be a last resort, with every peaceful means for resolving the dispute having first been tried and found to have failed, does not mean waiting for ever. In some circumstances undue delay is likely to strengthen the hand of an aggressor and may even make it impossible to force him to desist. So this condition is not only about taking time, it is about weighing all the factors and deciding what might or might not be possible at a particular time, with the probable consequences taken into account. In relation to this criterion, as all the others, it is a matter of judgement, with no exact calculus possible. There is clearly a spectrum between an illegitimate military action initiated when virtually nothing has been done to resolve the issue peacefully to delaying so long that the cost of putting right what has happened becomes very high indeed in terms of casualties and destruction.

The fact that just war thinking is not an exact science, but a matter of judgement in which many factors have to be weighed, is particularly pronounced in relation to the principle of proportion. This says that anyone contemplating military action has to weigh its cost, in terms of casualties and destruction, against the cost of doing nothing. But it is legitimate to take into account not only material factors, like death and injuries, but the destruction of basic human values, and this on a long-term, not just a short-term, perspective. But it is not only values that have to be taken into account but probabilities. Some threats might be very serious indeed but the probability of them occurring extremely slight. Another threat might be less massive but its probability certain.

Some would say that judgements in this area are bound to be totally subjective, with no possibility at all of arriving at a conclusion which is anything other than an expression of national self-interest. That is too pessimistic a view, though it is true, of course, that the values we champion will depend on the position from which we view life. Europeans as post-imperialist powers, hardened by bitter experience as a result of two world wars, may regard themselves as wiser in their search for diplomatic, international solutions to the world's problems. But this arises out of a European power base, weak in relation to the USA, just as much as an American perspective arises out of one that is at present strong: which doesn't mean to say that a European perspective is invalid. It merely means that it needs to be assessed in its own right, without either illusion or any sense of superiority or self-righteousness. It is important that considerations of relative power, though they need to be taken seriously into account, should not make us totally cynical about the possibility of making good judgements.

Amongst the values which were taken into account during the Second World War, and which are very much to the fore now, are those associated with liberal democracies. Not just the freedom of speech, of movement, of assembly and worship, but the freedom peacefully to change governments by democratic means. Democracy is a desirable good but not one to be imposed by force, and it has to be understood and assimilated in different cultural ways. Though it is a legitimate value, just war thinking warns against making the quest for democracy throughout the world a crusade. It is one highly important value that has to be taken into account along with others in the overall weighing of goods and evils.

It clearly follows as a logical consequence from the principle of proportion, that there is a need to have a reasonable chance of success, for the evil unleashed by war is bound to be greater than the evil which would have to be endured if the injustice is not rectified. But Britain, standing alone in 1940, certainly could not be sure of success or even think that success was very probable. So there is something which belongs to the human spirit which will resist oppression and injustice as a matter of fundamental integrity, honour and dignity, even if chances of success appear slim. The paradox of this is that a strong will to resist, come what may, is likely to increase the chance of success, whilst the lack of that will, even though forces on the ground may be greater than the enemy, as French forces were stronger in numbers than those of the Germans at the beginning of the Second World War, can drain the possibility of victory.

Traditional just war thinking distinguishes between *jus ad bellum*, the considerations that have to be taken into account in considering the moral legitimacy of a military action, and *jus in bello*, questions concerning the conduct of the action. The two key principles here are discrimination and, again, proportion. The principle of discrimination says that the only legitimate targets in a military action are those who are directly contributing to the military aspect of the war effort. A baker may be supplying bread to soldiers as well as civilians but his occupation is not such as to contribute to the military aspect of the war effort. A grandmother knitting socks for troops in the front line may be as much full of hate for the enemy as her soldier son who is there. But she is no threat and nor is she contributing to the military aspect of the war effort. The purpose of military action is not, at least in theory, to kill the enemy, but to render him harmless. So it is that once soldiers have laid down their arms, they are due all the rights of a prisoner of war. To kill an unthreatening prisoner of war is murder.

During the Cold War the main purpose of deterrence was to work on the minds of the adversary and to pose such a threat that they desisted from aggressive action. No doubt working on the minds of opponents has always been a feature of warfare, but it became the quintessential element during the years of nuclear stalemate. During the conflicts following the break-up of the former Yugoslavia, there were signs that this kind of targeting policy had taken hold of coalition forces. The purpose sometimes seemed not simply to destroy enemy military facilities but to impress Milosovic with the certainty that forces were around him, getting closer and closer, and he could not continue. Another dramatic example has been given by General Sir Rupert Smith.[4] When commanding in Bosnia, he became aware that in a Serbian culture a man's honour included taking care of one's parents' graves. So in targeting General Mladic he devised a bombing strategy that set down bombs closer and closer to the graves of Mladic's parents. In principle, there is no reason why such a bombing strategy should not be devised in such a way that it also conforms to traditional *jus in bello* criteria, but the question certainly has to be raised and pressed as to whether it does. With the current

---

[4] Rupert Smith, *The Utility of Force: The Art of War in the Modern World* (London: Allen Lane, 2005).

emphasis on 'effects-based warfare', this question, as Paul Cornish argues, remains highly pertinent.

The principle of proportion, taken together with the principle of discrimination, brings into play the traditional Christian concept of double effect. Those not directly contributing to the military aspect of the war effort (most civilians or non-combatants) may not be directly attacked. But direct attacks on military targets are likely to cause civilian casualties. These are foreseen but they are not directly intended either subjectively or objectively, in the sense that the weapons were directed against a military target. Civilian casualties as a result of a direct attack on a military target are not regarded as an intrinsic wrong, according to traditional just war thinking. However, they are always a tragedy, and they become wrong, in a moral sense, if civilian loss of life is disproportionate to the military gain of destroying the target. There is of course a very widespread view by those who regard themselves as consequentialists or utilitarians that there is no distinction between what is foreseen but unintended, as indicated above, and what is foreseen. Everything that is foreseen has to be regarded as intended and therefore civilian casualties have to be weighed in exactly the same scales as the deaths of soldiers. Though this way of making moral decisions is understandable, it is alien to just war thinking. This does indeed stress that everything has to be weighed and taken into account, but some actions are intrinsically wrong in a way that other actions become wrong only in the light of their consequences.

In weighing what needs to be taken into account, there arises a further question about how it is possible to weigh up the value of the lives of soldiers against those of civilians, and the lives of people on one's own side, whether soldiers or civilians, and the lives of those on the side of the enemy, whether soldiers or civilians. Francisco de Vitoria stressed that a war, otherwise justified, becomes wrong if the evil inflicted on Christendom as a whole outweighs any particular good. In other words, the widest possible good has to be taken into account, which in our time means the world, not just so-called Christian nations. It's highly unsatisfactory that those responsible for the forces of the USA and her allies being in Iraq have resisted obtaining accurate official figures of the deaths of Iraqi people.

Just war thinking has emphasised that *jus ad bellum* and *jus in bello* need to be seen as separate categories. That is true in one way; when there can be such divergent judgements about whether or not a war is just in the first place, it is important to try to inculcate universal standards about what is just conduct in war, whatever view is made about its justice, hence the Geneva Agreements on a range of issues. So a nation which fights war which is morally justified could find some of its commanders brought to court for committing war crimes. Conversely, a nation engaged in an unjust conflict may find that its commanders pay scrupulous attention to the laws of war. So, whilst for this reason it is important to keep the two categories distinct, it is also possible to make a judgement that if a military action is unjust, then all the actions that ensue as a result, whether against military targets or civilians, are in fact criminal. So, for example, the terrorist attack on the Pentagon would be regarded as a criminal activity, just as much as the terrorist attack on the Twin Towers, because the whole basis of the terrorist attack was fundamentally flawed. In South Africa, where under apartheid it was not possible to achieve change by democratic means, the ANC could reasonably be regarded as justified in trying to attack military targets. They, like a number of other liberation movements, sought to make a distinction between military targets and civilian ones. Most forms of current anti-Western terrorism do not of course accept that there is any distinction between military and civilian targets. Their purpose is to inflict as much damage and fear as possible, literally to terrorise, with no distinctions being made.

In conclusion, therefore, it can be seen that the traditional criteria for the justifiable use of force remain an indispensable tool of moral and intellectual analysis. They cannot simply be applied by rote but need to be thought through in relation to the actual circumstances, the enemy to be countered and the weapons in use, today. This is true in relation to almost every one of the criteria, as indicated above. But the principles themselves remain irreplaceable.

# BIBLIOGRAPHY

*A Human Security Doctrine for Europe: Report of the Barcelona Study Group on Europe's Security Capabilities*, Barcelona: Study Group on Europe's Security Capabilities, 15 September 2003.

*A More Secure World: Our Shared Responsibility*, Report of the Secretary-General's High-Level Panel on Threats, Challenges and Change, New York: United Nations Publications, December 2004.

Allison, Graham, *Nuclear Terrorism: The Ultimate Preventable Catastrophe*, New York: Time Books, 2004.

Andreani, Gilles, 'Why Institutions Matter', *Survival* 42/2 (2000): 81–95.

Annan, Kofi, 'Two Sovereignties', *The Economist*, 18 September 1999, p. 8.

Anscombe, G. E. M., 'The Justice of the Present War Examined', in Richard B. Miller (ed.), *War in the Twentieth Century: Sources in Theological Ethics*, Louisville, KY: Westminster/John Knox Press, 1992, pp. 24–57.

Aoláin, Fionnuala Ní, *The Politics of Force: Conflict Management and State Violence in Northern Ireland*, Belfast: Blackstaff Press, 2000.

Arendt, Hannah, *On Violence*, New York: Harcourt Brace, 1969.

Aylwin-Foster, N., 'Changing the Army for Counterinsurgency Operations', *Military Review* (November–December 2005): 6–7.

Bailes, Alyson, *The European Security Strategy: An Evolutionary History*, Stockholm: SIPRI, 2005.

Bailey, J., 'Land Warfare: A Contemporary Perspective', in C. Finn (ed.), *Effects-based Warfare*, London: Stationery Office, 2002, pp. 68–93.

Bailey, Sydney D., *War and Conscience in the Nuclear Age*, Basingstoke: Macmillan, 1987.

Barth, Karl, 'The Christian Community in the Midst of Political Change', in *Against the Stream: Shorter Post-War Writings, 1946–52*, New York: Philosophical Library, 1954, pp. 77–93.

Baur, Michael 'What Is Distinctive about Terrorism', unpublished manuscript.

Beach, Hugh, 'Interventions and Just Wars: The Case of Kosovo', *Studies in Christian Ethics* 13/2 (2000): 15–31.

Bederman, David J., *International Law in Antiquity*, Cambridge: Cambridge University Press, 2001.

Bellamy, Alex, *Just Wars*, Cambridge: Polity Press, 2006.

Bellamy, C., 'Cause or Effect?', *Defence Director* 6 (2004): 48–63.

Berman, Frank, 'The Authorization Model: Resolution 678 and Its Effects', in David M. Malone (ed.), *The UN Security Council: From the Cold War to the Twenty-First Century*, Boulder: Lynne Rienner, 2004, pp. 153–66.

Bettati, Mario and Kouchner, Bernard, *Le Devoir d'Ingérence*, Paris: Denöel, 1987.

Bicheno, Hugh, *Rebels and Redcoats: The American Revolutionary War*, London: HarperCollins, 2003.

Biggar, Nigel, 'Christianity and Weapons of Mass Destruction', in Sohail Hashmi and Steven Lee (eds.), *Ethics and Weapons of Mass Destruction*, Cambridge: Cambridge University Press, 2004, pp. 168–99.

'On Giving the Devil Benefit of Law in Kosovo', in William J. Buckley (ed.), *Kosovo: Contending Voices on Balkan Conflicts*, Grand Rapids, MI: Eerdmans, 2000, pp. 409–18.

Blanchard, Christopher M., 'Al-Qaeda: Statements and Evolving Ideologies', *CRS Report for Congress*, RL32759, p. 10.

Bugnion, François, 'Just Wars, Wars of Aggression and International Humanitarian Law', *International Review of the Red Cross* 84 (2002): 523–46.

Bull, Hedley, 'Conclusion', in Hedley Bull (ed.), *Intervention in World Politics*, Oxford: Oxford University Press, 1984, pp. 187–211.

Burke, Anthony, 'Just War or Ethical Peace? Moral Discourses of Strategic Violence After 9/11', *International Affairs* 80 (2004): 239–353.

Brown, Peter, *Augustine of Hippo*, Berkeley, CA: University of California Press, 1967.

Catholic Bishops' Conference of England and Wales, 'The Aftermath of the Attacks on the USA', *Briefing*, London: Catholic Media Trust, 31/12 (12 December 2001): 8–9.

Chesterton, Simon, *Just War or Just Peace*, Oxford: Oxford University Press, 2001.

Childress, James F., 'Just War Criteria', *Theological Studies* 39 (1978): 427–45.

Chinkin, Christine, 'An International Law Framework for a European Security Strategy', in Marlies Glasius and Mary Kaldor (eds.), *A Human Security Doctrine for Europe: Project; Principles; Practicalities*, Oxford: Routledge, forthcoming.

Church of England: General Synod, *Report of the Proceedings*, London: Church House, 2003.

*Report of the Proceedings*, London: Church House, 2002.

*Report of the Proceedings*, London: Church House, 1999.

*Report of the Proceedings*, London: Church House, 1990.

Church of England: General Synod: Board for Social Responsibility, *Iraq: Would Military Action Be Justified? The Church's Contribution to the Debate*, GS Report 1475, London: Church House, 2002.

*Peacemaking in a Nuclear Age*, Report of a Working Party, London: Church House, 1988.

*The Church and the Bomb: Nuclear Weapons and Christian Conscience*, Report of a Working Party, London: Hodder and Stoughton, 1982.

Church of England: General Synod: Public Affairs Unit, 'A Submission to the House of Commons' Foreign Affairs Select Committee's Inquiry into the Decision to go to War in Iraq', 9 June 2003.

Church of England: House of Bishops, *Countering Terrorism: Power, Violence and Democracy Post 9/11*, Report of a Working Party, London: Church House, 2005.

Church of Scotland: Committee on Church and Nation, 'The War in Iraq', Supplementary Report to the General Assembly, Edinburgh: Church of Scotland, 2003.

'The Terrorist Attacks on the United States of America and the War in Afghanistan', Supplementary Report to the General Assembly, 2002.

'Statement on the Military Campaign in Afghanistan', Edinburgh: Church of Scotland, 1 November 2001.

'Kosovo Press Release', Edinburgh: Church of Scotland, 2000.

'The Legacy of the Kosovo War', Edinburgh: Church of Scotland, n.d.

Church of Scotland: General Assembly, *Report of the Proceedings* (1991), Committee on Church and Nation, 'The Gulf Crisis', Edinburgh: Church of Scotland, 1991.

Clausewitz, Carl von, *On War*, ed. and trans. Michael Howard and Peter Paret, Princeton, NJ: Princeton University Press, 1976.

Coates, Anthony, *The Ethics of War*, Manchester: Manchester University Press, 1997.

Cooke, Jacob E. (ed.), *The Federalist*, Middletown, CT: Wesleyan University Press, 1961.

Cooper, Robert, *The Breaking of Nations: Order and Chaos in the Twenty-first Century*, New York: Grove Press, 2003.

'The Next Empire', *Prospect* (October 2001): 22–6.

Cordesman, Anthony, *The Iraq War: Strategy, Tactics and Military Lessons*, Westport, CT: Praeger Publishers, 2003.

Cornish, Paul, 'Clausewitz and the Ethics of Armed Force: Five Propositions', *Journal of Military Ethics* 2/3 (2003): 218–27.

Cornish, Paul and Edwards, Geoffrey, 'Beyond the EU/NATO Dichotomy? The Beginnings of a European Strategic Culture', *International Affairs* 77/3 (2001): 587–603.

Cornish, Paul and Harbour, F., 'NATO and the Individual Soldier as Moral Agents with Reciprocal Duties: Imbalance in the Kosovo Campaign', in T. Erskine (ed.), *Can Institutions Have Responsibilities: Collective Moral Agency and International Relations*, London: Palgrave, 2003, pp. 212–49.

Crahan, Margaret, Goering, John and Weiss, Thomas G. (eds.), *Wars on Terrorism and Iraq: The US and the World*, London: Routledge, 2004.

Crowder, G. L., 'Effects-Based Operations: The Impact of Precision Strike Weapons on Air Warfare Doctrines', *Military Technology* (June 2003): 16–18.

Department of the Army, *Field Manual 3.09-32: J-Fires*, Washington, DC, November 2002.

*Law of Land Warfare, US Army Field Manual 27-10*, Washington, DC, 1956.

der Derian, James, *Virtuous War: Mapping the Military-Industrial-Media-Entertainment Network*, Boulder, CO: Westview Press, 2001.

DG Joint Doctrine and Concepts, *Joint Operations*, London: UK Joint Warfare Publication 3-00, 30 March 2000.

Diez, Thomas, 'Constructing the Self and Changing Others: Reconsidering "Normative Power Europe"', *Millennium* 33/3 (2004): 22–33.

Dorr, Donal, *Option for the Poor: One Hundred Years of Vatican Social Teaching*, Maryknoll, NY: Orbis Books, 1992.

Dostoyevsky, Feodor, *The Brothers Karamazov*, trans. David Magarshack, London: Penguin Books, 1982.

Elshtain, Jean Bethke, *Just War against Terror: The Burden of American Power in a Violent World*, New York: Basic Books, 2003.

Evans, Michael, 'Conflict Opens Way to New International Community: Blair's Mission', *The Times*, 23 April 1999, p. 2.

Fanon, Franz, *The Wretched of the Earth*, New York: Grove Press, 1981.

Finn, C., 'Air Power and Effects-Based Warfare', *World Defence Systems* 7/1 (Spring 2004): 12–13.

Finnis, John, Boyle, Joseph M. and Grisez, Germain (eds.), *Nuclear Deterrence, Morality and Realism*, Oxford: Clarendon Press, 1987.

Fisher, David, 'Some Corner of a Foreign Field', in Roger Williamson (ed.), *Some Corner of a Foreign Field: Intervention and World Order*, Basingstoke: Macmillan Press, 1998, pp. 28–37.

'The Ethics of Intervention and Former Yugoslavia', in Roger Williamson (ed.), *Some Corner of a Foreign Field: Intervention and World Order*, Basingstoke: Macmillan Press, 1998, pp. 166–73.

'The Ethics of Intervention', *Survival* (Spring, 1994): 51–60.

*Morality and the Bomb: An Ethical Assessment of Nuclear Deterrence*, London: Croom Helm, 1985.

Forbes, Ian, 'NATO Transformation', *World Defence Systems* 7/1 (Spring 2004): 18.

Freedman, Lawrence, 'Can the EU Develop an Effective Military Doctrine?', in Charles Grant (ed.), *A European Way of War*, London: Centre for Reform, 2004, pp. 13–26.

French, Shannon E., *The Code of the Warrior: Exploring Warrior Values, Past and Present*, Lanham and New York: Rowman and Littlefield Publishers, 2003.

Giegerich, Bastian and Wallace, William, 'Not Such a Soft Power? The Deployment of European Troops outside Europe', *Survival* 46/2 (2004): 163–82.

*The Globe Illustrated Shakespeare*, New York: Greenwich House, 1986.

Goulding, M. *Peacemonger*, London: John Murray, 2002.

Graham, Bradley, 'Pentagon Prepares to Rethink Focus on Conventional Warfare', *Washington Post*, 26 January 2005, p. 5.

Gray, Colin, *Modern Strategy*, Oxford: Oxford University Press, 1999.

Haas, Richard N., *The Opportunity: America's Moment to Alter History's Course*, New York: Public Affairs, 2005.

Harbour, F. and Cornish, Paul, 'Planning for Casualties: Insights from World War II and Kosovo', paper presented to the International Studies Association, Chicago, February 2001.

*Christianity and War in a Nuclear Age*, London and Oxford: Mowbray, 1986.

*Should a Christian Support Guerrillas?* Guildford: Lutterworth, 1982.

Hart, H. L. A., *The Concept of Law*, Oxford: Clarendon Press, 1961; 2nd edn, 1994.

Harvey, R., *A Few Bloody Noses: The American War of Independence*, London: John Murray, 2001.

Hobbes, Thomas, *Leviathan*, New York: Penguin Books, 1986.

Howard, Michael, *The Invention of Peace*, New Haven: Yale University Press, 2000.

Ignatieff, Michael, *The Lesser Evil: Political Ethics in an Age of Terror*, Edinburgh: Edinburgh University Press, 2005.

*Empire Lite: Nation Building in Bosnia, Kosovo, Afghanistan*, London: Vintage Books, 2003.

*Virtual War: Kosovo and Beyond*, London: Chatto and Windus, 2000.

*The Warrior's Honour: Ethnic War and the Modern Consciousness*, London: Vintage, 1999.

Iklé, Fred Charles, *Every War Must End*, 2nd rev. edn, New York: Columbia University Press, 2005.

Jablonsky, D., *The Owl of Minerva Flies at Twilight: Doctrinal Change and Continuity and the Revolution in Military Affairs*, US Army War College, Strategic Studies Institute, May 1994.

Jackson, Robert H. *International Order* (Havana, 27 March 1941), http://www.roberthjackson.org/theman2-7-6-2.asp, p. 1.

Janis, Mark Weston, *The American Tradition of International Law: Great Expectations, 1789–1914*, Oxford: Clarendon Press, 2004.

Jefferson, Thomas, *Thomas Jefferson: Writings*, New York: Library of America, 1984.

John Paul II, Pope, 'Address to the Diplomatic Corps', 12 January 1991, *Briefing*, London: Catholic Media Trust, 21/1 (14 February 1991): 2–4.

'Address to the Vicariate of Rome', 16 January 1991, *Briefing*, London: Catholic Media Trust, 21/3 (31 January 1991): 15.

Johnson, James Turner, 'Just War, as It Was and Is', *First Things* 149 (2005): 14–24.

*Just War Tradition and the Restraint of War: A Moral and Historical Enquiry*, Princeton, NJ: Princeton University Press, 1981.

Johnson, James Turner and Weigel, George (eds.), *Just War and the Gulf War*, Washington, DC: Ethics and Public Policy Centre, 1991.

Kagan, Robert, *Of Paradise and Power: America and Europe in the New World Order*, New York: Knopf, 2003.

Kaplan, Robert, *Warrior Politics: Why Leadership Demands a Pagan Ethos*, New York: Random House, 2002.

Katzenstein, Peter (ed.), *The Culture of National Security: Norms and Identity in World Politics*, New York: Columbia University Press, 1996.

Kelsey, F., *Classics of International Law*, Oxford: Clarendon Press, 1925.

Kenny, Anthony, *The Logic of Deterrence*, London: Firethorn, 1985.

Kolenda, Chrsitopher, 'Technology, Leadership and Effectiveness', *Military Review* (July–August 2000): 87–91.

Krueger, Alan B. and Maleckova, Jitka, 'Does Poverty Cause Terrorism?', *New Republic*, 24 June 2002, pp. 27–33.

Krulak, Charles, 'Strategic Corporal: Leadership in the Three Block War', *Marines: Official Magazine of the Marine Corps* (January 1999).

Lammers, Stephen, 'William Temple and the Bombing of Germany: An Exploration in the Just War Tradition', *Journal of Religious Ethics* 19/1 (Spring 1991): 72–82.

Lane, Rupert, 'The Challenges of Expeditionary Operations for NATO', *World Defence Systems* 7/1 (Spring 2004): 59–60.

Langan, John, 'The Elements of St Augustine's Just War Theory', *Journal of Religious Ethics* 12/1 (1984): 19–38.

Le Carré, John, *Tinker, Tailor, Soldier, Spy*, New York: Alfred A. Knopf, 1974.

Levinson, Sanford (ed.), *Torture: A Collection*, Oxford: Oxford University Press, 2005.

Lewis, Bernard, *The Political Language of Islam*, Chicago: University of Chicago Press, 1988.

Longley, Clifford, *Chosen People: The Big Idea that Shaped England and America*, London: Hodder and Stoughton, 2002.

Low, Anthony, *Lion Rampant: Essays in the Study of British Imperialism*, London: Cass, 1973.

Lugard, Frederick, *Political Memoranda: Revision of Instructions to Political Officers on Subjects Chiefly Political and Administrative, 1913–18*, London: Cass, 1970.

Macgregor, Douglas, *Transformation under Fire: Revolutionizing How America Fights*, London: Praeger, 2003.

McMahan, Jeff, 'Just Cause for Just War', *Ethics and International Affairs* 19 (2005): 1–21.

'War and Peace', in Peter Singer (ed.), *A Companion to Ethics*, Oxford: Blackwell, 1994, pp. 384–98.

Maritain, Jacques, *Rights of Man and Natural Law*, trans. Doris Anson, New York: Scribner's Sons, 1943.

Marten, Kimberly, *Enforcing the Peace: Learning from the Imperial Past*, New York: Columbia University Press, 2004.

Mazarr, M. J., *The Revolution in Military Affairs: A Framework for Defense Planning*, US Army War College, Strategic Studies Institute, June 1994.

Miller, Fred D., Jr, *Nature, Justice and Rights in Aristotle's Politics*, Oxford: Clarendon Press, 1995.

Müllerson, Rein, *Ordering Anarchy: International Law in International Society*, The Hague: Martinus Nijhoff, 2000.

Murphy-O'Connor, Cormac and Williams, Rowan, 'Catholic and Anglican Archbishops' Joint Statement on Iraq', 20 February 2003.

Murray, John Courtney, *We Hold These Truths: Catholic Reflections on the American Proposition*, New York: Sheed and Ward, 1960.

Musto, Ronald G., *The Catholic Peace Tradition*, Maryknoll, NY: Orbis Books, 1986.

Nagl, John, *Counterinsurgency Lessons from Malaya and Vietnam: Learning to Eat Soup with a Knife*, New York: Praeger, 2002.

National Conference of Catholic Bishops, *The Harvest of Justice Is Sown in Peace*, Washington, DC: United States Catholic Conference, 1993.

*The Challenge of Peace: God's Promise and Our Response*, Washington, DC: United States Catholic Conference, 1983.

Niblett, Robin and Wallace, William (eds.), *Rethinking European Order: West European Responses, 1989–1997*, Basingstoke: Macmillan, 2001.

Niebuhr, Reinhold, *Moral Man and Immoral Society*, Louisville, KY: Westminster Knox Press, 1960.

Nitschke, Stefan, 'Network-Centric Warfare – The European Initiatives', *Military Technology*, 28 (March 2004): 12–29.

O'Brien, David J. and Shannon, Thomas (eds.), *Catholic Social Thought: The Documentary Heritage*, Maryknoll, NY: Orbis Books, 1992.

O'Donovan, Oliver, *The Just War Revisited*, Cambridge: Cambridge University Press, 2003.

*Peace and Certainty: A Theological Essay on Deterrence*, Oxford: Clarendon Press, 1989.

*In Pursuit of a Christian View of War*, Bramcote, Nottingham: Grove Books, 1977.

Ogata, Sadako *et al.*, *Human Security Now: Final Report of the Commission on Human Security*, New York: United Nations Publications, 2003.

Osiel, Mark, *Obeying Orders: Atrocity, Military Discipline, and the Law of War*, New Brunswick and London: Transaction Publishers, 1999.

*Pacem in Terris: Encyclical of Pope John XXIII on Establishing Universal Peace in Truth, Justice, Charity and Liberty, 11 April 1963*.

Pagden, Anthony and Lawrence, Jeremy (eds.), *Political Writings*, Cambridge: Cambridge University Press, 1991.

Paz, Reuven, 'Yes to WMD: The First Islamist Fatwah on the use of Weapons of Mass Destruction', *Global Research in International Affairs (GLORIA) Centre, The Project for the Research of Islamist Movements (PRISM) Special Dispatches* (2003): 16–35.

Pinnock, Kenneth, 'November Thoughts', *Oriel Record 2002*, Oxford: Oriel College, 2002, pp. 35–38.

Pollack, Kenneth, *The Threatening Storm: The Case for Invading Iraq*, New York: Random House, 2002.

Pontifical Council for Justice and Peace, 'Peace Is Possible in the Balkans', *Briefing*, London: Catholic Media Trust, 24/2 (27 January 1994): 14–15.

Porter, Bruce D., *War and the Rise of the State: The Military Foundations of Modern Politics*, London: Free Press, 1994.

Pringle, Philip and Jacobson, Philip (eds.), *Those Are Real Bullets, Aren't They?* London, Fourth Estate, 2000.

Prins, Gwyn, *The Heart of War: On Power, Conflict and Responsibility in the Twenty-First Century*, London: Routledge, 2002.

Ramsey, Paul, *Speak Up for Just War or Pacifism: A Critique of the United Methodist Bishops' Pastoral Letter 'In Defense of Creation'*, University Park, PA, and London: Pennsylvania State University Press, 1988.

*The Just War: Force and Political Responsibility*, New York: Charles Scribner's Sons, 1968.

*War and the Christian Conscience*, Durham, NC: Duke University Press, 1961.

Rawls, John, 'The Idea of an Overlapping Consensus', in Samuel Freedman (ed.), *Collected Papers*, Cambridge, MA: Harvard, 1999, pp. 432–44.

Reed, Charles, *Just War?* London: SPCK, 2004.

Reiss, Hans (ed.), *Kant's Political Writing*, Cambridge: Cambridge University Press, 1992.

Roberts, Adam, *Humanitarian Action in War*, Oxford: Oxford University Press, 1996.

Roberts, Les, Lafta, Riyadh, Garfield, Richard, Khudhairi, Jamal and Burnham, Gilbert, 'Mortality before and after the 2003 Invasion of Iraq: Cluster Sample Survey', *Lancet* 364/9448 (29 October 2004): 1857–64.

Rostow, Eugene V., *Toward Managed Peace: The National Security Interests of the United States, 1759 to the Present*, New Haven: Yale University Press, 1993.

Russell, Frederick, *The Just War in the Middle Ages*, Cambridge: Cambridge University Press, 1975.

Russett, Bruce, *Grasping the Democratic Peace*, Princeton, NJ: Princeton University Press, 1993.

Schmitt, Carl, *The Concept of the Political*, Chicago: University of Chicago Press, 1990.

Seidentop, Larry, *Democracy in Europe*, London: Penguin, 2001.

Shawcross, William, *Deliver Us from Evil*, London: Bloomsbury Publishing, 2000.

Shay, Jonathan, *Achilles in Vietnam: Combat Trauma and the Undoing of Character*, New York: Simon and Schuster, 1994.

Shurtleff, D. K., 'Deleting the Human Factor: An Ethical Inquiry into Armed Unmanned Vehicles', *World Defence Systems* (December 2002): 10–11, 14–15.

Slaughter, Anne-Marie, *A New World Order*, Princeton, NJ: Princeton University Press, 2004.

'A Chance to Reshape the UN', *Washington Post*, 13 April 2003, p. 7.

Smith, Rupert, *The Utility of Force: The Art of War in the Modern World*, London: Penguin Allen Lane, 2005.

Smith, R., 'Wars in Our Time: A Survey of Recent and Continuing Conflicts', *World Defence Systems* 3/2 (2001): 4–5.

Stokes, Eric, *The Peasant and the Raj: Studies in Agrarian Society and Peasant Rebellion*, Cambridge: Cambridge University Press, 1978.

Sun Tzu, *The Art of War*, trans. S. B. Griffith, Oxford: Oxford University Press, 1963.

Tibi, Bassam, 'War and Peace in Islam', in Terry Nardin (ed.), *The Ethics of War and Peace*, Princeton, NJ: Princeton University Press, 1996, pp. 128–45.

Toner, J. H., *Military Ethics: Dr Jekyll and Mr Hyde* (US Air Force Academy, Joseph A. Reich Lectures on War, Morality and the Military Profession, 9 November 1999).

Tooke, Joan D., *The Just War in Aquinas and Grotius*, London: SPCK, 1965.

Troeltsch, Ernst, *The Social Teaching of the Christian Churches*, New York: Harper and Brothers, 1960.

United Methodist Bishops, *In Defence of Creation: The Nuclear Crisis and a Just Peace*, Nashville, TN: Graded Press, 1986.

United Nations General Assembly, *2005 World Summit Outcome*, 15 September 2005.

Vesely, M., 'A Different Kind of War', *Middle East*, February 2003, pp. 6–13.

Walter, Abbott S. J., *The Documents of Vatican II: Gaudium et Spes*, Baltimore: Geoffrey Chapman, 1966.

Walzer, Michael, *Arguing about War*, New Haven: Yale University Press, 2004.

'First, Define the Battlefield', *New York Times*, 21 September 2001, p. 8.

*Just and Unjust Wars: A Moral Argument with Historical Illustrations*, 3rd edn, New York: Basic Books, 2000.

*Just and Unjust Wars, A Moral Argument with Historical Illustrations*, New York: Basic Books, 1977.

Weigel, George, *Tranquillitas Ordinis: The Present Failure and Future Promise of American Catholic Thought on War and Peace*, New York: University Press, 1987.

Weigley, Russell F., *The American Way of War*, Bloomington: Indiana University Press, 1973.

Williams, Ian, 'Annan Has Paid His Dues', *Guardian*, 20 September 2005, p. 8.

Williams, John, 'Network-Enabled Capability – The Concept', *World Defence Systems* 7/1 (2004): 6–7.

Wulf, Herbert, 'The Challenges of Re-Establishing a Public Monopoly of Violence', in Marlies Glasius and Mary Kaldor (eds.), *A Human Security Doctrine for Europe: Project; Principles; Practicalities*, Oxford: Routledge, forthcoming.

Yeago, David S., 'Just War Reflections from the Lutheran Tradition in a Time of Crisis', *Pro Ecclesia* 10 (2001): 401–27.

Zagorin, Perez, *How the Idea of Religious Toleration Came to the West*, Princeton, NJ: Princeton University Press, 2003.

# INDEX